PN 1998 .A2 B47 1 **W9-DBD-958**

Between action and cut

DATE DUE

~~MAR 2 2 1993~~		
~~FEB 2 7 1995~~		
~~MAR 2 7 1995~~		

DEMCO 38-297

BETWEEN ACTION ☐
☐ AND CUT:
Five American Directors

edited by
Frank Thompson

The Scarecrow Press, Inc.
Metuchen, N.J., & London
1985

Library of Congress Cataloging in Publication Data
Main entry under title:

Between action and cut.

   Includes filmographies and index.
   Contents: Introduction / by Frank Thompson -- Victor
Fleming / by John A. Gallagher -- William K. Howard / by
William K. Everson -- Roland West / by Scott MacQueen --
[etc.]
   1. Moving-picture producers and directors--United
States--Addresses, essays, lectures. 2. Moving-pictures
--United States--History--Addresses, essays, lectures.
3. Moving-picture plays--History and criticism--Ad-
dresses, essays, lectures. I. Thompson, Frank T.,

1952-   ·
PN1998.A2B47 1985   791.43'0233'0922   84-23540
ISBN 0-8108-1744-6

"Before shooting a scene, the director calls: Action. When the scene is finished, he calls: Cut. All the secrets of the cinema lie there, in what happens in the mind of the director between action and cut."

--Francois Truffaut

This book is dedicated to

Herman G. Weinberg

CONTENTS

INTRODUCTION

The genesis of this book can be traced back to a brisk April afternoon in 1979. I had just begun research for a book about director William A. Wellman and had come out to Los Angeles to talk with those who knew and had worked with him. I imagined that, once my intentions were known throughout Hollywood, a queue would begin forming outside my door, each person in it brimming with amusing anecdotes and surprising revelations about Wild Bill. Somehow word never got out and at the end of a week I had little more data than I had brought with me from Chicago.

David Shepard of the Director's Guild helped turn the tide. He gave me the names and phone numbers of several technical people who had worked with Wellman and one day, as a sort of afterthought, suggested, "You should talk with Charlie Barton; he worked with Wellman." Since I wasn't having much luck with my "A" list, I figured I could do worse than to see Barton. A little rudimentary checking turned up the fact that Barton had been Wellman's assistant director on Young Eagles (1930) and had acted in Beau Geste (1939). It wasn't much, but it was a start. Besides, I reasoned, I could hone my interviewing skills on Barton so that I'd be ready when I talked with someone really important.

I called the number that Shepard provided and Barton answered. He had a voice that seemed to be filtered through gravel and dense smoke. I told him that I was writing a book about Wellman and he burst into laughter. While I was trying to figure out what was so funny, he said, "I'll be glad to help ya out. Wanta come over today?"

An hour later I was driving toward Santa Monica to meet Barton in his beach-front apartment. I didn't hold very high hopes for any startling information, but he sounded pleasant and Beau Geste was one of my favorite films.

1

Late that afternoon, on my drive back home, I realized how wrong I had been. Barton turned out to be a wonderful raconteur with a razor-sharp memory and an endless
supply of patience and good humor. I blanched when I recalled how easily I might never have gotten around to seeing
him, for it was already quite apparent that I was unlikely to
talk with anyone who had worked with Wellman more often
or under more diverse circumstances: Barton had been
prop boy or Assistant Director on eleven of Wellman's films
and on projects of the caliber of Wings (1927) and Beggars
of Life (1928). More importantly, I had received my first
inkling of what a staggeringly varied and prolific career
Barton had had: actor, prop boy, A. D. , writer, and finally, director of over sixty feature films and six hundred
television shows: his professional life spanned more than
sixty years. I had the opportunity to talk with Barton many
more times, once, memorably, before an enthusiastic audience at a National Film Society affair. I became more and
more interested in his work and started seeking out his
films. Later I wrote a brief, affectionate profile of him
for American Classic Screen magazine, but he died a few
weeks before it appeared in print.

Barton will never be the subject of a book. He is
not even mentioned in the great majority of books on film,
and understandably so. His work is of wildly variable quality, few of his films would stand up to any rigorous analysis, and his personality was always subordinate to the style
of whatever studio he was under contract to. He was a good
director, but no more than that. He was a contract man,
an efficient cog in the movie factory. Still, I find his career fascinating and it occurred to me that there were many
directors like him: men of varied skills and approaches,
studio workhorses or eccentric mavericks, men who could
make no claim to the Pantheon but whose work is evocative
of the period in which they worked, who mixed technical experimentation with routine studio assignments, or who simply kept working, up through the silents, the coming of
sound, color, widescreen, 3-D. Adaptable filmmakers.
Professionals.

When I decided to put this book together, I made up
a list of about fifty directors who, I felt, met the rather
loose criteria that I imposed. With some thought, I easily
came up with fifty more. That done, I felt there were three
steps that I needed to take. First, I had to find out if any
publisher would be interested in a book about directors of

whom virtually nothing had previously been written. Happily, the Scarecrow Press (which had published my book on Wellman in 1983) agreed to the project immediately. Second, I sent the list around to various writers and film scholars of my acquaintance to see what they thought of such a project. The response (with the exception of a few Signs-and-Meaning-in-the-Cinema types) was overwhelmingly positive. Finally, the most difficult part: would anyone be interested in tackling a chapter? Again, I had good luck and the requisite number of entries was spoken for by the end of the week. I could have done a book twice the size of this one (or two books, or more) from the number of directors who were spoken for. Some writers even approached me with names that had not been on my original list (and two of those are represented in this volume).

The guidelines for the contributors were simple and few: the subject had to be an American film director; his career had to be over, so that the study could take into account the arc of his development (as it happened, all five of the directors in this book are deceased); any director who had been the subject of a book was ineligible; each chapter was to be provided with as detailed a filmography as possible, down to the most minor credit. Beyond these suggestions, each contributor was left to his own devices to take any approach he pleased, with the chapter's length being the author's only limitation. Consequently, the entries range from the biographical (Fleming and Barton) to the analytical (Brown and West).

Among the first people with whom I shared the idea for the book was my friend John Gallagher. I sent him the list so that he could have an early choice of subjects. He countered with an idea that was, at first, surprising. How about, he asked, a chapter on Victor Fleming? My initial response was to say no. This book was to be about "underknown" directors and Fleming had put his name to at least two of the most famous of all films: Gone with the Wind and The Wizard of Oz. Beyond those two films, however, not much has been written about Fleming's career and the rest of his work is not much better known than that of anyone else covered in this volume. Even "comprehensive" works like Richard Roud's Cinema: A Critical Dictionary and Jean-Pierre Coursodon's American Directors don't find Fleming worthy of inclusion (actually none of the directors covered here is mentioned in either of those works). So, I was convinced and the Fleming chapter was the first on the roster.

When I was making up my first list, I barely knew
who Roland West was. His films are very difficult to find
and I had seen none of them. If I knew him at all, it was
through his connection with the death of actress Thelma
Todd. An article in American Classic Screen introduced me
to West the filmmaker and I became interested in knowing
more about him and seeing (particularly) The Bat Whispers
(1931). Coincidentally, at about that time, the author of that
article, Scott MacQueen, wrote to ask if I thought West was
a worthy entry in this book. I was delighted to provide an
opportunity for Scott to expand his article to nearly triple
its original length. The West that emerges from this fine
piece of work is a fascinating director, a technical innovator,
a second-rate writer, a master of mise-en-scène, a poor
handler of actors and, possibly, a murderer.

John Tibbetts contributed the chapter on Rowland
Brown. Brown is something of a puzzle. He directed only
three feature films, but each one is absolutely first-rate--
quirky, eccentric, funny, bizarre, beautifully paced and nu-
anced. Proportionately, I suppose, this makes Brown the
most artistically successful director in the history of the
medium. Tibbetts provides concise readings of Brown's
work, pointing out his thematic consistencies and the extent
to which Brown drew upon his own life and interests in the
creation of his characters and stories.

In the final analysis, the aim of this book is not to
over-praise these five directors nor to attempt to apply any
radical or revisionist readings to their oeuvre in order to
qualify them for entry into some Pantheon of Great Artists.
Our approach has not been to claim that their work has
been misunderstood, just that, by and large, it's been ignored. The rise of the auteur theory beginning in the mid-
'50s led to the reappraisal of several directors who were
originally dismissed as being studio hacks or, at best, simply "entertainers" (Howard Hawks, Nicholas Ray and Alfred
Hitchcock are three filmmakers whose critical standing is a
full 180 degrees from what it once was), but the auteur theory did not allow for men like Barton, West or Fleming.
Their efforts have largely gone unsung because their directorial skills were subordinated to the demands of genre or
the anti-individualistic rigors of series films (Barton), the
career-long association with major studios and the factory-
like aspect which was imposed on even their best work
(Fleming), or the general unavailability of their work (West).

Of course, re-evaluation is inevitable in the case of a director like Rowland Brown; the very touches and odd tones of his films that make them so fresh and alive were generally reviled by contemporary critics, who seemingly couldn't understand why Brown wouldn't deliver a straight-forward melodrama or cops 'n' robbers picture. William K. Howard, too, is a director whose work deserves major reappraisal. Bill Everson's fine career study of Howard should start the ball rolling, though it remains a mystery why Howard has never taken his place as one of the masters of American film. Certainly White Gold, The Power and the Glory and Mary Burns, Fugitive can stand beside any films of their periods.

This book, then, is not first and foremost a work of criticism. It is a celebration of a manner of filmmaking and a breed of filmmaker that, for good or ill, has passed from the scene. Their work ranges from the ridiculous to the sublime but the work of Charles Barton, Victor Fleming, Roland West, William K. Howard and Rowland Brown deserves, at least, a respectful salute.

Frank Thompson

February 15, 1984
Atlanta, GA

Victor Fleming (The Museum of Modern Art/
Film Stills Archive)

VICTOR FLEMING

by John A. Gallagher

Vic Fleming was one of the best directors that
ever lived. The funny thing is, nobody mentions
him anymore. ... [1]

> --Mervyn LeRoy (director of Little Cae-
> sar, I Am a Fugitive from a Chain Gang,
> Johnny Eager, Quo Vadis, The F. B. I
> Story, Gypsy)

By any critical standards, 1939 was a remarkable
year for the American cinema. Consider this partial list:
Frank Capra's Mr. Smith Goes to Washington, George Cuk-
or's The Women, Michael Curtiz' Dodge City, Cecil B. De-
Mille's Union Pacific, William Dieterle's The Hunchback of
Notre Dame, Edmund Goulding's Dark Victory, Howard Hawks'
Only Angels Have Wings, Mitchell Leisen's Midnight, Anatole
Litvak's Confessions of a Nazi Spy, Ernst Lubitsch's Ninotch-
ka, Leo McCarey's Love Affair, George Stevens' Gunga Din,
Raoul Walsh's The Roaring Twenties, William Wellman's
Beau Geste, Sam Wood's Goodbye, Mr. Chips, William Wy-
ler's Wuthering Heights, King Vidor's Northwest Passage,
and no less than three John Ford classics: Young Mr. Lin-
coln, Stagecoach, and Drums Along the Mohawk.

That extraordinary year also saw the release of two
of the most beloved, most written about movies ever made,
The Wizard of Oz and Gone with the Wind. Both of these
pictures bear the credit "Directed by Victor Fleming," but
while the films' popularity has mushroomed over the years,
Fleming has been all but forgotten. He was one of the most
important directors of his day, and for sheer entertainment
value his record is unsurpassed, but his contributions to

The Wizard of Oz and Gone with the Wind have completely
overshadowed his other work.

Fleming created movies of enduring appeal. Such
films as The Virginian with Gary Cooper, Red Dust with
Gable and Harlow, Treasure Island with Wallace Beery,
Captains Courageous with Spencer Tracy, Test Pilot with
Gable, Tracy, and Myrna Loy, Dr. Jekyll and Mr. Hyde
with Tracy, Ingrid Bergman, and Lana Turner, A Guy
Named Joe with Tracy and Irene Dunne, Adventure with
Gable and Greer Garson, and Joan of Arc with Bergman.
Fleming's lesser-known pictures deserve to be revived regu-
larly: his first two films, the delightful Douglas Fairbanks
movies, When the Clouds Roll By and The Mollycoddle; the
Clara Bow comedy, Mantrap; the exotic Foreign Legion ad-
venture, Renegades; the satirical gem, Bombshell; the gentle
Americana of The Farmer Takes a Wife and Tortilla Flat.

Both The Wizard of Oz and Gone with the Wind are
"producer's pictures," definitive examples of a studio system in which the producer pulled together script, cast, production, and multiple directors to achieve a cohesive work.
Though Fleming won an Academy Award for Best Directing
with Gone with the Wind, he was one of a half dozen directors on the epic, and the film's true auteur was producer
David O. Selznick.

From 1932 through 1945, Fleming was the top director at Hollywood's richest studio, Metro-Goldwyn-Mayer.
The Metro machinery tended to swallow up directors, but
Fleming's movies were accorded the credit, "A Victor Fleming Production," prominently displayed in prints and advertising. As Andrew Sarris said in The American Cinema,
"aside from Cukor, he was the only Metro director who
could occasionally make the lion roar."[2]

Fleming's close friend and fellow director Tay Garnett told this story:

> Victor Fleming was once visited by a producer on
> his set [at M-G-M]. He asked the producer how
> long he planned to stay on the set. The producer
> said he wasn't sure, so Fleming went home and
> said, 'Call me when you leave the set.'[3]

The films of Victor Fleming are blessed with many
virtues. John Howard Reid wrote that "first and foremost,

he was a subtle creator of atmosphere.   Secondly, he was
an exponent of 'action. '   And thirdly, he was a director of
acting.   No one ever gave a bad performance in a Fleming
film. "[4]   Historian John Baxter has pointed out that "Victor
Fleming shared with [Jack] Conway the ability to impose on
most of his films a distinctive style, but where Conway was
fast, hard-hitting, witty, Fleming was, like William Wyler,
contemplative and elegant. "[5]

Fleming helped shape the careers of Gary Cooper,
Clara Bow, Jean Harlow, Myrna Loy, Spencer Tracy, Henry
Fonda, Judy Garland and, most importantly, Clark Gable.
Director Henry Hathaway (Lives of a Bengal Lancer, Kiss
of Death, True Grit) was Fleming's assistant director during
the Twenties, and he once commented:

> As for Vic, every man that ever worked for him
> patterned himself after him.   Clark Gable, Spencer
> Tracy, all of them.   He had a strong personality,
> not to the point of imposing himself on anybody,
> but just forceful and masculine.   Every leading
> lady that ever worked for him fell in love with
> him.   And he generally reciprocated, at least for
> that picture. [6]

Fleming handled his male stars with a combination of
boyish camaraderie and strong-armed authority, directing
some of Gable's best performances (Red Dust, The White
Sister, Test Pilot, Gone with the Wind, Adventure), as well
as Tracy's (Captains Courageous, Test Pilot, Dr. Jekyll and
Mr. Hyde, Tortilla Flat, A Guy Named Joe).   Columnist
Hedda Hopper revealed:

> [When Fleming], Tracy, and Gable get together,
> they don't talk pictures or books.   Can you see
> those three lugs discussing the classics?   Or Vic
> saying to Gable, 'Read me Hamlet's soliloquy--my
> nerves are razzled to a frazzle!'   Why, Clark
> would hit him with a monkey wrench.   In many
> ways, tho, these three are very much alike--lusty,
> moody, frank--brutally frank.   Yet each can be
> tender if and when the moment is propitious.   What
> they do talk about when they get together is horses,
> cattle breeding, oil wells, dogs, or guns ... Spen-
> cer Tracy's description of Victor Fleming is 'the
> Clark Gable of directors,' and he has most every
> player in Hollywood agreeing with him.... Men

fight to work with Vic.   Women think he should be
in front of the camera, not behind it. [7]

Despite a reputation for being tough on actresses,
Fleming got along wonderfully with Clara Bow, Jean Harlow,
and Ingrid Bergman.   He detested Vivien Leigh, however,
and while shooting Gone with the Wind, his nickname for her
was "Fiddle-Dee-Dee." Fleming's methods could sometimes
be primitive.   On A Guy Named Joe, Irene Dunne complained
bitterly of the practical jokes played on her by Tracy and Fleming.   During a scene with Cowardly Lion Bert Lahr on the set
of Wizard, young Judy Garland had a severe case of the gig-
gles that turned into hysterical laughter.   Fleming slapped
Judy across the face, and sent her to her dressing room to
regain her composure.   On Dr. Jekyll and Mr. Hyde, Lana
Turner was unable to conjure up tears for a scene until Fleming slapped her, and on the same film, the director used a
similar ploy with Ingrid Bergman.   Despite, or perhaps because of, these occasional outbursts, Fleming's films were
consistently praised by critics for their superior acting.

Like Raoul Walsh, Fleming worked for the master,
D.W. Griffith, early in his career, and like George Stevens
he learned the movie business as a cinematographer, developing in the process a keen eye that served him well when he
became a director.   Fleming's favorite cameraman, Harold
G. "Hal" Rosson, told Leonard Maltin:

> I always believed he was a master showman as far
> as the mechanics of the making of films were con-
> cerned.   Victor always knew what he wanted, and
> if by chance you didn't quite know how to do it, he
> would come up with a solution.   Victor Fleming
> knew as much about the making of pictures as any
> man I've ever known--all departments.   He was a
> craftsman of the first order, he was a machinist,
> he did the mechanics.   I doubt very much if he
> lacked the knowledge to answer any solution me-
> chanically. [8]

Fleming belonged to the "man's man" school of Hem-
ingwayesque director, flying planes, racing cars and motor-
cycles, globe-trotting, drinking, hunting, womanizing.   He
lived life to the fullest, invigorated by the example set by
Douglas Fairbanks, a creative collaborator and good friend.
Fleming and Fairbanks reveled in extravagant stunts and gags,
and did not confine their shenanigans to the set.   Even after

he reached fifty, Fleming could be found on most Sunday
afternoons riding his motorcycle through the Hollywood hills.
His cronies in this "Spit and Polish Club" included Gable,
Ward Bond, Howard Hawks, William Wellman, Keenan Wynn,
Robert Young, and Andy Devine.   "Fleming," wrote Lyn Tornabene in the definitive Gable biography, "was the only wild one
of the bunch. "[9]

   In her excellent The Making of The Wizard of Oz, Aljean Harmetz paints the most complete portrait of Fleming to
be found in print.   She quotes his daughter Victoria describing
him as a loving father but a cross between Patton and Mac-
Arthur, and related the nauseating story of the time Fleming
"killed a fly, mashed it with his knife, sprinkled it with salt
and pepper, and licked the knife clean.   To prove he had actually eaten the fly, he opened his mouth.   One black leg was
still on his tongue. "[10]

   During his Metro heyday, Fleming lived in Bel Air at
1050 Moraga Drive, where his neighbors included Gable and
Lombard, W.C. Fields, Gene Raymond and Jeannette Mac-
Donald, and writer-producer Carey Wilson.   Fleming also
kept a ranch at Rancho Santa Fe, and enjoyed farming and
harvesting several acres of produce.   He married once, on
September 26, 1933, to Lucille Rosson, and they had two
daughters, Victoria Susan, born in 1935, and Sara Elizabeth,
born in 1937 (on the last day of shooting for Captains Courageous).

   Politically, Fleming was a staunch Republican and
vehement anti-Communist.   He was a founding member of
the Motion Picture Alliance for the Preservation of American
Ideals, formed in February of 1944.   The right-wing organization boasted an impressive roster, including John Wayne,
Gary Cooper, Cecil B. DeMille, Barbara Stanwyck, John
Ford, Ward Bond, Irene Dunne, Leo McCarey, Ginger Rogers, Morrie Ryskind, Donald Crisp, King Vidor, Pat O'Brien,
Adolphe Menjou, Sam Wood, and Robert Taylor.

   Fleming was a paradoxical man.   Screenwriter Ben
Hecht remembered him as "aloof and poetical. "[11]   To director King Vidor, he was "a close friend, but he played the
part of being gruff, brusque, taciturn. "[12]   Henry Hathaway
called him "a real tough man.   Fleming was a very serious
man.   He wasn't quite the egotist that Jo [von Sternberg] was,
but he was a very demanding man and very positive in what
he wanted to get. "[13]

Fleming and close friend Howard Hawks met when both
men were driving in a car race.   Hawks recalled,

> I put him through a fence and wrecked his car.   I
> won the race and saw him coming; I thought I was
> gonna have a fight with him.   Instead of that, he
> came up with a grin and he said, 'That was pretty
> good, but don't ever try it again, because I'll just
> run into you!"   We became very good friends.   He
> came up to my house for a while when he was look-
> ing for a place, and he stayed five years. [14]

The pair worked together at Paramount in the mid-
Twenties, when Hawks was in the story department and Fleming was a staff director.   It was Hawks who bought the rights
to several properties that Fleming turned into successful films,
such as Zane Grey's To the Last Man and The Call of the
Canyon, Jack London's Adventure, and Joseph Conrad's Lord
Jim.   Over the years, Hawks claimed to have contributed uncredited ideas and dialogue for Fleming's Red Dust, Captains
Courageous, Test Pilot and Gone with the Wind, although this
has been disputed by John Lee Mahin, who worked on these
pictures.

There is no denying the mutual influence of Hawks and
Fleming, the famed "male bonding" found in Hawks' films was
no doubt inspired by his friendship with Fleming.   Hawks
reminisced that Vic would say, "'Dan, what are you gonna
do?'   And I'd say, 'Dan, I don't know.'   And we'd go out
and get into some kind of trouble. "[15]   That Hawks and Fleming enjoyed a mutual creative consultation is indicated by two
scenes in Fleming's 1946 Adventure in which Gable is given
virtually the same bit of business--of playfully acting effemi-
nate while flirting with Greer Garson--that Bogart would do
later the same year in the bookstore scene in Hawks' The
Big Sleep.   Another Hawksian similarity is present in Adventure in Thomas Mitchell's death sequence, although it is
not nearly as eloquent as Mitchell's equivalent scene in Hawks'
Only Angels Have Wings or an identical one in Fleming's Test
Pilot.

Despite Fleming's friendship with Hawks, he has most
in common professionally with William Wellman; there are remarkable parallels in their respective careers.   Both Wellman
and Fleming made their mark in the movies with Douglas Fairbanks, and both started off making action melodramas, Wellman at Fox and Fleming at First National and then Paramount.

Both men were under contract to Paramount in the mid-
Twenties, and both made sweeping historical roadshows for
that studio in 1926-27: Wellman's Wings and Fleming's The
Rough Riders, shot simultaneously on location in San Antonio,
Texas. In the first Academy Awards sweepstakes, Wings won
Best Picture, while Fleming directed Emil Jannings to a Best
Actor Oscar in The Way of All Flesh.

Fleming and Wellman each adapted easily to sound in
the late '20s--Fleming with the Western, The Virginian, Wellman with the boxing film, The Man I Love, and both directed
pictures that helped provoke the establishment of the Production Code: Fleming's sexy Red Dust, and Wellman's violent
The Public Enemy. Both directors made screwball comedy
gems, Fleming with Bombshell and Wellman with Nothing
Sacred. Both men did popular "family classics"--Fleming's
Treasure Island and Wellman's The Call of the Wild, and
adaptations of Kipling: Captains Courageous by Fleming and
The Light That Failed by Wellman. And finally, both directors made aviation movies released in 1938, Wellman's Men
with Wings and Fleming's Test Pilot.

Victor Fleming was born on February 23, 1883 in
Pasadena, California, the only son of W. R. L. Fleming and
Evelyn Hartman. Fleming's father came from Virginia Eng-
lish stock, and had moved to Pasadena from Texas. He be-
came the first engineer to install a water supply system in
Pasadena, and passed along his knowledge of irrigation to
Victor. Fleming's mother was of Pennsylvania Dutch extrac-
tion, and in addition to Victor, gave birth to three daughters,
Arletta, Ruth, and Caroline.

When Victor was four, Mr. Fleming died, and Victor
moved into the household of an uncle, Edwin Hartman, a San
Dimas citrus farmer. The boy went to grade school in San
Dimas, and when his mother remarried he moved with her to
Los Angeles. It was still a rough country and had yet to be
invaded by moviemakers from the East. When Victor reached
the age of fourteen, he quit school during the seventh grade,
to work in a machine and bicycle shop. It was an exciting
age of inventions, from automobiles to airplanes to motion
pictures, and with his innate mechanical skill, Fleming became a master of each.

His initiation to auto driving reveals his flair for

machines.   Foreman Ed Ballard asked Fleming to drive a
brand new Oldsmobile runabout to a doctor in Santa Monica,
twenty-five miles away.   The car was a curved dash affair,
steered by a stick.   It was a full day's journey from Los
Angeles to Santa Monica, by way of the old National Boulevard through Culver City.   Outside Los Angeles, the key that
held the car's timing gear fell off.   Fleming walked to a
nearby smithy, where a bemused blacksmith gave him a
square-headed horseshoe nail to replace the key.   Fleming
resumed his trip, but past Culver City, near what later became Clover Field Airport, the gas line broke.   Unperturbed,
and brimming with ingenuity, Fleming acquired a strip of
rubber tubing from a farmhouse and made a plug with a piece
of dead tree limb, creating a crude, makeshift gas line so
that he could complete his mission.

        By 1908, Fleming was an accomplished mechanic,
working in the "pit" for car races featuring Barney Oldfield's
teammate Charley Soules.   As pit mechanic, Fleming worked
the first Vanderbilt Cup Race, and in 1910 he drove as a
Vanderbilt racer himself, competing with Oldfield, Barney
Blitzen and "the Peerless Green Dragon," and Joe Nikrent,
all pioneers in auto racing.   Vic also barnstormed at county fairs, racing on the circular mile course.   His interest
in auto racing led to flying, and his extra money went for
fuel and repairs on second-hand planes.   Fleming would later
own several planes, and on several occasions used them to
scout locations for his films.

        Fleming had always been intrigued by the mechanics
of photography, and with an old box camera had begun to
take pictures of race cars in action.   With cars, cameras,
and the movies still at the formative stages, a fluke incident
provided Fleming with the key to his life's work.   He told
the story years later:

                    The motion picture business was beginning to get
                    a foothold in California in 1910, but I had given it
                    little thought.   Few people rated it as more than a
                    temporary insanity which would wear off when the
                    victims lost enough money....
                        I was walking along the beach at Santa Barbara
                    one Sunday afternoon when someone shouted at me
                    from an automobile that had balked.   We had Sun-
                    day drivers even then.   It was an actor I had met
                    around town and he was seated in the car with a
                    companion, both of them helpless.

The motor had stalled and its owner, who was
Allan Dwan, the director, was resorting to language
that almost curled back the breakers on the Pacific.

'The kid might be able to fix it,' the actor suggested. 'He knows something about the darned
things.'

Dwan turned a cold and doubtful gaze on me as
I went to work. The trouble was minor and in a
few minutes the engine was turning over. Dwan
was surprised and appreciative.

'Look here,' he offered, 'maybe you can fix
cameras, too.'

I had never seen a motion picture camera. But
it was a mechanical contrivance and I had served
my apprenticeship in a machine shop. It was my
guess that I could fix cameras and Dwan took me
up on it.

'You come out to the American Film Company
tomorrow morning,' he instructed me.

My introduction to the business was an order to
repair an old Williamson camera that had been
chewing up good film in the manner of a buzzsaw
with cordwood. I discovered that the brass plate
was fouling the film and replaced it with a new
aperture plate of steel. The thing worked and I
had a job. [16]

Dwan told Peter Bogdanovich in an interview that he
had found Fleming working as a chauffeur for a wealthy Mon-
tecito family when he was unable to fix his car. According
to Dwan, Fleming was shooting target practice in the family's
garage with a .22 at the time, and using a silencer as well.
Fleming repaired Dwan's auto, while the director checked out
the young man's camera equipment in a corner. Dwan was
impressed by some still photos taken by Fleming, and invited
him to join his company. However it happened, Victor Fleming had entered the movie business.

Fleming already knew Dwan's regular cameramen, Roy
Overbaugh and "Army" Armstrong, through their mutual interest in photography. Fleming worked initially in the lab
at the American Film Company, or "Flying A" Studios in
Santa Barbara, then was quickly promoted to Overbaugh's
assistant, staying with the company when it relocated to La
Mesa. Camera expert Charles Ziebarth, later an executive
for the Bell and Howell Company, was also with "Flying A,"
and he taught Fleming a great deal about the technical aspects of cinematography.

Dwan was making one and two-reel action films, mostly Westerns, starring J. Warren "Jack" Kerrigan (the model
for Charles Dana Gibson's "Gibson Man") and Pauline Bush,
with Wallace Reid and William Russell in support, Marshall
"Mickey" Neilan as the juvenile, George Pierlott and Jack
Richardson as "heavies," and ten-year-old Henry Hathaway
when the plot called for a little boy.   This "Flying A" unit
turned out two of these shorts a week.   Since Fleming could
drive, he often doubled for the stars in chase scenes, and
also drove the crew out to locations, in addition to learning
his craft as an assistant cameraman and camera operator.
It was a wild and woolly time in the fledgling film industry,
with many of the independent movie companies warring for
control.   At La Mesa, Fleming once had his camera fired at
while he was operating.

In mid-1913, Dwan took his "Flying A" company to
Universal, and Neilan began directing his own comedy shorts
at Kalem on Sunset Boulevard.   Fleming worked with both,
serving a well-rounded apprenticeship with Dwan on the action
pieces and with Neilan on the comedy films.   By 1915, Fleming was working for Triangle with Dwan under the supervision
of D. W. Griffith.   He probably worked a camera on Griffith's
Intolerance (1916).   When Dwan moved to Triangle's New York
studio in 1915, he took Fleming with him as first cameraman.

Triangle had snared Broadway star Douglas Fairbanks,
and teamed him with director Dwan and cinematographer Fleming in a series of action pictures that established the Fairbanks trademark of dashing vitality.   The public embraced
him as the ideal American male, living life with physical
gusto, high moral values, a sense of humor, and athletic
powers of Olympian proportions.   A disciple of the like-
minded Teddy Roosevelt, Douglas Fairbanks possessed these
qualities in abundance.   Fairbanks and Fleming became fast
friends, and shared many high-jinks.   The most famous occurred when Doug, Vic, and Dwan were aboard the speeding
Santa Fe Express, horrifying their fellow passengers by
changing rail cars by jumping from roof to roof, after climbing out of the train's windows!   Fleming wrote of their relationship,

> We agreed that life was a thing to be taken not too
> seriously.   We enjoyed a mutual yearning for trav-
> el.   And, we agreed in the theory that moving pic-
> tures either would move ahead, or lose what they
> had gained by lack of action....   Fairbanks and I

preferred laughter and fun at any cost. He was
the sort who would play leapfrog over the stuffed
furniture in a Broadway hotel lobby and I was
likely to join him, although it was never possible
for me to jump so high, or to shin up a polished
marble pillar with equal agility. We had parallel
contempt for stuffed furniture and stuffed shirts.
As a result, we raised the devil generally and enjoyed ourselves doing it. [17]

Fleming proved to be an innovative cinematographer
on the Fairbanks pictures, specializing in trick camerawork.
With Fleming as director of photography, such pictures as
The Good Bad Man (1916), The Americano (1916), In Again,
Out Again (1917), Wild and Wooly (1917), Down to Earth
(1917), and The Man from Painted Post (1917) established
Fairbanks as the top action star in Hollywood. In 1917,
Fairbanks was successful enough to form his own production
company, releasing through Paramount, and two years later
he founded United Artists, along with Mary Pickford, Charles
Chaplin, and his former boss, D. W. Griffith.

With the United States' entry into World War One,
Fleming enlisted in the Officers' Training Corps, but before
his commission came through he was drafted and wound up
peeling potatoes at Camp Lewis. When the Army learned of
his photographic experience, Fleming was promoted to the
rank of Sergeant and sent to Fort Sill, Oklahoma to train in
the school for aerial photography. The United States Army
was employing film as a war tool for the first time in history, and Fleming was in the vanguard of this military inno-
vation. In addition to developing cameras to spot enemy tar-
gets for artillery, Fleming made fifteen one-reel training
films for gunnery crews, working under the supervision of
Majors Ellis and Gerry, the co-authors of The Plattsburgh
Manual.

Fleming was next sent to Columbia University in
Manhattan, where the Army Signal Corps was conducting a
school of photography to train movie, still, and lab technicians for overseas duty. Commissioned a First Lieutenant,
he also worked extensively in military intelligence, testing
explosives and making training films in the propaganda divi-
sion of the Army War College, where his fellow filmmakers
included Ernest Schoedsack, George Hill, and Josef von Sternberg. He tried several times, without success, to transfer
to aviation but the brass felt that Lt. Fleming was more

valuable teaching his skills to Signal Corps recruits. He
didn't go "over there" until after the armistice.

When he did ship abroad, it was with an historical
distinction. Fleming was designated Presidential Cameraman
and assigned to President Woodrow Wilson's entourage to the
Versailles Peace Conference. The contingent sailed for Paris
on December 4, 1918, and the famous footage of Wilson with
Clemenceau of France, Orlando of Italy, and Lloyd George
of Britain was shot by Fleming. He was asked to go on the
President's second diplomatic trip to Europe, but Fleming requested a discharge, and returned to Hollywood.

Fleming promptly went back to work for Fairbanks,
who by now was the undisputed King of Hollywood, reigning
at his Pickfair mansion with his Queen, wife Mary Pickford.
As one of Doug's cronies, Fleming was an integral part of
the court. After shooting His Majesty, the American (1919),
the first picture released by United Artists, Fleming was
urged by Doug to move into directing with the next Fairbanks
film, When the Clouds Roll By (1919), which followed the
early Dwan formula of blending bravado action with raucous
humor.

When the Clouds Roll By is one of the most inventive
of all silent films, and an impressive directorial debut.
Fleming was given a literal introduction to audiences in the
main title, which featured on-camera credit clips of Fairbanks, screenwriter Tom Geraghty, cameramen William Mc-
Gann and Harry Thorpe, and director Fleming. Fairbanks
plays Daniel Boone Brown, a "dumfuddle" who works for his
uncle's investment firm. As the unknowing guinea pig for
the crazed Dr. Metz (Herbert Grimwood), he is subjected to
a series of ruses aimed at convincing the young man that he
is going insane. The picture contains one of the first references in American films to mental telepathy and "thought
transmission," which it satirizes gleefully. Fairbanks' psyche
is represented with symbolic figures of "Reason," "Despair,"
and "Sense of Humor," enacted in an expressionistic setting
reminiscent of The Cabinet of Dr. Caligari (1919).

While the climax of the film is a devastating flood set
piece, brilliantly achieved with miniatures, the most extraordinary section is the imaginative nightmare and chase sequence. Fairbanks eats a heart-burning meal of raw onions,
lobster, Welsh rarebit, and mince pie. Fleming cuts to the
inside of Doug's stomach, where actors dressed like food-

stuffs cavort, frolic, and tumble about. A title ("The stuff
that dreams are made of") introduces Doug's nightmare, an
apparition of a crazed strong man (Bull Montana) who looms
at the foot of his bed.   Out-sized, grasping hands are superimposed on the screen, reaching for Doug. He runs frantically out of the room, right into a women's meeting, as
he struggles to keep his pajama bottoms from falling.   Fairbanks escapes the women by jumping through a painting into
an outdoor pool, but he spies the foodstuffs in pursuit. He
runs from them in slow-motion as they gain on him in regular speed.   Doug takes a slow-motion leap onto a horse, rides,
dismounts, and runs through a brick wall into a drawing room.
Here, he walks up the walls, across the ceiling, and down
the wall to the floor, much as Fred Astaire would do thirty
years later in Royal Wedding (1951).   When the foodstuffs
enter the room, Doug exits and leaps across the roof top,
and jumps down a chimney, falling helplessly down the chute.
Fairbanks grapples with his bedsheets, and his surrealistic
nightmare is over.

     Since Fairbanks' character is portrayed as superstitious,
the filmmakers have a wide range of situations to demonstrate
Doug's protean feats, as when he climbs a building to avoid
crossing a black cat's path. He even repeats his Santa Fe
Express stunt, jumping from one railroad car to another.
When the Clouds Roll By, a splendid vehicle for the Fairbanks technique and satirical tone, prompted Motion Picture
News to report, "Fairbanks, cameraman and director are entitled to full credit for producing a picture which will stand
as a masterpiece of its kind for amny a day."[18]

     As producer, writer, and star, Fairbanks was very
much in creative control of his pictures, but he valued Fleming for his pictorial sense and his technical knowledge, as
well as their close friendship. He asked Fleming to direct
him again, in The Mollycoddle (1920). This time, Doug played
Richard Marshall IV, descended from a family of "God-
fearing, hell-bustin', fighting adventurers and two-fisted
pioneers." Unlike his hardy ancestors, Marshall is an ef-
feminate, monocled fop, raised in Monte Carlo society instead of the Arizona canyon country, "where all my people
were cow persons," as he puts it via a title card.

     Fairbanks' skill as a farceur is evident throughout
The Mollycoddle, whether he is playing the dandy plucked
out of the sea in a fish net and thrown into the ship's hold
with hundreds of fresh fish, or dancing with the Hopis in

a delirious jig.   Except for The Nut (1921), The Mollycoddle
was the last "contemporary" Fairbanks film prior to his series
of big-budgeted costume adventures: The Three Musketeers
(1921), Robin Hood (1922), Thief of Bagdad (1924), Don Q,
Son of Zorro (1925), The Black Pirate (1926), The Gaucho
(1927), The Iron Mask(1929), and The Taming of the Shrew
(1929).   These epics, unfortunately, have overshadowed the
excellence of the Fleming-Fairbanks collaborations.

The Mollycoddle has many moments of visual interest.
In a prologue, Marshall's grandfather (also played by Doug),
is seen fighting off Indians while taking refuge in a water
hole, in a faithful recreation of the Remington painting.   A
clever fantasy illustrates his image of New York City as a
Wild West town, complete with cowboys on horseback shooting
up Wall Street.   In an unusual touch, Wallace Beery's smuggling
operation is explained with animation that is surprisingly effective
for 1920.   There is also a fluid use of subjective camera
when Fairbanks gets seasick in the ship's stokehole, and the
camera tilts and rotates to simulate his nausea.

The highlight of The Mollycoddle is the exhilarating
finale, an elaborate avalanche scene followed by a spectacular
fist fight between Fairbanks and Beery.   Doug leaps over a
small gorge at Beery, who is crouched in a tree.   They slide
painfully down the tree, ripping off branches, and tumble down
a steep slope through an adobe roof into an Indian house.
Fairbanks throws Beery through the wall of the house, then
dives after him, and they maul each other as they slide down
a rock-strewn hill, into a rushing river, and over a water-
fall!

Motion Picture News said, "Wallace Beery deserves
mention for risking his life in such a realistic manner.   This
scene is the biggest thrill that ever came out of a Fairbanks
picture and it will be hard to duplicate in the future....   Victor Fleming has turned out a production which entitles him to
the highest praise."19 Both When the Clouds Roll By with its
flood and The Mollycoddle with its avalanche and brawl were
box office bonanzas, and hold up very well today as solid
entertainments.

It was under Fairbanks' aegis that Victor Fleming made
a smooth and successful transition from cinematographer to
director, and it was with his blessing that Fleming moved to
the 48th Street Studio in New York to direct three Anita Loos-
John Emerson photoplays, Mamma's Affair (1921), A Woman's

Place (1921), and Red Hot Romance (1922). Emerson had
directed and co-written with Loos several of the best Fairbanks pictures, such as His Picture in the Papers (1916),
The Americano (1917), and Wild and Wooly (1917), so it
was a reunion of sorts for the new director. Mamma's Affair opened with an Adam and Eve prologue, then told the
story of the suffering daughter (Constance Talmadge) of a
hypochondriac. Though Talmadge was primarily known as
a romantic comedienne, this picture gave her the opportunity
to play high drama.

    Talmadge also starred in A Woman's Place, a farce
in which she plays a flapper who runs for mayor against her
fiancé. She loses the election, but wins the love of the
town's political boss, and since he gives the mayor his orders, she is soon running the political machine. This includes putting females in key administrative offices. Women
had won the vote only a year earlier, so A Woman's Place
was quite a timely piece of satire, and the New York Times
cited it as one of the year's best pictures. Red Hot Romance
was an even wilder farce, starring Basil Sydney as Rowland
Stone, an heir to a fortune who is forced by the demands of
his father's will to sell life insurance for one year before
winning his inheritance. Stone goes to the Caribbean country
of Bunkonia to insure King Caramba XIII, and finds himself
mixed up in an assassination attempt planned by Enrico de
Castanet and the Countess Puloff de Plotz. Motion Picture
News called Red Hot Romance "the very acme of comedy
perfection ... one corking comedy that would get a broad
smile from the Sphinx."[20]

    These films were released by First National, but in
late 1921 Fleming signed a seven-year contract with Famous
Players-Lasky, the production company distributed by Paramount. It was here that Fleming's directing capabilities became fully developed; he made twenty pictures, only a handful of which survive today. His first assignments for Paramount were melodramas. The Lane That Had No Turning
gave Agnes Ayres (of The Sheik fame) her first starring role,
in a heavy story about a woman who gives up an operatic
career to care for her crippled husband (Theodore Kosloff).
Anna Ascends (1922) cast Alice Brady in a repeat of her stage
success as Anna Ayyob, a Syrian immigrant who is innocently
involved in diamond smuggling. She kills one of the smug-
glers, disappears to escape the law, then emerges after she
has written a best-selling novel under a different name.
She learns that the "murdered" man is still alive, and she

lives happily ever after.   The outlandish plot didn't stop the
movie from becoming a hit.   Motion Picture News reported,
"The director's atmosphere is first rate and he has done good
work with a story which is mostly colorless aside from its
characterization. "21

Dark Secrets (1923) was the first of six Fleming films
photographed by Hal Rosson, and was written by Edmund
Goulding.   His story revolved around Dorothy Dalton's struggle between her love for her American sweetheart and the
mysterious seductive powers of the Egyptian Dr. Mohamed
Ali.   The picture was considered topical because it dealt
with medical cures by "auto-suggestion," or "the laying on
of hands. " Dalton also starred in The Law of the Lawless
(1923), yet another implausible storyline translated to the
screen with finesse, according to contemporary reviewers,
by director Fleming.   Paramount made an effort here to
turn Charles DeRoche into a new Valentino, with a narrative
pitting Gypsies against Russian Tartars in eastern Europe.
Variety said "In direction the picture is well handled, with
the detail in production likewise well looked after. "22

Fleming was tiring of these melodramas, and because
of his good box office track record, he was rewarded with
material better suited to his "action is the word" philosophy.
He proved his prowess in handling action with two Zane Grey
Westerns, To the Last Man (1923) and The Call of the Canyon (1923), both starring Richard Dix and Lois Wilson, and
photographed by the twenty-four-year old James Wong Howe
on location in Arizona's Tonto Rim basin, previously seen in
The Mollycoddle.

To the Last Man, classic cattleman-versus-sheepherder
fare, drew praise from Variety as "a well made feudal Western
that should click on the strength of its story and the work of
the cast ... Fleming, in directing, has trailed pretty close
to the narrative as laid down when a novel and outside of per-
mitting a few overly dramatic subtitles to get by has turned
in a creditable piece of work as his bit.... The feature is
'pie' for all the younger theatre-goers throughout the country
while the older members should also get a 'kick' out of this
fast moving vehicle. "23

The Call of the Canyon featured twenty-three-year old
Mervyn LeRoy, later the producer of Fleming's The Wizard
of Oz, in a supporting juvenile role.   According to Motion
Picture News, the film "has red blooded Western scenes,

thrilling physical combats, wonderful shots of the Arizona
canyon country, a terrific prairie sand storm.... There
are some of the most beautiful exteriors we've ever seen
in a screen play.... Victor Fleming has injected some
very appealing situations in the various reels as well as
a number of real dramatic wallops and true comedy moments. "24

     This James Wong Howe anecdote demonstrates the in-
genuity of these filmmakers of the silent era:

> Vic said one day, 'Jimmy, we're going to take our
> box lunches and climb up that hill over there. I
> want a silhouette picture of Richard Dix under the
> tree. ' In those days we didn't have portable lights,
> and we didn't have generators--we lit with reflec-
> tors.... Vic said, 'Don't bring any reflectors be-
> cause I'm not going to do any close-ups and I don't
> want to take those big reflectors if I don't have to. '
> So we went up and had lunch and made the long shot
> and then he said, 'Jimmy, I've got to have a close-
> up. ' And I said, 'Dammit, Vic, you told me you
> weren't going to, so we didn't bring any reflectors
> up here. ' Then I looked down at my tin coffee cup
> (this was in the days before we had paper cups)
> and at Vic Fleming's large hands, and I said, 'Vic,
> how many of these tin cups do you think you can
> hold in one hand?' 'Oh, I think I can hold about
> six, ' he said. So I said, 'Good, put two of them
> together. ' Then we got the grips together and I
> took the tin cups and reflected the light off them
> onto Richard Dix. And they shook a little so it
> looked just like the shadows of leaves on the guy's
> face. 25

     The popularity of To the Last Man and The Call of the
Canyon spawned a series of Zane Grey Westerns that Paramount would churn out for over a decade, such titles as
Wanderer of the Wasteland (1924), The Heritage of the Desert
(1924), The Thundering Herd (1925), The Vanishing American
(1925), Man of the Forest (1926), and Nevada (1927). Fleming's assistant director, Henry Hathaway, would make his directorial bow in the early Thirties, directing eight of these
Zane Grey Westerns in sound remakes, including To the Last
Man. Hathaway incorporated a good deal of footage from
Fleming's originals.

Fleming's next feature was a nautical adventure, Code of the Sea (1924). Rod LaRocque starred as a captain who fears he has inherited the cowardice of his father, who left his post in a storm. In the course of the 61-minute running time, LaRocque proves himself by saving a vessel and co-star Jacqueline Logan. Code of the Sea was "an attractive program thriller of little more than average merit," according to Variety. "The story itself allows for great photography and the ship models necessarily used in several shots are strikingly good replicas. The thrill scenes are developed nearly to their utmost, and while the story isn't given particularly inspired direction, its continuity is good and the cast competent."[26]

Fleming introduced a new star, Norma Shearer, in Empty Hands (1924), an action tale set in the Canadian wilderness. Shearer plays a spoiled rich girl taken on a fishing trip to the Northwest Territory by her millionaire father. When she is caught in the rapids, Jack Holt attempts to save her, but they are both swept away, and become lost in the forest. They fall in love, of course, before they are rescued by airplane. Variety called the film "a corking story, excellently directed, filled with matchless exterior shots ... while it has been more or less unheralded, [Empty Hands] can take its place as a first-rate first run."[27]

A period picture followed for Fleming, The Devil's Cargo (1925). Against the background of the California Gold Rush of 1849, the story tells of a couple(Pauline Starke and William Collier, Jr.) who are run out of Sacramento by vigilantes for alleged immorality. Placed on a cargo ship, they are at the mercy of a mutinous seaman (Wallace Beery) before they escape his clutches. Variety again approved of Fleming's work, terming the film "capably directed ... a good standard melodrama done much better than usual."[28]

With Jack London's Adventure (1925), Fleming directed his first literary adaptation of a classic novel. Adventure was a South Seas drama set on a coconut plantation overrun with "blackwater fever" and a slave uprising. Pauline Starke and Wallace Beery were again in the cast. Variety reported, "There are a couple of good fights, several thrills and a lot of love interest, all carried out in a natural manner and never too mushy ... Victor Fleming has directed the picture skillfully and held it down in footage so that it never drags."[29]

A Son of His Father (1925) was a Western melodrama,

based on a novel by Harold Bell Wright, a best-selling writer
whose popularity resulted in screen versions of his books,
The Winning of Barbara Worth (1926) and The Shepherd of
the Hills (1928, 1941). Bessie Love, a favorite Fairbanks
heroine, and Warner Baxter were starred in this tale of
smuggling and kidnapping. In her autobiography, Miss Love
remembered Victor Fleming:

> He was as big as a moose and one of my beaux.
> After A Son of His Father had been made I asked
> him, frankly, why he had agreed to make such
> a bad film and he asked me, frankly, if I knew
> how much money the film had made. [30]

Variety commented, "Fleming's direction and excellent in-
jection of nice bits saved the whole business from being a
loss. "[31]

As the contemporary reviews indicate, Fleming was
receiving good notices for his direction on even his most
mediocre pictures. With his version of the Joseph Conrad
classic Lord Jim (1925), however, Fleming stepped up to
quality material and secured his reputation as a top director.
The exotic tragedy of cowardice and redemption starred Percy
Marmont in the title role, was given an expensive production,
and was slated as Paramount's Christmas attraction for 1925.
The studio located an old steamship which had run aground
off the coast of Wilmington, California, and used the vessel
for Conrad's Patna.

Exceptional Photoplays praised Lord Jim as "an interesting example of what a fine story by a great writer can
do for the screen when that story has been translated with
a fair amount of accuracy and understanding into the language
of motion pictures ... it has a quality that lifts it above the
average run of pictures. "[32]

Sam Goldwyn's 1925 production of Stella Dallas had
been one of the year's biggest hits, so Paramount assigned
Fleming to The Blind Goddess (1926), a glossy production
with similar plot elements, Louise Dresser plays a mother
who deserted her husband and daughter twenty years before.
She comes back to find her husband (Ernest Torrence) has risen
to become a strong-arm politician, and her little girl grown
into a beautiful young woman (Esther Ralston). When Torrence is killed by his politically corrupt partner (Richard
Tucker), Dresser takes the rap. By the fadeout, Ralston's

Clara Bow and Victor Fleming
(Museum of Modern Art/Film Stills Archive)

fiancé (Jack Holt) has proven her innocence, and mother and
daughter are tearfully reunited. Variety said, "The picture
is perfectly played and the direction by Victor Fleming carries the story along at a pace that keeps the audience keyed
up all the way. "[33]

Paramount had bought Sinclair Lewis' novel Mantrap
immediately upon its publication, and scheduled the comedy
about a flapper in the wilderness as an Allan Dwan production.
The picture was re-assigned to Fleming for a start date in
the middle of April, 1926, on locations in the Rockies. As
the flapper, the studio cast their promising young star, Clara
Bow, the fiery redhead who personified the vivacious playgirl
of the Roaring Twenties. Fleming rounded out the cast with
Percy Marmont from Lord Jim and Ernest Torrence from
The Blind Goddess.

Mantrap is sex comedy Twenties style, with Clara Bow
stealing the show. It is her picture all the way, and she is
a fireball of bubbly and bouncy energy. The picture made her
a full-fledged star. In Bow, starmaker Fleming gave audiences
a sex symbol for their time, as he would later with Gable and
Harlow in Red Dust. A romance blossomed between Bow and
her director on Mantrap that would last intermittently for three
years.

James Wong Howe was again the cameraman, and he
captured magnificent mountain panoramas. He and Fleming
concocted an interesting visual in which Bow is peeking out
of her tent and shining a pocket mirror on Marmont's face
to wake him. They achieved the effect by flaring frames of
film optically to create a flashing motion. Mantrap did big
business for Paramount, and Variety raved: "Clara Bow!
And how! What a 'mantrap' she is! And how this picture
is going to make her! ... The picture itself is a wow for
laughs, action and corking titles. "[34]

Paramount was pursuing a policy of expensive epics
with historical themes, such as the naval adventure, Old
Ironsides (1926) and the aviation drama, Wings (1927). Fleming was handed the reins for The Rough Riders (1927), based
on the adventures of Teddy Roosevelt's cavalry corps during
the Spanish-American War of 1898, billed by the studio as
"A Cyclonic Epic of American Courage. " It was shot on
location in San Antonio, Texas, concurrent with the filming
of Wellman's Wings, and used the same Exposition Fair
Grounds where Roosevelt had drilled his riders thirty years
earlier.

The studio launched a massive publicity search for an unknown to play Col. Roosevelt, and settled on a Los Angeles book dealer named Frank T. Hopper.   The leading roles were enacted by Charles Farrell, who had scored in Old Ironsides, as an aristocratic New Yorker, with Noah Beery and George Bancroft as two battling Texans.   Mary Astor supplied the love interest and referred later to "Victor Fleming's great talents as a director ... he did get the feel of the period, the zeal for a cause, the heat and dust of Texas. "35

The Rough Riders opens with Roosevelt as Assistant Secretary of the Navy, then traces his exploits as he recruits his troop, trains the men, sails for Cuba, and fights the Battle of San Juan Hill.   For the last scene, which recreated Roosevelt's Presidential inauguration, Fleming intercut studio-staged close-ups of Hopper with actual newsreel footage of the event.   Location work in Texas lasted from August to October of 1926, with studio work and some exteriors filmed in Hollywood in November.   Post production carried on through the winter and the New York premiere took place on March 15, 1927 at the George M. Cohan Theatre.   Film Daily labeled the show, "Vastly entertaining ... sure for big money, "36 and the New York Times termed it "a bully entertainment. "37   At thirteen reels, the picture was deemed too long by studio brass, and it was trimmed by three reels for its general release in October, 1927.

Like most of Fleming's silents, The Rough Riders is a "lost" film, callously destroyed by Paramount along with hundreds of other movies.   It would be especially interesting to see for its technical innovations.   The most impressive sequences were reputedly the landing on Cuba, in which Fleming used a portable radio transmitter to direct 2000 men in fifty boats, and the climactic charge up San Juan Hill.

Cameraman James Wong Howe invented an early version of the crab dolly for The Rough Riders.   Howe recalled to Charles Higham,

> He [Fleming] asked me to figure something out to
> follow the action.   I figured out with a camera de-
> partment man named Madigan a device like a cart
> on aeroplane wheels and a two-armed thing with a
> counter-balance and a camera on each arm.   You
> could lift them up or drop them down as you pulled
> the cart along to follow the action.   It worked
> well ... I always remember the sight of 400

buckjumpers trying out their skill in breaking in
horses for our tests at San Antonio; there was so
much dust you couldn't see anything except vague
figures flying dismounted through the air. Teddy
Roosevelt had made the sport popular and everyone wanted to be in the picture. 38

Fleming had another major box office hit in 1927:
The Way of All Flesh, a melodrama that introduced German
star Emil Jannings to American audiences after his triumphs
in Murnau's The Last Laugh (1924) and Faust (1926), and Dupont's Variety (1925). Jannings' performance as a secure,
middle-aged businessman who forsakes his family for a wanton woman won him the first Academy Award for Best Actor
(shared with his role in Sternberg's The Last Command).

Critics were unanimous in their praise for The Way
of All Flesh. The New York Times called it "a great artistic triumph ... a marvel of simplicity, a poignant character study that bristles with carefully thought out detail ...
compelling. "39

Film Daily pointed out that "more of these 'better' pictures and the public would find itself gradually educated to
expect, and look for, just this kind of entertainment. They
should be made to enjoy such things as Emil Jannings and
Victor Fleming offer them here. There is life, reality, with
the joys and sorrows familiar to all, entirely realistic in
their presentation. "40

In The Film Spectator, Welford Beaton wrote, "Victor
Fleming's direction places him among the few really capable
directors. In my opinion the bank sequence is one of the best
acted and best directed parts of a picture that I have ever
seen. Jannings's subtlety and his nuances, his extraordinary
ability to talk with his eyes, and the ever-present impression
of a sense of humor, make him magnificent in this sequence;
and Fleming has handled it with consummate skill. "41

Fleming and Clara Bow were reteamed for Hula (1927),
and while box office was hot, critical reception was not up to
the level of Mantrap. The New York Times found Miss Bow
"vivacious and charming," but thought it "nothing short of
astounding that anything like Hula ... could have been issued
by the same concern that was responsible for Service for
Ladies and Underworld. "42 The actress played "Hula" Cal-
houn, and the action in the romantic melodrama took place

Victor Fleming drives his star, Nancy Carroll, to the set of Abie's Irish Rose.

on a Hawaiian plantation. Variety cracked, "Miss Bow's
mouth has such an overdose of carmine that it seemed as
though the horse she wouldn't get off had kicked her there.
Or a cold sore or just a bad spot that she and everyone
else around overlooked, unless the director, Victor Fleming, was running this thing through on a time limit. At
other times Clara's sometimes pouting lips resembled a
raspberry ice. And Clara is no stranger to makeup. "[43]

Anne Nichols' 1924 play, Abie's Irish Rose, had en-
joyed long-running success on Broadway and on the road, and
Paramount had a completely pre-sold property when it bought
the film rights. Fleming directed Nancy Carroll as Rosemary Murphy and Buddy Rogers as Abie Levy in the overly
sentimental comedy-drama about their marriage on New York's
Lower East Side. A quaint picture of life in the Irish and
Jewish ghettos was painted, and the ethnic bigotries of the
Murphys and the Levys were satirized. Paramount released
Abie's Irish Rose in an exclusive roadshow engagement on
Broadway in April of 1928, at the unreasonable length of 129
minutes. Business was poor, the new phenomenon of sound
was sweeping the industry, and the film was pulled to add
several talking sequences. These included tap-dancing and
singing by Nancy Carroll. For the re-release at Christmas,
Paramount trimmed the film by 49 minutes.

Fleming was not on hand to shoot the new sequences,
having been loaned to independent producer Sam Goldwyn, an
indication of Fleming's growing prestige.

The picture was The Awakening (1928), a World War
One romance with Vilma Banky in her first starring vehicle
after a series of successes with Ronald Colman and Rudolph
Valentino. The Samuel Goldwyn Company reports that The
Awakening no longer exists. "It is equipped," wrote Variety,
"with charming photography (by George Barnes and assistant
cameraman Gregg Toland), artistically arranged scenes, and,
for most of its length, clever direction. "[44] The Awakening
was released with sound effects and an Irving Berlin song,
"Marie, " featured in the score, but it had no dialogue scenes.

Back at Paramount, Fleming was in his element with
Wolf Song (1929), set in California during the 1802s, with
young Gary Cooper as a trapper who comes down from the
mountains to woo Lupe Velez. Wolf Song featured Fleming's
first talking sequence, an interlude between the two leads
that develops into a song by Lupe. Paramount exploited

this scene to label the picture "the first musical film romance. " The picture was a reasonable adaptation of Harvey Fergusson's novel, co-scripted by John Farrow, who
would become one of the studio's best directors, making
Wake Island (1942), Two Years Before the Mast (1946), and
The Big Clock (1948).

     Reviews of Wolf Song were not very good, though
business was. Variety called it "a sluggish western of un-
distinguished caliber ... Cooper does his strong silent man
role conventionally, and Miss Velez overacts in the emotional scenes, particularly with those ludicrous chest-heavings,
as much the fault of direction. As a heaver, Lupe's a
champ. "45

     Owen Wister's novel The Virginian had already been
filmed twice by the time Fleming adapted it for his first
all-talking feature in 1929. He created the definitive version, and managed to overcome the technical limitations of
the new medium. After a series of small roles in "A"
pictures and leads in programmers, Gary Cooper was boosted
to star status as The Virginian, and later named it his favorite film. His understated performance set the standard for
much of his work, with a laconic presence and delivery ex-
emplified by his famous line to the oily Trampas (Walter Huston): "If you want to call me that, smile. " Fleming employed an aspiring young actor named Randolph Scott to coach
Cooper in his Virginia drawl.

     For this classic 1880s Western, the director took his
cameras outdoors to the High Sierras, near the old mining
town of Sonora, California, and used sound in a naturalistic
fashion to capture the feeling of the range. For a three-
hundred-head stampede across the Stanislaus River at Byrne's
Ferry, twenty miles from Sonora, microphones were set up
three hundred yards behind the cameras, and formed the first
sequence of the film. The main titles are seen over long
shots of the herd, with sound effects replacing music.

     We are introduced to Cooper with a long tracking shot
as he tends herd on horseback. Fleming lends mobility to
the early sound cinema, and later tracks in front of a slow-
moving train to shoot Mary Brian on the platform as Richard
Arlen and Eugene Pallette ride alongside her.

     The early sections of the film develop the easy cama-
raderie between Cooper and Arlen, and their friendly rivalry

for the affections of Brian, the schoolmarm from Vermont.
Fleming keeps the tone light with a rowdy schoolroom full
of children harmonizing a terribly off-key "Three Blind
Mice. " Cooper and Arlen play an elaborate practical joke
when all the new babies in town are brought together for
a mass christening. While the parents socialize in the next
room, the cowboys switch the infants around. "Wonder what
these little varmints think about all day long?" asks Coop.
"Not a gol' durned thing," replies Arlen. "Gettin' mighty
swampy around this bed. " The joke provokes confusion and
hysteria among the mothers, and Cooper pins the blame on
Arlen.

The mood of the picture shifts dramatically when Arlen joins Huston's gang of rustlers. He is caught by a
posse and Cooper is forced to oversee the hanging of his
friend. The lynch scene is a visual triumph, with close-ups
of tightening nooses, cutting away from the faces of the condemned men. The camera focuses behind the horses, as
Cooper slowly, painfully, nods his head. The horses are
lashed, their tails fly in the air, indicating that the rustlers
have been hanged, in an admirable use of the power of off-
screen suggestion.

This incident sets up the climactic showdown, on
Cooper's wedding day, between him and Huston--a scene
that would by played many times but rarely so well. "The
Virginian," wrote Variety, "is truly a nugget of rare entertainment. Victor Fleming has done a great job, preserved
in the cutting room. "46

The success of The Virginian, Abie's Irish Rose,
The Way of All Flesh, The Rough Riders and his Clara Bow
pictures had catapulted Fleming into the ranks of Hollywood's
high-priced directors. His Paramount contract ended in 1929,
and rather than renew, he accepted a lucrative two-picture
deal at Fox. He hit box office paydirt with the tearjerking
Common Clay (1930), the talking version of a popular play
and silent film. Constance Bennett solidified her bid for
stardom as a good girl gone wrong. The critics were unimpressed, though the Times called it "considerably above
the average. "47

An exotic Foreign Legion adventure, Renegades (1930)
was next for Fox. As he had done on Common Clay, Fleming asked for his frequent Paramount writer, Jules Furthman,
as scenarist, and while the script was written, the director

went aerial location scouting, flying his own plane, and set-
tling on the Eastern edge of the Mojave Desert near the
Nevada line for his recreation of North Africa. Fleming
was teamed for the first time with Myrna Loy, here playing
a sexy spy who sinks her nefarious hooks into Legionnaire
Warner Baxter. The Times found it "a muddled and tedious
offering."[48] Furthman would write another film with a Foreign Legion setting later in 1930, the far more successful
Morocco, for Josef von Sternberg with Marlene Dietrich and
Gary Cooper at Paramount.

        Fleming and his old friend Douglas Fairbanks both
felt their inherent wanderlust, and decided to make a trip
around the world, focusing on the Orient and filming along
the way. They sailed for the Far East in January, 1931,
with production manager Chuck Lewis, cinematographer Henry Sharp (The Black Pirate, The Iron Mask), and lightweight
camera and sound equipment. The footage reached the screen
as an entertaining travelogue originally titled Around the
World with Douglas Fairbanks (1931), but also known as
Around the World in Eighty Minutes. It is a seldom seen
curio, fascinating for its informal glimpses of Fairbanks
and Fleming at play in the Orient.

        The movie opens with Fairbanks stepping out of a
life-size photograph of himself, and using a golf club as
a pointer to show the itinerary of the tour. "We've got
the hemispheres a little mixed up," he explains, "a little
cock-eyed, but, uh ... that's the kind of a picture this is."

        He introduced Fleming as "the menace of the story.
He made me work when I wanted to play." After a ship-
board demonstration of Fairbanks acrobatics, the first stop
is Honolulu, where Doug leaps out of a car feet first, and
surfs with champion Duke Kahanamoku, who had appeared
in Fleming's Lord Jim. In Japan, we visit Yokohama and
Mt. Fuji, meet Sessue Hayakawa and Sojin (the Mongol
Prince of Fairbanks' Thief of Bagdad), and watch Doug play
golf.

        There is a cute scene in which Fairbanks is luxuri-
ating in a Japanese bath. Fleming walks in and asks, "How
'bout some work?" Fairbanks gulps, "Work?" and submerges
underwater. "Yeah," growls Fleming, "Moving pictures,
that's what you're supposed to be doing. Leave the golf to
the golfers."

   Fairbanks sends Vic out "window shopping," and Fleming peeks in on a geisha girl as she is made up and has her
hair done.   Fairbanks joins him at the window, but confesses, "I didn't want to peek, but that guy Fleming made
me. "   The pair are chased away as the girl is about to take
a bath, but she catches up with Doug and asks for his auto-
graph.   While Fairganks flirts, Fleming warns him from off-
screen: "I'll tell Mary on you, young fella!"

   Fairbanks' commentary, written by Robert E. Sherwood, guides us through Hong Kong, China, the Philippines,
Siam (Cambodia), and India, but is overloaded with puns and
wisecracks, such as "The Japanese carry courtesy to an extreme.   They're even polite to their own relatives," or "On
the morning we arrived in Peking, two Eskimos were found
frozen to death on the street," and "These elephants bathe
with nothing on but their trunks. "   At one point, Fairbanks
wears an absurd pork pie hat, and confesses, "I told Fleming I wanted some comedy in this picture.   He said, don't
worry, just keep wearing that hat. "

   One section is devoted to the manly pursuit of big
game, and Great White Hunters Fairbanks and Fleming indulge in stalking tigers and leopards.   Documentary scenes
of their safari hunt through the jungle, with Fleming wound-
ing a tiger, shift smoothly into satirical fantasy.   In an elaborate studio jungle, the tiger carries off a native, with much
of the action seen from the tiger's point-of-view.   Doug races
off after the man-eater, attacking the beast in a ferocious
struggle.   In a deft spoof of their macho images, Fleming
dissolves to Fairbanks wrestling with a tiger skin in his tent.
Vic enters to find a bewildered Doug: "I dreamt I was Trader Horn. "

   The finale is another staged sequence.   Fairbanks,
Fleming, Lewis, and Sharp are entertained by an Indian rope
trick, and then, in a reference to Thief of Bagdad, they lift
off on a rear-projected magic carpet ride across a process
screen over the Atlantic, to New York City and on past Chicago, where they dodge machine gun bullets.   The adventurers
finally soar over Hollywood, pointing out their houses, and
land on a crowded set in front of a screen at the United Artists Studio on Formosa Avenue.

   The illusion is revealed, and we are suddenly on a
busy set.   Fairbanks admits that they need an ending for
their picture, so Fleming pulls the plug on the lights.   A

match flares up and Doug invites the audience along for his
next trip.   He is about to reveal the trade secret of the rope
trick and the magic carpet ride when Fleming, the craftsman,
blows out the light.   In that by-gone "Golden Era," filmmakers never divulged their production practices and techniques, the way audiences today are inundated with illusion-
shattering "The making of ... " specials.   Fleming and his
contemporaries preserved the mystery of their movies, and
it is fitting that Around the World with Douglas Fairbanks
ends with the director extinguishing the Fairbanks flame.

   The picture is a valuable novelty, with a seldom noted
cameo appearance by Mickey Mouse, performing a hilarious
dance to Siamese music.   Fleming and Fairbanks are presented as two All-American, red-blooded, over-grown boys,
seeking adventure in exotic ports of call.   Although Cecil De-
Mille and Frank Capra were well known to audiences, and
Tay Garnett had cameos in virtually all of his films, and
William Wellman and Mitchell Leisen were seen to a much
lesser degree, no major Hollywood director of this period
was seen as thoroughly as Fleming was in Around the World.
His camaraderie with Fairbanks creates an informality that
gives the movie a great charm and fascination.

   "Jaded?" asked the show's advertising.   "Tired of
gangster, sex and problem pictures? Want something new?
Here it is!   The Chance of a Lifetime, for only 'Doug'
could take you to the places you'll be going in this grand
adventure!"   This pitch was supplemented by ads of Fairbanks crying, "Zowie! We're off today! Be my pal in adventure!"   Around the World played off quickly, and although
he next sailed for Europe with director Lewis Milestone and
humorist Robert Benchley, Fairbanks did not continue his
planned travelogue series.

   When Fleming returned to Hollywood to cut Around
the World, he was offered a substantial contract with Metro-
Goldwyn-Mayer.   Under Louis B. Mayer and Irving G. Thalberg, M-G-M had become the richest studio in town, and
Fleming joined a directorial staff that included King Vidor,
Clarence Brown, W. S. Van Dyke, Jack Conway, Sidney Franklin, Edmund Goulding, Richard Boleslavski, Robert Z. Leonard, Monta Bell, Tod Browning, and such imports from other
studios as Hawks, Capra, Wellman, and Rouben Mamoulian.
At the grandest studio of all, Fleming could draw from a talent pool that included Metro's tremendous resources, such
as Cedric Gibbons' art department, top cameramen like Hal

Rosson, Joe Ruttenberg, George Folsey, and William Daniels,
and editors Margaret Booth, Blanche Sewell and later Frank
Sullivan. Metro had "more stars than there are in heaven,"
as studio flacks put it, and a first-rate writing staff. Thalberg understood the importance of story. Mervyn LeRoy
says,

> Irving Thalberg knew more about stories. He was
> a fantastic genius, and there were only two that I
> know of, him and Disney. Mr. Mayer was a show-
> man, and they made a terrific combination.
> Shakespeare agrees with me, the play's the thing.
> You gotta have it on paper. If you have real pros
> like Tracy, Gable, Fleming, they don't do it unless
> the script is right. [49]

Fleming brought Jules Furthman to Metro as a writer,
but it was 30-year-old John Lee Mahin who became his favorite
screenwriter. They became good friends, and Mahin worked
on the scripts for Fleming's The Wet Parade, Red Dust,
Bombshell, Treasure Island, Captains Courageous, The Wizard of Oz, Gone with the Wind, Dr. Jekyll and Mr. Hyde,
and Tortilla Flat.

Fleming would become one of Metro's most successful
directors, with one hit after another, but ironically his first
picture, The Wet Parade (1932), lost over $100,000 on an
investment of $366,000 Depression dollars. This disjointed,
hybrid, and overlong adaptation of Upton Sinclair's novel about
the effects of alcohol upon society was stripped of the author's social message and whitewashed into an all-star soap
opera. Metro gave it the Grand Hotel treatment, plugging
the picture as a follow-up to The Big Parade, with which it
had nothing in common save a similar title. The ad campaign
touted The Wet Parade as "The Greatest Drama of the Century ... of Vital Importance to Every Home in America!"
The cast for this opus included Walter Huston, Neil Hamilton,
Lewis Stone, Wallace Ford, Dorothy Jordan, Myrna Loy, and
the unlikely team of Robert Young and Jimmy Durante as
Prohibition gangbusters patterned after Izzy and Moe. Metro's
pressbook claimed that Fleming employed a surly ex-bootlegger
named "Rudy," who whispered advice to the director on the
set. Variety was negative: "This second of the season's two
booze problem talkers--the first was D.W. Griffith's The
Struggle--is, like its predecessor, no more successful as
entertainment than prohibition itself has been as a law."[50]

After The Wet Parade, Fleming was off for another
adventure, this time aboard Captain Fred Lewis' The Stranger, sailing north to Alaska to bring back live specimens of
Arctic wolves and bear cubs for the San Diego Zoo.   In the
Bering Sea, headed for Kodiak Island, The Stranger sighted
another vessel.   It was the Nanuk, outfitted with Director
Woody Van Dyke's M-G-M crew for the picture Eskimo.   The
two ships sailed close together and exchanged greetings.
Fleming wrote about the trip later:

> We ran into the usual ice troubles in the Arctic,
> but nothing beyond routine until we had to blast a
> glacier.   We put out in small boats to pack our
> dynamite where we reasoned it would do the great-
> est damage to the ice and the least to us.
>   Our calculations were all right about the berg,
> but we forgot to figure on nature.   When the blast
> let go, the berg rocked and partly shattered.   As
> a great block went over into the sea, it displaced
> the water, of course, creating a tidal wave that
> nearly sent us all to the bottom.   The Stranger
> righted herself.   But for a few moments, her keel
> was showing up to the Arctic sky and water was
> rushing in by the ton. [51]

Back at Metro, Fleming directed one of his best known
pictures, Red Dust. (1932).   Originally intended as a John
Gilbert vehicle to be directed by Jacques Feyder, Red Dust
was based on a 1928 Broadway play by Wilson Collison which
had proved a flop.   John Lee Mahin breathed life into his
screen adaptation, and suggested to producer Hunt Stromberg
that studio contract player Clark Gable would be ideal in the
he-man lead.   Stromberg agreed, and also turned over the
property to Fleming.   Red Dust established the sexual mag-
netism between Gable and co-star Jean Harlow.   A romantic
melodrama set on a rubber plantation near "Say-gon" (as
Gable pronounces it) in French Indo-China (later Vietman),
the picture seethes with a steamy eroticism that overrides
the frailties of the plot, a triangle situation involving Gable,
Harlow, and Mary Astor.   Fleming created an atmosphere of
incessant heat and rain on the Metro soundstages, the perfect
background for his performers' passionate emotions.   He chose
to keep the film devoid of music, which enhances the oppres-
siveness of the jungle setting (built on a Metro stage by Cedric Gibbons).

In Red Dust, Fleming created the screen images for

both Gable and Harlow. The "Platinum Blonde" spoofs the fallen-woman-type prevalent in Depression films, calling Gable "big boy" and exhibiting the wisecracking sexpot qualities that sustained her throughout her tragically short-lived career. She is an absolute delight in Red Dust as the prostitute Vantine, in a parody of Sadie Thompson. At one point, she looks into a parrot cage and cracks to the bird, "Whatcha been eatin', cement?" When a stalking tiger (reminiscent of Around the World) growls in the jungle, she shivers, "Did you hear that hungry pussycat out there? I feel like a porterhouse steak!"

Harlow and Gable sling insults at each other (She: "This room's full of lizards and cockroaches." He: "One more won't hurt."), while Gable exhibits his macho persona, calling Harlow "a cute little trick, at that." Their on-screen rapport becomes complete in the final scene, when Harlow tells Gable the story of "Little Molly Cottontail," his fingers marching up her thigh as she reads "Hippity hop, hippity hop" in baby talk. Some states cut out the famous scene in which Harlow takes a bath in a rain barrel, bickering all the while with Gable, but despite the controversy, Red Dust made it clear that the pair were box office gold.

In Gable, Fleming found his ideal actor. Henry Hathaway once commented that "there was more of Fleming in Gable at the end than there was Gable in Gable. I think that Gable really mimicked Victor Fleming and became that kind of a man on the screen."[52] Fleming and Gable would work together with the same empathy as John Ford and John Wayne, Raoul Walsh and James Cagney, Frank Capra and James Stewart, and such latter-day teams as Don Siegel and Clint Eastwood and Martin Scorsese and Robert DeNiro. Fleming and Gable were close pals, and the star trusted the director implicitly. Fleming guided Gable through five key films.

Red Dust was shot on a 44-day schedule at a cost of $408,000, making a tidy profit of $399,000 for M-G-M. The shooting was interrupted by the death of Harlow's husband, Paul Bern, a Metro production executive, but the scandal did not hurt the star, who was well protected by Louis Mayer. In her autobiography, Mary Astor offers a fascinating memoir of the making of Red Dust, and records a comment by Fleming when Harlow returned to the set after the funeral and mourning period: "How are we going to get a sexy performance with that look in her eyes?"[53]

Critics liked Red Dust as well as the audiences did.
Time called it "a rowdy exposition of bed manners,"[54] while
Pare Lorentz in Vanity Fair said, "Red Dust is lusty and
fresh simply because, instead of one trader and one woman
and one softy in the tropics, all suffering from damp rot and
sex starvation, we have thrown in for good measure two ladies and three gentlemen, troubled with the same movie dis-
eases."[55]

An immediate contrast to Red Dust, Fleming's The
White Sister (1933) presented Gable and delicate Helen Hayes
in a tender love story that proved Gable was capable of sensitivity as well as macho bluster. A remake of the Lillian
Gish-Ronald Colman silent, The White Sister is a reverent
and spiritual picture that can stand with the most ethereal of
Frank Borzage's work, and reminds one particularly of his
A Farewell to Arms (1932) with Hayes and Cooper. Both
these pictures won large grosses from the female audience.

Fleming employed two technical innovations in the film.
A special camera crane was constructed to move up three
flights of stairs in one scene, and in another, a percussion
blast used hundreds of pounds of compressed air to smash
windows and break doors in an air raid sequence.

The director was interviewed at the time of The White
Sister's release and expressed his feelings about picture making:

> Because I was a cameraman, I am particularly
> aware of one of the most common faults we have
> in picture studios, namely, the tendency of both
> director and cameraman to become absorbed in
> the beauty of particular compositions and to for-
> get that the plot of the story must move ahead or
> the public will grow bored.
> In the carnival scenes and the convent episodes
> of The White Sister, there were many temptations
> to stop, to spend a great deal of time catching this
> bit of landscape, that group of picturesque char-
> acters, a lovely corner here and there. This story
> abounds in such pictorial possibilities. We tried to
> take advantage of some of them but were careful not
> to let them overbalance the production. Beauty we
> must have in pictures, but it should be beauty in
> action. When beauty becomes static and slows down
> the action, it is a hindrance, rather than a value.[56]

After The White Sister wrapped up production, Fleming was off again, on a pleasure trip to the South Seas.

Throughout his career, Fleming seesawed from one end of the dramatic spectrum to the other, and after The White Sister he moved easily into raucous screwball comedy with Bombshell (1933), a showcase for Harlow's considerable talents as a comedienne. She shines in the picture with her devastating satire of a Hollywood star, based on Fleming's old flame, Clara Bow. Harlow is ingenuous, by turns harried, charming, exasperated, glamorous, and always sexy.

Questioned by an inquisitive gossip columnist, Harlow replies, "I ask you as one lady to another ... isn't that a load of clams?" In another scene, Franchot Tone tells her, "I'd like to run barefoot through your hair." Their romantic revelry is interrupted by press agent Lee Tracy, cracking. "He looks like an athlete. I wouldn't want him puttin' his foot in my scalp." Tracy is in top form as "Space" Hanlon, pulling one outrageous stunt after another to keep Harlow in the headlines.

Bombshell includes an in-joke with Harlow filming retakes for Red Dust, with director Jim Brogan (Pat O'Brien). One can be reasonably certain that O'Brien's tough-talking, hard-nosed, no-nonsense portrait of a director is a mirror image of Victor Fleming. Critics and audiences alike loved Bombshell, and the New York Times praised it as "a merry, fast-paced diversion. Victor Fleming, the director, sometimes mystifies one with noise ... but he does his share to sustain the wild fun."57

Fleming was involved in some embarrassing headlines on December 19, 1933, when he was named in a $150,000 alienation of affections suit filed by cameraman Paul Lockwood, charging that the director had promised his wife Margaret DeHaven Lockwood (daughter of stage star Carter DeHaven) a career, and had engaged in a six-month affair with her before walking out. On March 14, 1934, Lockwood brought divorce proceedings against his wife, claiming mental cruelty. Fleming, who had married Lu Rosson on September 26, 1933, denied all charges.

The director plunged into his next assignment with enthusiasm to create one of his most memorable movies, the classic adventure, Treasure Island (1934), from Robert Louis Stevenson's perennial novel. As a reaction to the new Production Code, which Red Dust had ironically helped bring

about, Hollywood began to turn away from seedy contemporary
melodramas and began manufacturing "family classics" versions of literary greats.   This trend was most prevalent from
late 1933 through 1936, beginning with Cukor's Little Women
(1933) and continuing with his David Copperfield (1935) and
Romeo and Juliet (1936) at M-G-M.   A Tale of Two Cities
(1935) and Anna Karenina (1935) were also made at Metro,
and such works as Oliver Twist, Jane Eyre, The Count of
Monte Cristo, Great Expectations, The Three Museketeers,
The Call of the Wild, and The Last of the Mohicans were
all brought to the screen by various studios during this period.   Few filmmakers captured the spirit of the original as
completely as Fleming did with Treasure Island, bringing
Stevenson's cutthroats and rogues to lusty life.

          Fleming wanted to shoot his pirate picture in Techni-
color, but Mayer vetoed the idea because of the expense, and
it would remain for Mamoulian to make the first three-strip
Technicolor feature with Becky Sharp (1935).   Wallace Beery
and child actor Jackie Cooper had proved a potent box-office
team in Vidor's The Champ (1931) and Walsh's The Bowery
(1933), so they were cast as Long John Silver and Jim Hawkins, respectively.   Cooper remembered that "Fleming would
tell me not to whine, to try to act more mature.   It was the
first time anyone had me think about what I was doing, really
to consider any character and make him come alive."[58]

          Wallace Beery had appeared in the early Fleming films,
The Mollycoddle, The Devil's Cargo, and Adventure, and by
1934 he was a major Metro star.   His Long John Silver, the
one-legged rascal and rogue, is the role for which he is best
remembered.   He deceives his young friend Jim into thinking
that he is a harmless sea cook.   When they speak of sword-
play, for example, Beery lies: "I'd swoon like a lady of
quality.   I guess I'm kind of sensitive, like."   Another brilliant serio-comic performance is given in the picture by Chic
Sale as the eccentric castaway, Ben Gunn, who dreams of
cheese, and whose appearance on-screen is accompanied by
a bizarre and quirky piece of music by composer Herbert
Stothart.

          Treasure Island is full of exciting moments.   There
is the nocturnal pirate attack on the Benbow to steal Billy
Bones' treasure map.   The buccaneers batter down the door
to the inn while Jim and his mother (Dorothy Peterson) escape.   Dr. Livesey (Otto Kruger) comes to the rescue by
coach, as the blind murderer Pew (William V. Mong) is

stranded in front of the tavern. In long shot, Pew is knocked
down by Livesey's charging horses, then Fleming cuts closer
for brutally graphic violence as the coach wheels roll over
Pew's body and crush him. Later, on the island, there is a
well staged assault on our heroes' stockade, followed by hand-
to-hand cutlass combat.

Treasure Island reveals Fleming's obsession with detail and atmosphere. The Nanuk, the former whaling ship
used on Eskimo, was remodeled with a completely new upper
structure, and transformed into the three-masted Hispaniola,
complete with dressing rooms and production offices. Fleming
worked closely with Dwight Franklin, artist and historical authority, who had designed Fairbanks' The Black Pirate. Magnificent photography was provided by Fleming's three cinema-
tographers--Hal Rosson, Clyde DeVinna (Trader Horn, Tarzan
the Ape Man), and Ray June (Alibi, Arrowsmith, China Seas),
with whom the director had worked in the Signal Corps. Cedric Gibbons referred to N. C. Wyeth's famous pirate illustra-
tions in preparing the picture's sets.

For the port of Bristol, England, an estuary near the
wharf of the Alaska Packers Company in Oakland, California
was transformed into a bustling 18th-Century waterfront. On
location on Catalina Island, the moviemakers used 500 heavy
pine logs shipped from Northern California to construct the
stockade. A fenced-in area was filled with rare tropical birds
from the William Wrigley, Jr. Collection for additional island
atmosphere.

Treasure Island took sixty-six days to shoot, at a cost
of $825,000. Fleming talked about some of the production's
challenges:

> The most difficult scene mechanically was that off
> Catalina Island where the boat is capsized amidst
> four dynamite explosions. The cannon being fired
> from the ship and the men in the small boat firing
> muskets back required several days to photograph.
> It was necessary repeatedly to re-mine the ocean,
> dry off the guns and the players, and reshoot the
> scene, although it consumes less than two minutes
> on the screen. Another difficult scene was the
> knife-throwing incident in which Hands falls into
> the ocean. Jackie's perch sixty feet above the deck
> was precarious. The roll of the boat made it hard
> to maintain the balance of the cameras built on par-
> allels over the edge of the boat. It was necessary

to cover the mike boom to avoid the whistling
of the wind. [59]

The movie was a big summer hit for Metro, and made
a profit of $565,000 for the company. "Physically," wrote
Richard Watts, Jr. in the New York Herald Tribune, "the
film possesses considerable charm and illusion, and the direction of Victor Fleming seems to have been helpful on both
scores."[60] Treasure Island is frequently revived today, especially on television during holiday seasons, and stands up
as both the definitive pirate movie and one of the best entertainments of all time.

On September 9, 1934, Metro announced that Fleming's
next project would be a musical starring Joan Crawford and
William Powell, his first production with David O. Selznick.
Selznick (under the pseudonym of Oliver Jeffries) and Fleming
came up with an original story about a Broadway star and a
sports promoter. She marries an alcoholic who shoots himself, leaving her with a baby and front-page scandal. The
promoter marries her and she makes a big comeback on stage.
The film was unofficially based on the Libby Holman-Smith
Reynolds tragedy, in which tobacco heir Reynolds had com-
mitted suicide, leaving wife Holman to dispel wagging tongues.
Selznick had in mind a follow-up to his 1933 musical drama,
Dancing Lady, which had starred Crawford.

Selznick and Fleming were horrified to learn that the
front office had replaced Crawford with Harlow, because of
the similarities between the script and the Paul Bern case.
Despite protests, the film went into production as Reckless
(1935). Metro spared no expense, with elaborate musical
numbers and a title song by Jerome Kern, but the result
was an uneven mish-mash of melodrama, comedy, and music.
Harlow's singing and dancing were performed by doubles, and
in their attempt to make her into a musical star, the studio
made a costly mistake. Letters came in from exhibitors re-
questing that the musical numbers be cut and the film released
as a straight drama.

Fleming was loaned to Fox for The Farmer Takes a
Wife (1935), the film version of a popular Broadway play.
Set in the 1850s, it was a rustic comedy-drama about life
along the Erie Canal in upper New York State. Fox produc-
tion chief Winfield Sheehan wanted Gary Cooper or Joel Mc-
Crea to co-star opposite Janet Gaynor, but producer Walter
Wanger convinced him to cast the young man who had played

the part on the stage, Henry Fonda. Wanger had already
signed Fonda to a contract, and loaned him to Fox to make
his screen debut.

Fonda learned an important lesson from Fleming. On
the first day of shooting, Fonda was told by his director that
he was mugging. This, of course, is the ultimate insult to
an actor, but as a newcomer to films Fonda was playing to
a theatrical back row, instead of underplaying for the camera.
Fleming pointed this out to a grateful young Hank, and Fonda
always credited him with teaching him screen acting technique.

The Farmer Takes a Wife, like Fox's earlier Gaynor
hit, State Fair (1933), was pure Americana, and seems more
like a Ford film with its folk singing and brawling, and its
reference to Abraham Lincoln when the boy John Wilkes Booth
passes through the canal. The picture also addresses another
favorite Fordian theme, that of the coming of a new order, as
railroads threaten to make the canal obsolete. Although there
is an expertly realized fight scene between Fonda and Charles
Bickford for a finale, The Farmer Takes a Wife ultimately
suffers from an exceedingly slow pace. The New York Times
called the movie "a rich and leisurely comedy of American
manners, " and proved prophetic about Fonda: "He plays with
an immensely winning simplicity which will quickly make him
one of our most attractive screen actors. "61

After a safari trip hunting big game in Africa, Fleming
reported to Irving Thalberg with the assignment to direct
Pearl Buck's The Good Earth (1936). Pre-production had
begun with George Hill (The Big House), but his alcoholism
led him to a tragic suicide. Fleming worked with Thalberg
in preparing the epic, but was forced off the picture when
he was hospitalized for an operation. Sidney Franklin eventually directed The Good Earth.

Back on his feet, Fleming made one of his best films,
Captains Courageous (1937), based on Rudyard Kipling's novel.
Sea picutres were big business, with the success of Metro's
Mutiny on the Bounty (1935) and China Seas (1935), Para-
mount's Souls at Sea (1937), and 20th Century-Fox's Slave
Ship. Fleming made the best one of all.

A schooner, the Oretha F. Spinney, was bought in
Gloucester, Massachusetts to simulate Kipling's We're Here
fishing boat. It was sailed to Newfoundland for background
shots, then through the Panama Canal to California, where

Long Beach Harbor doubled for Gloucester. Another vessel
was dispatched north along the Pacific Coast for fog scenes,
and to further recreate the New England atmosphere, live
cod were brought down from Washington State for use as
props!

Most of the shoot took place on a sound stage facsimile
of the ship. A first-rate cast was assembled, including Spencer Tracy as the Portuguese fisherman Manuel, Freddie Bartholomew as spoiled rich kid Harvey, Melvyn Douglas as his
neglectful father, Lionel Barrymore as Captain Disko Troop,
Mickey Rooney as Troop's son, and John Carradine, borrowed
from Fox, as Long Jack.

Captains Courageous presents both sides of Fleming
the filmmaker, with lusty action scenes and poignant, poetic
sequences. He handled the heart-tugging friendship between
Manuel and Harvey sensitively; indeed, the whole picture is
beautifully directed. Manuel teaches Harvey the ways of the
sea, and the lad grows from brat to man. With Manuel's
death at sea in a spectacular storm sequence, we feel Harvey's
loss, and hardened is the viewer who does not shed a tear at
his passing.

The film was made at a cost to Metro of $1,645,000,
and became one of the biggest grossers in its history. When
Fleming had to undergo minor surgery, Jack Conway stepped
in briefly to help him out (Fleming would return the favor in
1940 on Conway's Boom Town). Spencer Tracy took a real
chance on Captains Courageous: he had his hair curled for
the part, and speaking with a Portuguese accent, called Bartholomew "leetle feesh." He even sang in a baritone. The
result: Tracy won an Academy Award for Best Actor in this
first of his five Fleming films. Frank Nugent, later a screenwriter for John Ford, praised Captains Courageous in Cinema
Arts as "really a great motion picture."[62]

By 1937, Fleming was making $2500 a week at Metro,
and his next picture, Test Pilot (1938), was yet another winner, Clark Gable played a dashing flier, Spencer Tracy his
mechanic, and Myrna Loy a girl from Kansas, and the chemistry among the trio made it M-G-M's biggest hit of the year.
The superb aerial sequences were shot at the Metropolitan and
Union Air Terminals in Los Angeles, Lindbergh Field in San
Diego, and the March Field army post near Riverside.

The critics were happy too, and Test Pilot was

nominated for Best Picture. The film, still tremendously
watchable today, is a smashing indication of what 1938 America considered top-notch entertainment. It is a bit on the
sentimental side, but Myrna Loy has called Test Pilot her
favorite film. Its phenomenal popularity was most evident
when Ed Sullivan crowned Gable and Loy the King and Queen
of Hollywood soon after its release. Fleming had been flying
for twenty-five years and had logged over 1400 hours by the
time he made Test Pilot, and his aerial expertise is apparent
in the finished film. The stunt pilot was Paul Mantz.

When M-G-M decided to mount its elaborate musical
fantasy, The Wizard of Oz (1939), Mervyn LeRoy was assigned to produce. LeRoy says,

> I wanted to make The Wizard of Oz since I was a
> little boy. But Mr. Mayer wouldn't let me direct
> it. I wanted to both produce and direct it, but he
> said it was too much, too tough a thing. 63

Richard Thorpe (Night Must Fall) was chosen to direct,
but lasted only two weeks. George Cukor then signed on, but
left after three days to direct Selznick's Gone with the Wind
(1939). LeRoy comments,

> So I did The Wizard of Oz with one of the greatest
> directors, Vic Fleming. He was not only a great
> director but a great man. We got along like a
> couple of kids, but The Wizard of Oz was a very
> tough picture to make, production-wise, shooting-
> wise, sets-wise, effects-wise. M-G-M wanted
> Shirley Temple to play Dorothy, but I wanted Judy
> Garland because I saw her in a Fox picture, Pig-
> skin Parade. I heard this kid sing and that was
> enough for me. 64

Fleming accepted the job to please his young daughters,
but he proved just the man to handle the elaborate special
effects and Technicolor photography as well as the charming
comedy and drama. Margaret Hamilton, cast as the Wicked
Witch of the West, and who had worked with him on The
Farmer Takes a Wife, said, "Vic was an excellent director
who knew exactly what he wanted."65 The Wizard of Oz is,
of course, a time-honored classic. The reader is referred
to Aljean Harmetz's superb account of the film's making,
and little can be added to her wonderfully detailed volume.

On the set of Gone with the Wind, Victor Fleming checks
Vivien Leigh's make-up. Clark Gable is on horseback.
(Museum of Modern Art/Film Stills Archive)

With a week and a half left to shoot on Wizard (including the unforgettable "Over the Rainbow" scene), Selznick
asked Fleming to replace Cukor on Gone with the Wind.
Fleming wanted no part of what he, and many in the film
community, considered "a white elephant," but was finally
pressured into the job by Mayer and his close friend
Clark Gable. Gable chose Fleming over King Vidor, Jack
Conway, and Robert Leonard, and in a chain of events possible only under the studio system, Vidor replaced Fleming
on Wizard, who had been prepping Northwest Passage, which
was eventually made by Vidor. Even though he began re-

working the GWTW script with Selznick and Ben Hecht, he continued to oversee post-production on The Wizard of Oz.

Gone with the Wind is the most famous movie in history, and there are numerous books available about its making. The best account is the section devoted to it in Ron Haver's spectacular David O. Selznick's Hollywood. Film buffs are familiar with Fleming's well-publicized fights with Vivien Leigh, his intention to direct the movie as an old-fashioned melodrama, his objections and violent disagreements over Selznick's constant interference. Fleming faked a nervous breakdown and walked off the picture, and Sam Wood worked with another unit before Fleming came back to finish. Gavin Lambert has estimated that Fleming directed 45 per cent of GWTW, including all of Gable's Rhett Butler scenes (excepting his visit to Aunt Pittypat); the barbecue and bazaar; the escape from Atlanta; and, in the second part of the film, all of Rhett and Scarlett's scenes together.

John Lee Mahin dispelled the myths about Fleming and Cukor that have been perpetuated over the years:

> Vic was a great admirer of Cukor. Vic has gotten so much bad publicity on Gone with the Wind. I remember him saying to somebody, 'George would have done just as good a job as I. He'd probably have done better on the intimate scenes. I think I did pretty well on some of the bigger stuff.' ...
> Vic was very fair. I heard him say that many times. And he's never been given that credit. 66

At any rate, it is with Gone with the Wind that Fleming's name is most often associated and he was awarded an Oscar for Best Direction of 1939. When the film was trade-shown in December of that year, ecstatic reviews hailed him for his work. Motion Picture Daily said, "Victor Fleming's direction of the production sets him permanently in the front rank of his craft."67 The Showmen's Trade Review wrote, "Great tribute should be paid Victor Fleming who, with this picture, becomes one of the greatest directors ever to contribute to the screen."68 And the Hollywood Reporter added to the praise: "Victor Fleming goes automatically into the ranks of the greatest directors in film annals with his magnificent work on this picture. It is flawless perfection."69

But this reception was tempered with a great loss for Fleming. On December 12, 1939, shortly after midnight,

Douglas Fairbanks passed away. Vic was grief-stricken, and
flooded with youthful memories of picture-making and hell-
raising with Doug. Since he was a pallbearer at the funeral,
he was unable to attend the world premiere of Gone with the
Wind in Atlanta on December 15th.

After what was undoubtedly the best deserved vacation
in filmland, Fleming reported back to M-G-M in March of
1941 to direct a new film of Robert Louis Stevenson's Dr.
Jekyll and Mr. Hyde (1941), with Spencer Tracy in the title
roles. It was not up to Rouben Mamoulian's definitive 1931
version with Oscar-winner Fredric March, but Fleming's picture was nonetheless a creditable effort. The director played
down the macabre elements, concentrating instead on the psy-
chological overtones to create a Freudian horror show, played
mostly at night in fog-enshrouded London against a background
of repressed Victorian morality.

Katharine Hepburn was reportedly interested in playing
both female leads, but Fleming opted for sultry Ingrid Bergman
and a pouting Lana Turner. He originally had Bergman
in mind for the part of Jekyll's fiancée, with Turner as the
low-life barmaid Ivy, but Bergman was tired of her "goody
two shoes" image and campaigned to play Ivy. She made a
screen test that convinced Fleming to make the casting switch,
and Bergman gave one of her best performances. As she
revealed in her autobiography, the actress fell in love with
an unreciprocating Fleming.

Dr. Jekyll and Mr. Hyde was a surprisingly dark film
for M-G-M, and indicates Fleming's power at the studio.
Louis Mayer, purveyor of Mom, apple pie and Andy Hardy,
must have been horrified at Tracy's lusting after Lana and
Ingrid, the brutal beating of Donald Crisp as Turner's father,
and the overtones of sadism in the Tracy-Bergman scenes.

The picture's most striking moments come with the
transformation sequence when "good" Dr. Jekyll turns into
"evil" Mr. Hyde. When Tracy drinks the mind-altering
potion, there is a mad, surrealistic swirl of kaleidoscope,
then lilies floating on a pond, followed by low-angle shots
of bare-shouldered Turner and Bergman being whipped by
Tracy, then their images turning into charging horses! Later,
the struggle in Tracy's psyche is represented with a corkscrew
uncorking a wine bottle, with Bergman superimposed "in" the
bottle. The cork is pulled out, and Bergman escapes the bottle with a great explosion.

Because of its sensationalistic sensuality, the film was
a big grosser for Metro. Variety accurately prophesied,
"It'll draw 'em out in droves. The promise, however, of
something superlative in filmmaking, in the combination of
the star, the Robert Louis Stevenson classic and Victor
Fleming's direction, is not completely fulfilled. It won't
matter much to the customers.... It may be that Fleming,
keeping closer to the literal than to the spirit of the text,
missed some of the more subtle points. "[70]

The Hollywood Reporter gave the picture a rave review: "Victor Fleming's production of Dr. Jekyll and Mr.
Hyde is a master screen work and a first-calibre dramatic
hit. Magnificent are the performances of both Spencer Tracy
and Ingrid Bergman, the thoughtful direction of Fleming, and
the artful screenplay writing of John Lee Mahin. They have
dared to be intelligent in discarding the horror spectacle that
usually results from dramatizations of the Robert Louis Stevenson novel.... Tracy wisely chooses to play Hyde with the
smallest application of makeup, and his face, though radically
altered with the assistance of Jack Dawn's creations, is no
longer a visage designed to haunt little children. Tracy's
interpretation reaches deeper into the characterization ...
His Jekyll and Hyde is the top portrayal of a top actor's
career. "[71]

Fleming was next set to direct The Yearling, based
on Marjorie Kinnan Rawlings' 1938 novel. Metro sent Fleming, Spencer Tracy, Anne Revere and child actor Gene Eckman to the Florida Everglades with Mahin's script, but the
company was faced with severe problems. Fleming fought
bitterly with producer Sidney Franklin, the location was rife
with insects and several varieties of poisonous snakes, and
the fawn that figured so prominently in the story grew too
quickly and threatened to wreak havoc with continuity. After
a month, the demoralized company returned to Hollywood,
Fleming withdrew from the project, and the picture was postponed after Metro had spent nearly half a million dollars.
The Yearling was eventually filmed and released in 1946 by
director Clarence Brown, with Gregory Peck, Jane Wyman,
and Claude Jarman, Jr. in the Tracy, Revere, and Eckman
roles. It proved to be enormously popular.

Fleming turned to Tortilla Flat (1942), John Steinbeck's earthy tale of the California paisanos. The 1935
novel had been bought by Paramount with the intention of
starring George Raft in a musical version, but that film

never materialized. With the adaptations of Steinbeck's Of
Mice and Men (1939) by Lewis Milestone and The Grapes of
Wrath (1940) by John Ford, there was renewed interest in
the author's work, and M-G-M staged an expensive production.

     Steinbeck's novel was episodic and strong on atmos-
phere, and Fleming's film reflected the author's intentions
of leisurely portraying a slice of California life. Tortilla
Flat has an appropriately lethargic pace, with a great deal
of emotional warmth emanating from the characters. There
is a beautifully uplifting, sun-filtered scene in the redwood
forest, as Frank Morgan kneels in prayer to St. Francis.
As in many Fleming films, one has the feeling of a celebration of nature. All of the picture's performances are excellent.

     Tortilla Flat opened at Radio City Music Hall in May
of 1942. Bosley Crowther of the New York Times termed it
"as genial a bit of propaganda for common vagrancy as has
ever been shown ... Victor Fleming has directed with deep
understanding ... Tortilla Flat is really a little idyll which
turns its back on a workaday world. But it is filled with
solid humor and compassion--and that is pleasant, even for
folks who have to work. "[72] Variety noted, "Victor Fleming,
with careful skill and expert understanding, has made the
most of the simple tale and the carefree characters that people it to win first-rank directing honors. "[73]

     Metro announced that Fleming's next production would
be Shadow of the Wing, an Army Air Corps drama starring
Gable. The director also wanted Gable to star in a proposed
biography of World War One ace Eddie Rickenbacker. Gable,
however, was off to the real war, and in August, 1942,
mourning the tragic loss of wife Carole Lombard, he enlisted
in the United States Army. The Rickenbacker story, eventually filmed as Captain Eddie (1945) at 20th Century-Fox,
was directed by Lloyd Bacon, with Fred MacMurray in the
title role. Shadow of the Wing was permanently shelved.

     Producer Everett Riskin had scored a smash hit with
his 1941 Columbia fantasy, Here Comes Mr. Jordan (remade
by Warren Beatty as Heaven Can Wait), and he came to M-
G-M to make a similarly themed picture, A Guy Named Joe.
Fleming was assigned to direct Spencer Tracy for the third
time. Dalton Trumbo's screenplay concerned a World War
Two fighter pilot (Tracy) who is killed in combat and sent
to that big command post in the sky. He gets orders from

a celestial general (Lionel Barrymore) to serve as guardian
angel for a young pilot (Van Johnson), who also happens to
be wooing Tracy's former fiancée (Irene Dunne). The title
came from General Claire Chennault's famous line: "When
I'm behind the wheel, I'm just a guy named Joe. "

Fleming handled the fragile material with great sensitivity. Dunne's grief at the loss of Tracy was delicately and
poignantly portrayed, and the blend of comedy, tragedy, and
fantasy well integrated. The film is one of the better examples of a genre that enjoyed great popularity in the Forties,
with movies such as Hal Roach's Topper series, Alexander
Hall's Here Comes Mr. Jordan, Ernst Lubitsch's Heaven Can
Wait, Archie Mayo's Angel on My Shoulder, Charles Barton's
The Time of Their Lives, and Frank Capra's It's a Wonderful Life.

The shooting of A Guy Named Joe was beset by problems and took eleven months to complete. When Van Johnson was injured in a car accident, Fleming and Tracy in-
sisted that filming be rescheduled to accommodate the young
actor. This meant that Irene Dunne was forced to begin her
next Metro film, The White Cliffs of Dover, and alternate
between the two pictures, which caused tension on the set.
After the release of A Guy Named Joe, however, M-G-M
had a new star in Johnson.

The picture originally ended with Dunne being killed
in action and joining Tracy at the Pearly Gates. Riskin and
Metro were convinced, though, that this ruined the picture
for their wartime audience, and demanded that the ending
be reshot so that Dunne survives and ends up in Johnson's
arms. Fleming was irate, and walked off the lot, but the
new ending was shot nevertheless.

A Guy Named Joe was yet another Fleming hit for
Metro, and grossed over $4 million in its first release.
The Hollywood Reporter praised it as an "extraordinary
boxoffice attraction ... Riskin and Fleming are to be congratulated for not filming the returned heroes as ghosts or
unsubstantial wraiths. The men are simply there to com-
municate thoughts to their students, and there are no tricks
in the clear-cut photography by George Folsey and Karl
Freund. "[74] Recently, Steven Spielberg announced his intention of remaking A Guy Named Joe, and even included a
short clip in his production of Poltergeist (1982).

Fleming vowed never to return to Metro, and it took
Clark Gable to get him back to the studio.   The movie was
Adventure (1946) and for his first post-war picture, the studio
teamed Gable with Greer Garson, the studio's most popular
female star and an Oscar winner for William Wyler's Mrs.
Miniver (1942).   The glossy Adventure was ballyhooed with
one of the most famous advertising slogans in movie history: "Gable's Back and Garson's Got Him!"

Gone with the Wind was no doubt reverberating in the
minds of the Metro chieftains.   Like Vivien Leigh, Greer
Garson was a strong dramatic actress from the United King-
dom, and Gable and Fleming were reunited with GWTW's
Thomas Mitchell and Harry Davenport.   Adventure also contains a famous dolly shot, a reverse of the Gable-Leigh clinch
from the earlier picture.   Gable berates Garson, telling her,
"I'm sick to death of you."   He storms outside and she fol-
lows.   They embrace in close-up, and them Fleming's camera
swiftly dollies out to a long shot of the couple against a rustic background.

As Variety noted in its review, Adventure "has everything but a worthwhile story ... Victor Fleming's direction
overcomes to a great extent the unbelievable plotting."[75]   The
mistitled picture concerns an unlikely romance between Gable's
virile, rowdy Merchant Marine and Garson's inhibited librar-
ian.   They meet in San Francisco, fall in love, run off to
Reno to marry, separate after three days when Garson realizes that Gable will never forsake his carousing, seafaring
ways, and then divorce.   The couple is reconciled nine
months later for the touch-and-go birth of their baby!

Fortunately, some comic relief was provided by Mitchell as Gable's drunken Irish mate and Joan Blondell as a
breezy "dame."   Gable was right at home with his character,
brawling, gambling, calling Garson "screwy," even singing
and whistling "The Trolley Song" from Meet Me in St. Louis
(1944, M-G-M).   His camaraderie with Mitchell is lively and
entertaining, but there is a disparaging contrast between the
men's scenes and those featuring Garson and Blondell.   Fleming had proven many times that he could direct actresses
(Bow, Harlow, Bergman, Lamarr), but perhaps Greer Garson
was too refined for his roughhouse style.   She is not well
matched with Gable, though she gets a chance to break into
dance at one point.   She fared much better during this period
at Metro in Garnett's Mrs. Parkington (1944) and The Valley
of Decision (1945).

Long lines queued up for a preview of Adventure at
the Village Theatre in Westwood on December 14, 1945, and
William Weaver of Motion Picture Herald reported that "a
largely student audience ... shrieked itself hoarse when the
name of Gable was flashed on the screen, again when Miss
Garson's name followed it, and ... went along enthusiastically
with the picture for something over half its length, chafing a
bit after that, in a good natured way, but staying it out."76

When the picture opened in New York at Radio City
Music Hall, Bosley Crowther of the New York Times cracked
that "Adventure, which should have been a bombshell, is about
as explosive as a slightly ancient egg. Truly, a more con-
spicuous fizzle than this new film ... cannot be readily imagined.... The writers provided a shamefully foolish script,
and Victor Fleming, who surely knows better, directed in a
shrill and calmorous (sic) style."79 Audiences disagreed
and flocked to the picture, making Adventure one of 1946's
biggest moneymakers.

Fleming was 64 years old when he saw Ingrid Bergman play Maxwell Anderson's Joan of Lorraine on the Broadway stage. She had followed Dr. Jekyll and Mr. Hyde with
a dazzling series of films: Curtiz's Casablanca (1942), Wood's
For Whom the Bell Tolls (1943) and Saratoga Trunk (1945),
Cukor's Gaslight (1944), McCarey's The Bells of St. Mary's
(1945), Hitchcock's Spellbound (1945) and Notorious (1946), to
become Hollywood's hottest actresses before conquering Broadway. Fleming was dazzled by her virtuoso performance as
the 15th-Century maid Jeanne d'Arc, who claimed to hear
heavenly voices exhorting her to lead France to victory. Bergman had tried, without success, to persuade David O. Selznick (who had imported her from Sweden and owned her contract) to produce a Joan of Arc epic for her on many occasions, so she was delighted when Fleming convinced producer
Walter Wanger to buy the screen rights. Bergman, Fleming,
and Wanger became partners, and Sierra Pictures was born.

Sierra represented the latest group of major filmmakers breaking away from studio control to produce their
own pictures. The late Forties saw the proliferation of such
production entities as Arrowhead Productions (Mervyn LeRoy),
Rainbow Pictures (Leo McCarey), Transatlantic Pictures (Alfred Hitchcock), Monterey/Winchester (Howard Hawks), Ar-
gosy Pictures (John Ford and Merian Cooper), and Liberty
Films (Frank Capra, William Wyler, George Stevens).

Walter Wanger had known Fleming since World War
One, when he too served on President Wilson's peace conference in Paris. He had been a high-ranking executive
with Paramount, Columbia, and M-G-M, before turning independent producer and had an excellent reputation with directors. He and Fleming enjoyed a healthy working relationship.

Anderson's Joan of Lorraine had used the backdrop
of a stage production for his story of an actress trying to
get a handle on her portrayal of Saint Joan, and the problems she encounters in bringing Joan's spirituality to a
theater audience. Anderson wanted to repeat this concept
for film, but such a stylized angle was unacceptable to Hollywood veterans Fleming and Wanger. They steered him
into a straight-forward historical approach, and brought in
movie writer Andrew Solt (The Jolson Story) as a collaborator.

After a prologue that chronicles Joan's sainthood by
the Catholic Church, with a parallel between 15th-Century
France and World War-torn France, the story opens in
December 1428 at Domremy, the d'Arc family's native village. The scenario was made up of six sections--Joan's
roots in Domremy; at Vaucouleurs in February, 1429, when
she publicly pronounces that her voices compel her to lead
France to victory over English domination; at the court of
the Dauphin, Charles VII, at Chinon in March, 1429; leading
the French army at the Battle of Orleans in May, 1429; her
trial at Rouen and her eventual execution by burning at the
stake.

Wanger and Fleming engaged RKO-Radio to distribute
their epic production of Joan of Arc (1948). They leased
Hal Roach's Culver City studioes for a two-year period, and
attacked the movie's tremendous logistical problems with fervor and professionalism. The enormous task of production
design went to Richard Day, who gathered 71 ancient cannons,
500 crossbows, 110 Percheron horses, two medieval dog col-
lars, and 150 suits of non-clinking armor for the production.
Principal photography commenced on September 16, 1947.
With a budget of $4,600,000 (one million dollars more than
Gone with the Wind), Joan of Arc was one of the most expensive Hollywood movies of its day.

Winton Hoch was a cameraman for the Technicolor
Company, and was assigned to Joan of Arc with William

Skall, under the overall supervision of Director of Photography
Joseph Valentine.   He recalled his experience working on <u>Joan
of Arc</u>:

> That was a picture I didn't even expect screen credit
> on.   I was surprised when I got it.   I started out
> on the second unit work when the picture began in
> the fall of '47.   Slavko Vorkapich was directing all
> this battle stuff on the stage.   When I met Vorky,
> he had some sketches of what he wanted to get on
> camera.   He was a pretty good artist himself, and
> he was going to show Fleming these sketches, and
> I gulped when I saw them.
>
> I said, 'Vorky, you're not going to get these in
> the camera.   You've cheated on perspective.   Be-
> fore you show them to Fleming, let's get a still
> camera and go out on the set and we'll demonstrate
> exactly what we can get.
>
> We did, and then he revised his sketches.   We
> didn't promise Fleming something we couldn't de-
> liver, which I thought was quite important.   We
> slugged our way through the battle stuff.   It was
> very interesting and quite a challenge. [78]

Production was shut down for the Christmas holidays,
and resumed in January, 1948.   Hoch remembered,

> When they reactivated the picture, they called me
> back to work with Fleming on the first unit, with
> Ingrid Bergman.   They did a bunch of retakes, and
> some scenes he still had to finish.   Vic was very
> easy to work with, and Bergman was very nice, no
> problems at all.   On the last day of rushes she
> was there, and when the final scene went off she
> said to me, 'Those were very beautiful.   Let's
> shoot the rest of the picture over again.'
>
> Vic tested me once, though.   I had a dolly shot
> that went down through the rafters of the church
> to a close-up of Joan, the last time that she hears
> the voices.   Of course, when the camera is in the
> back position, the boom track is rigged.   The tech-
> nique is time-honored--you wing back so when the
> camera has gotten into a certain position you smooth
> the tracks back into position so you can keep on
> going.   It's all rehearsed and timed.   It's not easy,
> but you do it.

It was especially tricky because you have to pull
the beams apart to let the camera through, yet it's
done in such a manner that you don't realize the
beams are moving. It's an art of its own, the
cinematographer coordinating the move with the
head grip.

When I got things all set up, lighted with Miss
Bergman's stand-in, and ready to go, Victor came
along and said, 'I don't want you to wing the tracks
back. Make the shot without winging the tracks.'

I said, 'That's the only way I can make the
shot.'

He pretended he didn't hear me and walked away.

The grip looked at me, and he didn't know what
to do. I looked at the grip and I said, 'Wing it
back." Vic tested me there, just to get my goat. [79]
But after that, he was very pleasant to work with.

Working on Joan of Arc had happy consequences for
Winton Hoch. He shared an Oscar for Best Color Cinematography with Valentine and Skall, and Ward Bond, who played
a French Captain, recommended Hoch to his good friend John
Ford while they were still in production. Wanger invited Ford
to Culver City to screen some of the battle footage. Ford was
greatly impressed with Hoch's camerawork and hired him to
shoot his next picture. Three Godfathers (1948), and later
She Wore a Yellow Ribbon (1949), The Quiet Man (1952), and
Mr. Roberts (1955).

Hoch credited Fleming as a strong technical influence:

Vic, as you know, started as a cameraman, and he
would drop me a cue once in awhile. For instance,
there was a scene where Joan was praying, and she
lifts up her face. A key light here is deadly, but
when the face is down, you do have to have a key
light. So when Vic gave me that set-up he said,
'If I were you I'd hang a light over her head and
bring it on as she lifts her face.'

In those days that was a no-no. You never put
a light on a dimmer. But those no-no's all have
to be taken with a grain of salt. I put each key
light on a dimmer, so as she raised her head, one
light faded out and the other light came in. There
was a color temperature change, but in the movement and the spirit of the scene you didn't mind or
notice. It's dramatic, not technical. If you're

gonna sit there with a color temperature meter,
sure, it's wrong, but this is drama and entertainment you're putting onto this technology. This is
what so many people tend to forget. But not Fleming or Ford. They took risks. [80]

After 86 shooting days, Fleming wrapped Joan of Arc.
A rough version was previewed to favorable response in Phoe-
nix, Arizona and Santa Barbara, and the final work print was
delivered to Technicolor for processing on June 1, 1948.
The musical score was completed by July 1, and the effects
and titles were perfected by John Fulton, Jack Cosgrove, and
William Cameron Menzies (the latter two from Gone with the
Wind). The picture was trade-shown at RKO on October 18,
to generally good reviews.

The Independent Film Journal wrote, "Sierra Productions' Joan of Arc emerges on the screen as a triumph in picture making ... filmed with all the sweep and pageantry of
that colorful period and has all the necessary ingredients for
maximum box office returns. This must-see, expensively
mounted film should be given an opportunity to reach the
widest possible audience. Victor Fleming handled the directorial reins expertly. "[81]

"Never surpassed for values and beauty," said Variety,
"an impressive undertaking but ... lacks the one sure thing
which makes a picture great--popular ingredients. First half
of film is an exciting, action-packed melodrama ... second
portion of the film is what the average spectator will find
dull and uninspired.... Victor Fleming gave rugged polish
to his direction, particularly in the battle sequences. "[82]

The Hollywood Reporter raved, "It is a hit in every
sense of that much abused word.... A wiser choice than
Victor Fleming for the directorial assignment is impossible
to imagine. Fleming is at home in the atmosphere of Joan
with its mob scenes and spectacle elements. But more than
this, he is a director whose sensitivity can merge subtle
characterization and human emotions into the pageantry. It
is a tribute to his own finesse.... "[83]

RKO opened the movie in reserved seat, roadshow
engagements for Christmas, 1948. Contrary to popular belief, Joan of Arc was not a financial disaster, and became,
in fact, one of the top grossers for 1948-49. The reviews,
however, were devastating. The L. A. Daily News condemned

it as "a masterwork of cinematic archaisms. Joan of Arc is neither real drama nor historical pageant; its exposition of the spiritual theme that has fascinated all succeeding generations is told more on a Sunday School catechism level. There should have been one adjective for this film--inspirational; we submit two--pretentious and hollow. "[84]

"The main trouble with this script," said Commonweal, "as well as with the direction of Victor Fleming, is that the film makers were overawed by their subject. "[85] Herman G. Weinberg summed it up in Sight and Sound, berating the film as "childishly oversimplified, its battles papier-mache, its heroine far too worldly, its spiritual content that of a chromo art calendar. "[86]

Joan of Arc, all agreed, was a beautiful production, exquisitely photographed in Technicolor, with outstanding art direction. In the title role, Ingrid Bergman brought sincerity and passion, but she was harnessed by the long soliloquies, weighed down by the heavy-handed script. The whole affair is ponderous, solemn, and talky, with little relief from the heavy dramatics, and at 145 minutes in its original release, quite long and tedious. The set pieces, such as the coronation sequence, are slowly paced, while Joan's trial is interminable. The film is too studio-bound, and there is no sense of the dirt and realism of medieval history, as in Anthony Harvey's brilliant The Lion in Winter (1968).

The only exception is the stirring siege of Orleans, with medieval warfare staged against red Technicolor skies, the French fleur-de-lys fluttering through the smoke of combat. Beaten back by the English, Joan is wounded, yet leads a rally against the fort. The British Commander duels with Ward Bond, damning Joan as a witch. Bond fights him back towards a blazing fire, and rather than surrender, the Englishman is consumed in flames, screaming to her, "Burn in hell!" as the wooden ramparts crumble from the fire. John Fulton's mattework also deserves mention, especially the infinite perspective of lit candles in the opening montage; the long shot of Joan's rural village; the French forces moving towards Orleans; and the Fort at Tourelles. This is Hollywood craftsmanship at its best.

In her autobiography, Ingrid Bergman wrote movingly of her relationship with Fleming, how he had fallen very much in love with her and devoted all his energies to make Joan of Arc a success for her. Fleming realized with a heavy heart that a romance with Bergman was impossible, because of his age, his marital status, and the fact that the actress from Dr. Jekyll and Mr. Hyde who had been infatuated with Fleming in her early Hollywood period was now master of her own destiny.   Although she cared deeply for Fleming, his love was unrequited, and she would soon move to Italy to be with director Roberto Rossellini.

The past two years had taken a heavy toll on Fleming. At Christmas of 1948, as the grosses for Joan of Arc were coming in to RKO, he underwent severe and depleting dental surgery.   On December 28th, he left Los Angeles with wife Lu and daughters Victoria and Sara for Beaver Creek, Arizona, the ranch home of his good friend Louis Lighton, the producer of The Virginian and Test Pilot.   They celebrated New Year's 1949 together at the ranch, and Vic tried to recuperate from his gargantuan labors on Joan of Arc.

On Thursday, January 6, 1949, Fleming was suddenly stricken at the ranch with a massive heart attack.   He was rushed twenty five miles south to Cottonwood, but he died en route, in Lu's arms.   He was pronounced dead on arrival at Marcus Lawrence Memorial Hospital.   He was a month and a half short of his sixty-sixth birthday.

Fleming's death came as a shock to the film community that had known and emulated him for thirty years as a robust adventurer.   On Monday, January 10th, simple rites were held for him at St. Alban's Episcopal Church in West Los Angeles, before a congregation of over two hundred Hollywood luminaries, including his longtime Metro boss Louis B. Mayer, Sam Goldwyn, John Wayne, and James Stewart. The Reverend John A. Bryant read the Episcopal service and Psalm 23 ("The Lord is my Shepherd"), and a eulogy written by John Lee Mahin.

The active pallbearers for Fleming's funeral were Clark Gable, Hal Rosson, Charles Cotton, Sterling Hebbard, Al Menasco, Lee Bowman, Victor Ford Collins, and Mahin. Honorary pallbearers were Ward Bond, Spencer Tracy, Walter Wanger, Eddie Mannix, Leland Hayward, Sam Zimbalist, Jack Conway, King Vidor, Howard Hawks, Jules Furthman, Robert Peyton, Laurence Stallings, Douglas Shearer, John Farquis, Ormond Ruthven, Major C. Moseley, Richard Rosson, Lew Wasserman, Louis D. Lighton, Henry Hathaway, Fred Lewis, Vance Breese, A. T. Tergen, John Boyle, Paul Whittier, and Cedric Gibbons.

Fleming mastered his medium with an expert control of acting, narrative, action, and cinematography, always with first-rate production values and maximum entertainment appeal. While one is hard-pressed to identify themes and motifs in his films, there is a recurring moment in many of his finest pictures, that of the memorable farewell. It was a device used by Fleming for its inherent dramatic impact, rather than as preconceived cinematic subtext.

In The Virginian, for example, there is the ironic farewell between Gary Cooper and Richard Arlen, and in The White Sister, Gable leaves Helen Hayes to go off to war. In the last sequence of Treasure Island, a tearful Jackie Cooper waves goodbye as crusty Wallace Beery rows off into the night. There is the equally poignant farewell between young Freddie Bartholomew and the mortally wounded Spencer Tracy in Captains Courageous, Tracy's death in Gable's arms in Test Pilot, and Thomas Mitchell dying in Gable's arms in Adventure. And of course, two of the most unforgettable farewells in movie history, both directed by Fleming: Dorothy's goodbye to the Wizard, the Scarecrow, the Tin Woodsman, and the Lion in The Wizard of Oz, and Rhett Butler's "Frankly my dear, I don't give a damn" to Scarlett O'Hara in Gone with the Wind.

Fleming did not live to see the rise of the auteur theory, Hollywood's revival through television, the establishment of repertory cinemas, the expansion of film history into major educational curricula, and the era of the director-as-star. Like John Ford, and like his protégé Henry Hathaway, Fleming probably would have had little patience with methodological and semiotic dissection of his work; Victor Fleming was, after all, an unpretentious, self-taught craftsman who made movies. He gave much to that craft, and left us a timeless legacy of entertaining motion pictures.

Acknowledgments

Portions of this monograph appeared in a different form in Films in Review (March 1983), and are reprinted by permission of the National Board of Review. I would like to thank former FIR editor Brendan Ward, and the magazine's current editor, Robin Little.

For graciously enabling me to see key Fleming films, I am grateful to William K. Everson; Bill Kenly of Paramount

Pictures; and Charles Silver and the staff of the Museum of
Modern Art Film Study Center.

Valuable research assistance was provided by Val Al-
mendarez of the National Film Information Service at the
Academy of Motion Picture Arts and Sciences; James Cavanaugh of the State Historical Society of Wisconsin; and the
staffs of the Philadelphia Free Library Theater Collection
and the New York Public Library at Lincoln Center.

I am indebted to Douglas Whitney for the accompanying
stills, and to John Cocchi for additions to my Fleming filmography. My special thanks to Mervyn LeRoy, Leon Ames,
Margaret Hamilton, and the late Winton Hoch for sharing
their memories of Victor Fleming.

For assorted kindnesses, friendship, and encourage-
ment, I would like to express my gratitude and appreciation
to John Springer, Frank Thompson, Sam Sarowitz, Mark Car-
ducci, Jennifer Kelley of Gotham Entertainment, Karin Reid
of Equestrian Reels, Ira Gallen of Video Resources New York,
and especially Mary Hickey.

Notes

1. Interview with Mervyn LeRoy, Los Angeles, January 16,
   1978, by the author, Marino Amoruso, and Sam Sarowitz.

2. Andrew Sarris, The American Cinema (New York: E. P.
   Dutton, 1968), pp. 258-59. Also Andrew Sarris, "The
   American Cinema," Film Culture, No. 28, Spring 1963,
   pp. 36-37.

3. Rick Fernandez, "Tay Garnett Speaking," The Velvet
   Light Trap, No. 18, Spring 1978, p. 16.

4. John Howard Reid, "The Man Who Made G. W. T. W. ,"
   Films and Filming, December 1967, p. 14.

5. John Baxter, Hollywood in the Thirties (New York: A. S.
   Barnes, 1968), p. 28.

6. Scott Eyman, "I Made Movies: An Interview with Henry
   Hathaway," Take One February 1976, p. 7.

7. Hedda Hopper, "Looking at Hollywood," Chicago Tribune,
   January 23, 1944.

8. Leonard Maltin, Behind the Camera (New York: Signet, 1971), p. 146.

9. Lyn Tornabene, Long Live the King: A Biography of Clark Gable (New York: G. P. Putnam's Sons, 1976), p. 313.

10. Aljean Harmetz, The Making of The Wizard of Oz (New York: Alfred A. Knopf, 1977), p. 143.

11. Ben Hecht, A Child of the Century (New York: Simon & Schuster, 1954), p. 450.

12. Aljean Harmetz, The Making of The Wizard of Oz, p. 164.

13. Rui Nogueira, "Henry Hathaway Interview," Focus on Film, No. 7, 1971, p. 12.

14. Joseph McBride, Hawks on Hawks (Berkeley: University of California Press, 1982), p. 12.

15. Ibid. , p. 34.

16. Victor Fleming, Action Is the Word: Life Story of Victor Fleming, M-G-M Publicity Department, 1939, pp. 1-2.

17. Ibid. , p. 20.

18. J. S. Dickerson, "When the Clouds Roll By," Motion Picture News, January 10, 1920.

19. Laurence Reid, "The Mollycoddle," Motion Picture News, June 26, 1920.

20. Lillian R. Gale, "Red Hot Romance," Motion Picture News, November 19, 1921.

21. Laurence Reid, "Anna Ascends," Motion Picture News, November 25, 1922.

22. Fred. , "The Law of the Lawless," Variety, June 21, 1923.

23. Skig. , "To the Last Man," Variety, August 30, 1923.

24. Frank Elliott, "The Call of the Canyon," Motion Picture News, December 22, 1923.

25. Win Sharples, Jr., "James Wong Howe: An Interview," Filmmakers Newsletter, February 1973, pp. 22-23.

26. Sisk., "Code of the Sea," Variety, May 28, 1924.

27. Sisk., "Empty Hands," Variety, August 20, 1924.

28. Sisk., "The Devil's Cargo," Variety, February 4, 1925.

29. Fred., "Adventure," Variety, April 22, 1925.

30. Bessie Love, From Hollywood with Love (London: Elm Tree Books, 1977), pp. 100-101.

31. Sisk., "A Son of His Father," Variety, September 30, 1925.

32. National Board of Review, "Lord Jim," Exceptional Photoplays, November-December, 1925, p. 4.

33. Fred., "The Blind Goddess," Variety, April 7, 1926.

34. Fred., "Mantrap," Variety, July 14, 1926.

35. Mary Astor, A Life on Film (New York: Delacorte, 1967), p. 59.

36. "The Rough Riders," Film Daily, March 20, 1927.

37. "The Spanish-American War," New York Times, March 16, 1927.

38. Charles Higham, Hollywood Cameramen (Bloomington: University of Indiana Press, 1970), p. 82.

39. "Emil Jannings Triumphs," New York Times, June 27, 1927.

40. "The Way of All Flesh," Film Daily, July 3, 1927.

41. Welford Beaton, The Film Spectator, August 4, 1927, in Anthony Slide, Selected Film Criticism: 1921-1930 (Metuchen: Scarecrow Press, 1983), p. 306.

42. "Beauty and Banalities," New York Times, August 29, 1927.

43.   Sime. , "Hula," Variety, August 31, 1927.

44.   Land. , "The Awakening," Variety, January 9, 1929.

45.   Abel. , "Wolf Song," Variety, February 27, 1929.

46.   Waly. , "The Virginian," Variety, December 25, 1929.

47.   "About 'Nice People'," New York Times, August 2,
      1930.

48.   "The Four Legionnaires," New York Times, November
      8, 1930.

49.   Mervyn LeRoy Interview.

50.   Bige. , "The Wet Parade," Variety, April 26, 1932.

51.   Fleming, Action Is the Word: Life Story of Victor Flem-
      ing, p. 39.

52.   Nogueira, "Henry Hathaway Interview," Focus on Film,
      p. 12.

53.   Astor, A Life on Film, p. 95.

54.   "Red Dust," Time, October 17, 1932.

55.   Pare Lorentz, "Red Dust," Vanity Fair, December
      1932, p. 64.

56.   Undated newspaper clipping in the files of the Theater
      Collection, Free Library, Philadelphia, Pennsylvania.

57.   Mordaunt Hall, "Bombshell," New York Times, Octo-
      ber 21, 1933.

58.   Jackie Cooper with Dick Kleiner, Please Don't Shoot My
      Dog: The Autobiography of Jackie Cooper (New York:
      William Morrow, 1981), pp. 54-55.

59.   Teacher's Key to Treasure Island, M-G-M Publicity
      Department, 1934, p. 14.

60.   Richard Watts, Jr. , "Treasure Island," New York Her-
      ald Tribune, August 18, 1934.

Victor Fleming 67

61. Andre Sennwald, "The Farmer Takes a Wife," New York Times, August 9, 1939.

62. Frank S. Nugent, "Captains Courageous," Cinema Arts, July 1937.

63. Mervyn LeRoy interview.

64. Mervyn LeRoy interview.

65. Interview with Margaret Hamilton by the author, New York City, March 11, 1982.

66. Joseph McBride and Todd McCarthy, "Bombshell Days in the Golden Age," Film Comment, March-April, 1980.

67. William R. Weaver, "Gone with the Wind," Motion Picture Daily, December 13, 1939.

68. "The Box Office Slant: Gone with the Wind," Showmen's Trade Review, December 16, 1939.

69. "Gone with the Wind Magnificent; Supreme Triumph of Film History," The Hollywood Reporter, December 13, 1939.

70. Flin., "Dr. Jekyll and Mr. Hyde," Variety, July 23, 1941.

71. "Dr. Jekyll and Mr. Hyde," The Hollywood Reporter, July 22, 1941.

72. Bosley Crowther, "Tortilla Flat," New York Times, May 22, 1942.

73. "Tortilla Flat," Variety, April 22, 1942.

74. "A Guy Named Joe," The Hollywood Reporter, December 24, 1943.

75. "Adventure," Variety, December 17, 1945.

76. William R. Weaver, "Adventure: Gable Meets Garson," Motion Picture Herald, December 22, 1945.

77. Bosley Crowther, "Clark Gable, Returned From War, and Greer Garson, Seen in 'Adventure,' His First Film in Three Years, at Music Hall," New York Times, February 8, 1946.

78. Interview with Winton C. Hoch, Hollywood, January 4, 1978, by the author, Marino Amoruso, and Sam Sarowitz.

79. Winton Hoch Interview.

80. Winton Hoch Interview.

81. "Joan of Arc," The Independent Film Journal, October 23, 1948.

82. "Joan of Arc," Variety, October 20, 1948.

83. "Joan of Arc," The Hollywood Reporter, October 20, 1948.

84. Frank Eng, "Joan of Arc," Los Angeles Daily News, December 23, 1948.

85. Philip T. Hartung, "Joan of Arc," The Commonweal, November 19, 1949, in Anthony Slide, Selected Film Criticism: 1941-1950 (Metuchen: Scarecrow Press, 1983), p. 96.

86. Herman G. Weinberg, "Joan of Arc," Sight and Sound, Spring 1949.

WILLIAM K. HOWARD

by William K. Everson

It was in 1968 in his <u>The American Cinema</u>, a survey of American directors, that Andrew Sarris placed William K. Howard under the category of "Subjects for Further Research. " It was a fair assessment, and the fact that Howard's compatriots in that category included Clarence Brown, Sidney Franklin, Henry King, Rex Ingram, Malcolm St. Clair, Victor Sjostrom and Maurice Tourneur makes it apparent that it was an honorable company, not a collection of directors being given a quick brush-off. In the intervening years, some of those directors, especially Brown, King and Tourneur, have received the benefit of further research. Howard, whose career neatly parallels that of another underrated director, W. S. Van Dyke (they were even born in the same year, 1899), has not. Both Howard and Van Dyke started in the silent period with action quickies, made their most personal and arguably most "artistic" films at the end of the silents, and then veered into a string of ultra-glossy studio products with a stress on melodrama. Only at the end do their paths diverge: Van Dyke remained on top, commercially at least, as a major M-G-M director and died in harness. Howard followed the more familiar path: a faltering career sustained only by "B" pictures. Actually the absence of a worthwhile critical study of Van Dyke's work is harder to understand; from the late '20s, all of his films were made for M-G-M and virtually all of them, until his last film in 1942, are available.

Howard presented a more complex problem. When a major company product was finally released to television*

---

*I don't mean to imply that historical research in film should be done via television. Quite the contrary in fact. But making these films available to television also made them available for theatrical reissue, archival exposure and individual viewing. In many cases, no prints existed at all until new prints were struck for TV release.

Howard was represented primarily by his group of five
M-G-M films of the mid-'30s, backed up by two Paramounts
and his last ten movies, covering ten years of activity in
England, for independents and in "B" movies. Understandably the M-G-Ms would have been considered the high point
of those films. But as we know from the careers of Clarence Brown and W. S. Van Dyke, M-G-M was essentially a
"star" studio, and directors, even the best and most individual of them, were expected to subordinate their talents to
better showcase the stars.

Good directors, and among the M-G-M directors
Brown is the best example, were able to do this and still
retain a style that was both tasteful and individual, but it
was often difficult to recognize that style at work unless
one was familiar with that director's overall body of work,
and especially those made outside M-G-M.

Howard's best work in the sound period was done at
Fox between 1929 and 1933. As a body of work this has
only comparatively recently been restored, let alone made
available. Even now these films can be seen, if at all,
only under archival auspices. The majority of his silents
are lost, though fortuitously those that do survive contain
examples of both his best and his most typical work. The
later "B" films and programmers as his career spiraled
downwards are not preserved as a single group anywhere,
and have to be hunted out individually--an increasingly difficult task given the much-reduced commercial value of these
films in terms of television (or videocassette) usage. Complete reconstitution of Howard's full body of work seems now
to be a virtual impossibility, though one hopes for the un-
foreseen miracle that might restore to us (via a forgotten
print discovered in an old vault or an exhibitor's attic) his
very first feature. Such miracles did restore to us the
first films of John Ford and Raoul Walsh, and they proved
to be incredibly valuable in pin-pointing elements of their
style that were clearly present from the very beginning.

An overriding problem, of course, is that Howard was
essentially a craftsman rather than an artist, and was always
honest with himself about that. He loved making films, and
like Robert Florey (yet another director long overdue for
study and reappraisal) enjoyed making them in a manner far
superior to what their budgets would normally permit, or that
the studios really expected. But so many of today's
structuralist-oriented researchers and historians are only

interested in <u>what</u> a director says, and <u>how</u> he says it is of
lesser concern to them.   In such a cli<u>ma</u>te, Howard may
well be permanently exiled to that no-man's-land of "Subjects for Further Research. "

<u>William K. Howard (June 16, 1899-February 21, 1954)</u>

1.   The Career

Howard's parents were Irish emigrants who settled in
St. Mary's Ohio, where Howard was born in 1899.   His father prospered sufficiently to send him to Ohio State's law
and engineering schools, but Howard apparently decided rather
quickly that those careers were not for him, and while still
in his teens he drifted into the film world--a much easier
world to enter into in those days when film work was neither
fashionable nor even particularly respectable, and certainly
not restricted by powerful unions.   Howard's first job was
as a kind of jack of all trades for a film distributor in Cin-
cinnati, followed by a period working on the exhibition side
on the industry.   Then, while still in his mid-teens, he became sales manager for Vitagraph's Minnesota exchange,
where he used his instinctive talents for drama and storytelling by acting out the plots of Vitagraph releases for un-
decided theatre owners.

Returning from France in 1919, after eighteen months'
service in the War, he tried to return to the film business
via the sales and distribution offices in New York's Seventh
Avenue--as much of a jungle then as now, though at least
concentrated into a specific geographic area where the lions,
the sheep and the watering holes were all instantly recog-
nizable.   However, Howard made no impression on anybody
in New York, and assumed that the logical place to go was
where the films were being made.   His rise in Hollywood
may not have been exactly spectacular, but it was fast.   In
very short order, he sold himself to Carl Laemmle at Universal as a sales adviser who would plan and develop publicity and selling angles <u>while</u> the films were being made.
Such activity enabled him to observe experienced directors
at work, and to gain experience himself by being promoted
to an Assistant Director position.   In a few months he had
learned the rudiments of directing and considered himself
capable of directing a film.   One wonders why a man of his
obvious go-getting qualities and apparently persuasive gift of
gab was unable to sell himself to Universal as a director,

especially given the success at Universal of John Ford and
Erich von Stroheim, who likewise had had to cajole Laemmle
into those all-important first-feature breaks.

Inexplicably, most biographies of Howard give East of
Broadway, a 1924 Ince film, as Howard's directorial debut.
Actually he landed a deal at Fox in 1921, and made some 13
films (for Fox and various independents) before East of Broadway. The Fox deal began with a brief apprenticeship. His
very first film, Get Your Man, was made in late 1920 and
released in early 1921. A Buck Jones melodrama, it allotted
Howard a co-director credit with George Hill, oddly enough
not the experienced director that would often be assigned to
guide a new talent, but a newcomer himself and soon to assume a major directorial berth at Metro.

Howard's second credit was on another Jones vehicle,
One Man Trial (released in March of 1921), but as the scenarist, while Bernard Durning directed. Howard's first solo
directing credit came with Play Square, released in August
of 1921. From that point on, Howard was established as a
director and never again shared directorial billing, though
much later in his career he was twice called in to "doctor"
films directed by others. There were also more scenario
credits for Howard (on three silents that he did not direct),
but essentially he was not a writer. The scenarios that he
did were all screen treatments of originals written by others,
and the essence of his writing talent was in translating the
written word into visual terms.

His early Fox films were exceptionally short in running
time, usually 4000 to 5000 feet. In the sound period they
would have been considered "B" movies, but such a classifi-
cation did not exist in the early silent period. Obviously
there was an enormous range in the variety, cost and importance of given movies, but each was designed to stand
on its own as a single bill, the Howard actioners finding
their key audiences in relatively unimportant time-slots or
at Saturday matinees. Nevertheless, since each film was
regarded as single-bill material (though the shorter and
lesser ones needed extra-strength help from short subjects)
it was usually afforded the best production values that the
budget could allow, and a major studio like Fox would be
concerned about maintaining its "class" image even on smaller films.

It is particularly unfortunate that none of Howard's

early Fox films is available for study today. Buck Jones
was an important Fox star, and a good actor as well as a
likable Western type. Moreover, he had much in common
with Jack Holt, with whom Howard was to work so well at
Paramount in just a few years. Too, in these early Fox
films Howard was already making associations that would
last throughout his career. His third film, Play Square,
introduced him to Johnnie Walker, a slightly built yet rugged
player who, rather curiously, looked a little like Howard and
had much the same kind of temperament. Walker starred in
later Howard films, too, and remained a lifelong friend; as
late as 1939 Howard used him as a production associate (and
small part player) in Backdoor to Heaven. The visual quality
was always of paramount importance to Howard; once he was
established and had sufficient clout, he built up team association with such cameramen as Lucien Andriot (on his De-
Mille films) and James Wong Howe (at Fox) as well as one
of the top art directors, Anton Grot. Howard's cameraman
on his initial Fox films was Frank Good, an excellent cinematographer who seemed forever wasted on independent and "B"
product, but whose crystal-clear focus and intricate lighting
raised the level of many an otherwise unimportant film. Presumably the "look" he brought to the early Howard actioners
had a lot to do with their success, and may have influenced
Howard a great deal.

Of Howard's first 18 films (1921-1925) only two are
known to survive. Since they (Let's Go and Captain Fly by
Night) were made for independent companies on shoestring
budgets, their quality raises expectations about the other
sixteen, most of which, small films or not, were made under conditions providing better studio facilities and budgets.
From 1926 on the picture is a little brighter and while there
are frustrating gaps in the Howard chronology, at least the
available films are thoroughly representative and do contain
the titles reputed to be his best.

On the strength of his promising independent work
(and perhaps because Paramount was a notoriously cheap
company that would naturally gravitate to a director who
could turn out a class product on a small budget) Paramount
signed Howard to a contract in 1924. The only film to survive is 1926's Volcano, a Bebe Daniels vehicle, which unfortunately cannot be reliably appraised in the extant version.
An elaborate but rather silly romantic melodrama, it was
clearly saving most of its energies for the big climax of
the volcanic eruption--all of which was removed from

Returning from the Arizona location of the Thundering Herd
(l. to r.): Noah Beery, Noah Beery, Jr. , Lucien Andriot,
Howard and Jack Holt.

Paramount's negative for use as stock footage in other films.
No prints were saved, and new prints--made up from the
emasculated negative--are missing the melodramatic highlight which presumably showed Howard at his best! Far
more successful, both commercially and critically, were
four large-scale Westerns based on Zane Grey novels.
Again, none has survived, but from other isolated Westerns
in this prolific Grey series one can see that Paramount did
devote real care to this series, and that they maintained an
overall high standard. Moreover, much of Howard's action
footage was re-used by Paramount when they remade the
films as talkies, and Howard's handling of action and spectacle was done with real style and vigor. The best of Howard's quartet would seem to be The Thundering Herd (his
last Paramount film of 1925), which starred Jack Holt, Tim
McCoy and Noah Beery. Impressive footage from this film
was used not only in the 1933 remake, but also as late as
1940 in Geronimo. Howard was much impressed by Jack
Holt, and they remained firm friends until Holt's death in
1952.

     Howard's stay at Famous Players /Paramount was

short-lived, though not through any dissatisfaction with his work there.   When Cecil B. DeMille withdrew from the company following disagreements over the production and handling of The Ten Commandments (and resentment of rather shabby treatment of him personally by Paramount executives) he took some key people with him--including stars Leatrice Joy, Rod la Rocque and William Boyd--and invited William K. Howard to join him too as the "prestige" director (next to DeMille himself!) in his newly organized Producers Distributing Corporation.   Howard accepted with alacrity, seeing PDC as a parallel company to United Artists, and one which would give him greater opportunities than Paramount had.   In one sense his judgment was good.   PDC did give him the chance to make his two best films to date, and as it happened, two that would remain among his best: White Gold and A Ship Comes In. But PDC faced the same basic problem that United Artists had faced--an inability to exist on prestige product alone, and the need for a constant flow of bread-and-butter movies.   Considering the difficulties it faced, PDC did rather well.   The star vehicles kept the fans happy, and cameramen like Arthur Miller and Peverell Marley, and art directors such as Anton Grot, Mitchell Leisen and Paul Iribe worked wonders with set designs and glass shots that expanded the horizons of limited budgets.   Less distinguished directors--Elmer Clifton, Donald Crisp and Paul Sloane--kept the run-of-the-mill product running efficiently and new talent, John Farrow and Tay Garnett in particular, was being broken in via the title writing and scenario route.   Although it had its fair share of mediocrities, PDC turned out showmanlike pictures.   However, releasing through Pathé, it had no guaranteed theater outlets, and the coming of sound presented real financial problems.   Although Pathé eventually evolved into RKO Pathé and then RKO-Radio, in 1929 most of its major talent assets broke up.   DeMille went to M-G-M for a brief stay before returning to Paramount under much happier and more powerful circumstances, and Howard was signed to a particularly felicitous contract at Fox.

Fox at that time had virtually no leadership and a relatively weak roster of stars.   If M-G-M was a star studio, then Fox was a director studio.   Raoul Walsh, John Ford, Frank Borzage, Howard Hawks and the great F. W. Murnau were already there, and William Dieterle, Erich von Stroheim, Rowland Brown, James Cruze and others would be arriving within a year or two.   It was a marvelous opportunity for any director to experiment and establish a personal style, and Howard took full advantage of it.   Long an admirer of Germanic style and technique, and prone to reflect that admiration

in his own films (White Gold especially), he found that Fox
was still so much in awe of Murnau (despite films subsequent
to Sunrise that had not maintained its momentum in terms of
critical response) that emulating German style even in essentially commercial films was encouraged rather than frowned
upon.   Howard became great friends with Murnau in that relatively short period before Murnau's tragic death in 1931, and
was one of the pallbearers at his funeral.   Even though the
Germanic echoes in Howard's melodramas derive more directly from Lang than from Murnau, it was undoubtedly his
association with Murnau that most influenced Howard.   (Indeed, the individual Lang scenes that are recognizably used
as the pattern for Howard scenes are, for the most part,
from later Lang movies.)

        The 13 Fox films came to their climax with the crit-
ically acclaimed The Power and The Glory (1933), largely on
the strength of which Howard was offered a contract at
M-G-M.   The five glossy star vehicles (Helen Hayes, William
Powell, Myrna Loy) that resulted were all good, extremely
well-crafted and well-mounted films, but even when their subject matter veered to melodrama, the Howard penchant for
fast cutting and stylish angles had to be soft-pedaled.   There
was nothing wrong with the films, which were well received
by both critics and public, but they caused Howard to mark
time precisely when he should have been striding forward
from his Fox period.   This waste of his talent was confirmed
when he moved back to Paramount in 1935 for a brace of
films, the first of which, Mary Burns, Fugitive, was a dynamic thriller in the best Lang tradition (even its flaws were
Langian!).   In 1937 Howard was invited to England by Alexander Korda--a measure of the prestige he had achieved,
since by that time Korda, aiming at an international market
for his films, was importing both the top Hollywood and European names (stars, cameramen, directors) to help achieve
that end.   Howard, re-united with one of his favorite Hollywood cameramen, James Wong Howe, was assigned to one
of the most important British films of the year, Fire Over
England.   Then, however, things began--slowly and without
any definite pattern--to go wrong.   Howard's second Korda
film, The Squeaker, was a good one, but no more than that.
Howard actually gave it far more style than its relatively
simple crime story needed, but it was still an anti-climactic
follow-up to Fire Over England.   Then he was asked to doctor a third Korda film, and virtually salvage a fourth one
that had turned out badly.   The association with second-
string assignments certainly did his career no good at that
point.

Back in Hollywood in 1938--a year of relative doldrums for Hollywood--he was confronted with two problems. One, his kind of high-powered melodrama had virtually (though only temporarily) disappeared from the screen, pushed into hibernation by the Production Code's fostering of more "wholesome," family-oriented entertainment. Raoul Walsh, who had been a contemporary of Howard's at Fox and made the same gutsy kind of melodramas (and who had also made a brief trip to England seeking better and more virile material), was working out his Paramount contract on puerile musicals and simple romances, exactly the kind of film he was least suited to. Seeking to re-establish himself with a really personal film, Howard promoted a pet project of his from one of his own stories, Back Door to Heaven. It was--and is--a remarkable little film, albeit a trifle old-fashioned in its narrative technique and reminding one (though not unfavorably) of some of his silents. However, it was virtually a film-noir, an unremittingly downbeat film which, devoid of a star like Muni or Tracy who could have made such a film commercially viable, had virtually no chance of success. Moreover, it was made--extremely economically--at the old Paramount Studios in Astoria, New York, and it clearly lacked the polish and gloss for which Howard was famous.

Howard began to drink; not enough to impair his reliability or to affect his work--when it came--but enough certainly that he became a difficult man to deal with, and not one to inspire confidence should a major project have come along. However, the six final films that followed Back Door to Heaven were neither devoid of interest, nor did they represent a steady decline. One of his best opportunities for some time came when James Cagney, producing independently, offered Howard the chance to direct Johnny Come Lately (1943), from a novel by Louis Bromfield. Unfortunately, Cagney was trying to establish himself as an artist as well as a personality; it was deliberately different and gentle. Howard did a good job with it, but the Cagney fans were disappointed. Cagney himself wouldn't fully recover his lost momentum until he returned to Warners in 1949 and re-established himself with White Heat. For Howard, however, it was too late.

In 1946 Republic offered him a contract for a group of films--presumably the same kind of contract (for the same kind of "B" actioners) that they had offered James Cruze in 1938. The four Cruze films had been minor, but nothing to be ashamed of, and they had kept him usefully busy. The first of the Howard films, rather unfortunately titled A

Guy Could Change, indicated that it was following the same
pattern. It was neat, economical and efficient. It was also
the last film he made.

One often wonders, rather sadly, just how much
friendship really counts in Hollywood. Why are so many
eminently employable talents allowed to go to waste? Why,
for example, did Boris Karloff (who certainly had the clout
to do so) not try to bring James Whale into the Val Lewton
horror unit at RKO in the early '40s? Why didn't Tay Garnett, an old friend and colleague of Howard's, who on many
occasions expressed tremendous admiration for him and felt
him to be one of the best directors in the business, not try
to bring him into M-G-M where he (Garnett) was riding high,
and where Howard could certainly have fitted honorably into
Dore Schary's so-called "B" unit? Questions like that can
never be answered, of course; nor, knowing the pressures
and politics of the studio system of the time, is it really fair
to imply some kind of failing on the part of friends and colleagues who did not provide aid when it was needed.

Howard, in any case, had not lost confidence in him-
self--nor had he lost the enthusiasm for making movies. Rea-
soning (not without some logic) that since his White Gold had
been acclaimed a silent masterpiece, yet was essentially a
non-action piece that depended on the evocation of mood, and
might benefit from the addition of dialogue, he hit upon the
idea of remaking it. Curiously, rights had been passed on
in the late '30s to the Charles Laughton-Erich Pommer May-
flower group, but after three extremely interesting Laughton
vehicles (presumably he would have played the lesser role
of the father, had the film in fact been remade then) the war
intervened, and the company dissolved. Howard, locating
himself in New York, acquired the property and set about
promoting its remake. Unfortunately, his old literary short-
coming--he was a functional writer rather than a genuinely
creative one--proved its downfall. Instead of working with
a writer, he wrote the new script himself, merely adding
dialogue to the original material rather than coming up with
a new concept. Quite possibly, had the project gotten underway, that would have been sufficient. Howard as a director
was certainly creative and innovative enough to transform a
script into a real film merely by his dazzling technique. The
routine script of The Trial of Vivienne Ware (1932) and the
dynamic film that he made of it are ample proof of that. But
it wasn't enough to arouse interest in the film where it
counted--from the distributors or independent financiers.

When Howard died in 1954 he was still trying to sell <u>White</u>
<u>Gold</u>--and happily was convinced that he would do so, and
that a major comeback was thus imminent.

2.   The Films

Since "lost" films are still turning up (though with
far less frequency than hitherto) it would be unnecessarily
defeatist to state categorically that all of the early Howards
are irrevocably lost.   But in realistic terms, their redis-
covery is extremely unlikely, and in any case time is running out.   Time--and essentially the hot summers--is the
perennial enemy of silent nitrate film, and if anything exists
it has to be found and transferred to safety stock without de-
lay.

One would give much to see Howard's initial Fox
melodramas and westerns, and especially <u>Deserted at the</u>
<u>Altar</u>, made in late 1922, and the seventh film with which
he was associated.   <u>Deserted at the Altar</u> is, minus the
spectacular climax, an adaptation of a play that was a direct
steal from <u>Way Down East</u>.   Not only does the film use a
former Griffith leading lady (Bessie Love), who was a contemporary of Lillian Gish and a similar "type," but it even
has the temerity to give her the same character name as
<u>Way Down East</u>'s heroine, Anna Moore!   (It's surprising the
number of small-scale independent productions that <u>Way Down</u>
<u>East</u> influenced; William Seiter's <u>The White Sin</u>, of 1924, was
a later example.   One would have thought that the original,
with Gish's incredible performance and its remarkable ice-
floe climax, was so "definitive" as to discourage any imita-
tion, let alone those produced on extremely limited budgets.)

The earliest extant Howard is <u>Captain Fly By Night</u>,
film number five.   Although it is basically a rip-off of Fairbanks' <u>The Mark of Zorro</u>, the pilfering was done by the
original author, Johnston McCulley.   The characters and
swashbuckling action remain almost identical, but there is
an element of mystery in that one never knows for sure
until the end just <u>who</u> the titular captain is, and whether
he is a good badman or a bad badman!   Howard, assisted
by a cameraman who would work with him a great deal in
the future, Lucien Andriot, manages to make an obviously
cheap film look quite glossy.   Scenes are neatly composed,
and Howard's penchant for exciting editing and angling is
already well in evidence.   A climactic duel atop a bell-

tower is particularly well done. Even the inter-titles manage
to elevate the film's intentions from routine western to would-
be epic, referring to the decidedly unimpressive posse of
villains as "conspirators," and to the lead villain's fairly
orthodox chicanery as a plot to overthrow the government!
The few surviving prints of this interesting and still entertaining little film are all printed on vibrant amber stock,
reminding one how the use of toned stock (enhanced of
course by the incredible vitality of the old nitrate prints)
could add real polish and an illusion of higher production
values to even the most economical silent quickie.

Curiously, the last of Howard's silent quickies, Let's
Go (1923), Howard's thirteenth film, has also survived.   A
vehicle for Richard Talmadge, stuntman/star, double for
Douglas Fairbanks, and in the later sound period a notable
second-unit director for stunt and action sequences, it is
literally no more than three prolonged stunt-action sequences
linked by a serviceable tale of a ne'er-do-well son of a big
city business man landing in a small town, rounding up local
crooks, and saving his father from involvement in a fraudu-
lent scheme.   Talmadge's speciality was spectacular acrobatic
leaps--aboard moving vehicles, from building to building or
from building to passing truck--and Howard keeps the camera
in close in all these scenes, stressing the lack of doubles and
back projection.   The chase and action scenes aboard a moving
train are particularly well done.   Let's Go also uses a favorite trick of silent quickies by employing a number of fairly
well-known players (Fairbanks' leading-lady Eileen Percy,
character actors George Nicholls, Tully Marshall, Mathew
Betz and others), giving each of them about a day's work, and
and spacing their appearances so that there's always a known
face on screen, and an aura of production-respectability is
thus maintained.   Only in the frenetic but not very convincing
fisticuffs does the action element falter.   Howard made a
number of Talmadge vehicles in the early '20s and one of
them, Danger Ahead, was virtually remade by Talmadge as
a mid-30s talkie, Now or Never.

It is unfortunate that of all Howard's Paramounts, only
Volcano (1926) survives, and that in an incomplete print.
It's a silly and outdated romantic melodrama in which the
main issue is the apparent "black blood" in the veins of
heroine Bebe Daniels.   Ultimately her 100% pure French
ancestry is established, paving the way for her happy marriage to aristocrat Ricardo Cortez.   (Raoul Walsh's much-
later Band of Angels presented a similar story, but without

the climactic racial compromise and cop-out). Such an artificial tale can only work if the budget allows the mise-en-
scène to be of a bravura nature. Paramount allowed such
extravagance to von Sternberg in the '30s, but in the '20s
was notoriously reticent about expanding budgets for any but
the real super-specials. Volcano thus not only seems silly
and lurid, but also very cheap; how much all that was com-
pensated for by the climactic volcanic eruption of Mount
Pelée can only be surmised. With Lucien Andriot photo-
graphing, one has high hopes, but critics of the time were
not impressed. In any event, the entire climax is now lost,
having been re-routed to the stock shot vault and periodically
decimated.

However, from 1926 on, most of the Howard films do
exist. Bachelor Brides, from the DeMille group for Producers Distributing Corp., is one of the many film versions
of the many plays ("One Exciting Night," "The Bat," "The
Gorilla," "The Cat and the Canary") that established an "old
dark house" school in the '20s. The play veered more to
comedy and satire than chills; Howard, backed by cameraman Andriot, tries to redress the balance somewhat in the
film version. Stylistically and photographically it is atmos-
pheric and exciting, but the plot remains singularly devoid
of real menace and the miscreants are ultimately revealed
to be no more than jewel thieves. Rod la Rocque's broad
playing also tends to undermine any efforts to take the film
at least partially out of the comedy field.

La Rocque is also something of a liability to Gigolo,
a typically involved Edna Ferber story taking in a big business family's travails prior to, during, and following World
War One. The titular material is confined to the latter portions of the film and (presumably) softened somewhat from
Ferber's original since the gigolos involved (one a companion
to the hero's mother, the other the hero himself following
service in the Lafayette Escadrille) never get off the dance-
floor. However, Howard and Andriot cover a lot of ground
very stylishly in a little over 7000 feet--surely the briskest
treatment ever afforded a Ferber chronicle.

Another DeMille production, Red Dice, benefited from
a more suitable role for Rod la Rocque (and a more sober
playing of it) and a strong if somewhat contrived original
story by Octavus Roy Cohen: a suicidal down-and-out, in
order to raise money, makes a deal with a gambler who in-
sures him for a large amount, with his death to follow by

a certain date.   Love and restored fortunes cause la Rocque
to want to retrieve himself from the deal, and in doing so he
becomes involved with the underworld and rum-runners.   It's
a very solid, well-paced and handsomely mounted melodrama,
quite superior to the still interesting early sound remake (The
Big Gamble, 1931, with William Body).

    The current unavailability of The Main Event is a mat-
ter of considerable frustration, since although its basic storyline (a triangle romance with a prize-fighting background) is
relatively ordinary and familiar, the scenario and art-direction
are both by Rochus Gliese, Murnau's production designer on
Sunrise.   However, the reviews make no mention of a Gliese
contribution, and concentrate on applauding Howard's rescue of
of a routine story by clever technique, including a stress on
dissolves.   Howard's first full-scale collaboration with a German craftsman whose style he so much admired would, however, be particularly rewarding if available for study today.
One must remember that critics in 1927 had recently been
dramatically alerted to Howard's talents via White Gold, and
at that time, either through being uninformed themselves or
because they felt the matter of small interest to their readers, tended to ignore the contributions of such "lesser" craftsmen as art directors and cinematographers.   Unquestionably,
however, Howard was "growing" as an artist, and two of his
finest films came close to the end of his period with DeMille.

    White Gold (1927) was long thought lost; a major loss
since Howard had always considered it his one important film.
Reviews at the time clearly indicated that it was something of
a masterpiece; and this in a period when Hollywood's influence
by European filmmakers was often considered suspect and un-
desirable.   When White Gold finally did re-emerge in the
1960s (oddly enough both an American and a French print,
slightly different in small details, were found at the same
time) it proved to be one of those rarities, a legendary lost
film that did indeed live up to its reputation.   Like most
great films, it did not exist in a vacuum; in some ways it
bears a resemblance to William Beaudine's The Canadian
(which preceded it) and Victor Sjostrom's The Wind and F. W.
Murnau's City Girl (which followed it), as well as a number
of lesser films influenced by one or the other of them.   The
late silent period was one of simplification and subtlety.   The
great individual directors cut down on the number of inter-
titles, and dispensed with color-tinted stock in favor of the
effects that could be achieved via lighting and black-and-white
photography.   A greater stress on close-ups enabled nuances

of mood and motivation to be conveyed purely by subtle
changes in expression.   One of the most spartan backdrops
for this technique was the theme of the city woman in a
wilderness, coping with harsh realities, the rigors of the
elements, and often a decidedly unromantic marriage.   White
Gold and all of the other titles mentioned had these plot elements in common, even though their basic narratives were
quite different.   Despite being the most economical of the
four, and the only one not to benefit from exterior location
shooting, White Gold is one of the most powerful of the
group both for its directorial stylization and for its decidedly
modern, even feminist, plot.

The title refers to sheep, although at most only two
or three are ever shown, and the plot is developed almost
entirely within the confines of a studio-created and deliberately claustrophobic ranch-house set.   Jetta Goudal is the
Eastern woman with an implied dubious past who has married
the son (Kenneth Thompson) of a sheep-rancher (George Nicholls) and encounters not only the boredom of ranch life, but
the antagonism of the father and ultimately the lack of faith
of her husband.   When she shoots and kills a ranch-hand who
presumably has tried to rape her (George Bancroft), the killing is not shown, so that the audience, like the husband, is
forced into the position of having to trust her without explana-
tion.   The husband, tied too closely to his father, is unable
to express the faith in her that she needs, so she leaves in
a climax that is both ambiguous and satisfying, accompanied
by a sub-title in which she states that her destiny is un-
certain--she may be going to prison, but whatever happens,
she'll be free.   Anton Grot's sets--appropriately drab but
evocative--and Lucien Andriot's camerawork do much to off-
set the potentially static quality of the story, and there are
a number of visual tours-de-force.   Prior to the rape attempt,
George Bancroft is shown literally wrestling with his own conscience, playing cards with himself in multiple exposures as
he delays making his decision--all of this cross-cut with a
ticking clock (a recurring device of Howard's to stress tension and the pressure of time)--before he makes his move to
the heroine's bedroom and bursts in at the height of an elec-
tric storm.   Adroit editing and the repetition of certain visual
motifs--the continual, relentless rocking of the father's chair
on the porch--at times so effectively create the illusion of
sound that one forgets that this is a silent film.   Critically
the film was exceptionally well reviewed.   Harrison's Reports, an exhibitor journal known to be box-office oriented
and prone to be critical of artistic experimentation (it

literally crucified Potemkin and Greed), wrote:

> From the standpoints of production, scenario con-
> struction, directing and acting, White Gold com-
> pares most favorably with the best German films
> that have been brought to America. The produc-
> tion style is of the same order as The Last Laugh.
> Deeper psychology is revealed in this film than in
> any other ever produced in America.

To say that White Gold was a box-office failure is an
over-simplification.   Greed, after all, has been touted as one
of the spectacular box-office fiascos, whereas actually, even
initially, it did return a small profit.   White Gold was not
an expensive film to produce, its stars were popular, and it
undoubtedly broke even.   However, it didn't do the business
its critical reception entitled it to, nor did it afford Howard
the prestige and autonomy that a major commercial success
might have.   Disappointed or not, Howard was enough of a
realist to accept the situation.   He said in an interview that
"those who etch on celluloid live only for a day," that he had
no intention of trying to carve a filmic monument to his ge-
nius, and that he'd prefer to make Standing Room Only pictures rather than award-winners.   (John Ford, of course, has
uttered identical sentiments on many occasions.)   Even the
fan magazines acknowledged White Gold as a masterpiece, and
Howard was the subject of interviews and articles in Photoplay and the like.   But masterpieces and serious analyses of
directorial style didn't sell fan magazines then--nor were
there many writers around then who were interested in such
an approach.   For all of the press coverage that Howard got,
most of the articles were of a typical rags-to-riches variety,
boosted him as a director of romantic films, stressed his
happy marriage to wife Nan, and capitalizing on his Irish
heritage--the "K" is for Kerrigan--filled the articles with so
much blarney that only one factual element ever seemed to
emerge: namely, Howard's tremendous admiration for Murnau.

A Ship Comes In (1928) tried in essence to capitalize
on White Gold in much the same way that, the same year,
Frank Borzage's Street Angel tried to weld the prestige of
Sunrise to the commercial success of Seventh Heaven. (That
result was a misfire, though an interesting one.)   A Ship
Comes In was clearly designed to cash in on the artistic
reputation that Howard had secured, but was not about to
repeat White Gold's commercial shortcomings.   It was a

mother-love story, always a reliable genre, but particularly
so in 1928 when, earlier in the year, Four Sons had been a
smash success--in terms of individual ticket sales, probably
the biggest success John Ford ever had.   But if A Ship Comes
In was suggested by Four Sons, it was no case of lazy borrowing.   Though set in the same period (before, during, and
after World War One), it was a vastly different film, dealing
primarily with the problems of newly arrived emmigrants.
(The emigrants in Four Sons had no problems at all, and indeed the mother only arrived in time for the films' ultra-
emotional climax.)   While Ford milked the film's honest
sentiment (without subtlety but to great emotional effect),
Howard tended to underplay the emotional highlights in his
film: the mother's farewell as her boy leaves for war is
played largely off-screen, in shadows, and reminds one of
the homecoming scene in Griffith's The Birth of a Nation.
But if Howard downplays the emotionalism, he attacks the
(limited) melodramatic content with bravura virtuosity.   One
of the film's sub-plots involves Bolshevik agitators and ter-
rorists.   An underground conspiratorial meeting is done with
the moody, expressionist style of Lang's Mabuse films, and
when the chief conspirator (Fritz Feld) later has pangs of
conscience over a bomb outrage that he perpetrated precisely
at ten o'clock, a dynamic montage of clocks ticking towards
the fatal hour causes him to break down and rush to his doom
under a truck.

     But essentially A Ship Comes In is a warm, human,
restrained film, with its titles couched in the peasant vernac-
ular of the immigrant protagonists.   Rudolph Schildkraut as
the father, in one of his meatiest roles, perhaps jumps a little too joyfully into the thespian opportunities it offers him,
but Louise Dresser as his wife compensates with a beautifully
modulated performance.   DeMille realized what a potential
winner the studio had in the film and afforded it far more
advertising than was given to the average release.   Reviews
were excellent.   But the film came several months after Four
Sons, and the talkie revolution was now sufficiently underway
for a "pure" silent of the old school to seem old-hat.   Although it did well enough, A Ship Comes In was rather lost
in the shuffle.   Very fortunately, however, it wasn't totally
lost to posterity.   In the 1950s one solitary (and good condition) 16mm print was found in a Connecticut camera store;
it was rescued and has since been copied and preserved by
the American Film Institute.   Interestingly, its realistic depiction of the immigration process, the rituals at Ellis Island
and the first exposure of the newcomers to busy 1900's New

York streets, has made the film invaluable as a source of
stock footage for documentaries on immigration!

      With the dissolving of the DeMille company and with
Howard's record of both artistic and commercial successes,
Howard was offered an excellent contract at Fox, and there-
upon entered the most exciting and productive phase of his
career. Howard's thirteen Fox films started out on fairly
safe grounds with a melodrama, The River Pirate, that was
also a part-talkie, though for the most part its rich visuals
were accompanied only by music and effects. A fairly familiar and trite story about the reformation of a potential criminal (Nick Stuart) and his divided loyalties between a hardened
if sentimental criminal who has befriended him (Victor McLaglen) and the girl who loves him (Lois Moran), it nevertheless
breezes through its narrative in a brisk seven reels, and
uses its Sternbergian waterfront sets so effectively that the
images linger in the mind long after the story has been forgotten. Fortunately, one excellent 35mm nitrate print survived and has been copied, though it has not yet been made
available.

      Howard's second Fox Film, Christina, has apparently
been irrevocably lost. A modern fairy-story set in a very
picturesque Holland (judging from surviving stills), it was
more Borzage territory than Howard, especially in that it
was a Janet Gaynor vehicle to boot. Howard, who had had
the clout to bring Lucien Andriot with him to Fox, also
brought Rudolph Schildkraut over from the old DeMille unit
to play Gaynor's father--a toymaker--in what was to be his
last role. The film had music and sound effects, but--per-
haps wisely in view of the Cinderella-like quality of the
story--no dialogue. The sets of windmills and old-world vil-
lages were elaborate and impressive, and while it was probably not a major Howard, it would have been interesting to
see what he did with such untypical but still richly visual
material. Phil Ford, son of Francis, was Howard's assistant
director on the film.

      Fortunately, all of the remaining Fox films survive,
though not all are readily available as yet outside of archival
facilities.

      The Valiant, made in the Spring of 1929, is important
not only as Howard's first talkie and the first movie of stage
actor Paul Muni, but it could be an invaluable teaching tool
as a virtual textbook on many of the problems of the very

early talkie. Howard clearly wishes to weld sound and image:
he sets the early scenes in city streets, and captures naturalistic sound and direct dialogue. As the story progresses, he
attempts to retain the camera mobility and visual design of
his silents. But the story is already an expansion of a one-
act play, dealing with a condemned man's final days before
execution, and his refusal to explain the murder he has committed, and thus possibly save his life. Inevitably, as the
story nears its conclusion and zeroes in on long dialogue ex-
changes among the prisoner (Muni), his sister (Marguerite
Churchill), the warden and others, it becomes more and more
of a talk-fest. Howard can do little but turn the film over to
Muni. In some ways a primitive film, it has a great deal of
power, although its open sentimentality (and some unfortunate
changes of meaning in then-colloquial phrases) render it rather
vulnerable to insensitive audiences today. This film, too,
has been saved by a fluke. Just before the only surviving
35mm print was turned over to the Museum of Modern Art,
one 16mm reversal reference print was struck. The Museum
then proceeded to lose the original, and the reversal--for-
tunately a very good one--then became the preservation "master" from which the American Film Institute was forced to
make a protection negative. Howard's later The Trial of
Vivienne Ware (1932) makes a perfect mate for the film in
an educational sense, since it shows how in only three years
Howard had totally mastered sound and was using it creatively
and as an inherent part of the film's pacing. Each film runs
about 58 minutes, so in less than two hours, these two films
provide a perfect object lesson in the development of sound
at that critical juncture in Hollywood history, with the added
cohesive advantage that both films are from the same studio
and the same director. Furthermore, one is from a play and
the other from a novel, so that they illustrate additionally
the problems facing the then new art of screen-writing for
the sound film.

Its academic value outweighs its entertainment value,
but The Valiant is one of Howard's more interesting films,
and deserves to be more generally accessible than it probably
ever will be. Incidentally, Fox also made a Spanish-language
version in 1930, and remade it (as The Man Who Wouldn't
Talk) in the early '40s, though with its downbeat film noir
quality reshaped to provide more melodramatic excitement
and a happy ending!

Many of the top silent directors--and certainly John
Ford, a Howard contemporary at Fox at this period--were

having their problems in adjusting to sound, and the 1929-30
period generally represents a kind of marking time intermission for them, wherein they could work with sound, learn
and overcome its pitfalls, on the kind of films where mistakes
could neither harm the films nor do their reputations serious
damage. (Films made such remarkable progress in terms of
technical virtuosity that a movie made at the beginning of a
year could seem totally outdated by the end of it. Usually
such films were withdrawn from circulation promptly, and
few achieved sufficient stature to warrant later reissue. This
practice certainly kept audiences from being reminded of
directors'--or stars--misfires, though it also made it difficult for critics to see and reappraise these films). Between
The Valiant and 1931's Transatlantic, the film that really enabled Howard to hit his stride again and establish himself as
a major sound director, came four interesting but generally
forgettable movies.

First was Love, Live and Laugh, released in the Winter of 1929, one of several ultra-sentimental tales that George
Jessel made at the time, as though to compensate for having
turned down the chance to star in the film version of The
Jazz Singer. Like many early talkies, it carried a "Staged
By" credit to an actor (in this case Henry Kolker), which
usually meant that additional dialogue scenes were done independent of the basic film, or after its completion, in order
to further exploit the novelty of sound. (Oddly, the directors
who were best able to carry a story visually, and didn't need
such assistance, were the ones most affected by this irksome
but temporary practice. John Ford had his share of this
problem too.) In any event, its 90 minutes slowed by such
typically Jessel pseudo-Jolson songs as "Two Little Baby
Arms" and much dialogue written by Jessel himself, the film
was slow and plodding.

Good Intentions, which followed, was likewise afflicted
with Kolker's assistance, but at least it was a melodrama and was
some two reels shorter than the Jessel film. Moreover, it introduced Howard to star Edmund Lowe. They proved to be a most
felicitous combination, and made a total of seven films together.
Though not quite equaling the box-office chemistry of Wayne and
Ford, they worked well together, in "A" films and "B", in Hollywood and Britain. Lowe's screen persona has just the right blend
of toughness and elegance to match the quality of Howard's own
work. Good Intentions, however, was perhaps more of an
enigma in 1930 than it seems today. Howard is credited

with the original story (about a crook's reformation and self-
sacrifice) but it is such a glib reshuffling of John Ford's Born
Reckless, released slightly earlier, fortuitously also by Fox,
that the "originality" can be taken with raised eyebrows.
Since it featured the same two stars, Lowe and Marguerite
Churchill, in the same kind of relationship, the "influence"
would have been quite apparent at the time.

     Lowe and Howard followed up with another melodrama,
Scotland Yard (1930). Exploiting sound and the magic of the
camera by presenting an actor in a dual role was almost
something of a sub-genre then, supplemented by films like
Such Men Are Dangerous, in which an actor (in this case,
Warner Baxter) starts out with one face, undergoes plastic
surgery, and emerges with a new face and a new personality
to match. The sheer novelty (or at least popularity) of the
situation undoubtedly carried Scotland Yard in 1930, since
it was one of the earlier entries of its breed. But it dates
rather badly today, not least because the wonderfully atmos-
pheric opening exterior scenes are soon supplanted by rather
stagey interior dialogues, and the far-fetched plot becomes
even wilder as it progresses. (It was remade, updated to
World War Two, in 1941, when it was no more logical but
a bit more subdued.)

     Howard continued his association with Lowe into his
next film. Don't Bet on Women (1931) suggested that he was
at last beginning to hit his stride again. It was a short and
peppy sex comedy, Lubitsch style, cramming a lot of plot
into seventy minutes and moving fast enough that its absurdities
and complications were over before they really had a chance
to register. It probably seemed a lot better in 1931 than it
does today, since it came out a year before such silken comedies as Love Me Tonight, Trouble in Paradise and One Hour
with You (two of which also starred Jeanette MacDonald, the
star of Don't Bet on Women, but exploited her singing voice,
which Howard's film did not). In direct contrast with them,
it inevitably suffers today. But a year was a long time in the
early sound period, and by the standards of 1931 it was a
good and even advanced comedy. The New York Times praised both the film and specifically Howard's direction. Although
a 35mm print does exist, it is incomplete by a reel or more,
and so its preservation priorities are presumably not too high.

     Howard rounded out 1931 with two films that put him
right back among the front rank of movie stylists. They remain two of his best films: Transatlantic and Surrender.

Although highly individual and personal productions, they also
tend to confirm that Howard was not really an "auteur" in the
sense that that ambiguous word is usually interpreted today.
There are rarely signs of Howard reshaping the content of a
script to reflect a personal point of view, as such true au-
teurs as Whale, Ford and Walsh did frequently. True, there
are visual motifs and editing patterns that Howard returns to
frequently, but they are essentially stylistic trademarks rather
than statements. If some insist that this is auteurism, then
it is team-auteurism. When Howard had a project that he
felt needed a specifically Germanic design, then he turned to
an art director like Anton Grot, and presumably gave him his
head. (Grot had a fondness for sweeping, circular stairways;
one shows up on cue in Surrender, but not in other Howard
films.) Similarly, when Howard envisioned a photographic
style that would make use of beams of light piercing the
night, illuminating dark interiors or coming dramatically
through prison bars, he would turn to a cameraman who was
also a lighting specialist, James Wong Howe, who achieved
just those effects in Transatlantic, The Squeaker, Surrender
and Fire Over England. Even in his casting and in his stock
companies, Howard drew largely on the resources of the studio he was currently with, only very occasionally insisting
(as with Rudolph Schildkraut) on a player from outside. Ad-
mittedly, Edmund Lowe plays a crook or a victim who is (in
varying ways) reformed by love in five of the six films they
made together, undoubtedly because Lowe did this so well
and type-casting was fairly rampant in the '30s and '40s.
Given a script with such a character, Howard would probably
automatically seek out Lowe. To attempt to establish Howard
as essentially a craftsman and specifically not an auteur is
in no way to minimize his talent, although it may explain the
lack of attention given to the body of his work and his relatively low status (if indeed he has one at all) among the "serious" critics.

    Transatlantic was both an artistic and a commercial
success, a kind of ocean-going Grand Hotel (though of course
it preceded that film) unhindered by the need to cater to big
name stars. The underlying mood was one of melodrama with
strong visual contrasts between foggy exteriors on the deck and
slick, bright, art-deco design in the salons and cabins. Unfortunately the original negative no longer exists, and a new
preservation negative had to be constructed from a combination
of French, American and even Spanish prints. The matching-
up (sometimes using sound track from one version over picture from another) was smoothly done, given all the problems,

but the pictorial results are sub-standard; those contrasting
visual moods somehow evened out so that the whole film now
has a unified, greyish tone.   Nevertheless, it's too good and
important a film to have been lost entirely.   Laboratories in
the U.S. have shown little real interest in preservation nega-
tives and prints, since the subsequent print orders are mini-
mal, and frequently adopt a take it or leave it attitude with
the results they come up with.   Gordon Wiles won an Academy
Award for his Art Direction and James Wong Howe's mobile
and superbly lit photography represented one of his best screen
credits, and both artists are short-changed by the washed-out
prints of this film that are now available.

        Surrender, Howard's final 1931 film, was equally styl-
ish, though it was not promoted too heavily by Fox, perhaps
because they had a plethora of films starring Warner Baxter
on their hands at that time.   Apparently it did not even get
a New York first-run.   Based on the novel Axelle by Pierre
Benoit, an essentially romantic story laid in a World War
One German prisoner-of-war camp (the romance, and the
commentary on changing social values, are centered in an
aristocratic family living in an adjacent chateau commandeered
by the German authorities), it must have influenced Jean
Renoir's La Grande Illusion considerably, with Ralph Bellamy's
disfigured commandant clearly foreshadowing Erich von Stroheim in the later film.   The romantic complications are somewhat superficial and that sturdy old Englishman, C. Aubrey
Smith, is no more convincing as a German aristocrat than
he would be as a French one the following year in Love Me
Tonight.   But Howard dwells on the romantic elements as
little as he can, and spends far more time on scenes and
sequences that can benefit from his visual flair, ranging
from a stunning long shot of a soldier playing the organ in
a cathedral-like chamber of the castle, sunlight streaming
through a high window, to an exciting and economically staged
prison-break at night, all shadows, searchlights piercing the
gloom and vicious guard-dogs straining at their leashes.   Never
as moving or as emotionally involving as Renoir's later film
(its script only makes passing stabs at social comment), it
is nevertheless one of the most interesting and one of the
least known of Howard's Fox films.

        The Trial of Vivienne Ware (1932) must have looked
in script form to have the substance of a solid 75-minute
melodrama.   In an astonishing display of editing virtuosity
and camera mobility, Howard rushes through it in less than
an hour, using rapid-fire overlapping dialogue, swish pans

and lightning transitions from different locations and time periods. It is still just about the fastest film ever made, with Dieterle's Fog over Frisco (1934) running an honorable second. As noted earlier, it emphasizes how totally Howard had overcome all the problems of sound in the relatively short time since his first talkie. Quite apart from the artificial speed inflicted on the film, snatches of musical numbers, almost thrown-away wisecracks and stunning art deco design distract one's attention from a routine who-dun-it story and outrageous trial behavior (from judge, attorneys and casual assassins!) that would never have been coutenanced in any courtroom.

Inevitably, there was a slackening of pace for Howard's next film, The First Year, a remake of a silent Frank Borzage movie, itself an adaptation of a serio-comic play about the travails of the first year of a marriage. In 1926 it had been minor though pleasing Borzage; in 1932 Howard, possibly trying to create a deliberate contrast with his prior film, stretched it out to a tedious 80 minutes. Moreover, the silent version had benefited from non-star casting, Matt Moore and especially the charming Kathryn Perry, whereas Howard was stuck with the by now too-often co-starred Janet Gaynor and Charles Farrell. Not only did the use of that team result in a predictable quality that the original didn't have, but it also meant reshaping the material so that the story became subordinated to "business" designed for them. While not a disaster, it certainly confirmed--as other films did--that romantic comedy was not Howard's forte.

Almost as if to emphasize this, Howard reverted to melodrama with a vengeance in Sherlock Holmes, ostensibly a remake of the old William Gillette play, but basically a new script pitting Holmes and some minor sci-fi gadgets against imported American gangsters. All that was left of the original was the Holmes (Clive Brook) and Alice Faulkner (Miriam Jordan) romance, though the intricate schemings of Moriarty (Ernest Torrence) had a genuine Doyle flavor. The film was short and fast paced, giving Watson (Reginald Owen) a mere two token appearances. There was also perhaps a shade too much comedy, partially to highlight a new character comedian that Fox was developing (Herbert Mundin) and also to allow for a mildly amusing if singularly unconvincing episode in which Holmes masquerades as his own elderly aunt in an encounter with a too-easily fooled Moriarty. But at its best, it was Howard back to his favorite UFA/Lang style. The film opens with Moriarty's trial and conviction for murder,

all done with silhouettes and shadows, and not long after there's
a magnificent prison-break sequence, done in Howard's best
manner: short takes, sharp angles, a cunning mixture of
sound and image, climaxed by a lengthy tracking shot down
a prison corridor, past the body of a murdered guard and
into Moriarty's empty cell wherein he has scrawled on the
wall the message, "Tell Holmes I'm OUT!"   The climactic
shoot-out and round-up of the gang, staged in the cellars of
a bank, and with all of the participants wearing masks and
shields to protect them from the acetylene torches they are
using to break into the vault, their clothing powdered with
white dust, reminds one of many a similar Lang-Mabuse
caper.

      Howard's final film for Fox, The Power and the Glory
(1933), was critically hailed at the time for its "revolutionary" technique (a series of flashbacks) although actually it
was a refinement and an exploitation of existing techniques,
and press puffery latched on to this as a selling angle.   Ret-
rospectively, of course, it has been recognized, justifiably,
as the forerunner of Citizen Kane, and as an early example
of Preston Sturges' scripting capabilities.   Possibly it is too
short a film, at some seven reels, to do full justice to the
theme.   Too many important elements (particularly in the
tycoon's initial rise to power) seem glossed over, though this
may be an unfair criticism since circulating prints today derive from Fox's sole studio vault print--itself well-used, dam-
aged at the beginnings and ends of reels, and clearly lacking
substantial footage.   As a pre-Code film, it was relatively
outspoken and uncompromising.   It was one of the best of the
twenty films, mainly quickly produced programmers, that
Spencer Tracy made in the early phase of his career at Fox.
It did much to bolster his growing reputation as a major new
screen actor, and also underlined Howard's reputation as a
"serious" director as well as a commercially reliable one.
Howard accepted an offer from M-G-M, and Tracy would follow him there shortly thereafter.

      Just as German directors in the '20s longed to get to
Hollywood and the unleashed budgets and the great pool of
equipment and expertise that would be made available to them,
so did most directors of the '30s set their sights on the biggest of the major studios, M-G-M.   But if the studio afforded
them the production facilities they expected, it also removed
much of the freedom that they had enjoyed at other, smaller
studios.   M-G-M films were built around their stars, and
directors were expected to turn out vehicles for those stars.

Even Clarence Brown, who had a long and enviable record
at M-G-M, working there exclusively (except for one picture) from 1927 through 1952, went on record as saying that
his most enjoyable directing experience was on that one "away"
picture (1939's The Rains Came) because at Fox the picture
came first, before star considerations, and because all units
collaborated in the picture's best interests.   At M-G-M apart
from catering to star considerations, each distinct department
competed with one another to stress how indispensable it was
and to impress the higher-ups.   The result often was an extreme imbalance in the final work, which perhaps accounted
for the over-produced look that was always a hallmark of
M-G-M product.

Howard's five M-G-M films in the mid-thirties are all
enjoyable and well crafted films, and the first two can even
be considered among his better films, but none was among his
very best works.   As was its custom, and despite his earlier
prestige, M-G-M let its new director get himself acclima-
tized with a fairly unimportant film where he could do little
real damage if something went wrong.   The presence of Lionel Barrymore on the star roster at M-G-M was of immense
help to directors who wanted to make the more personal, or
at least non-formula, film.   Barrymore was a big name, and
an expensive one.   He had to be kept busy, and putting him
in support roles in the big Garbo and other prestige films
didn't fully pay his way.   He was occasionally shunted into
starring roles in smaller films which had a habit of becoming
some of the studio's more interesting releases in their respective years: Vidor's The Stranger's Return, for example,
and The Voice of Bugle Ann and On Borrowed Time.

This Side of Heaven was the Barrymore starring film
(with Mae Clarke as its leading lady) that was given to Howard for his M-G-M debut.   It was a warm, human story, but
also richly dramatic, and turned out to be a surprise hit.
M-G-M recognizing its superior qualities and without waiting
for the January '34 release and reviews to confirm it, assigned Howard to a far more important property, The Cat and
the Fiddle, which was produced quickly and efficiently, and
followed This Side of Heaven into release a month later.
Howard was still considered more of a coup by M-G-M than
the film's two stars.   Jeanette MacDonald, a new acquisition
from Paramount, was making her first film for M-G-M and
did not yet enjoy the prestige that would follow her teaming
with Nelson Eddy.   Ramon Novarro, a former major M-G-M
star, was slipping drastically in popular appeal and was

merely working out his contract. Neither of these two stars
would need to be catered to as much as Gable, Harlow, Crawford and the well-established M-G-M stars.

Although hampered by the new restrictions of the
Production Code (and M-G-M tended to be more nervously
respectful of those restrictions than the other major companies), the European-localed and flavored musical romance
had much of the risqué quality of the earlier Lubitsch films,
and a great deal of charm. If comedy was never to be Howard's basic forte, he certainly showed here that, given the
material, he could deliver with maximum efficiency, if not
inspiration. The film's commercial success was also boosted
by a Technicolor sequence, then still very much of a novelty,
and it holds up well as a tasteful and sprightly entertainment
some fifty years later. However, these two initial Howards
were to be the only ones of his M-G-M group in which the
contribution of the director was recognizably present. Convinced of his abilities, M-G-M promoted him to bigger "prestige" star vehicles where it would be hard to retain the in-
dividuality he had been permitted thus far.

The first of them was Evelyn Prentice, coming so hot
on the heels of The Thin Man that clearly uppermost in the
M-G-M collective mind was the need to sustain the perfect-
marriage image of William Powell and Myrna Loy. The film
combines both soap opera travails and murder mystery elements with a court room climax, and seems to be operating
under instructions to maintain as light a tone as possible.
The very real possibilities for strong and exciting melodrama
are played down in the script, though in his handling of actress Isabel Jewell, and in his steering away from conventional editing of conventional material, Howard does manage to
inject a note of sustained suspense into the climax, even though
the "surprise" denouement does telegraph some of its revelations. It's still a good, glossy, entertaining trifle, but looking at it without its director credit one could reasonably place
authorship with those other M-G-M perennials, W. S. Van Dyke
and Jack Conway, as readily as with Howard.

Vanessa, Her Love Story, which followed, was even
more of a disappointment. A prestige production by David O.
Selznick, it was based on (though much watered-down from)
a Hugh Walpole novel, and was dominated by Helen Hayes and
a miscast Robert Montgomery. Its English locale and its
wildly melodramatic plot (at least in film form, where stra-
tegically isolated incidents in Walpole's long original work were

jammed in together as though the film was a serial thriller)
would have been magnificently suited to the bravura theatrical
style of James Whale.   Howard was more than submerged by
it all, but managed to make a creditable swan song to his
M-G-M period with Rendezvous (1935).   Again it was slanted
more to star vehicle needs than to exploiting its qualities as
a melodrama.   If played to the hilt in the latter direction, it
could have been a winner, since it was based (somewhat
loosely) on the actual exploits of an ace American code-buster
in World War One.   The suspense of breaking an enemy code
under pressure of time gave Howard the chance to indulge in
effective pacing and editing, and Powell was first-rate in the
role.   Unfortunately the script contained little of the physical
action at which Howard was so adept, and far too much irri-
tating comedy with an obnoxious and intrusive "heroine," a
role that even Rosalind Russell couldn't (and didn't make likable.

    Back at Paramount for the first time since his silent
days, Howard turned out his best melodrama in ages--one of
his best from any period, in fact--and quickly established that
his marking-time period at M-G-M had in no way impaired
his ability to turn out fast, taut thrillers.   Mary Burns,
Fugitive had plot motivations and complications that wouldn't
hold up to close scrutiny.   The hapless heroine, played by
Sylvia Sidney, was often her own worst enemy, and a courtroom scene in which she is sent to prison on the flimsiest
of circumstantial evidence is hard to accept.   Although fast-
paced, the film is just long enough for one to have time to
ponder its incongruities, unlike the frenetic The Trial of
Vivienne Ware with its narrative pace of head-long hysteria.
However, it is so well crafted that one doesn't feel inclined
to argue its illogicalities.   Howard had returned in top melodramatic form with fancy lighting and editing, one of his several dynamic jail-break episodes coming early enough in the
film to signal that the old Howard was back.   Alan Baxter,
as the near-psycho villain, has one scene that is a direct
homage to Lang's Dr. Mabuse, while Melvyn Douglas, the
film's nominal hero, appears only at the midway point and
as a recuperating patient spends most of the film in bed,
or resting, surely the most passive of all Howard heroes.

    There was a long wait before Howard's second Para-
mount film, The Princess Comes Across (a neat pun-title),
and after the forceful renaissance with Mary Burns, Fugitive
it was frankly a disappointment.   Although an "A" film, it
was fairly short and unprepossessing one.   Moreover, it was

of a mixture that has proven not to wear too well--screwball
comedy mated with murder mystery. Most of Howard's sym-
pathies seem to go to the thriller half of his script: the fight
and pursuit scenes on the fog-bound decks of an ocean liner
were well and atmospherically done, recalling Transatlantic.
But while the comedy was amiable enough, it lacked bite.
Perhaps the fault was partially with the stars, since as a
team Fred MacMurray and Carole Lombard (who also teamed
in the much inferior True Confession the following year) lacked
chemistry. The rough-hewn qualities of MacMurray drew
more sparks when matched against the sophistication of a
Claudette Colbert, while Lombard, with a rough-hewn quality
herself, likewise worked better when partnered by the urbane smoothness of a William Powell or a Frederic March.
Moreover, Lombard had a tendency to mug and overplay
comedy; tough directors like Hawks and Wellman would slap
her down and discipline her into delivering a subtle, controlled comic performance. Howard was either too much
of a gentleman--or just not tough enough--and let her have
her way too much in The Princess Comes Across. It remains an enjoyably slick movie but no more. It had the ingredients and the potential to match the goofy excesses of
those other great screwball comedy thrillers, Remember Last
Night? and It's A Wonderful World. Sadly, too, The Princess Comes Across marked the end of a period in which the
Howard name was to really mean anything in Hollywood, although at the time this was by no means apparent, since Howard had an invitation to go to England from Alexander Korda
to make one of the year's biggest films, Fire Over England.

        Korda, as usual, spared no expense to acquire the
top names to ensure a film created with so much talent behind and in front of the cameras that it couldn't fail to achieve
world-wide acceptance. Erich Pommer produced, James Wong
Howe photographed, and scenario, art direction, music and
other credits were all out of the top drawer, while the cast
was headed by Laurence Olivier, Vivien Leigh (at the height
of her youthful loveliness and stunningly photographed by
Howe), Flora Robson, and Raymond Massey, with a supporting
cast ranging through such names as Robert Newton and Leslie Banks down to an unbilled James Mason. Like Eisenstein's
Alexander Nevsky, made in Russia the same year, it was
partially designed as a propagandist call to arms at home,
and a warning to Nazi Germany that invasion and conquest
had failed before and would fail again. It was typical that a
European outsider like Korda had the acumen to see the need
for such a warning, while Britain as a whole, ostrich-like,

Howard and cinematographer James Wong Howe leave for London to work with Alexander Korda and London Films, Ltd. , April 1936.

was pretending that the German threat did not exist. But if
the British public as a whole ignored its propagandist warning, they rallied to its patriotic call. (The coronation of a
new King and the launching of the Queen Mary were big events
in royalty-conscious Britain of the '30s, and Fire Over England certainly benefited from this new surge of nationalism.)
For a British film--even a Korda production--it was unusually
glossy and polished, and British critics were delighted to ap-
plaud the film as one that proved that Britain could make them
"as good as Hollywood, " rather ignoring the fact that it was
an American director and an American cinematographer who
were largely responsible for this feat. Only in one respect
did it fail. British expertise at staging action sequences
(whether a simple fist-fight or a full-scale sea encounter)
fell far short of Hollywood's at this time. Their stunt men
and second unit directors just didn't have the know-how to
put over slick action material and this film, coming in the
wake of Flynn's Captain Blood, was a let-down in the swashbuckling department. Olivier seemed clumsy and ill at ease
in his brief sword-fighting scenes, and the climactic sequence
of the burning of the Armada, though cunningly done, was
mainly a matter of montage and models that couldn't match
Hollywood standards--especially when, in America, in an effort to give the film some extra novelty appeal, this sequence
was sometimes shown on the enlarged Magnascope screens,
the sheer size of which only made the model work all the
more obvious. However, in Britain this drawback was seen
as a minor one in view of the film's other very tangible assets, which included an extremely literate script and some
excellent acting, especially in the smaller roles: Leslie
Banks' subtle performance stood out, as did the warmly human one by Morton Selton. In Britain, too, its all-star cast
gained in value through the years, and as players like Robert
Newton and James Mason gained prominence, the film would
be reissued with their names given far greater prominence in
the advertising. Sequences from it were used in wartime
propaganda films, as well.

      While in England, Howard made another film for Kor-
da, a melodrama that re-united him with star Edmund Lowe.
An Edgar Wallace thriller, The Squeaker (retitled Murder on
Diamond Row in the U. S.), it was unfortunately essentially a
"B" handsomely dressed up, and with appropriate running
time, to masquerade as an "A". It was full of interesting
little visual touches: the unknown master criminal writing
his demands in the moisture on an automobile window; an
unexpected burst of sharply edited violence when petty crim-

inal Robert Newton escapes from a police station; and best
of all, another Langian climax when the chief villain, for
all his near-genius, breaks down and confesses in a prison
when he thinks he is being confronted by the shades of his
former victims--a trick rather more convincing in Lang's
world than in the more mundane cops-and-robbers London
of Edgar Wallace. Although an anti-climax after Fire Over
England, it was an enjoyably stylist exercise (most Edgar
Wallace films of the period were "B"s and showed it) and
had a good cast in support of Lowe: Ann Todd, Sebastian
Shaw, Robert Newton, Alastair Sim and others.

Howard was also asked to doctor two other films.
Why Korda had him intervene on Over the Moon is something of a mystery. The Rex Harrison-Merle Oberon comedy
had been quite capably directed (as far as one can tell) by
another American, Thornton Freeland, and in any case direction hardly mattered on this film. The script was light and
amusing, and the film was really just a showcase for the
new three-color Technicolor, used to excellent advantage as
it followed the adventures of sudden heiress Oberon as she
buys herself expensive make-up treatments and fancy and
colorful clothes, and tours all the picturesque beauty spots
of Europe. It seemed to do its job well enough, and could
have been as effective even if less well-directed. There's no
obvious sign of Howard's intervention. An interestingly atmos-
pheric opening scene on a country road across a fog-shrouded
moor looked like Howard and might have been his, but the
film hardly needed to start off looking like another Edgar
Wallace film! William Cameron Menzies had also shot a
low-budget thriller entitled The Green Cockatoo, a curious
assignment indeed as a follow-through on his spectacular
Things to Come. Whether Menzies was irked at the assignment, or possibly just not able to function on the extreme
paucity of budget available, the results were not deemed sat-
isfactory. Howard moved in and was able to turn it into a
serviceable little picture, although Menzies retained screen
credit. Disappointing or not, by virtue of the fact that its
two stars--John Mills and Robert Newton--were about to at-
tain major stardom, it remained in constant distribution,
sold for reissue many times and afforded a U.S. release
as well, so it undoubtedly returned a tidy little profit in
due time.

Back in America with no major studio contract to return to, Howard found it difficult getting re-established, but
he did manage to promote backing for a pet project of his,

a story that he'd written himself, and a film that turned out
to be his most personal and deeply felt work since White
Gold, a film called Back Door to Heaven. Produced at the
old Paramount Studios in Astoria, Long Island, with some
location work in Cleveland, it was a curious film indeed--
very much of a film noir long before that term had been
coined, and unfortunately long before there was much interest in that kind of a film. A public still very much in
the throes of a depression exhibited little excitement about
this very downbeat tale of a born loser and ex-convict (extremely well played by Wallace Ford) who manages to return
to a high school reunion before being shot down in a hail of
bullets. It had many of the eventual standard themes and
images of the noir school, including the sub-theme (best ex-
emplified by The Asphalt Jungle) of the protagonist's desire
to return to the simplicity of rural America from the cor-
ruption and doom-laden destiny of the city. Although a trifle
over-emphatic in its treatment, and with a mildly if pleasing-
ly old-fashioned visual style reminiscent of Howard's silents,
it also stressed its affinity to the silent period with a musical score (using Home Town as a recurring theme) that
was less a punctuation and accompaniment than an emphasized
and possibly overdone adjunct to the whole film. A sensitive
and moving film, with an interestingly serious and non-
condescending attitude to black characters (an attitude still
depressingly rare as late as 1938), it was in essence Lang's
You Only Live Once but without its production polish or the
box-office insurance of star names. Johnnie Walker was re-
associated with Howard as a production assistant, and both
Walker and Howard (as a prosecuting attorney) had effective
small acting parts. Although not a success at the time (and
an awkward film to place with its "A" running time and "B"
cast and marketability) it achieved some recognition in later
years, although prints have never been easy to find.

     Once settled back in to a "B" niche, Howard found it
hard to get out of it. In 1940 he made Money and the Woman for Warners, a film that holds the distinction (though this
is hardly Howard's doing) of being the closest and most faithful adaptation of any James Cain story. (It came from The
Embezzler). Well-mounted and photographed, with a good
cast of contract players well-selected and handled, it came
to roaring life in its two main physical action sequences (a
bank hold-up and a climactic car chase) and generally was
a very creditable production, showing both that Howard had
lost none of his flair, and that he could still turn out a cheap
picture that was efficiently made and looked more expensive

William K. Howard in 1939.

than it was. He followed up with another Warner "B", Bullets for O'Hara. Most of the Warner "B" thrillers at this
time were remakes of Cagney and other big-budget thrillers
of the '30s, and were bolstered by big chunks of stock footage lifted from them. Bullets for O'Hara was a re-working
of 1936's Public Enemy's Wife, and Howard was unusually
adroit at setting up newly filmed scenes to match the old,
and intercutting them skillfully. It was another thoroughly
enjoyable, crisply paced melodrama.

In 1942, there was a slight upswing in his career
when the new producing team of the King Brothers assigned
him to direct their most ambitious production to date, Klondike Fury, for Monogram release. Although it would be dismissed casually as another "B" today, when the phrase is
used far too casually and most writers do not understand the

subtle variations in "B" movies from period to period and
studio to studio, in 1942 it was one of Monogram's bigger
pictures, and was a good money-maker for them. A remake of a much earlier Monogram film titled simply Klondike (and also quite similar to The Outcast, a film that Robert Florey made for Paramount in the late '30s), it was a
more elaborate and psychologically better developed film than
its predecessor. Howard was allowed very much of a free
hand. He acquired his old friend Edmund Lowe for the lead
(a typical role, that of a disgraced doctor gradually re-
establishing his self-respect) and brought in old friends from
the silent era (Kenneth Harlan, Monte Blue) for supporting
roles. Some interesting editing effects--tense cross-cutting
between clocks before a dangerous operation--recalled Howard's
earlier visual excitements, and one love scene played in silhouette against a frost-encrusted cabin window was particularly
pleasing.

Reviews (and business) were good, and interest in Howard revived. In 1943 the William Cagney group offered him
James Cagney's new vehicle, Johnny Come Lately. It was
Howard's best break in years, and he made a good job of it,
evoking the small-town atmosphere well, though held in check
by a deliberately low-key script that, apart from one action
sequence, denied him the kind of material that he did best.
(And to his credit, he didn't try to jazz up the leisurely style
of the film by injecting his own dynamic style of editing and
camera angling.) The failure of the film (discussed earlier)
was due more to audiences rejecting Cagney in a non-typical
role than any shortcomings in Howard's handling of the material, but that late in his career, it was too big a black
mark against him to be overcome easily.

He made just two more films. When the Lights Go
on Again was, by PRC standards (and they were about the
cheapest and least respected studio in operation at that time)
an even bigger and more important film than Klondike Fury
had been for Monogram. PRC, with its meager budgets, had
a way of bringing out the best in really talented directors
(Edgar Ulmer, Joseph H. Lewis), who managed to eke out
well-made films despite the lack of facilities, and When the
Lights Go on Again even had a more generous budget than
was usual with that studio. It was by no means a film to
be ashamed of. Howard's last film was for Republic in 1946,
A Guy Could Change, a short, lean, well-made little "B"
with Allan Lane and Jane Frazee, with a well-staged fist-
fight as the wrap-up of a melodramatic climax. One might

have wished that Howard's career hadn't come so completely full circle, going out as he began with a five-reel melodrama, but at that it was a respectable and professional fadeout.

ROLAND WEST

by Scott MacQueen

For Mae Whitehead, December 16th, 1935 was a Monday morning like any other. She left her modest home midmorning and started her drive up the Pacific Coast Highway. Mae was employed as a maid and Sunday had been her day off. Now, only a week until Christmas, her thoughts were of her family and the holiday just ahead. As Mrs. Whitehead passed Santa Monica, the familiar breakers of the Pacific Ocean sweeping up on Topanga Beach reminded her that she was nearing her destination. Her thoughts shifted to the beautiful lady for whom she worked, whose home she was nearing. There had been a party for the beautiful lady on Saturday night; Mae anticipated the stories her blonde employer would have to share. Mae also remembered a spot of unpleasantness with the boyfriend. She had been concerned enough to insist that the lady take a spare key with her--Mae had personally put it into the lady's evening bag. The gentleman had seemed to mean it when he said he would lock her out.

Mae took the car up Posetano Drive. Below her, along the highway, was the sprawling three-story building that housed a restaurant on the ground floor. "Thelma Todd's Sidewalk Cafe," declared the sign to star-struck tourists and movie colony glitterati who frequented it. Mae's employer, Thelma Todd, lived in an apartment above the club.

Built into the side of the hill overlooking the Cafe on Posetano Drive was another imposing Spanish structure, "Castillo del Mar." This was the boyfriend's house, though he lived now in the apartments over the Cafe with Miss Todd. The boyfriend's wife used to live in the big house, but she hadn't been there for a long time.

105

Roland West: Studio portrait circa 1923.

About 10:30 the black woman stopped her car in front of the garage next to the big house.   As was her custom she would bring Miss Todd's big chocolate-colored car out, put her own car away in the garage, and take the Lincoln phaeton down to the Cafe for her mistress's convenience.

One of the sliding doors to the garage was partly open. Mae pushed the heavy, hand-carved oak door open all the way. There were two cars in the dark garage, Miss Todd's Lincoln convertible and the boyfriend's car.   There was something else as well.

Mae was so startled by what she saw next that she nearly dropped the bundles she was carrying in her arms. There was Miss Todd, in the front seat of the car, sleeping! Surprised and concerned, Mae walked quickly around to the right side of the open touring car.

The beautiful blonde movie star looked strangely passive.   Thelma Todd sat upright behind the steering wheel, her hands resting in her lap.   She still wore the blue silk evening gown and a single camellia still rode on her shoulder. Thelma's big fur coat was draped around her immobile shoulders.   The only sign of life in the silent garage was the twinkle of $20,000 worth of diamonds, little points of light on the still form of the beautiful woman.

Beautiful!   As Mae tried to wake her the maid already knew that she was beyond sleep; a strange, dull black pallor stretched across her complexion.   Her bottom lip was slightly discolored, and clots of dried blood were caked beneath her nostrils and above the mouth.

By evening the newspapers had it.

"My daughter has been murdered!" cried a devastated Mrs. Alice Todd.   If it was murder, and there seemed little doubt of it, it was well-nigh the perfect crime; fifty years later it remains an unresolved mystery.   As newspaper headlines coast to coast shrieked out TODD DEATH CLUE IN GAMBLER'S WAR and FILM STAR'S GHOST TELLS OF TERRORS, the investigation focused on The Boyfriend, prominent film director Roland West.   In the weeks following the death, West was interrogated many times.   His alibi always remained substantially the same but the telling details of his story became changeable and contradictory.   Just before New Year's an exhausted but well-rehearsed West, still

denying that he and Miss Todd were anything but business
partners and "best friends," told the press:

> You know, I always thought third degrees were
> conducted in a room. I never knew it was any-
> thing like this. It is pounding, pounding, rush and
> wait.
> Thelma Todd's death was the greatest shock of
> my life. For three days after her death I could
> hardly talk. My mouth dried up. My throat burn-
> ed. Yet police investigators and detectives plied
> me with questions. They have taken five state-
> ments from me so far. Now I'm to be the last
> witness in this inquiry. That's all right with me.
> I don't think anyone knew Thelma Todd better than
> I did. She was keen, witty, a powerful person-
> ality. We were partners ... She had everything
> to live for--money, position, beauty. Those were
> the only things I ever concerned myself with in
> Thelma Todd's life--her work and her beauty. [1]

Roland West, long dead and forgotten, strove to maintain a reclusive and mysterious air around himself and his
activities. Most of his films are gone; so are most of the
people who knew and worked with him.

But the few films that exist are exciting, surprising
oddities that exist to defy conventional film histories. They
do things that, we are told, films of their day didn't do.

"Who is Roland West?" began an article in The New
York Times, shortly after the young man had scored a
Broadway success in 1918. More than sixty years later,
that question still can't be answered with any certainty.

"I liked him very, very much," said Hal Kern, who
edited five pictures for him, "but he was a very 'close' fellow, very closed-in. I would say that he kept to himself
entirely."[2]

Actor Regis Toomey recalled, "He was a very odd
man. A nice, pleasant man--nothing 'weird' about him; he
was a difficult man to get to know. He was rather shy,
very reticent, a very retiring man. He had very little to
say."[3]

He was also an enigma to actress Una Merkel, who
remembers him as "not too pleasant."

He was nice enough to me.   When I say not too
pleasant I don't mean he was nasty or said nasty
things to anybody.   I just mean, like you work
with some people and the whole atmosphere is
pleasant.   Well with him, it was kind of vacant:
no particular feeling of any kind.   I think he had
a lot in his own mind that he kept to himself. [4]

Who was Roland West?

He was born Roland Van Ziemer in Cleveland, Ohio
in 1887.   His mother was Margaret Van Tassel, an actress
of the legitimate stage.   It was his aunt, Cora Van Tassel,
a noted theater personality and producer of the Cleveland
stage, who initiated him to the theater, casting the twelve-
year old boy in a Cleveland show she was producing, The
Volunteers, [5] in 1899.

When he answered his cue a sea of faces swam
before his eyes.   He hadn't known an audience
could be so terrifying.   His voice trembled and
his knees shook. [6]

On the second night he had conquered his stage fright, and
he remained with the show for the entire run.

Perhaps the surname "Van Ziemer" rankled in print
on a theatrical programme; perhaps the strong-willed boy,
electing to succeed or fail on his own, chose not to trade
on the name "Van Tassel. " A stage name was in order, and
Roland Van Ziemer became Roland West.

In 1904 the seventeen-year old West replaced Emmet
Corrigan in a touring edition of Jockey Jones.   In New York,
eager to make a name for himself, he determined that he
would get himself arrested, if necessary, to let the town
know that Roland West had arrived.

An extortionist, representing himself as West, was
offering ambitious young ladies "opportunities" in the theater.
Each gave him $8.00 but the bogus West failed to appear for
the call-backs.   The more clever ladies rushed down to Pas-
tor's where the real West was performing.

It was about this time also that West's press agent
learned what had been going on....   It would be a
great card ... to have his principal arrested and

taken into court, where of course he would have
been released. A cog slipped, however, and the
arrest was not accomplished. [7]

West, to his chagrin, had the perfect alibi, he looked
nothing like the swindler.

At nineteen, now an accomplished performer, West became a writer. In collaboration with W. H. Clifford he
wrote a twenty-five minute vaudeville sketch titled The Criminal. It was a "protean" sketch, a histrionic showcase for
the young actor's chameleon instincts. The Criminal is
West's career in embryo: its melodramatic turns of plot
and preoccupation with the criminal mind occur in every one
of his later projects.

> This tale of murder, robbery and police in-
> quisitions is worked out rapidly, tensely and with
> impelling dramatic effect.... Five distinct char-
> acters are drawn by West, with a remarkably
> short time elapsing for changes, running the range
> of a stylish young newspaper detective, doddering
> old man, Hebrew pawnbroker, youthful newsboy and
> a young tough.... Voice, action, manner and
> method are completely changed with each.... The
> special setting includes a vision scene which de-
> picts the crime of which the old man is accused
> and which, to shield his wayward son, he confesses
> to under third degree police methods. [8]

For the next five years he toured the act throughout
the country, changing its title in 1909 to The Under World but
embellishing and refining his portryal of the dark side of human nature.

Back in New York, with The Under World generating
good reviews, West's engagement to frequent girlfriend Anna
Howard was announced to the press on October 2, 1911, [9]
with a typically brash stunt. While visiting at the home of
the actress, so went the tale, West was overcome with pa-
ralysis. Medical advice was that he not be moved, and so
for two weeks Miss Howard ministered to her invalid fiancée.
There is no record of the marriage ever having occurred.

The years with the Loew's Circuit were profitable for
West, and he acquired a measure of accomplishment as a
writer/performer. He also formed the most important

acquaintance of his life with Joseph Schenck, then working for
Marcus Loew as General Manager in charge of bookings. It
was a friendship that endured more than a quarter of a century until West's death, weathering success and scandal in the
lives of both men.   Always ambitious, West abandoned acting
in the early 'teens to produce independently.   At his peak he
boasted of fifty-three acts playing simultanteously.

Crime, mystery, and police methods were the elements
in these playlets.   The idea of concealed and inverted iden-
tity--a good man who is really a bad man, the bad man who
is actually good--which is so central to all of his mature
films, is graphically present in these early, inconsequentially
brief sketches.

In January of 1913 he produced Who Was He?, a four-
teen-minute playlet:

> ... With the slangy visitor whom the wife guesses
> immediately to be a burglar, and his knowledge of
> the crime of the theft of an heirloom, together with
> the return of the husband along with the impending
> disclosure, the audience is held.   The wife asks the
> visitor how he knew the jewel had been lost and she
> had stolen it, but he declines to divulge trade se-
> crets. [10]

The audience was left to ponder whether the burglar
was perhaps not a crook, but actually a detective.   No such
vague twist occured in Thro' the Skylight, a nineteen-minute
offering in January of 1914:

> ... A female appealing for protection to two col-
> lege boys against an allegedly insane husband who
> believes he is a detective, is in reality a sneak
> thief, hitting upon the ruse to escape from a gen-
> uine officer close upon her trail ... (at the end
> she leaves) a couple of pieces of jewelry she had
> stolen from her saviors, and silently depart(s),
> with the sketch giving the wrong right. [11]

Malvina, How Could You?, a seventeen-minute act in
March of 1914,

> ... is the tale of an adventuress from New York
> who does not disguise her profession. ...   The
> hotel detective, as an Italian Count, uncovers her. [12]

The Auto Bandit, in September 1914, is self-explana-
tory, cops 'n' robbers stuff, though West's stage effects were
becoming ambitious:

> The final scene is an up-to-date version of the
> familiar race scene from Ben Hur, an automobile
> and a motorcycle being the contestants in the race. [13]

In fifteen years West had paid his dues and climbed to
the top of his profession.   Financially he was well off.   The
fledgling movie shows that had accompanied the vaudeville
shows were coming into their own.   West began writing and
submitting scenarios, and they were being accepted. [14]

Joe Schenck had done exceedingly well for himself,
too.   With $26,000 he and West established The Roland West
Film Corporation. [15]

Lost Souls, probably filmed during the last months of
1915, starred an English comic-opera performer, Jose Collins.
Helene (Jose Collins), an Italian peasant girl, marries her
sweetheart Roberto in a civil ceremony just before he leaves
for the New World, intending to send for Helene once he has
made their fortune.   Helene's mother dies and the orphaned
girl goes to Naples where she falls victim to a bordello pro-
prietress, "La Terribula," and her partner, Tochetti.   After
two weeks Helene escapes from the brothel, manages the
steamship fare to America, and arrives in a Pennsylvania
mining town in time for Roberto to die in her arms.   Fatally
injured in a mine explosion, he admonishes her to avenge her
honor.

In New York City, Helene loses her job in a sweatshop
when she rejects the foreman's romantic advances.   Finding
work as an artist's model, she falls in love and agrees to
marry a young Italian lawyer, Guido Ferrari.   Guido informs
her that they must go to Naples and obtain permission from
his uncle, the head of the family.

The uncle turns out to be the Madame's consort, Tochetti.   Plotting vengeance, Helene feigns a liking for Tochetti, who gives her a key to his apartment.   At a rendezvous the following evening, Helene poisons Tochetti's drink
and he dies before he can summon help.   Helene arrives at
the bordello just as "La Terribula" is about to induct Helene's
little sister, Maria, into the ranks of courtesans; Helene
strangles the Madame with her bare hands.   Maria's boyfriend, a police official, enters the bordello just in time to

conceal the only clue linking Helene to the murder.   When
Helene confesses the whole tale to Guido, he happily for-
gives her and they sail back to America to be married.

Location shooting gave Lost Soul's exteriors some
veracity; the city scenes were filmed in New York, and
the production traveled to Shamokin, Pennsylvania--the quin-
tessential mining town of that region and period--for the sequences of Roberto's travails and death.   The European War
put Italy off-limits for location filming, so the company com-
promised by embarking to Cuba for an approximation of the
Neapolitan look. [16]

West entered Lost Souls for copyright on April 7,
1916.   It was sold to William Fox, who retitled it A Woman's
Honor before applying for a new copyright on June 11, 1916.
Though all of West's later publicity always referred to this
initial venture as Lost Souls, it was as a William Fox picture, A Woman's Honor, that the film was distributed and
reviewed.

"This is a picture that hardly any releasing company
except Fox would consider putting on the market,"[17] declared
a trade reviewer.   He found the acting uniformly terrible,
with Arthur Donaldson's Tochetti all but ruined by his "wop
villain" make-up.   West's craft as a filmmaker would seem
to be inordinately clumsy, even for this early date.   Certainly for a five-reel feature that followed The Birth of a
Nation such lapses are lazy and inexcusable:

> Josie saw the messenger [from Tochetti] talking
> to Friend Hero, and indignantly accused him of
> being a friend of the willun (sic) in Naples.   She
> left his home in a rage.   Following this scene
> came a title, "Love Surmounts all Obstacles," and
> we saw the hero proposing to Josie.   For jumps,
> that is one of the worst I have ever seen. [18]

Helene and company were bounced between New York
and Naples with the case of ping pong balls:

> By means of another title and a short scene or
> two (and believe me some of the scenes in this
> film were short), hero and shero (sic) were landed
> in Naples ... that was one of the best things [the
> director] did. [19]

Potentially in the film's favor was its speed, as "this thing

moves so very fast that it does not at any time really register, " though the cumulative result placed the film somewhere between "pitiful" and "truly funny. "[20]

Whatever the critical opinion, West, Schenck and Fox
were astute businessmen who gave audiences what they wanted:
sex and wickedness.   A party scene was so tasteless that it
was deemed riotous even by William Fox's licentious standards, and advertising sold the film as a sex picture, with the
tag line "A beautiful woman faced ruin in Naples" over a picture of a beaming Jose Collins in pantaloons cut a good six
inches above her knee, looking very pleased at the prospect.
Anticipating trouble, Fox provided copy like "What a Great
American Legal Authority Says of Censorship and Its Injus-
tice to Workmen, " with the admonition, " ... we suggest that
you get your local papers to republish this soon. "[21]

Financial figures for A Woman's Honor are unknown,
but historian Jack Spears describes the venture as "none-too-
successful. "[22]   If this is true, it didn't dampen West's enthusiasm one bit.

In 1917 thirty-six-year-old Joe Schenck reorganized the
career of his twenty-one-year-old wife, Norma Talmadge,
founding the New York-based Norma Talmadge Company exclusively for her.   West, the General Manager of the company, was entrusted with the third picture, De Luxe Annie,
released in 1918.   It was a popular and financial success,
though reviews of the Talmadge performance varied from
praise to damnation.   Cited as a "grand and glorious melodrama ... directed with speed and discretion, "[23] the story
must have appealed to West.

Suffering a blow on the head, Talmadge, as the well-
bred Julie Kendall, descends to a life of crime.   After she
spends a period of years as the wanton woman in a badger
game peppered with "unbelievable coincidences that are
really the properties of her half-remembered life, " a brain
operation restores her gentle personality and Julie is re-
united with husband and child.

Next West dusted off an old trunk item, a motion
picture scenario called The Vanishing Man, and struggled
to shape it into a stageplay.   He had written the story in
1912 and refused a $10,000 purchase offer from a film
producer, figuring that a greater profit could be realized
by developing the property himself.   In succession West

took his story to writers Carlyle Moore, Jasper Ewing
Brady, and Edward Clarke.   When West brought it back
to him Moore agreed to spend the spring of 1918 working
it over.   Refused backing by every Broadway producer to
whom he pitched the idea, West used $50,000 of his own
money to bankroll the play, now called The Unknown Purple. [24]

How to put over with conviction an invisible protagonist was a task West solved himself, as lighting was not
only of major interest to him, but a skilled specialty.   Much
of the money was squandered on ultimately impractical electrical equipment to achieve a purple glow that indicates the
presence of the invisible one.   When The Unknown Purple
finally opened in Long Branch, New Jersey during the early
summer the invisibility gimmick, which Carlyle Moore had
wanted to scuttle, proved to be the major drawing card.

Out-of-town tryouts followed in Atlantic City and Washington, D. C. as West was deluged with offers from Broadway.   He didn't need them now.   The Unknown Purple opened
at the Lyric Theatre in New York on September 14, 1918,
produced by Roland West.   Though the problematical lighting
effects misbehaved on opening night, word of mouth had preceded the company and the play was an overnight success.
West gave a small interest in the show to Schenck and two
of the company's staff, and sold Norma Talmadge a five per
cent interest for $5000.   Apart from these awards to a few
close associates, the fledging producer was satisfied to retain the profits of a gamble that no one else had been interested in.

Helen MacKellar starred as Jewel Marchmont, named
for Roland West's new bride, Jewel Carmen, a petite blonde
William Fox star.   Also in the cast were Richard Bennett
as Peter Marchmont (alias "Victor Cromport"), the inventor /
protagonist; Earle Brown as Jewel's scheming lover, James
Dawson; and Lorraine Frost as Jewel's good sister, Ruth.

Plowing through The Unknown Purple sixty-five years
later, one is painfully aware of the naïve and heavy-handed
writing, germane to the period and genre, so far removed
are we from the post-Victorian sensibility that found melodrama and sentimentality vital, exciting entertainment.

"Why think of it, Ruthie," says Peter Marchmont,
describing his discovery to his sister-in-law, "--with a

piece of it in my hand no bigger than a dollar, I can render
my body invisible to the human eye.   All you can see of me
is just a purple glow.   Why, it's stronger than radium; more
powerful than the X-ray. "25

Peter also has a new dye process, potentially worth
a fortune, that is appropriated by Jewel's lover, Dawson,
who blackmails Jewel into framing Peter for theft of company funds.

> JEWEL: If that will make Peter wealthy, that's
>   what I want.   The things other women
>   have.
> DAWSON: (quietly threatening) Then all these
>   months you've known that I'm dependent
>   on my uncle, who keeps me in his office
>   on a rotten salary, and yet you have
>   taken dresses--everything--from me, and
>   what have you given in return?   Prom-
>   ises!   Promises!   But now you'll make
>   good.
> JEWEL: You are in no position to threaten me,
>   Jimmy.
> DAWSON: Then perhaps you can explain where you
>   get all your new dresses.
> JEWEL: Explain to whom?   Why, my husband--
> DAWSON: They represent to a penny the shortages
>   occurring in my uncle's office during the
>   past three months.
> JEWEL: Jimmy!26

Peter, believing Jewel has appropriated the money to
take their little Bobby to the country, assumes the burden of
guilt and a jail term.

Act Two finds Dawson and Jewel living in splendor
from the profits of the stolen dye process.   But a mysterious, unseen presence has been haunting Dawson.   Peter, released from jail and disguised as Victor Cromport, returns
and reveals himself to Jewel, and persuades her to poison
Dawson's nerve tonic:

> A VOICE: Jimmy! (Dawson stops, galvanized)
>   Jimmy! (back of Dawson develops
>   the strange purple light and in the
>   midst of it is Cromport, speaking
>   in Peter Marchmont's voice.)

DAWSON: I know you're here--but I can't see
               you.
CROMPORT: You know who it is, don't you, Jim-
               my?
DAWSON: Yes, damn you, you're Peter March-
               mont! But you can't hurt me. You're
               dead.
CROMPORT: But I'm not dead in your mind, Jim-
               my. [27]

Marchmont reveals Jewel's betrayal and Dawson attacks her with a knife. Peter is overcome by the drug. He
admits that it was merely a sleeping potion, that he has been
toying with Jewel, and in reality loves her sister, Ruth.

JEWEL: So that's it, eh? (sarcastic)
               So it's Ruth that you love. (anger)
               If you think that you can take every-
               thing I've got and then walk calmly
               to eternal happiness, you're mistaken.
CROMPORT: Stop--
JEWEL: (rushes up to door) Stop, hell!
               You try to stop me; and when I'm
               through with you--you jailbird--she
               or anyone else will be welcome to
               what's left of you--Damn you! [28]

Detective Alison and his men swarm in to arrest Peter, who
is slowly enveloped by the purple ray.

CROMPORT: I'm sorry I can't remain longer; but
               I'm going to a far greater happiness
               --one you could never understand.
               Listen, Alison, I am the Purple Ray--
               Good-by and good luck, Mr. Alison.
ALISON: He's gone! [29]

West reveled in his accomplishment; this wasn't
vaudeville, this was Broadway, the legitimate stage. Within forty-eight hours of the opening, tickets were sold out
eight weeks in advance. When a road company of The Unknown Purple hit West's home town in March, 1920, the
papers referred to West as a "Cleveland Playwright," wrap-
ping banner headlines around their civic pride: "Another
Cleveland Boy at Top of Ladder." [30]

With the Broadway run ended and road companies

heading out to the provinces, West returned to the aegis of
Joe Schenck and Marcus Loew, who had just purchased Metro
Pictures. He returned to films as what might today be called
a "total filmmaker." He didn't need the money; West made
movies now solely because he wanted to, limiting himself to
one carefully prepared and meticulously mounted production
a year. For a director West's position was an enviable one.
He was his own producer and writer. He gathered around
him a network of trusted associates including Willard Mack,
Hal Kern, Ned Mann, William Cameron Menzies, Ray June,
Charles Smith, and Chester Morris, with all of whom he
worked closely and consistently.

        The stories of West's pictures are seemingly inter-
changeable. People parade about in dual or concealed iden-
tities, indulging in murder, vice, theft and racketeering.
The Police and the Social Order are either ineffectual or as
unscrupulous as the underworld they would restrain. Solutions
are reached via an internal moral code which often verges on
vigilantism. The disturbing sameness of incident in his
scripts is more properly a single recurring theme. In an
era of growth and rampant opportunism marked by robber
barons operating within the fringes of the law, and equally
capitalistic gangsters at work just beyond its perimeter,
West's films don a guise of melodrama to meet this contra-
diction.

        West's villains have enormous appeal. The title char-
acter in The Bat is a master criminal who commands our
respect for his supreme skill as a criminal, while in the
same story the initial bank robbery is committed by the bank's
own president! In Alibi a hardened criminal adopts middle
class mannerisms, while the frustrated police must finally
act like criminals to catch him.

        Amnesia and schizophrenia finally enter the stories,
until all clear conceptions of personality and morality become hopelessly muddled. Probably the key scene in any
West story occurs in The Monster. The lonesome, ineffectual hero finds himself out at night alone in a thunderstorm. Daffy Dan, a weird but harmless character, approaches him, halting while he gleefully rolls, then smokes,
an imaginary cigarette. He ambles up to Johnny and politely
asks him, "Do you know who I am?" Our hero is sorry, and
shakes his head, "No." "Neither do I!" confides Dan, before merrily going about his business.

We can discuss theme and story by recalling the plots
of West's pictures. We can't always discern their tone or
attitude because so few of the films actually exist. The
films that do survive show that West was a weak dramatist,
but an overwhelming stylist. The loss of seven of the eleven
films he directed (including all but one of the silents) makes
it impossible to fully chart his development as an artist.
With a director more committed to how he told a story than
to the story itself, synopses are a frail substitute for the
experience of seeing.

West's original story The Silver Lining was a vehicle
for his wife, Jewel Carmen, produced in 1920 for release in
early 1921. It opens with a frame: at an upper crust wedding reception, Secret Service agent John Strong overhears a
discussion among the guests and contradicts their contention
that heredity determines a child's destiny by telling a story.

Two orphaned girls are adopted; one by the Schofields,
who raise her as a lady of society; the other by criminals,
who train her as a pickpocket, "The Angel." Johnson, a
confidence man, catches the thieving Angel and forces the
girl and her mentors to go to Havana with him.

In Cuba "The Angel" falls in love with writer Robert
Ellington, who just happens to be orphan sister Evelyn Schofield's estranged fiancé. Johnson forces "The Angel" to
swindle $25,000 from Robert, but she confesses the scheme
and stages a mock love scene with Johnson to break off her
affair with Ellington. Johnson is touched by the girl's love
for the writer, and reveals to Robert that he is a Secret
Service agent. Robert and "The Angel" marry.

Did society accept the couple, asks John Strong's audience? Strong points to the contentment of the hosts at the
reception and admits that he is the Johnson of the story.

The Silver Lining takes the Jekyll/Hyde aspects of
De Luxe Annie a step further by illustrating the dual identity
theme with twin sisters, then resolving the conflict by allowing the gutter girl to assume the respectable sister's station
in life. Existing synopses are annoyingly vague and don't
indicate a reason for the Secret Service agent's prolonged
(and presumably expensive) masquerade. His most unpro-
fessional decision, to overlook "The Angel's" life of crime
(he has probably been sent to apprehend her) and deliver her
to wedded and material bliss, is a sentimental gesture typical

of West, and derived from that "internal moral code." What
Strong's superiors would say to an operations agent playing
fairy godmother and assuming such initiative in dispensing
with a Federal investigation doesn't seem to be relevant!
West's most outrageous flaunting of guiltless profiteering,
however, would occur in his last film, Corsair.

Nobody, released the summer of 1921, was similarly
a vehicle for Jewel Carmen and shared a like narrative
framework.   Financier John Rossmore is the victim in a
"locked room" murder for which his butler is about to be
found guilty.   As the jury deliberates, Tom Smith holds out
for acquittal and tells his fellow jurors an odd story.

Smith and his wife meet Rossmore while vacationing
in Palm Beach.   As Tom is called back to New York on
business, Rossmore invites little Mrs. Smith out on his
yacht, where she is drugged and raped by her host, who
then blackmails her into silence.   Terrified, little Mrs.
Smith goes to Rossmore's home, admits herself with a key,
and shoots him dead.

The jurors agree never to repeat Tom's story, and
acquit the butler of murder.   A sentimental recital of an
unproven crime is sufficient grounds for jury tampering in
Nobody.   The wrongs suffered by the little Mrs., told by
someone who could not possibly have witnessed the events,
again activate the "internal moral code" for an incredibly
gullible and irresponsible jury.

West's persistence in spelling out the lady's distress
by flashback illustration seemed labored justification to The
New York Times' critic, since

> on the screen, with its continual dependence upon
> words and the merciless exposure of its skeleton
> by literal pictures ... [the movie is] clearly a
> consciously fabricated piece. [31]

West seems to have hit his stride with the motion picture adaptation of his play, The Unknown Purple, in 1923.
He made much of color tinting for the highlight thrill scenes,
so that Marchmont's purple halo was transferred intact.   Additionally he tackled effects he could never have achieved on
stage:

> ... a purple cone strikes the center of the room

and a hand is seen writing a note.... [This scene] is much more effective than those where the whole screen is tinted purple. [32]

The Unknown Purple received generally positive reviews, but the following item from the New York Sun probably contains as much truth as sarcasm:

> [The Unknown Purple is] a first cousin to the trashy old Fantomus (sic) series ... [it's plot] is worth 10¢ any day in the canned goods market of melodrama....
>   We were rather disappointed that he didn't kill his faithless wife and her wicked husband. Instead, after he has ruined one of their dinner parties and scared the guests pretty badly, he only gives [them] a bad scolding and leaves them together to hate one another.
>   The ray is colored in the picture. The purple, however, has too much red in it, which gives it a very cheap theatrical look.... As it moves about on the screen ... it resembles a ham vaudeville spotlight searching for an actor. But this is probably what the director meant for it to resemble as the actor in the case is Mr. Henry B. Walthal (sic), than whom no one has more savoir faire and the coolness commonly attributed to cucumbers. [33]

The Unknown Purple was distributed by Truart, which announced that the writer/director West had just signed a six-year contract, calling for two films per year. [34] West apparently had other ideas, as the only work he did for Truart was an adaptation of a Redbook magazine story, "Driftwood," which was released as Daring Love. His collaborator was Willard Mack.

An odd footnote to the Truart contract is that Daring Love was directed by Roland G. Edwards, whose only other known credit is another 1924 Truart release, Drums of Jeopardy, for which he was Production Supervisor. Could West have partially fulfilled his contract and signed these pictures with an alias?

The Monster (1925) is the only surviving example of West's silents and though largely a comedy it is one of the few genuine "horror" films Lon Chaney made. West adapted a 1922 "clutching hand" play by Crane Wilbur which transfers

to film as a leaden burlesque, dependent on childish titles.
The action and thrill sequences are a good deal better but
the mixture is an uneasy one.

In a rural Mid-Western town the disappearance of a
prominent citizen has caused the biggest excitement since
"the grocer's wife ran off with the milkman. " Our hero,
a wispy little loser named Johnny, has ambition, which in
Danburg is "like having eczema. " Johnny wants to be a
detective, and brandishing handcuffs, tin star and diploma
from the Kankakee School of Detectives he sets out to solve
the disappearances which center around Dr. Ziska's sanitar-
ium.   Taking a cue from Caligari, the inmates have overrun the asylum.   The presiding Dr. Ziska is the worst maniac of the lot; having incarcerated the staff in a basement
dungeon he lowers a diabolical mirror across the nighttime
highway to create auto accidents.   The survivors are sal-
vaged as experimental subjects in Ziska's scheme to transfer souls between the bodies of men and women.

West's stylistic trademarks are fully developed in The
Monster, though he approaches the subject as theater rather
than film.   He never abandoned the fondness demonstrated
here for long shots and arranging his action as though framed
by a proscenium.   Typically, the story is set almost entirely
at night, which allows West and the excellent cameraman Hal
Mohr to indulge in some sophisticated lighting set-ups and
shadow play.   Spotlights and dimmer lights emphasize and
reveal events within West's carefully posed tableaux.   Ziska's
entrance is impeccably staged: shadowy fingers writhing on
the wall herald his descent of a steep staircase into a pool
of light.   While drawing on an elegantly mounted cigarette
that wreaths him in wisps of smoke, Ziska uses some artful
hand gestures to casually resurrect a corpse.   "Rigo--a patient of mine, " he explains, "... sometimes he gets out ...
does terrible things.   A strange case ... but I deal in strange
cases. "

"Doctor, " asks Johnny, "Shall we see you in the
morning?"   With the aplomb of the ham actor Ziska draws
himself up for the obvious incantation, "Who knows if one
will ever see the morning?"

West moves his cameras outdoors for an offbeat sequence in which the heroes and the ghouls battle while perched on high-tension power lines at the height of a midnight
thunderstorm.   There is also a clever moment as Johnny's

party arrives at the asylum, to be greeted by a hulking giant
who moves behind the door as he opens it for them. The
door slowly swings closed and the brute has vanished--a giddy
but theatrical joke. In later years West would achieve the
same punchline with camerawork and editing.

        The Monster had been filmed at the Hal Roach Studio
and was distributed by M-G-M; but a shakeup in the structure
of United Artists resulted in Joe Schenck assuming UA's
chairmanship. West was given a financing and distribution
deal with UA that allowed him a secure, free hand. In the
scant six years remaining in his film career West never
worked for anyone else--or should we say with?--for Roland
West made films only to please Roland West.

        In adapting the phenomenally popular Mary Roberts
Rinehart/Avery Hopwood play The Bat in 1926, West made
his reputation. Though as late as 1964 a 35mm print was
"rumored to be at large in the Mid-West,"[35] The Bat has
never surfaced and is perhaps the most sorely missed of
all of West's silents. It is a key "old dark house" movie,
was the most well received of all of West's silents and,
unaffected by the post-1926 influences of montage, moving
camera and German Expressionism, would be the single most
valuable barometer of West's silent style.

        The Bat is a master criminal who, dressed as his
namesake, has eluded capture by the police. When his robbery of a bank is thwarted by another thief who beats him to
the punch, The Bat trails the robber to a gloomy Long Island
mansion rented by Cornelia Van Gorder. Cornelia's maid
Lizzie witnesses the manifestations of The Bat and another
mysteriously masked man. Dale, the daughter of the house's
owner, is terrorized also and Mrs. Van Gorder sends for
Detective Moletti. Dale's brother, Richard Fleming, is
killed for a blueprint that shows a secret room where the
money may be hidden. Anderson, a bumbling country detective, arrives as suspicion falls on the sinister Dr. Wells,
the Japanese houseboy Billy, and Brooks the gardener, who
is really the missing cashier of the bank. A disheveled,
badly beaten stranger solves the mystery when he reveals
that he is the genuine Detective Moletti, attacked and im-
prisoned by The Bat upon his arrival. Dale's father, the
owner of the plundered bank, had conspired with Dr. Wells
and robbed it himself. The unmasked Bat makes a break
for freedom and is caught in a bear trap set on the lawn
by the simple-minded Lizzie.

The delicate balance of thrills and comedy that eluded
West in The Monster worked in The Bat. Its comedy was
confined to Lizzie's character, played here by Louise Fazenda,
and served as counterpoint to The Bat's undiluted reign of
terror. "Nobody is permitted to forget The Bat ... if this
thief does not appear in his ungainly make-up, then a moth
on the headlight of an automobile is magnified into a bat
against the ceiling," said the New York Times. "In translating [the play] to the screen ... Roland West has profited
by the wide scope of the camera."36   The grass roots Harrison's Reports was equally pleased:

> Few pictures have been released lately that
> hold the spectator as breathless as does The Bat,
> and not only does it hold him breathless but it
> thrills him and at the same time makes him laugh
> to his heart's content. 37

The Bat was photographed by Arthur Edeson, whose
later camera work on Frankenstein and The Old Dark House
itself would set the style for gothic thrillers of the 'thirties.
It was the first of three pictures designed for West by the
brilliant William Cameron Menzies, though he may have over-
indulged his taste for the fanciful:

> There is a scene in which a structure that looks
> like Warwick Castle is in full blaze. It is rather
> surprising when one reads on a caption that this
> building is only the garage. 38

In adapting the story West made it his own. The
original play focuses on Mrs. Van Gorder's calm, method-
ical solution of the mystery, but West gave equal emphasis
to The Bat and his criminal activities. As he would also
do in his later remake of the story, he opened the film with
an extensive prologue showing The Bat plundering millionaire
Gideon Bell, the thwarted bank robbery, and the flight to
the countryside.

By 1937 Schenck's marriage to Norma Talmadge had
eroded to the degree that they separated, though he continued
to manage her career. With the expiration of her First
National contract he brought her into the fold at United Artists. Her career was slipping, and would end in 1930 after
two abortive talkies. A reunion with West seemed a good
idea, and in an interview Miss Talmadge announced that
she and West were about to do a picture at the UFA Studio

in Berlin, to take advantage of the "exciting new techniques of the German film industry. "[39]

This statement is important for its affirmation of
West's acute awareness of German films and for the implication that he wished to emulate them. It confirms influences on the visual style of his late films, and perhaps
explains some stray, individual images which might otherwise seem mere coincidences.

The UFA project never materialized and West remained in Hollywood where he directed Talmadge in The
Dove (1928). Willard Mack, West's collaborator on The
Monster, assisted him and playwright Wallace Smith in
adapting Mack's Broadway hit about a corrupt Mexican des-
pot. To appease Mexican authorities, ever sensitive to Hollywood's portrayal of such matters, the locale was trans-
posed to "Costa Roja" in the Mediterranean, fooling absolutely
no one.

Talmadge played Dolores, a dance hall girl known as
"The Dove," who falls in love with croupier Johnny Powell.
The wealthy and egotistical Don José desires the girl. José's
cousin, Gomez, is killed by Johnny in self-defense when he
is caught cheating at the gambling house. Johnny is jailed,
and Dolores gives herself to Don José on condition that he
will free her lover.

Johnny appears at Don José's hacienda the morning
of the wedding, and escapes with Dolores. They are re-
captured and sentenced to be shot. As Johnny is prepared
for the firing squad, Dolores runs to him, insisting that she
die alongside her lover. The onlooking crowd is touched,
and Don José quickly orders the execution to proceed. Ad-
dressing the mob, Dolores ridicules Don José's boast that
he is "the bes' dam caballero in all Costa Roja,"

> Go, damn you! Mak' the shoot! But all my life
> I say--an' everybody say--the bes' dam caballero
> in Costa Roja was my Johnny Powell!

To save his face, the Don is forced to release them,
and he gives them a splendid carriage to depart in. "Who
is the bes' dam caballero in all Costa Roja' now?" he asks
her.

"Senor Don José Maria Lopez y Sandoval--you betcha
my life! "[40]

"Courage and imagination have entered into its direction, " commented a critic.   If West couldn't go to Germany to use their techniques, he would bring German techniques-- particularly the moving camera of Murnau and Lang--to Hollywood:

> In the introduction ... West has the temerity to keep his camera going without a soul on the horizon.   It is a fine idea, for it creates quite a nice illusion, that of the audience being taken over the byways of Costa Roja to where the story is laid. You fly along the rough roads, over a mountain or two, and then come, to a place that has been smoothed over by José's minions. [41]

The very first Academy Award for Art Direction was given to William Cameron Menzies for his work on both The Dove and Tempest.   When we consider this description of The Dove's opening, not only does Mephisto's tour of the world in Murnau's Faust spring to mind; so do the extended traveling camera shots in the opening of Tempest.   The rich, silent storytelling we will soon encounter in the prelude to Alibi, like the silent, pictorially coherent openings of other Menzies-designed pictures as disparate as Bulldog Drummond (1929) and The Devil and Miss Jones (1941), also strongly suggest Menzies' signature on West's films.   At the very least we cannot under-estimate the importance of Menzies' presence on West's staff.

West had closed to all visitors the stages where The Dove was filming, in order to protect the special nature of his camerawork.   Trick shots and close-ups, he felt, should be used "psychologically ... unless it means something, it should be left out. "[42]   This artistic credo stopped short with the boss's wife, and Norma Talmadge's close-ups in The Dove were soft-focus often enough to draw attention, and negative comments, to them.

Noah Beery, as Don José, received most of the critics' accolades in a part that was as showy as it was outrageous.   This was the second of a string of films that Talmadge would make with Gilbert Roland, with whom she was conducting a torrid and much-publicized love affair while still married to Schenck.   History remains divided on The Dove's qualities: William K. Everson calls it "one of the best Norma Talmadge silents, "[43] but Jack Spears deemed it "slow-moving and unrealistic, " marred by the slangy

intertitles.   These were not uncommon in a Talmadge vehicle,
although in this case they were transliterated for a Spanish
dialect, emerging with such howlers as "You betcha my
life!"[44]

As West left the stage one day during a lunch hour
he found himself under siege by an agitated, nondescript girl.
"Are you Roland West?" she asked.   When he admitted he
was, the girl announced that she was desperate to write for
the movies.   "I know that you made The Bat," she stam-
mered, fingering a portfolio under her arm, "and I read that
you were filming The Dove."   She opened the portfolio and
thrust a copy of her original story, "The Lark," into his
hands, explaining that since he was interested in bird stories
her script might be just the thing for him. [45]   But West already had his next project: another Broadway play, Nightstick.

Nightstick is a story of the New York underworld.
Gangster Chick Williams, recently released from prison, is
engaged to Joan Manning, the daughter of a cop.   Chick
swears that he has gone straight, but Joan's father, Pete,
and another policeman, Tommy Glennon, are convinced otherwise and oppose the marriage.   With Buck Bachman's nightclub as a front, Chick reactivates the gang.   A fur warehouse is robbed and a policeman is killed.   Chick is sus-
pected but he has an alibi: he was at the theater with Joan.
Tommy reconstructs the crime, proving that Chick could have
left the theater at intermission, robbed the warehouse, and
returned just as the second act was beginning.   Detective Danny McGann, having infiltrated the mob, is killed when Chick
discovers the deception.   Tommy confronts Chick at the nightclub, where he tells Chick that he will kill him to avenge
Danny's death.   Chick becomes hysterical, and as he pleads
for his life Tommy fires his revolver: but the bullets are
blank, and Chick has only fainted from fear.   He regains
consciousness and attempts to escape from the roof by jumping to the roof of an adjoining building.   He loses his footing
and plummets to his death.

West was determined that his movie, now called Alibi,
should have an unknown in the pivotal role of Chick Williams.
Sifting through film in the United Artists vaults, he came upon
a screen test that D. W. Griffith had made of a New York
stage actor, Chester Morris.   As West watched the silent
footage he leapt to his feet, exclaiming, "That's my Chick
Williams!"[46]

Morris, under contract to producer Al Woods, was still appearing on Broadway in <u>Crime</u> and was due to begin the show <u>Jealousy</u> when West contacted him.   Morris declined the offer to go to Los Angeles, citing his contract with Woods and his ignorance of Hollywood.   The refusal made West twice as determined and he had Joe Schenck buy out Woods' contract. [47] Morris found himself, in late 1928, headed to Los Angeles with a six-month United Artists contract.

Production on the silent film was just beginning when West had second thoughts and decided to turn <u>Alibi</u> into UA's first talkie.   "We started it as a silent picture, then went right into sound," recalled film editor Hal Kern.

> A lot of people didn't believe in sound in those
> days.   I did, and Roland West did.   That was the
> main reason that I was on it.   I went to New York
> to the Bell Lab for two weeks to learn something
> about sound, because Warner Brothers' wouldn't
> let you know <u>anything</u>. [48]

By the time the cast reported in September, there was no question that <u>Alibi</u> would be anything other than 100% talking, though an auxilary silent edition was prepared simultaneously.   Regis Toomey, who played Danny McGann, the undercover detective, took exception with the suggestion that it was ever begun as a silent:

> ... it was always intended as a talking picture.
> What we <u>did</u> do, because at that time there weren't
> very many theaters wired for sound ... it was con-
> verted, if you will, into a silent picture by adding
> scenes that we shot to bridge gaps where the dia-
> logue was needed to follow the storyline. [49]

The camera was encased in a sound-proof booth on wheels.   <u>Alibi</u> is the first time we hear of West shooting at night, a fact that has been interpreted by some historians as bizarre and eccentric.

> There was nothing eccentric about it!   That's the
> way you had to make pictures then.   We didn't
> have sound stages.   In order to minimize the out-
> side noise we shot at night and covered the stages
> with blankets to act as a buffer against the street
> noises.   That's the way <u>everybody</u> was shooting
> until they got the sound <u>stages</u> built. [50]

THE "ALIBI" SOUND STAGE

Toomey recalls that six weeks of intensive rehearsal were conducted before anything was shot. "We rehearsed this picture as though it were a stage show; we could have gone with it into any theater afterward."[51] When production started in October, the thorough rehearsals were repeated before each take; then West would retire to a sound-proof, glassed-in tower where he could watch the take while monitoring the sound recording.[52] The Movietone sound-on-film process was used. It is claimed that a secondary, wax disc was cut for an immediately playable reference check,[53] but Hal Kern maintains that they never used wax but did have two optical sound-recording machines. Kern also indicated that they could mix their soundtrack electronically, that it was not necessary to record all music and sound effects "live." Looping was still unknown, so West recorded Virginia Flohri, singing off-camera, while Irma Harrison silently mouthed the words.[54] Harrison's own voice, retained in the dialogue sequences, had a distinct Betty-Boopish quality.

This is the precise technique that Hitchcock used in

William Cameron Menzies' "bighouse" set for Alibi: forced
perspective, painted shadows, echoes of Fritz Lang.

Blackmail, where Anny Ondra's lines were dubbed live by
Joan Barry.   Blackmail's sound technique has been much
discussed; it must be said that West did precisely the same
things in Alibi and he did them first.   Alibi was first shown
in mid-April of 1929, just when Blackmail was being changed
over to sound.   The famous "knife" sequence in Blackmail,
in which the repetition of a key phrase is accented for subjective suspense, also has a precursor in Alibi.   As Tommy
grills one of Chick's men, Soft Malone--clearly threatening
to murder him and make it look like self-defense if he does
not get the answer--the slow, laconic dialogue suddenly shifts
into a throbbing exchange: "Who killed O'Brien?" is repeated
non-stop, over and over, always met with the quick, curt,
"I don't know!" Tommy fires a shot; there is a pause.
"That was your shot at Pete," he says, then tells the other
officer, "Let him have it!" Malone begins to chatter, and
both Tommy and Pete descend on him:

TOMMY	PETE	MALONE
Come on...	Tell us!	It was--
Come on!	Tell us!	It was--
COME ON!		
TELL US!		It was--

This is repeated a dozen times in rapid succession until, almost breathless, Malone whispers Chick's name twice, then firmly, "WILLIAMS!"

In Blackmail Anny Ondra is driven to the point of distraction by a chirping bird in its cage, and predictably, we find that this noisy songbird is a member of the Manning household in West's film.

Sound as an abstract rhythm interested West, and the warehouse robbery is scored by a cacophony of police whistles and the frantic pavement tapping of nightsticks. The film opens with ten non-dialogue shots bridged by dissolves and harnessed to dramatically contrapuntal sound. We see the shadow of a prison guard on a stone wall, in front of which moves a policeman's nightstick; we hear the dull ring of the stick playing against the wall. A close-up of a policeman's hand ringing a bell dissolves to a medium-close shot of convicts' marching feet. Dissolve to a medium-long shot of a vigilant guard swinging his nightstick, his shadow looming behind him, and the distinct rhythms of the marching feet and the twirling nightstick weld together. Dissolve to a long-shot in false perspective of the cell block as the cell doors open and the convicts listlessly form ranks. Another dissolve to the Warden's Office, then a typed paper identifying "No. 1065" as "Chick Williams," then a two-shot as Williams, in civilian dress, examines his release form. He exits frame left and the guard continues to sort his convict suit in the dim light sifting through the barred window. A final dissolve and Williams appears, a free man, on the steps outside of the prison.

This prologue has the fluid brevity and conciseness of a model storyboard and bears a strong formal resemblance to the opening of Bulldog Drummond. The extent of Menzies' hand in this is not known but the internal evidence is most compelling.

The very next sequence in Alibi seems especially contrived to show off the central set. It is an expansive

Nightclub rooftop in Alibi: West's integration of signs into
his decor was learned from German films and graphic arts
of the twenties.

dolly shot of Bachman's nightclub, the lettering on the canopy
taking prominence as we dolly under the awning to the front
doors. We dissolve to another dolly shot, in perspective,
across the hallway as the camera picks out the name
B A C H M A N in huge tiles on the floor. Reaching the
end of the hall we hear merrymakers and music; dissolve
to a dolly across the floor of the nightclub with its tables
full of patrons, up to a chorus line and, in a final dissolve,
one particular chorine.

     The roof of the club is dominated by a huge advertising
sign that prefigures similar signs in The Bat Whispers and
Corsair and can be traced directly to German Expressionism.
That the sign reads "Brooks" is a private joke; this was the
name of Chester Morris's infant son. Chick's fall from the
roof plays suspensefully with our expectations as for a moment he seems to recover his balance before toppling back-
wards. The in-camera mattes and the certain substitution

of a dummy in mid-fall are flawless, defying frame-by-frame examination fifty years later.

"Roland West was not a good director," said Regis Toomey, "He didn't understand the theater very well. I'd say that he wasn't too bright. He had weird ideas about how certain scenes should be played."55 Danny McGann, as part of his cover as "Billy Morgan, the Boy Wonder of Wall Street," constantly feigns drunkeness in <u>Alibi</u> so that he can appear harmless and inattentive to the gangsters he is observing:

> West didn't like the way I played a drunk. He didn't know what he wanted, and I did; I'd played drunks in high school--it was the one thing I did well! Finally, with the Assistant Director's help, I convinced him that if he'd just let me alone it would be all right. It became sort of an issue; I had never been asked to do this in rehearsals but on the stage he had some sort of screwy idea of something mechanical that had to be done with the tongue in order to talk and sound drunk. I said, Well, hell, Mr. West, the audience won't understand what I'm talking about. This is a talking picture, not a silent picture. He didn't like my attitude and the Assistant Director stepped in--and he risked his job--and said, He's right Mr. West, he's absolutely right. Nobody can understand what he's saying when he's trying to do it the way you want him to read it.
> So he sulked a little while and finally that was the end of it; it blew over and I did it the only way I knew how to do it. 56

Toomey is incorrect in saying that West didn't understand theater, for West was a technical master of its mechanisms; his films are ample evidence of this. But West doesn't seem to have had much feeling for actors. His dramatic sensibilitites never aspired beyond the melodramatic world of vaudeville that shaped him. West's technique is eclectic: at one moment he reaches back to early silents by lap-dissolving rather than match-cutting between long and medium shots of the same subject, only to push ahead with experimental use of sound. By mixing his sound-track, West has the music of a dance band invade the club's back room as Chick is about to murder Danny McGann--but all hope of deliverance is shut out with the music as the door is closed. One sequence does not fade in until several

moments after Eleanor Griffith has begun speaking, but this
novelty is as easily supplanted by West's retreat to stage-
craft during McGann's death, an interminable, mawkishly
sentimental scene that has the detective dying in his brother
officer's arms. As Danny moans, "Gee, it's getting dark
in here, " West slowly dims a spotlight on his face and introduces a phantom choir gently chirping "Aloha Oe!"

   Alibi is West's clearest and most cogent statement of
his usual themes. Chick and Tommy, both alternately gentle
and savage, are really no different from each other; they
merely work different sides of the street. If Alibi had been
done fifteen years later during the film noir cycle it could
easily have been made to address the kinship of cop and killer, along the lines of I Wake Up Screaming. The closest
the text of Alibi comes to this admission occurs as Danny
prepares to infiltrate the mob:

> MANNING: They tell me you know more crooks
>   than any detective on the force.
> DANNY: Maybe I missed my vocation.

   Alibi was very much a collaborative effort, beginning
with West's astute casting of Morris. Ray June was the
cameraman and Hal Kern credits him as well as West with
the moving camera shots that distinguish West's best films.
Kern was frequently on the set during shooting and West gave
him a free hand as editor, never dictating shot structures.
"I don't even know whether Roland knew enough about editing
to do a thing like that, " he says. [57] Menzies did, however,
and Kern recalls that he was a frequent visitor in the cutting
room. West was most at home on the set, plying the skills
acquired in thirty years of stage and screen:

> He's the best little 'set-lighter' in the business,
> giving a cameraman several pointers on how to
> get effects from velvet drops and painted shadows
> without much aid from Kliegs and Cooper-Hewitts. [58]

   Alibi opened in New York in April, 1929 to tremendous
response, hailed as a breakthrough in the bastard art of
"talkies. " Its reception in gangster-riddled Chicago was
another matter. On August 23, a week before the scheduled
opening at Chicago's United Artists Theatre, Police Commis-
sioner William Russell refused the film a permit. An in-
junction was obtained by Judge Fisher, who felt that Russell
had "censored the film to stifle criticism of [the police] and

to continue more easily their illegal activities under the guise of law enforcement."[59] Alibi eventually played out in 175 Chicago houses, but the legal furor carried on for over a year. Within two years The Motion Picture Production Code would reduce such worries and America's taste for movies was satisfied by a wholly homogenized product.

Alibi had cost $600,000[60] and taken three months to film.[61] Morris's contract was for six months and until Alibi was ready for release, there was no work for him. The transplanted New Yorker began to get edgy. When his option wasn't picked up, Morris went to face West. "What do I do now?" he demanded nervously.

"Sit tight," said West, "I've got ideas, but it's not time for them yet."

Morris' money got low and one morning he realized that the two-hundred dollars left would just get him and his wife Susan back to New York.

At nine o'clock that morning he received a phone call inviting him to a preview of Alibi at ten.

"I went with my wife to the premiere, and also with qualms," said Morris. "About three-quarters way through the picture I rose and slunk out. I thought I was terrible, and expected the audience to start throwing bricks any minute."

A phone call from Roland West found Morris packing his suitcase. "Listen, Kid," said West, "this is your old friend, Roland West. You take the extra pair of socks out of your pocket and put your toothbrush back in the bathroom. Prepare yourself to have dinner with Mrs. West and me."

Morris would have none of it. "I saw that picture Alibi this morning," he started, but West interrupted him.

"You did not. You only saw half of it. You walked out when it was half over. What kind of a way is that to act?"

"I couldn't stand any more. It was terrible."

"Maybe it was," conceded West, "but a lot of folks don't think so. You gave a fine performance."

Morris brought up the fact that his option hadn't been
picked up, and West brushed it aside as "standard procedure."
Before the day was over, Morris' bags were unpacked and
West signed him to a personal contract. [62]   West began loan-
ing him out, and after Alibi became one of the season's un-
qualified successes Morris appeared in thirteen pictures before West decided it was time to implement those ideas he
had been so vague about.

His ideas included a spectacular remake of The Bat
using every state-of-the-art technique known to the motion
picture industry.   The new title, The Bat Whispers, stressed
that this Bat would be seen and heard, and West personally
purchased a 65mm camera[63] to take advantage of widescreen
film, which was threatening to loom as significantly as sound
had in 1927.   Ray June was set to supervise 35mm photography, and he brought on Robert Planck to effect his instructions for the 65mm version, since two versions were shot,
rather than "printing down" the large format negative for
standard engagements.   Menzies, already cramped with ten
productions on his schedule, was superseded by his chief
draughtsman, Paul Roe Crawley, who was promoted by West
to Art Director.

Hal Kern had been slated to cut The Bat Whispers,
but as production started he had an argument with West, who
removed him from the project.   It was the only disagreement
the two men ever had and West thought better of it.   Though
full credit for film editing was given to James Smith, West
ran into problems with the 65mm format, made amends and
brought Kern back. [64]

By mid-summer pre-production was in full gear and
West put his technicians to work implementing his ingenious
effects.   Planck designed a new viewfinder for the camera,
and Charles Cline and William McClellan created three novel
lighting machines, shaped like giant scissors, which were
encased in soundproof booths so that the contacting of the
carbon rods would not interfere with sound recording. [65]

Nearly one hundred sets, including some remarkable
miniatures designed by Ned Mann, were sprawled over the UA
stages.   Many of the sets were pre-lit stage fashion, and run
from a dimmer board incorporating automatic stop watches to
raise or lower the lamps to predetermined levels of illumination.   Since existing projection rooms could not accommodate
a large screen, a thirty-eight-foot-wide screen was installed
on a vacant stage so that 65mm rushes could be projected. [66]

Above all West determined that <u>The Bat Whispers</u>
would be a motion picture that really moved, a manifesto of
the power of visual storytelling that had all but disappeared
in Hollywood with the coming of sound. With production preceded by three weeks of tests, he pushed his staff to distraction to enact his vision.

> Another difficult feat was solved at West's instiga-
> tion by Charles Cline. He perfected a zoom shot
> needed for just one short scene. The zoom is a
> contrivance that sent a heavy camera a distance of
> 18 feet in the fraction of a second as straight and
> silently as a spear. It started with a long shot
> and ended in a close-up; in other words, from a
> distance showing the full figure of a man it came
> to a focus that showed only the man's eyes.
> Once before a zoom shot was used in Hollywood.
> It was built at the request of a famous [German
> director three years ago]. When it was completed
> it weighed five tons and cost $17,000. The one
> built by Cline and paid for by West was mounted
> on a light truck and cost only $400. [67]

The truck was twenty-four feet long, and a camera
mounted to the front of it could be positioned as low as
eight inches off the floor, or raised to a height of six feet.

> There were cameras on wheels, on elevator
> rigs, on catapults, cables, rails, trucks and
> perambulators. One of the cameras rode a huge
> tricycle, electrically controlled ... it was designed
> by Robert Planck. [68]

Additionally, a scaffold was constructed thirty feet
high and three-hundred feet long, from which a camera was
suspended on a track by steel cables and sent flying through
space. This shot is truncated in the final film, picking up
Chester Morris as he leaps from the balcony into the garden, but originally West had taken a

> ... trolley shot, following Chester Morris through
> a scene [that] went through several rooms of a
> house and across a wide expanse of gardens. [69]

Other technicians toiled in odd specialties. Thomas
Lawless, a young artist, was commissioned to paint original
portraits to hang on the walls of the old house. West's stage
training had taught him the value of <u>trompe l'oeil</u>, and

Harvey Meyers, who pioneers the method of painting shadows on walls and settings ... was retained
by West to handle this detail. Meyers' sole job is
to paint shadows for West's productions. [70]

The Bat Whispers went before the cameras in late
summer, with a seven-week shooting schedule. [71] Production
proved unorthodox and difficult for all concerned. Una Merkel, who appeared as the heroine, lost twenty pounds under
the hot lamps and recalled that West repeated from Alibi
his habit of shooting only at night. Call was at 6:00 p.m.,
with wrap usually called at 3:00 or 4:00 a.m. [72]

> We worked at night. He didn't want anybody
> else, anybody connected with the office, coming
> in and telling him what to do or watching. He
> just didn't want to be bothered with anybody.
> When he worked at night, there was nobody but
> him and the company. We all ate together at
> midnight, everybody at the same table. [73]

With the intense illumination needed to generate a
strong depth of field, and many hard close-ups of Morris's
face needed, not to mention the almost non-stop use of the
lightning machines, Morris developed a painful condition that
was called "klieg eye"--a euphemism of the 'thirties for
what is today known to be a scorched retina! [74] Morris was
a guest at a screening of The Bat Whispers held for him by
producer Alex Gordon many years later, where he waxed
rueful about the quality of his performance and indicated that
it had been shot under altogether very trying circumstances. [75]
Considering that it was his fifteenth picture in less than a
year, he must have been nearing exhaustion.

One evening, in mid-production, it appeared that Morris might indeed have gone mad from the strain. After receiving a telephone call he ran off the lot like one possessed,
never stopping to explain to his bewildered co-workers. Four
hours later a composed and smiling Chester reappeared,
boxes of cigars and candies in his arms.

"It's a girl!" he proudly announced, "We're going to
name her Cynthia. "[76]

Since the play and silent film had enjoyed tremendous
circulation, West made changes in the script to return some
mystery to the story. He dispensed with the Japanese

houseboy, making him an eccentric middle-aged caretaker. Detective Moletti, alias The Bat of the silent film, became Detective Anderson (as he had been in the original play). Dale was no longer Banker Fleming's daughter, but the niece of Mrs. Van Gorder, and Dr. Wells became Dr. Venrees to accommodate Gustav Von Seyffertitz's European accent. West retained the exposition added as prologue in 1926, though what stylistic changes exist between the two versions we will probably never know. As an added precaution, no ending was included in the published script of The Bat Whispers. [77] West kept it in his head, as if to suggest that he might fool everyone with a wildly alternate ending to the familiar story.

Stage conventions endemic to both the material and West's idiosyncrasies survive in the use of long shots to display the decaying majesty of Paul Crawley's sets, and dimmer lights subtly highlight the presence of phantoms in the shadows. The flickering firelight that bathes the trunk room's windows at the film's climax, when the villain has ignited the garage, is faithfully transferred stage lighting that, still, admits a shot of a burning miniature to fulfill its effect. The point of departure between proscenium and camera is demonstrated when the house phone rings and a voice from the garage begs for help. Detective Anderson makes what is essentially a stage exit; instead of letting him disappear into the wings, we cut to an already moving camera shot, following in quick pursuit as Anderson runs through the French windows, leaps off the balcony and dashes through the garden toward the garage, the camera gliding swiftly behind him as lightning flickers all around the garden.

The opening reel is one of the most dynamic, purely visual expositions on film. We pull back from a tolling clocktower at night, revealing the sleeping city against stormy skies. The camera tilts down the face of the massive, modern skyscraper, and suddenly plummets in a deadfall to the street some fifty stories below. Moments before hurtling into the cars and trucks passing beneath us, the camera levels off. Beneath a sign announcing "Police Headquarters" a squad car roars out, taunted by a newsboy whose latest extra concerns the newest caper of the Bat. "You won't get the Bat!" the newsboy shouts at the car, "The Bat'll make a chump out of you!"

Dissolve to the interior of the squadcar as it darts through the night, skirting streetcars and traffic. A police radio bulletin announces its destination--the townhouse of

millionaire Gideon Bell, whom the Bat has promised to rob.
Dissolve to the front of the townhouse as the cars arrive
and the police exchange tactical information.

"Which is Bell's window?" The camera tilts up to
the top floor where a lone window is lit. "Not even a fire
escape," the officers' off-screen voice notes as the camera
moves forward, flies up the six floors and dives through the
open window. Bell is seated at his desk and the camera continues swiftly across the room to him and peeks over his
shoulder to reach the note in his hand.

West has synthesized several ideas from Alibi into a
new style: his moving camera has gained speed and purpose
and the jump-cut technique by which Williams fell to his death
has been modified and combined with miniatures and forced
perspective. The result is a deific camera tour through
places and spaces inaccessible to the human eye. Most importantly, he has provided the sweeping moves with payoffs.

To convey the criminal's flight to the countryside, the
sound of a tolling bell returns us to the clocktower; then the
noise of a locomotive and a shot of rolling train wheels.
This too passes to a rapid panorama of the nighttime city as
seen from the moving train. These three moving shots climax
with a fourth, rolling down the railroad tracks as seen from
atop the engine. Moments before we hurtle into a sign announcing the town of Oakdale, the tracks abruptly swerve to
the right.

Another dissolve and we are speeding in a car down
a country lane. As the headlights strike the facade of the
Oakdale Bank in front of us, the huge shadow of a bat sweeps
fleetingly across the front of the building.

Borrowing from German Expressionism, The Bat is
shown as a shadow or silhouette. As the camera dollies up
to the bank's skylight to observe a robbery in progress,
West's Expressionistic sense of lettering is repeated in the
hugely exaggerated, three-dimensional B A N K sign atop
the building. The Bat's descent by rope from the rooftop
is in silhouette, framed by scraggly leafless trees. Flashes
of lightning reveal him perched in the treetops--a breathless,
high-angle shot from above and behind--wings spread ma-
jestically as he swoops down on his unsuspecting victim on
the walk below.

Shots from The Bat Whispers.   At top, terror and suspense
wrought by the mutable shadows of the Bat.   Below, Chester
Morris's ersatz Detective Anderson degenerates into the
super fiend, thanks to low-key lights and, later, sepulchral
facial make-up.

West compounds our dread of his presence. From a
great distance we see the Fleming mansion as the camera
races through the air over the manicured lawns of the estate
and picks out a window on an upper floor. Thunder rumbles
and lightning flashes, the darkness between the bursts cunningly masking the juncture of two distinct shots as the camera moves up to the window sill and into the house, gliding
autonomously along the ancient corridors as it approaches a
pencil of light bleeding under a door. We hear voices faintly
at first, then louder as we sneak up to the door and dissolve
into the room to meet Mrs. Van Gorder and her maid, Lizzie.

Later, we observe rather than share the sensations of
The Bat's penetration of the house. Lightning flashes illumi-
nate a black shape in the treetop beyond the window. As the
flash subsides the room is thrown into darkness. Another
flash: the figure is now on the balcony and moving toward
the window. Again darkness. In the next bolt of lightning,
the figure has vanished--but the window is open, The Bat now
in the house and absorbed into the shadows. Cut to the wall:
The Bat's hunched shadow slowly pivots into relief from the
darkness, hands outstretched, writhing fingers bleeding along
the wall as in Nosferatu.

The seemingly supernatural threat reaches a crescendo
when the young girl, Dale, separates herself from her com-
panions and becomes trapped with the Bat in a hidden room.
Sensing a presence, Dale looks up and sees the shadow of The
Bat etched on the wall. Slowly its wings fold about it, and
it loses shape, shrinking. Thunder rolls on the soundtrack
until the shadow has all but receded. Then suddenly, with
an uneven halting gait, the very real Bat materializes from
the darkness. "Quiet! Quiet!" he whispers, "Not a word!
Not a sound!" Dale's candle flickers out and the black figure
engulfs her. "I'm gonna get cha, do you hear?" he whispers
gleefully, "Stand still! Till I put my hands around your lily
white throat and squeeze and squeeze until you're dead!"

West plants visual clues and stylish flourishes that,
subtly, focus our suspicions on Detective Anderson. He is
introduced in silent film style by a close-up of his calling
card, which dissolves to a long shot of Anderson and Mrs.
Van Gorder before pulling up to a tight shot. This kind of
dreamy dissolve, existing in real time rather than elapsed
time, is used at several points to highlight detail or move
into a scene, causing the moment to stand out in our

perception. As he eavesdrops on Dale's telephone call, the
composition is much like a split screen, with Anderson on
the left and Dale's shadow on the right, the two figures separated by a band of shadow falling diagonally across the frame.
Light becomes flexible and wholly unreal, changing whimsi-
cally from shot to shot within a scene, so that Anderson's
interrogations of Dale and the amnesiac stranger are both
played in close two-shots against black backgrounds that im-
part no sense of the actual room, though long shots of the
same action are deliberately high-key. The shifts in lighting
climax with The Bat's unmasking, where the ersatz detective
is revealed in all of his hollow-eyed splendor beneath The
Bat's cowl. "There never was a jail built strong enough to
hold The Bat," he declares, "and after I've paid my respects
to your cheap lock-up ... I shall return ... at night!" A
final closeup of his tortured face, awash in flickering light
from the burning garage, ends the film. "The Bat always
flies at night..." he grins broadly, displaying his teeth, "and
always ... in a straight line!" He laughs hideously to himself, tossing his head back, cackling.

West caps this wildly eccentric nightmare with a whimsical curtain speech. "We're not through yet--keep your
seats, everybody!" hollers a voice as a theater proscenium
appears before us. The curtains open amid cries of "Where's
the Bat?" "Coming, coming," mumbles the harried super-
fiend as a spotlight is thrown on a white screen. With the
sound of a slide whistle, the Bat slips down by rope, crashing
into an urn that explodes with a conjurer's puff of smoke.
The spotlight dims, the houselights rise and an urbane Chester
Morris in evening dress rises in his place to plead on behalf
of his "very dear friend," The Bat.

"If people discover his identity, he's heartbroken ...
he goes around for days killing people without the slightest en-
joyment for his work ... so in order to keep the Bat happy
and contented ... promise me that you won't divulge his identity, and in return ... he promises not to haunt your homes,
steal your money or frighten your little children.... Is it a
bargain?"

The Bat Whispers was a tough proposition to sell, since
it was released at the height of a glut of "old house" pictures, having been beaten into release by a talkie remake of
The Gorilla and previewing on November 6th, the day before
Universal's talking The Cat Creeps was released. Variety
gave The Cat Creeps very good notices, simultaneously

dismissing the preview of West's film as "one of those mystery mellers with 90% of the action in dimly lit interiors. "[78]
Universal launched its film with a saturation advertising campaign which paid off in nice grosses; United Artists put most
of its muscle behind Hell's Angels and the Technicolor Whoop-
ee, in spite of Variety's later clear assessment that The Bat
Whispers "must follow all of the other mystery-haunted house
films. Needs and can stand plenty of heavy exploitation. "[79]
October had already seen the debut of several other, incom-
patible wide-screen processes.   Troubled by exhibitors' fears,
the motion picture industry's refusal to standardize, and the
apathy of the public toward widescreen, The Hays Office ruled
against further 70mm films in December, forbidding

> ... by word or gesture ... [to] permit the public's
> curiosity to be aroused about any new [motion pic-
> ture] invention for at least two years. [80]

The Bat Whispers opened in key engagements in 65mm.
Opening week figures reported to Variety show it earning
grosses of $20,000 in San Francisco and $16,000 in Baltimore, the latter considered bad since it was the holiday week
of December 17th.   By New Year's the take at two Baltimore
theaters was a dismal total of $5600.   At the Rialto in New
York City, a mid-January 1931 opening earned a four-day
figure of $26,400, escalating to $36,900 by the end of the
week--not too weak an opening, as compared with RKO's
wide-screen picture, Danger Lights, which pulled in $52,800
in New York after a ten-day run, with a one dollar admission.

Reviews were uniformly good, citing the production as
excellent, the story as familiar and old hat, and the wide-
screen of variable interest:

> In the opening sequences, it is true, the wide
> screen serves a purpose.   There it helps the cam-
> eraman and scenic artist describe the magnificent
> dimensions of a city and its skyscrapers.   [But]
> ... the stretching of a bedroom from one side of
> the Rivoli's proscenium to the other is no great
> advantage to the bedroom, the characters therein,
> or the credulity of the audience. [81]

There had been problems with the November 6th preview, with Variety claiming that the projection was grainy
and that the theater blamed this on a projector malfunction,

... but with most scenes underlit, it would seem
that the grain came from reduction of the negative. 82

Working with so little light, the slow emulsion and
equally slow lenses of the day, June might well have resorted
to forcing the negative in the developing bath--a not uncommon
procedure that leaves a tell-tale increase in the size of the
grain structure.   When the film opened in London, on a 31 x
16-foot screen, "one or two mild faults, notably a certain in-
distinctness at times,"83 were noted.   One critic found little
to recommend the 65mm format:

> Frequently I found the 30-foot width of the screen
> distracted attention from the action, so that the
> drama seemed diffused, and to lack the intensity
> of the silent film of the same subject made some
> years ago.
> The photography seemed to lack definition, par-
> ticularly in the backgrounds. 84

Though one or two relatively complete (82-minute)
16mm prints have endured, the film is known, if at all, via
dupes or an abbreviated 71-minute re-issue copy lacking most
of the first reel.   In its 65mm glory and first-run length of
89 minutes/7991 feet, The Bat Whispers has vanished.

Ownership of the property, including physical control
of both silent and sound adaptations, passed to Mary Pickford, who intended to produce yet another version in 1938
with Humphrey Bogart playing opposite Lillian Gish. 85   The
project was not born.   Blackhawk Films, now preparing the
Pickford films for re-issue, have expressed mild interest in
The Bat Whispers, but the clearest hope for preserving the
film, particularly in the wide-screen format, will occur when
the Pickford Collection is ultimately deposited with the Library of Congress.   An original, 65mm nitrate copy was
extant in the Pickford Collection in the early 1960s when it
was donated to the ill-fated Hollywood Museum.   At that
time, one reel was screened for an absolutely astounded
select audience.   Even this print is today unaccounted for.
One can only hope that it is located, that the nitrate has
persevered, and that the film can find a friend on the whimsical AFI committees.

I'm honestly sorry I can't be on hand tomorrow,"
Chester Morris told a New York journalist by telephone from
Hollywood, the evening in 1931 before the New York premiere

of The Bat Whispers, "because I think Roland did a swell job
of direction and that they ought to make other directors go and
study his methods so they can learn something about sight and
sound. "86

     Morris and West became good friends.   When Roland
and Jewel bought the "Castillo del Mar" property, Chester and
his wife Sue bought the Wests' former home.   The two couples
journeyed across the border to Agua Caliente, Mexico, to
celebrate New Years' Eve, 1931.   West was tiring of production work, but still felt strongly committed to Morris and
continued to scheme new projects for him.   During the production of The Bat Whispers, West had received an urgent
letter, dated August 11th, from E. M. Asher, a producer at
Universal:

          Dear Roland,

               We will start Dracula in about three weeks.
          Is there any possibility of getting Chester Morris
          to play Dracula?87

West declined:

          Dear Efe,

               Don't think I'd care for that part for Chester as
          we are looking for romance.88

     It was shortly announced in the press that West would
direct Morris in remakes of Valentino's The Sheik and Son of
the Sheik to build up that romantic image, but reason pre-
vailed.89   West also was toying with the Phil Merivale stage
hit, Death Takes a Holiday, which might have been an ideal v
vehicle for Morris, combining the needed romance with the
macabre world that West doted on.   He had gone as far as
securing the rights, only to sell them to Paramount on October 17th, 1930.90

     West was feeling no pressure to do anything he didn't
feel like doing.   "He'd only make them as he wanted to,
that's sure, " says Hal Kern.91   Financially, he had no com-
punction to work.   Drinking with Morris and their wives one
day, West was overheard by a reporter:

          And I says to Joe Schenck, I says, 'Joe, wanta
          know how I got wealthy? By selling all the

stocks you bought and buying all that you sold.
Sure, I did. '92

"West hates to work," announced a 1930 press release:

... he has amassed a fortune, and he is himself
authority for the statement that he remains in films
solely because of his interest and personal contract
with Chester Morris. 93

He was further described as

a quiet, modest man.   No one ever saw him hurry,
but he's never late.   No shouting, no loss of temper.   He keeps talking about retiring ... a cruise
around the world is his favorite topic. 94

Yachting was always a big interest of his, and he was
ready for that long cruise.   His next vehicle for Morris, Corsair, would allow him ample opportunity to indulge his love
for the water.   A high seas adventure of rum running would
be a perfect dry run for the real voyage.

Johnny Hawks is a college football hero who accepts a
position with Stephen Corning's Wall Street brokerage firm.
The job has been arranged by Corning's aloof and beautiful
daughter, Alison, but Johnny can't reconcile himself to Corning's business philosophy: "We fight for existence, get their
money while the getting is good ... it doesn't matter how
much money you make in this world; it's how much you've
got when you quit!"   When Corning insists that Johnny take
an old woman's savings for some bonds that he knows are
worthless, Johnny refuses and is fired.   Alison becomes dis-
enchanted with Johnny.

Johnny turns to honest crime, and navigates the Eastern seaboard in his yacht, The Corsair, pirating cargoes
of bootleg liquor from other rum runners.   Corning is also
one of the biggest bootleggers in New York, and Johnny's
revenge is complete when he tells Corning that the caches
he has sold him are his own goods.   Impressed by his in-
dustriousness, Corning welcomes the boy back and places
him in control of his new Venezuelan oil company.   Alison
shows renewed interest.

Much of Corsair was shot on Catalina Island, where
West established a production base.   Hal Kern recalls

renting a forty-foot power boat and, once a week, ferrying
the dailies to the island for screening. [95]   Two weeks were
spent shooting on the water, with West transmitting radio
telephone instructions to his three co-directors. [96]   Kern
says that there were no difficulties with the location shooting,
and much of the dialogue is recorded in the open air; but the
film also displays many awkwardly dubbed exterior shots, apparently taken with unmotorized cameras.   These sequences
make parts of Corsair appear to have been made much earlier
than 1931.

The feminine lead in Corsair was a bubbly Hal Roach
comedienne, Thelma Todd.   The forty-four-year-old West was
deeply affected by the twenty-five-year-old "ice cream blonde. "
As he had attempted to promote Jewel Carmen's waning career
by casting her in his productions, so now he pulled the strings
of his new love's career.   He changed her name to Alison
Lloyd, " in order that no taint of comedy might cling to her
skirts. "   This pious and melodramatic gesture annoyed and
amused Todd's manager, Hal Roach, who immediately countered that she would return to two-reel comedies as Susie
Dinkleberry, to "erase any taint of drama. "[97]

Corsair is a strange picture, full of the photographic
craft West, June and Planck developed in their first two
sound pictures.   The film bears little resemblance to Walton
Green's serial/book.   It is West's most virulent, wildly irresponsible, and reckless exercise of his recurring themes
of personal honor and anti-social moral codes.   Everyone
engages in guiltless profiteering, and no one is ever held
responsible for the many sadistic murders committed to advance the smuggling.   Johnny will seemingly work any profitable scheme with Corning, providing that he is answerable
only to his own tenets.   Is his refusal to squander the old
woman's savings genuinely noble?   Probably not--they're
merely small potatoes compared to the millions available
via liquor or petroleum.

Technically Corsair is a hodge-podge of images, exciting in themselves but not always germane to the structure.
With an optical printer available, West indulges in wipes and

---

*Opposite, shots from Corsair.   At top, in the smuggler's
hideout, West has adopted his beloved "proscenium" long-
shot to the camera eye by incorporating foreground detail.
Below, enigmatic shadows once again take on lives of their
own.

irises.   The camera movements are used melodramatically:
We rush up to a darkened washroom door where two strug-
gling figures are viewed behind the frosted glass; we cut inside, and Chub is helping Johnny fasten his necktie!   The
camera dives into a window at the Wall Street office to discover Corning, just as it had revealed Mr. Bell in The Bat
Whispers.   West anticipates James Whale with a long lateral
tracking shot through the cabins of The Corsair, taking us
through four rooms below deck.. Whale used this as conscious
theater, but West fails since the sudden awareness that we
are on a set and "crashing through" solid walls does not mesh
with an exterior that has been established by genuine location
footage.

West's penchant for the gruesome is fulfilled with Big
John's execution of Johnny's crew, wooden champagne boxes
tied to their feet as they are suspended over the ocean and
sent to their deaths.

Corsair's finest sequence is a protracted cat-and-
mouse game in which Sophie, a renegade member of Big
John's gang who has been supplying Johnny's operation with
vital information, is caught by "Fish Face."   Sophie's boyfriend, Slim, has signed on Big John's ship as a cook to
learn about their plans.   Fish Face and Sophie are alone
in the smuggler's hideout; West opens the scene in a low-
angle long shot, the two figures at table lit by an overhead
lamp, a liquor bottle in the foreground framing them.   The
black, almost theatrical stage space is retained as Fish
Face reveals to Sophie that Slim is a known spy.   Cagily
she feigns a sexual interest in Fish Face, and lies to him
that her interest in Slim isn't sexual--he's her brother.   She
really loves Fish Face, and has been reluctant to tell him.
Fish Face seems to soften, allowing her to leave the cabin
to warn Slim before he is killed.   Fish Face and Sophie embrace passionately, agreeing to rendezvous as soon as she
has warned her "brother."   As she opens the door, a shot
is fired off screen.   Sophie turns, surprised, and crashes
to the floor.   Fish Face, still holding the smoking pistol,
nudges the dead woman's face with his foot, muttering, "You
dirty little double-crossing pelican."

This scene is flawlessly built and directed, the shots
progressing closer, the emotional climax intercut with extreme close-ups of Mayo Methot's face.   West has judiciously
withheld close-ups until this point.   The only other close-ups
that arrest our attention in Corsair belong to Thelma Todd,

who is handled with the attention and glamor packaging of a coveted, sensual ingenue. It is discomforting to sense her vibrancy reduced to posing and primping, constrained in elegant but static shots. Todd must have sensed the gagging of her talent, and quickly returned to comedy.

West now took that trip around the world in a boat that he had custom built. Jewel accompanied him on the first leg of the voyage, from Mexico up the coast to Alaska. The trip was a difficult one for her, and for whatever reason they separated before it was concluded. When the trip was completed in 1934, Roland returned not to Jewel and his film career, but to Thelma Todd and a nightclub.

West had purchased a defunct "community center," a failed restaurant/shopping mall just down the hill from the Castillo del Mar mansion. It had been built in 1924 to service the Castellamare neighborhood, but was something of a white elephant. His intention was to make it into a "very classy roadhouse."[98]

On the ground floor was a cabaret. On the second floor was a private club, "Joya's," and a suite of apartments. Over Todd's objections a speakeasy was included on the hexagonal third floor.

Thelma was the front for the business, lending her name to "Thelma Todd's Sidewalk Cafe" and receiving a percentage of the profits. But it was a Roland West Production, complete with hand-picked staff. Charles Smith, West's frequent co-writer and assistant director, was the treasurer,[99] and lived in an apartment over the garage on the hill. Rudolph Schaeffer, Roland's brother-in-law, was the club's manager and took up residence in the mansion, now vacated by Jewel who was "living with friends." Roland and Thelma lived in apartments on the second floor of the club in what West later tried to represent as a platonic relationship.

On March 3, 1934 Todd ended a two-year-old marriage to Pasquale "Pat" De Cicco, a wealthy playboy. Thelma had always been promiscuous, and even while she was ensconced in her love nest with West, she had other lovers besides the short, pug-faced director who was nearly twenty years her senior.

The business venture prospered, becoming "the expense account restaurant along the beach. In the depths of the Depression, those who could afford Thelma Todd's Side-

walk Cafe were paying $50 for lunch!"[100]   It was axiomatic
then, as now, that high-volume, cash businesses were attractive to organized crime.   Lucky Luciano's mob had approached
West, and gaming rooms were to be added on the second floor
of the Cafe.   A Grand opening was planned for New Year's
Eve, 1936.   Thelma Todd is said to have resisted the plan. [101]

She had been receiving threatening letters since the
Spring.   Some were eventually traced to a psychotic fan in
Astoria, New York, but others of the "Pay or Die" mold,
including one that threatened to blow up the Cafe, remained
unexplained.

On Saturday evening, December 14, Thelma was guest
of honor at a party given for her at The Trocadero by Stanley
Lupino.   West was not pleased.   They quarreled.   Later, he
would minimize the fight as "lighthearted."

There was an unexpected, last-minute addition to the
guest list.   Pat De Cicco called Ida Lupino and requested an
invitation, adding that it was his and Thelma's mutual wish
that he be seated next to Thelma at dinner.   A chair next to
Thelma remained vacant through dinner, and De Cicco arrived
later with the actress Margaret Lindsay on his arm.   Thelma
laced into him in front of the guests, for there was no doubt-
ing his deliberate attempt to humiliate her.

Thelma drank little and was in good spirits that night.
She excitedly confided to Ida Lupino a new love affair she was
having with a San Francisco businessman.   A hat check girl
overheard Thelma make a hushed telephone call around 11
o'clock, about a half-hour after her outburst with De Cicco.

As the night went on her mood changed.   Actor Arthur
Brooks recalled that

> Around 2 o'clock she went over to Sid Graumann's
> table.   He was with three people.   When she came
> back she was totally different.   She seemed terribly
> depressed.   I was dancing with her when she said.
> "Arthur, I'm terribly tired.   Take me to my car. [102]

At her request, Sid Graumann had telephoned West just
before 2:00 a.m. to say that Thelma was on her way.   It was
now 3:15 as Brooks escorted her out.   Suddenly she turned to
him, almost warningly: "Don't let Hollywood change you.
Stay just the same."[103]

Thelma arrived at the Cafe about 3:45. Breaking with
their custom, Thelma informed her chauffeur that it was not
necessary for him to escort her to the door. "I can look
after myself," she said. The last time Thelma Todd was
seen alive, she was walking in a cold night breeze toward
the door of her apartment.

On Monday morning Mrs. Whitehead found Thelma's
body in the garage. Captain Bruce Clark of the West Los
Angeles police was satisfied that "no foul play" had occurred
and the theory was put forward that she had suffered a heart
attack. [104] Los Angeles County Autopsy Surgeon, Dr. A. F.
Wagner, announced that she had died of carbon monoxide
"that she breathed accidently," and fixed the time of death
at 5:00 a. m. Sunday morning. [105]

Amid Alice Todd's cries of murder came an insistent
statement from Mrs. Wallace Ford that she had talked to
Thelma Todd Sunday afternoon. Mrs. Ford had invited Thelma
to a cocktail party Sunday night, and Mrs. Whitehead had already accepted for her employer.

> [Thelma Todd] telephoned me about 4 o'clock in the
> afternoon to explain that she would be a little late.
> She asked if she could bring a guest. I agreed of
> course, and she told me, "You'll drop dead when
> you see who I'm bringing with me to your party. '
> I said, 'Okay, mystery lady. '[106]

"You know who this is, of course?" continued the
voice on the telephone, "It's Thelma--your Hot Toddy. Oh,
and another thing--I went to a party last night and I'm still
in evening clothes. Do you mind?" Mrs. Ford said she
didn't, and Thelma rang off after promising to be there in
half an hour. [107]

Jewel Carmen, when questioned, said she knew nothing
about the mystery. West became the prime suspect, and in
his statement broached the details that became the foundation
of his alibi.

> Thelma was a very stubborn girl. She was very
> independent. She had been getting home late, and
> as it was necessary for me to stay up and let her
> in, I told her when she started for the Cafe Troca-
> dero on Saturday night that she should be home by
> 2 o'clock in the morning.

She smiled, and told me that she would be home
at five minutes after two.
I stayed awake until after 2:30 a.m.   Then I
went to bed.   At about 3:30 I was awakened by my
bulldog whining.   I knew it must have been Miss
Todd who aroused the dog, because of the kind of
whining he was doing.   If it had been anybody other
than Miss Todd, the dog would have growled.
But Thelma didn't make any more noise, or try
to waken me.   Instead, she must have walked up
to the garage up on the hill.   She kept the car in
the garage at the home of my estranged wife Jewel
Carmen.   I think Thelma must have got cold, turned
on the motor. [108]

By Wednesday, December 18th, Thelma had been reported as seen Sunday morning, disheveled and tired, making
a phone call at a drug store.   Ernest Peters, the hired chauffer, who had maintained that Miss Todd said nothing on the
ride home, now declared that she urged him to speed to the
Cafe, babbling that she was afraid of being kidnapped or slain
by gangsters. [109]

Jewel Carmen, who knew nothing, now summoned police
to her home.   "I was evasive when I talked to you last night,"
she said,

I want to tell you everything I know now.   I saw
Thelma Todd with a man of dark complexion whom
I did not recognize about 11 p.m. Sunday.   I was
returning from San Fernando Valley and was traveling East on Sunset Boulevard when I saw a phaeton
which I immediately recognized as belonging to Miss
Todd.   I hurried in my own car and drew as close
as possible.   Seated next to the driver was Thelma
Todd.   I recognized her from the smart hat I knew
she wore, and her blonde curls.   Driving the phaeton was a foreign looking man. [110]

Jewel's statement doesn't bear close scrutiny, and she
eventually withdrew her testimony.   Thelma was found wearing
the same clothes she had worn to the Trocadero.   The outfit
did not include a smart little hat.   In a more complete statement, Jewel maintained that she followed the car until she
lost it.   Having recognized the car, why would Jewel have
drawn closer, and then tailed it?   Jewel was awkwardly trying to protect Roland West from a murder charge.   On

Thursday, December 19th, she enlisted Louella Parsons in her campaign. Louella's byline appeared under the title "Gossip Denounced By West's Wife":

> The staunchest friend Roland West will ever have is his blonde wife, Jewel Carmen, who has been living apart from him for nearly a year. Mrs. West contradicted today accounts that have linked his name with that of the dead motion picture star Thelma Todd. She hastened to talk to me because I had known her and Roland well in the days when they were happy. [111]

Jewel told Louella that she and Roland hadn't <u>really</u> parted, that her health was bad and she had been <u>staying</u> with friends for the past year. Louella waxed on:

> Roland ... confessed to an infatuation with Thelma Todd, but doubted that she returned his feelings, and had such respect for Jewel that he never wanted to cause her any grief. He said, 'I'll take a trip around the world and get it out of my system. I wouldn't hurt Jewel for anything in the world; she's too fine.' The sea voyage almost proved fatal to his wife ... 'It left me a physical wreck--no woman used to the comforts of life can endure the hardships of such a voyage. So I left our home and tried to rest my nerves after two years and a half away from civilization.'[112]

West also maintained the formality of his relations with Todd when Coroner Frank Nance questioned him at the inquest:

> -Your relations with Miss Todd were more or less intimate, weren't they?
> <u>She was my very best friend.</u>
> -Was there any reason for leaving you and returning to Mr. DeCicco?
> <u>She couldn't leave me because, except for being my partner, we weren't connected in any way.</u>
> -Was there anything said about the time she was coming back?
> <u>Well, I asked her jokingly to be back by two o'clock. She said smiling, five minutes after two. And I said two o'clock. She said right back, 'Five after two.' We repeated this several times. It was all in a joking way.</u>[113]

West repeated the basic story he had told originally, only in this version, when the dog whines at 3:30, Roland calls out to see if Miss Todd is home yet. There was no answer, and Roland thought he heard water running in the building. Thinking Thelma was in, he fell back asleep. [114]

In light of Mae Whitehead's certainty that she had put a key to the apartment into Thelma's handbag before the party, West now began insisting that he had bolted the door from the inside. But having staked his belief on this theory, Roland stated from the witness chair that when he became concerned about her on Sunday, he knocked on the locked sliding door of their apartments, and receiving no answer, let himself in.

> There was a couch in the living room which bore an impression as if someone had slept there. I supposed Miss Todd had come in late and had a few hours sleep and then gone out again. [115]

West was clumsily attempting to account for his actions, whether Thelma had gained entrance to the house or not.

The inquest dragged on almost until New Year's, when Coroner Wagner reverted to the initial conclusion that Thelma Todd died after accidentally inhaling carbon monoxide. The investigation was dropped, even though many points were never answered. Principally, the autopsy had disclosed undigested foods in Miss Todd's stomach, foods that had not been served at the Trocadero dinner. And after presumably climbing nearly 300 cement steps to reach the garage, Thelma Todd's evening slippers were hardly scuffed. [116]

West eventually reopened the Cafe, and for a period of years settled into the uneventful role of restauranteur. Jewel Carmen sued him for separate maintenance in 1939, this time claiming no nonsense about nervous breakdowns but insisting they had been separated since 1934. Divorce was granted in 1940.

In 1945 he married actress Lola Lane of "The Lane Sisters," and they divided their time between the Santa Monica property and a home in Eau Gallie, Florida. West sporadically occupied himself by writing, but the cloud of Thelma Todd's death hung over any lingering ambitions to return to production. On a trip to Santa Monica from their Florida home in 1951, West was hospitalized at Santa Monica

Hospital;[117] he had been fighting heart trouble for two years.
On the afternoon of March 31st, 1951, he died.   Funeral
Services were held at Forest Lawn Cemetery on April 3rd,
in the Wee Kirk o' the Heather.   A plain, Christian Science
service lasting only fifteen minutes was conducted by Paul
Licktenfels, who read from the Bible and the works of Mary
Baker Eddy.   The service was sparsely attended by Lola,
her sister Rosemary Lane and Rosemary's husband, Bud
Westmore; Mr. and Mrs. Ned Marin, Mr. and Mrs. Harry
Brand, Mr. and Mrs. Dick Lambertson, Mr. and Mrs. Lou
Wheeler, Lee Parks, Johnnie Gordon, and Joe Bonner.[118]

The obituaries recalled West as a "veteran" and "pioneer" filmmaker, though more space was devoted to reprising
the circumstances of the Todd tragedy and West's implication
in it.

An estate believed worth hundreds of thousands of dollars, including the Castillo del Mar and Sidewalk Cafe properties, was left to Lola Lane.   West's will indicated one dollar each to Jewel Carmen, Helen Knight and Queenie Shannon,
explaining that settlements had been made with the first two
women during his lifetime.   Of Queenie Shannon he indicated,
"She has squandered or wasted all previous sums given by me
to her. "   To Joe Schenck, "my friend of a half century, "
West left his great esteem and affection.   There were small
sums to a few other friends, and the will provided that West's
interests in five stories--The Unknown Purple, Alibi, Love in
Chicago, The Second Egg and False Dawn--be divided equally
between Harry Brand and Ned Marin.[119]

In the intervening years West the man and West the
filmmaker slipped into total eclipse.   The films themselves,
for the most part, vanished.   Attempting to find Alibi many
years later, Regis Toomey was told that many films, Alibi
among them, were missing from West's personal vault at UA
and it was assumed that he had destroyed them.[120]   Whenever
West's name did surface, it was in connection with the death
of Thelma Todd, and this was ultimately reinforced with the
publication of Hollywood Babylon.   To the Hollywood community at large, there was never any question of West's guilt.
Late in his life, actor Frank McHugh spoke for many when
he told historian Ray Cabana that the L. A. P. D. didn't close
the Todd file until West was dead and buried.[121]   Chester
Morris was less equivocal when he told producer Alex Gordon that Roland West had killed Thelma Todd.[122]

Theories about what actually happened the weekend of

December 14th, 1935 are many.   Through all of the shifting
evidence and wild extrapolations, only two things seem clear:
Thelma Todd was murdered, and Roland West probably murdered her.

But why?

The most reasonable assessment was provided by someone intimately involved with the personalities and events of the
time, and who prefers anonymity.   Thelma, it is known, was
partying very heavily, and as she announced her departure
from the Trocadero she and West exchanged angry words.
He locked her out that night.   The fight was resumed when
she returned so she stormed to the garage after announcing
that she'd go to any party she felt like, such as Mrs. Wallace
Ford's.   "You've just been to one party, you're not going to
any more!" announced West.   Thelma was now in the Lincoln,
ready to drive off.   To make good his threat and teach her
a lesson, West closed and locked the garage.   Stubborn Thelma sat, the engine on, waiting for Roland to open the doors.
She didn't consider, in her anger, the odorless carbon monoxide filling the garage.   Neither did Roland.

In this telling of events, West made a complete confession to the police, who believed him when he claimed her
death was not premeditated.   No charges were filed, and the
Coroner's verdict was fudged.   West's penance would be to
live out his days with his own conscience.

The evidence of West's films is incomplete, and no
certain verdict of his artistry is possible.   But we do draw
certain conclusions.

The evidence of West the man, and West the alleged
murderer, is also incomplete.   Again we draw conclusions,
but we can't be certain of them.

Emblematic ally, Thelma Todd's Sidewalk Cafe still
sits derelict and mute along the Pacific Coast Highway.   After
serving as a production base for Paulist Productions' Insight
TV show in the 'seventies, a legacy from Lola Lane, the
three-tiered nightclub is now shuttered and dark, again a
white elephant on the California landscape.

Lost in history are the answers to the Roland West
Murder/Movie Mystery.

Acknowledgments

Thanks to the following individuals:

Ron Borst, Ray Cabana, Jr., William K. Everson, Elisabeth Feldmann, John Gallagher, Alex Gordon, Hal C. Kern, Bill Littman, Leonard Maltin, Una Merkel, Chris Steinbrunner, Bill Tompkin, Regis Toomey, George Turner.

Thanks to the following individuals and institutions:

Val Almenderez and Sam Gill of The Academy of Motion Picture Arts & Sciences; Jim Cavanaugh of The Wisconsin Center for Film & Theater Research; The New York Public Library.

Notes

1. "Roland West Talks Freely," New York American, December 28, 1935.
2. Interview with Hal Kern, August 19, 1983.
3. Interview with Regis Toomey, September 17, 1983.
4. Interview with Una Merkel, August 8, 1983.
5. Later materials sometime refer to this production as The Volume.
6. "Roland West, Maker of 'Bat Whispers' ...," The Bat Whispers, pressbook.
7. "Roland West Is Still at Large," New York Telegraph, October 20, 1906.
8. "The Under World," Variety, November 6, 1909.
9. "Roland West to Create New Role," New York Telegraph, October 2, 1911.
10. Sime, "Who Was He?" Variety, January 31, 1913.
11. Sime, "Thro' The Skylight," Variety, January 16, 1914.
12. Sime, "Malvina, How Could You?" Variety, March 27, 1914.
13. "'The Auto Bandit' Leading Attraction ...," Hartford Courant, September 25, 1914.
14. "'New Dictator' and West Drama Come This Week," Cleveland Plain Dealer, March 29, 1920.
15. "Career of 'Alibi' Producer, Roland West, Mystery Expert," Alibi, pressbook.
16. A Woman's Honor, pressbook.
17. "A Woman's Honor," review, The New York Public Library.
18. Ibid.

19. Ibid.
20. Ibid.
21. A Woman's Honor, pressbook.
22. Jack Spears. Hollywood: The Golden Era (New York:
     Castle Books, 1977), p. 119.
23. "De Luxe Annie," Philadelphia Public Ledger, June 17,
     1918.
24. "Who Is Roland West?" The New York Times, Septem-
     ber 22, 1918.
25. "The Unknown Purple," Hearst's, April 1919.
26. Ibid.
27. Ibid.
28. Ibid.
29. Ibid.
30. "Another Cleveland Boy at Top of Ladder," Cleveland
     News Leader, n.d.
31. "Nobody," The New York Times, July 25, 1921.
32. "The Unknown Purple," The New York Times, March
     24, 1924.
33. "The Unknown Purple," The New York Sun, March 25,
     1924.
34. Caption on reverse of Roland West photograph, New
     York Public Library.
35. William K. Everson. The Theodore Huff Memorial Film
     Society, notes, February 5, 1964.
36. "The Bat," The New York Times, March 15, 1926.
37. "The Bat," Harrison's Reports, March 20, 1926.
38. "The Bat," Times, op. cit.
39. Spears, Hollywood..., p. 136.
40. "The Dove," United Artists official synopsis, Univer-
     sity of Wisconsin, Madison.
41. "The Dove," Times, op. cit.
42. The Dove, pressbook.
43. Everson, Huff, notes.
44. Spears, Hollywood, p. 136.
45. The Dove, pressbook.
46. Clipping, New York Public Library.
47. Dick Hyland. "Turned Down by Griffith," clipping,
     New York Public Library.
48. Kern, interview.
49. Toomey, interview.
50. Ibid.
51. Ibid.
52. Alibi, pressbook
53   Ibid.
54. Mark Larkin. "The Truth About Voice Doubling,"
     Photoplay, July 1929.

55. Toomey, interview.
56. Ibid.
57. Kern, interview.
58. Regina Cannon. New York American, 1929.
59. UAC vs. William Hale Thompson 1929-30, file 137-10, O'Brien Legal File, University of Wisconsin, Madison, Wisconsin.
60. UAC vs Thompson, op. cit.
61. Hyland, "Turned Down."
62. Ibid.
63. The Bat Whispers, pressbook.
64. Kern, interview.
65. "West Champion of the Film Aspirant," The Bat Whispers, pressbook.
66. "Mystery Effects...," The Bat Whispers, pressbook.
67. Ibid. No such shot appears in existing prints of The Bat Whispers.
68. Ibid.
69. Ibid.
70. "West Champion...", op. cit.
71. Leonard Maltin. "Interview with Una Merkel," Film Fan Monthly No. 115, January 1971.
72. The Bat Whispers, pressbook.
73. Merkel, interview.
74. Chester Morris, letter to Ray Cabana.
75. Alex Gordon, conversation with author, September 1983.
76. "Chester's New Daughter," clipping, The New York Public Library.
77. The Bat Whispers, pressbook.
78. Variety, November 12, 1930.
79. "The Bat Whispers," Variety, January 21, 1931.
80. "Wide Film Is Ruled Out," Variety, December 17, 1930.
81. "The Bat Groans With Age," clipping, NYPL.
82. Variety, November 12, 1930.
83. R.J.W., "Giant Film Screen," clipping, NYPL.
84. W.A.M., "Wide Screen Film," clipping, NYPL.
85. George Turner, conversation with author, September 1983.
86. Eileen Creelman. Picture Plays and Players, clipping, NYPL.
87. Letter, E.M. Asher, August 11, 1930, West Collection, Library of the Academy of Motion Picture Arts & Sciences.
88. Letter, Roland West, August 12, 1930, West Collection.
89. "Chester Morris Will Probably Play in Both The Sheik..." clipping, NYPL.
90. Letter, For Mr. West, October 17, 1930, West Collection.

91. Kern, interview.
92. "How He Did It," clipping, NYPL.
93. The Bat Whispers, pressbook.
94. Ibid.
95. Kern, interview.
96. Corsair, pressbook.
97. Tony Scott. "Southern California Landmarks Are Rich in Showbiz History," Daily Variety, October 26, 1982.
98. Ibid.
99. Other accounts indicate that Wallace Smith was the treasurer. Both men, probably relatives, had worked with West. A 1929 story, The Purple Mask, pre-served in the Academy's Roland West Collection, bears the names of all three men.
100. Scott, "Southern California...," op. cit.
101. "Todd Death Clue in Gambler's War," New York Daily News, Dec. 18, 1935.
102. New York American, December 18, 1935.
103. Ibid.
104. New York Evening Journal, December 17, 1935.
105. The New York Times, December 16, 1935.
106. New York American, December 18, 1935.
107. The New York Times, December 16, 1935.
108. The New York Sun, December 18, 1935.
109. Ibid.
110. New York Herald Tribune, December 19, 1935.
111. New York American, December 19, 1935.
112. Ibid.
113. New York Herald Tribune, December 19, 1935.
114. New York Daily News, December 19, 1935.
115. Scott, "Southern California...," op. cit.
116. Ibid.
117. "Roland West, Veteran Film Director, Dies," Los Angeles Times, April 1, 1952.
118. "Final Tribute Paid Director Roland West," Los Angeles Times, April 3, 1952.
119. "Bulk of Roland West's Estate Left to Widow," Los Angeles Times, May 13, 1952.
120. Toomey, interview.
121. Frank McHugh, conversation with Ray Cabana.
122. Alex Gordon, conversation with author, September 1983.

ROWLAND BROWN

by John C. Tibbetts

If today's moviegoers are familiar at all with the
name Rowland Brown, it is probably due solely to his story
credit (and subsequent Academy Award nomination) for Michael Curtiz's 1938 classic, Angels with Dirty Faces.   Recently, however, there have been signs that Brown's screen
work--both as a director and as a writer--is drawing some
renewed critical and popular interest. 1   Arguably his best
directorial effort, Blood Money (1933), was recently included
in Volume Two of Cult Movies.   Doorway to Hell, his first
screenplay for the talkies (directed by Archie Mayo in 1930),
is now regarded as an epoch-marking effort in the development of the gangster film.   And his other two directorial efforts, Quick Millions (1931) and Hell's Highway (1932), are
likewise drawing new audiences through their availability in
16mm non-theatrical form. 2

Initially, and despite a few respectable notices, Doorway to Hell, Quick Millions, Hell's Highway, and Blood Money
suffered from public indifference at the box office.   They bore
traces of studio tinkering, re-cutting, and divers contributions
from other hands than Brown's; moreover, they seemed slow
and quirky when compared with the typical slam-bang gangster movies of the day.   As for those films that Brown worked on as a writer only--State's Attorney (1932), What Price
Hollywood (1932), The Devil Is a Sissy (1936), Johnny Apollo
(1940), Nocturne (1946), and Kansas City Confidential (1952)
--his own contributions are difficult to assess.   Indeed, some
of these films languish in what some think is well-deserved
obscurity.

We see in Brown's films a peculiarly "modern" look
that is in striking contrast to the work of his contemporaries;
his work was highly idiosyncratic.   Unlike Hawks, Ford,

163

Walsh, and Curtiz, he was unable to go the distance--to
balance his unique gifts with the assembly-line demands and
stock formulas of the studios.   One has to look elsewhere
to find a comparable body of work in America in the 1930s
and 1940s--perhaps to the Hecht-MacArthur films, for ex-
ample--that displays the same insistently offbeat, even comic,
kind of cynicism.   It was not story so much that mattered in
Brown's films, but rather a broadly dispassionate view of
character and incident that brings him closer than anyone else
in the Hollywood fraternity (save John Ford) to Jean Renoir.
Like Renoir, he tends to undercut the emotional charge in his
films; his secondary characters and incidental situations sometime overshadow everything else; his narratives are deliberately
episodic and rambling; and he tends to avoid social preach-
ments and simplistic moralizings.   Withal, there is present
that kind of "casual" tone that André Bazin ascribed to the
work of Renoir: "[Renoir] is the only film maker in the
world who can afford to treat the cinema with such apparent
offhandedness"; with plots often "oblique to the situation."[3]
In the best sense, these things can also be said for Rowland
Brown.

        Rowland Brown was only thirty years old when his
screenplay to Doorway to Hell and his first directorial effort, Quick Millions, brought him to public attention.   He
had come a long way from his Akron boyhood (born November 6, 1900).   After completing his education at the University School in Cleveland, Ohio, the University of Detroit, and
the Detroit School of Fine Arts, he took brief excursions into
fashion illustrating and sports cartooning.   Later, he went to
Hollywood with a number of his short plays.   Universal bought
one of them and soon he worked with the Reginald Denny unit
as a writer and gagman.   The Denny comedies were typical
of a genre of light, breezily contemporary satires that had
begun with the Anita Loos/John Emerson/Douglas Fairbanks
films of the mid-teens and extended to the work of Wallace
Reid and Tommy Meighan in the 1920s.   Brown even wrote
a Hoot Gibson western, Points West (1929), his first screen
credit.

        None of the foregoing, however, could have prepared
anyone for what was to follow with his story, "A Handful of
Clouds," the basis for the tough and pessimistic Doorway to
Hell.[4]   The prototype for the classic gangster films of the
thirties, Doorway to Hell implied that success in hard times
was open to the gangster, and that the only forces capable

of stopping racketeering were those represented by other racketeers. Real life gangsters like Al Capone had held the public spotlight for several years with their colorful lifestyles and vaguely romantic exploits. In an America suffering from the downward spiral of the Depression, Capone and his contemporaries were figures of action. They seemed the only ones capable of dealing with problems like unemployment and urban entrapment. [5] Even if efforts to bring Capone himself to the screen were eventually defeated, Warner Bros. brought his likeness to the screen in the character of Louis Ricarno.

This smash hit boasted a $46,500 take in its first week at the New York Strand. Zanuck promoted its "front page" topicality and fairly reveled in its "inside-story" associations. Indeed, the suggestion brought out at the time, that Brown had racketeering connections, was to pursue him throughout his career; during the release of Quick Millions a year later, Fox was to claim that "through his varied experience [Brown] had frequent contact with gangster types and concededly knows more about them than any other person in motion pictures. "[6]

The story was about Louis Ricarno (Lew Ayres), a powerful bootlegger who had come up from the slums to rule the city with efficient yet ruthless methods. When Louis decides to marry a wealthy society girl and retire to Florida to write his memoirs, he places his operation in the hands of his friend Mileaway (James Cagney). But Mileaway is unable to maintain control over the rival bootleggers. They kidnap Louis' kid brother, who is accidentally killed. When a vengeful Louis returns to the city, Mileaway fingers him and has him jailed. Ironically, he is now safe in jail, so his rivals plot his escape. Subsequently, they trace him down to a sleazy hotel where he expires in a barrage of offstate gunfire.

The New Movie Magazine called the film "a grim and exciting presentation. It has enough kick to hold your attention all the way. "[7] Photoplay noted that Ricarno's character displayed a decided Napoleonic complex, an important ingredient in countless crime films to come. [8]

Quick Millions was Brown's first directorial effort. It was released through Fox and, though it dealt with a different kind of racketeer, it displayed marked similarities to Doorway to Hell. "Bugs" Raymond (Spencer Tracy) is a

Sally Eilers and Spencer Tracy in Quick Millions (Museum of Modern Art/Film Stills Archive).

young man on the rise, moving from starting a protection racket by vandalizing cars parked in city streets and then taking a percentage of the garage owners' profits, to extorting street peddlers, independent truckers, and building contractors.   Eventually, he takes over all the truckers and gives his racketeering a "respectable" facade, complete with ornate offices, fancy clothes, and a society girlfriend.   During a gangland dispute, a reformer is killed without Bugs' approval and Bugs has the culprit eliminated.   In retaliation, his gangster rivals abduct Bugs and deposit his lifeless body at the steps of a church.

Photoplay noted that the film was "as cold-blooded as the gangsters who are characterized"; that "apparently disjointed scenes" contrived to keep the thread of the story and the viewers' interest at the same time.   "It's a man's

picture," concluded the review, "and is utterly lacking in
wild histrionics. "[9] By contrast, Modern Screen's review
was more acerbic, complaining of its "garbled tale"; although it did praise those scenes "showing how the racket
men force law-abiding industries into nefarious partnerships. "[10]
Although Mordaunt Hall complained in the New York Times
that "too much footage was given to [the racketeers'] sneering
at the law and lawyers," he singled out for praise those sequences "where the ways of the lawless crew in forcing the
hands of business men are depicted. "[11]

Brown's next two projects were screenplays for State's
Attorney and What Price Hollywood?, both co-written with
Gene Fowler in 1932. The former was about a shrewd, witty,
and unscrupulous lawyer, Tim Cardigan (John Barrymore),
whose clientele was made up mostly of underworld characters.
When Tim becomes District Attorney, he is forced to turn
upon his former colleagues. Apparently, the production of
the film was something of a hash, and Mordaunt Hall complained that co-author Gene Fowler's adulation of John Barrymore (Fowler went on to write Barrymore's biography, Good-
night Sweet Prince) was all too apparent--especially in scenes
exploiting his eye-rolling histrionics. Brown reportedly began the direction of the film, but was replaced, first by Irving Pichel, and then later by George Archainbaud. Photoplay liked the picture primarily because of Barrymore's
performance, calling it "inimitable." Elsewhere, however,
the picture contained "nothing startling"; in sum, it was "an
adult picture and not for kids. "[12]

What Price Hollywood! was adapted from an original
story by Adela Rogers St. Johns. Lowell Sherman portrayed
a famous but perpetually inebriated film director who becomes entangled with a blonde Brown Derby waitress (Con-
tance Bennett), who wants to get into the movies. As her
career subsequently skyrockets, his falters and then declines
until, in despair, he commits suicide. This plot device later
formed the basis for the three versions of A Star Is Born--
in 1937 by William Wellman, in 1954 by George Cukor, and
in 1976 by Jon Peters. Photoplay was ecstatic, noting that
its story was an accurate depiction of Hollywood life. The
review then concluded, "All in all, it is one of the finest,
most fascinating movies ever made. It grabs the interest
in a death-grip, and holds on. "[13]

Rowland Brown resumed directorial control with the
project that came to be known as Hell's Highway. [14] This

RKO-Radio picture emphasizes its topicality by opening with
a flurry of newspaper headlines, such as "Prison Guards
Accused of Murder as Tortured Youth Dies Chained in Sweat
Box" and "'Naked Boy Was Chained by Throat to Overhead
Rafters,' Convicts Declare"; and then dedicating it "to an end
to the conditions portrayed herein which, though a throwback
to the Middle Ages, actually exist today." Duke Ellis (Richard Dix) is a convicted bank robber serving time in a chain
gang currently building a highway called, ironically, "Liberty
Road." The camp is run by the sadistic Blacksnake Skinner
(C. Henry Gordon) and his foreman, the brutal Pop Eye Jackson (Warner Richmond). Both are in league with a road contractor, Mr. Billings (Oscar Apfel), who had underbid other
road construction companies. Together, these men apply constant pressures to the convicts--including starvation and a
confining "sweat box" with neck chains--to get the road completed. Duke's plans to escape are postponed when his younger brother Johnny (Tom Brown) is incarcerated in the camp.
The rest of the film details Duke's attempts to insure that
his brother keeps out of trouble so he can leave with a clean
record. It is grimly amusing that Duke must work harder to
keep Johnny in than break him out! Eventually, after an
aborted prison break during which Skinner is killed and Johnny is seriously wounded, the shady operations of the camp
are exposed, and the road contractor is arrested.

Released shortly before Warner Bros.' I Am a Fugitive
from a Chain Gang, Hell's Highway seems comparatively cool
and detached. Nonetheless, critics at the time were impressed by its power. Photoplay noted that "it isn't a pleasant picture, for its brutal power is in every reel and no morbid detail has been left out."[15] Mordaunt Hall in the New York
Times complained that Duke's protests at the torturing of his
fellow convicts were ineffective to audiences since Duke himself was not "an upstanding character." At the same time,
Hall concluded, "the producers fail by being overeager to
horrify audiences by depicting the cruel treatment of the
chain-gang convicts."[16]

Blood Money, Brown's last directorial project, appeared late in 1933. It was the third film for Darryl F. Zanuck's
newly formed 20th Century Pictures. Its main character,
Bill Bailey (George Bancroft), is an ex-cop now making a
good living as a bail bondsman. Once on the skids, he had
been rescued by Ruby Darling (Judith Anderson), who runs a
nightclub and maintains a continuing affair with Bill. Bailey's
enterprise is run just this side of the law: his clientele range

from gangland characters (from whom he is in the habit of receiving stolen goods) to little old mothers (from whom he cheerfully demands house deeds in payment for services rendered). His newly kindled romance with wealthy socialite Elaine Talbert (Frances Dee) is interrupted when his protégé, young Drury (Chick Chandler), runs away with her. Drury, who is a compulsive bank robber, has, through a mix-up, left some stolen bonds in Bill's safe. The police find them and try to incriminate Bill. Bill thinks Drury has two-timed him and in revenge almost precipitates a city-wide gang war. Before he learns about Drury's innocence, he is almost killed during a pool game when one of his enemies slips a dynamite-filled eight-ball onto the table. The ever-faithful Ruby Darling saves him in the nick of time.

Photoplay lauded the film as an "unpretentious but hearty tale of a big shot bail bondsman who turns on the underworld which made him. " Frances Dee was singled out as a girl with "a criminality complex. "[17] Mordaunt Hall, however, was unimpressed. He thought it "flat stuff. " Some of the rest of his review is worth quoting at length:

> This whimsical little tale of thievery, thuggery and attempted slaughter was mistaken for entertainment by Darryl Zanuck, who obviously thought that the part of Bill Bailey, the racketeering bail expert, would give George Bancroft an opportunity to shine once more on the screen. Perhaps there are cinema patrons who delight in such pavement plots, so long as they are touched up with occasional embraces between a pretty girl and a dyed-in-the-wool burglar. Those, however, who are unfortunate enough to want some suggestion of logic in their motion pictures will be somewhat disappointed in this effusion.... [18]

Perhaps it was this kind of negative reaction--singling out for public scorn the very erratic and offbeat things that to us make Brown's work unique--that helped terminate his career as a director. Rowland Brown would direct no more films after Blood Money. In 1934 he went to England, where he worked on several projects as a writer. Two non-gangster farces, Leave It to Blanche (1934) and Widow's Might (1934) were released. Then Alexander Korda approached him to direct The Scarlet Pimpernel, Baroness Orczy's story of a Zorro-like character caught up in the French Revolution. The project, however, was short-lived from Brown's standpoint and the direction was given over to Korda and Harold Young. It has been speculated that the prospect of a hero named "Sir Percy" might have been too much for Brown to bear. Certainly, The Scarlet Pimpernel could have used some of Brown's "blood-and-thunder" sensibility. [19]

Back in America directorial control was again wrested from Brown--this time on The Devil Is a Sissy. W. S. Van Dyke is credited as director and Brown only for original story. It was a film about three boys on New York's Lower East Side. Freddie Bartholomew portrayed an English lad who, upon finding himself adrift in the street life, is so thoroughly "Americanized" that he plans a robbery and ends up in juvenile court!

From 1938 until 1952, when he wrote his last film, Kansas City Confidential, Brown continued in his preoccupation with the nature of crime and the city as a shaping environment. Boy of the Streets, from Monogram in 1938, was about a boy who goes bad when he learns that his father is merely a political stooge. Angels with Dirty Faces (1938) also deals with the fate of boys brought up in a crime-wrought environment. One of two boyhood pals turns away from crime to become a priest (Pat O'Brien), the other goes to reform school and there continues a life of crime (James Cagney). Johnny Apollo (1940) features Tyrone Power as a college boy who turns racketeer when his stockbroker father (Edward Arnold) goes to prison. Nocturne (1946) is a strange and ironic story of a detective (George Raft) pursuing a murder investigation. The detective, like the protagonists in Boy of the Streets and Angels with Dirty Faces, operates on both sides of the law; he seems an uneasy and elusive blend of light and shadow, his character a triumph of ambiguity.

Brown's last project, Kansas City Confidential, was directed by Phil Karlson, who claims most of the credit for the story. [20] Brown is generally acknowledged as the author; indeed, it is the kind of story he specialized in--a combination of reportorial style and sensibility with episodically constructed moments of violence. Retired police captain Timothy Foster (Preston Foster) turns to a life of crime, embittered by his meager pension. He masterminds an armored car robbery during which innocent ex-con Joe Rolfe (John Payne) is implicated. Upon his release from the police, Rolfe goes underground to track down Foster. Here again is Brown's consistent use of what might be called "reversible morality. " Foster's allegiance to law and order (and subsequently to a

life of crime) is strictly one of convenience. He remains
peculiarly equipped to pursue both. Putting it another way,
each way of life becomes for him (and us) indistinguishable
from the other. Once again, "justice" is served, not by the
police but by a gangster employing his own methods to track
down a rival. In that sense we have come full circle from
Doorway to Hell.

When Rowland Brown died on May 6, 1963, he had a
family of three sons and one daughter. At the time of his
death he was working on a television series based on the life
of his old friend, Gene Fowler. It's a delicious idea but,
like so many others, it was not to be.

Implicit in this brief survey of Brown's work are a
number of themes, stylistic characteristics, and preoccupa-
tions that need further elaboration. Carlos Clarens' rather
peevish comment that Brown's kinky attention to the idiosyncrasies of the ruling class furnished the sole consistent social comment in all three of his films is too hasty. [21] Granted, Brown's authority figures do demonstrate some decidedly
strange behavior, but beyond this, his films demonstrate other
profound thematic similarities that tell us much about his attitudes toward the nature of urban crime and its causes. Few
filmmakers in the 1930s have left so pronounced a statement
that racketeernig and legitimate business enterprises have dis-
comfiting similarities--or at least share fundamental patterns
that blur their boundaries. Eugene Rosow in Born to Lose
has reminded us that "Prohibition turned the profits of the
liquor and beer trade over to gangsters and provided them
with enough capital to expand their other activities, to secure
legal and political protection, and to buy a certain amount of
respectability. "[22]

Louis Ricarno in Doorway to Hell is a bootlegger. He
tells his rivals that they must conduct their enterprises as a
business: "The only thing wrong with [bootlegging] is that it
needs organizing and it needs a boss. I'm taking over both
jobs. I'm gonna lay this town out in zones--I'll give each
mob what I think is comin' to 'em and not one inch more.
Get that! Each gang'll kick into me and I'll take care of
everything...." Similarly, Bugs Raymond in Quick Millions
wrests control over the truckers from his rivals in order to
do things in a businesslike way: "Now if I controlled ... that
is, I mean if we, if we controlled all the trucks we could put
this town in our vest pocket. You know that, don't you? ...

Just a question of big business--you know--organization. "
(That's the dream of every racketeer, boys," he says later;
"--to have a legitimate racket!") When the District Attorney
speaks to a citizens' group near the end of the film, he too
acknowledges the contemporary, narrowing gap between legitimate business and criminal practices: "Now all crime is
based upon money and money must be banked; and in one of
our recent bank disasters it was found that they were financing crime, making it big business, hiding their profits under
assumed names in safety deposit boxes so that these millionaire racketeers could defeat the income tax. " Bail bondsmen
Bill Bailey runs a business that seems equal parts of crime
and of legitimate enterprise.   When Elaine's father asks Bill
what his business is, he replies, "Insurance ... the tougher
the times, the better my business.   I'm a bail bondsman.   I
get people out of jail. " When releasing the bank robber
Drury from jail, he actually urges him to go ahead and jump
bail, lest another arrest send him to prison for life.   Bill
helps the "little people," too--but then asks Mother's house
deed as payment.   In Hell's Highway, Mr. Skinner, the warden, and Mr. Billings, the road contractor, are trying to
undercut labor competition by building the "Liberty Road"
quicker and more cheaply.   They employ harsh methods to
complete the job, yet they both rationalize this as a legitimate work program for the convicts.   Consider this conversation between Skinner and an inquiring prison official
named Whiteside:

> WHITESIDE: You've allowed that contractor [Billings]
>   to hire a lot of local roughnecks for
>   guards whose idea of handling men is
>   treating them like a lot of mules.
> SKINNER: Billings and I are running this camp.
> WHITESIDE: Yea, but you can't go on running it in
>   violation of state laws that were passed
>   passed to stop that sort of abuse.
> SKINNER: I don't believe in coddling prisoners.

In State's Attorney, we see Tim Cardigan employing phony
and shamelessly theatrical tactics in court--all for the purpose of bringing "justice" to his clients.   His former gangland associations and experiences provide the very expertise
by which he may now defeat crime in the courts.   (We are
reminded that within just a few years Hollywood would begin
making film like Bullets or Ballots and G-Men, which featured lawmen whose methods are virtually indistinguishable
from those of their enemies.)

If the boundaries between crime and a life of law and order seem blurred in Brown's films, it should come as no surprise that Bugs, Duke, Louis, Father Connelly, Tim Cardigan, and Bill Bailey all harbor yearnings to achieve legitimacy. That they consider these ambitions compatible with their criminal pasts is very much the point. Brown sometimes demonstrates this by depicting their needs for relationships with society women and their drives toward material ostentation. Rosow calls these twin drives the gangster films' application of the old-fashioned Gospel of Wealth and the Myth of Success: "Pre-eminent until the Great Depression, the creed of exalting wealth and success dominated the popular culture of industrial urban America and gave the gangster film plot its basic shape."[23] Louis Ricarno, after grasping control of all the bootlegging interests, wants nothing more than to retire to Florida, get married to a wealthy society woman, and assume the role of a respectable littérateur. When Bugs Raymond falls in love with a society woman, he shakes down her father and becomes his business partner. He wants to get married, be respectable, and move up in a world of appropriately ornate offices and apartments. At the outset of Hell's Highway Duke's prime goal is to escape the chain gang--although that is defeated by his sterner obligation to protect and counsel his younger brother Johnny. In numerous conversations with Johnny, Duke's main advice is to stay straight and get out. Tim Cardigan, once a racketeer, goes straight as an attorney and eventually implicates a former associate. Even Bill Bailey, in retaliation for a frame-up, goes to the mayor and to the newspapers to spill information on the gangster element in his town.

These respectable ambitions are not intended to be some kind of saving grace--or even obeisance to the Production Code. Only Father Connelly "goes straight" because of a genuine desire to correct his early faults and benefit the world. What Louis Ricarno really wants is the self-aggrandizement of writing his own life story and, like Bugs, to live in the lap of fame and luxury. Tim Cardigan finds he can win more cases by parlaying his former racketeering experience. And Bill Bailey has held his underworld connections as an ace up his sleeve to protect himself from his enemies. Honesty, legitimacy, social reform--they are all trump cards employed by these master gamblers. It is their effectiveness and their convenience, not their morality, that counts.

This is why these characters are ironic role models

for young people in Brown's films. In Doorway to Hell, Louis Ricarno keeps his younger brother in a military school,
safe from any knowledge of Louis' racketeering. At another
level, Ricarno's boyhood memories of idolizing his gangster
heroes are brought out in a scene deleted from the final
release print: "We kids kind of worshipped Lefty Louie,
Gip The Blood and Dago Frank ... why, we even sent them
a letter telling them we hoped that they would die game. We
had a warm spot for the three of them." Of course, this
anticipates the closing portion of Angels with Dirty Faces, and
one also recalls the bragging of one of the delinquents in The
Devil Is a Sissy as he describes his father's electrocution:
"It took three jolts to kill him!" One suspects that Drury's
admiration for Bill Bailey in Blood Money began at a young
age, as did Elaine Talbert's fascination with gangsters in the
same film. As her father puts it: "[She's a] very fine girl
but she has a little too much, er ... imagination? That's it.
She has an underworld mania. She's very fond of underworld
pictures; always reading detective stories. I sometimes think
that ... she might have been inclined to match her wits with
the law--that is, just for the thrill of it, you understand."
Bailey's response is crisp: "There are lots of people like
that."

What is perhaps Brown's most enduring quality, however, is something less tangible than that which comes out of
a recitation of thematic consistencies; rather, it has to do
with that "modern" look, which often celebrates the casual,
the indirect, and the idiosyncratic at the expense of the films'
nominal subjects. In other words, as much as Brown's best
films are concerned with the ambiguities of law, order, and
racketeering, or with the shaping influences of environment
and role models, the films are really memorable for their
offbeat, subtle, and quirky character revelations.

Such qualities come close to those characteristics
that José Ortega y Gasset has delineated in the "modern
novel." Writing in 1925, he noted that motion pictures can
do what modern novelists were doing: reducing the importance of plot to character. "The interest in the outer mech-
anism of the plot is today reduced to a minimum," he wrote.
"Not in the invention of plots but in the invention of interesting characters lies the best hope of the novel."[24] As far as
a film might be concerned, for example, there may not be a
plot or even a series of episodes so much as a succession
of character revelations:

> A film in which the detective and the young
> American girl are attractive may go on indefinite-
> ly and never become boring. It does not matter
> what they do; we simply enjoy watching them.
> They interest us not because of what they are
> doing; rather the opposite, what they do interests
> us because it is they who do it. [25]

Film viewers, like readers, are not told who a character is,
but must seek definitions from a welter of visible cues. So
it is in real life, Gasset says: that "chance leads [people]
into the ambit of our life, and nobody bothers officially to
define them to us. "[26] We are never let into their secret,
as it were, and some part of them must remain forever--
and intriguingly so--unknown. Thus, the modern novel, like
these qualities of the cinema of Rowland Brown, presents
figures that you must account for on your own. Again,
quoting Gasset: "... but as their behavior varies from stage
to stage they display one facet after another and thus seem
to be shaped and assembled step by step before our eyes. "[27]

This is precisely what Brown does. Quick Millions
is full of little camera asides, as it were--seemingly chance
moments in which Bugs' gang reveal themselves to us: during
a party, for example, when George Raft casually goes into a
soft-shoe dance, the camera is apparently distracted at first,
then locates his feet for the rest of the dance; or when Raft
dresses for the opera and, in a fastidious afterthought, se-
lects with care a pearl-handled revolver that best matches
his tails. The race track sequence with Bugs and his girlfriend has really only one true purpose--to acquaint us not
with the racketeering nature of racing but with the lady's
feigned naïveté at the operations. Her play-acting tells us
a lot that we need to know about her. Gangster or socialite,
these are people who alternatively disguise and reveal them-
selves--but we must be alert to catch it.

Hell's Highway and Blood Money are both interrupted
with what might best be described as "musical" sequences,
each of which reveals more about character and situation
than the nominal plot line. The funeral of two slain convict
escapees in Hell's Highway is intercut with shots of a black
convict singing a spiritual and a series of images, cartoons,
drawn by an anonymous hand (and we remember that Brown
was himself a cartoonist). While the biers are drawn away
and the men in black preside, these reportorial comments
are pungent reminders that these dead men were all their

lives the subject of invasive public scrutiny and black-and-white headlines. They had become the stuff of printer's ink and editorial cartoons. We see this scene twice; first as the event itself, then as impersonalized line-drawings. Spirituals frequently accompany other scenes involving the convicts out on the road or resting in their bunks; there is one startling moment when Duke and his friends all join in a spiritual whose words have been altered to fit the various situations and backgrounds of the convicts. This is information that we normally have received at the beginning of the film as we first encounter the characters. Not so with Brown: we must wait and be alert for the casual and fleeting appearance of such scenes.

The "musical" sequence in Blood Money occurs when Ruby Darling realizes that her love for Bill Bailey is jeopardized by his infatuation with socialite Elaine Talbert. At just the moment when we might expect verbal fireworks between the jealous Ruby and the errant Bill, there ensues instead a virtually wordless scene. Bill slowly leaves the room and comes downstairs to the bar. He listens thoughtfully a moment to Blossom Seely singing "Melancholy Baby," mutters tersely, "That song kills me," and exits. Then Ruby appears at the doorway. She too listens for several moments, then quietly goes back inside to her office while the song drones on and on.... A lot has transpired between Bill and Ruby over the years. We know that; or rather, we feel it. By the midpoint of the film such moments give us the impression that we know far more than we really do.

Both Duke and Bill are complex characters, although their guarded terseness and occasionally bantering falseness continually throw us off the track. We must track our course of understanding them as best we can. Hell's Highway contains what at first seems to be the standard "visitation" scene present in most prison pictures of the day: that moment when the white-haired mother and/or the languishing girl friend (or even a priest) come to visit the convict with words or moral support and hope. Even as fine a film as I Am a Fugitive From a Chain Gang is marred by such sentimental moments. Here, the scene opens with convicts and guests filing into the visiting room. A young black man greets his mother with the assurance that he reads his Bible "every day." Oh, brother, one mutters at this point; here we go. But then Duke appears and confronts his mother and his brother's girlfriend. The ensuing dialogue takes an unexpected direction and, in the process, tells a lot about Duke, his past, his attitudes, and how others see him:

> DUKE: (to the girl) What are you chasing after
> Johnny for?
>
> MARY: Why, I'm not chasing him; I came up here
> to see him.
>
> DUKE: That's what I mean. Do you realize that
> 99 out of 100 men steal for some dame?
> And keep on stealing for her? I don't
> want to see Johnny get hooked for anyone;
> I don't want to see him go through what ...
> the rest of these mugs are going through.
>
> MARY: Johnny doesn't have to steal for me. He
> wouldn't anyway; he's no thief. The only
> thing's wrong with Johnny is, he thinks
> you're ... something wonderful.
>
> DUKE: (after a pause): Well, you got some spunk,
> anyway. That's <u>something</u> in your favor.

Nothing could be further from the typical sentimental treacle
that so frequently mars such pictures. At the same time,
Duke <u>allows</u> us just a glimpse at--well, not him, but "the
rest of these mugs" and their problems. That last-minute
deferential twist away from himself says it all. Later, when
he is flogged for inciting a fight between a convict and a
guard, there is a brief moment when the prison guard pauses
after stripping off Duke's shirt. He stands, whip poised, and
we see from his viewpoint a tattoo on Duke's back: "42nd
Machine Gun Co. /167th Inf." Compare this trenchant little
moment with the bitter social protest of Wellman's <u>Heroes
for Sale</u> and LeRoy's <u>Fugitive</u>, where the plight of the service
veteran in a hostile and forgetful society is depicted in broad-
er strokes and at greater length. Is this scene less memorable for its brief reticence? Or does its very brevity render
it all the more effective? Duke himself never alludes to his
service background at all.

As for Bill Bailey's character in <u>Blood Money</u>, he is
emblematic of that wonderful description literary critic Donald Sutherland has applied to the archetypal Byronic hero:
he is <u>splendidly</u> <u>self</u> <u>propelled</u>. Significantly, before we see
him, we see his <u>name</u>--emblazoned on cigars, on the towels
dispensed at a prize fight, and on his storefront. He is the
result of media hype and shrewd huckstering. It is only fitting that we would hear <u>about</u> <u>him</u> before actually meeting
him. And if you look closely at his intial appearance, he
is collecting bets on <u>losers</u>, not winners, at a prize fight.

He lives off the suckers of the world, as he himself boasts:
"I make all my money off losers!" At the end of film he
quips to his girl friend, Ruby, "Behind every Barnum there
is a Bailey. " He keeps his office phones tapped so he can
overhear his client's conversations. All in a day's work.
As for his clientele, we find out all we need to know when
an angry Ruby demands that his "clients" all jump bail at
the same time, leaving him responsible for their monies.
Our suspicions about his underworld connections are now
abundantly clear as every gangster in town flies the coop.

These scattered revelations also help delineate dozens
of incidental characters, providing Brown's films with a
richness and density that is striking. Who can forget the
deaf-and-dumb convict in Hell's Highway who is shot in the
back because he can't hear the warnings of an approaching
posse? The camera holds him in medium close-up as he
crosses himself, frantically trying to pantomine his final,
silent prayer as he sinks lifeless to the ground. Or the
fry-cook convict who, when he is lightly flickered with
Blacksnake Skinner's whip, ecstatically responds with "Oh,
Mr. Skinner.... " This same character later, during the
funeral, recalls another somber event in his life where the
coffin "was covered with big pansies. " Or take Matthew
the Hermit (Charles Middleton): like so many other Brown
characters, he is an elusive mixture of deceit and apparent
sincerity. One moment he will fake a Biblical prophecy
(already possessing through another source the requisite
knowledge) and the next he accurately (and with no apparent
foreknowledge) predicts the infidelity of a guard's wife.
Oddly, he is given the final scene in the film when Duke
asks him why he hasn't tried to escape. Escaping the camp
is one thing, Matthew mournfully intones; but escaping three
wives outside is impossible.

Amen.

Not all of these eccentric little moments are on the
kinky side, however. One of the most effective moments
comes when Johnny is shot while trying to escape the chain
gang during a fire. In a moment anticipating Benton and
Newman's anti-western, Bad Company (1971), a gang of
children tracks down Johnny as he thrashes through the under-
growth. When he pauses with his back to them, one little
boy raises an impossibly large rifle and opens fire, wound-
ing Johnny in the shoulder. Although he is seriously wounded, his reaction is more one of irritation, as if he had just

been stung by a pesky mosquito.   Indeed, Johnny is no more
than a kid himself.   We are reminded that children taking up
early the tools of violence is a favorite theme of Brown's.

Blood Money is also full of dark and occasionally
quirky moments.   We already know that Drury, Ruby Darling's younger brother, is a bank robber.   Does he do it
because he's impoverished and underprivileged, a child of
the tenements looking for a way out?   Well, although Brown
might depict this sort of thing with some of his characters,
not so with Drury.   He is simply a completely amoral character.   Not only does he rob banks seemingly just for the
hell of it, but he likes it.   Moreover, you have to give credit
to a guy who can jump bail and go on a honeymoon with his
best friend's girl, all at the same time!   As for the girl,
Elaine, she provides probably the most famous scenes in all
of Brown's work.   When she and Bill are at a luau, she
describes her own peculiar notions of the ideal romance:

> ELAINE: I want a man who's my master.   Who's
> not afraid of anybody in the world.   Who
> would shoot the first man that looked at
> me.
> BAILEY: You'd have been crazy about Al Capone.
> ELAINE: You think you're kidding.
> BAILEY: You need a darned good spanking.
> ELAINE: What I need is someone to give me a
> good thrashing.   I'd follow him around
> like a dog on a leash.

Although this sort of thing might make her a perfect companion for Drury, she must look elsewhere after he is taken
away to prison.   And so we come to the film's justly famous
closing scene when she meets a distraught young woman in a
hotel lobby.   Upon finding out that the girl is fleeing a man
upstairs who has threatened to beat her, Elaine's eyes light
up and she hurries upstairs.   "Elaine is like no female in
film history," declares Danny Peary in Cult Movies 2.   "She
has a crime mania, and is also a kleptomaniac, a nympho-
maniac, and a masochist.   She is turned on by anything
daring...."[28]

At such times, of course, Brown's films seem to
wander off somewhere, away from the main plot, away from
the central situations, away from our expectations of Hollywood formulas.   And yet, are not such things more memorable than the intended social commentary?   As much as Brown

might have wanted to be a social commentator, he inevitably
becomes in our eyes an artist of the bizarre, a man whose
quick eye glitters at the use of a hemorrhoid cushion in the
chair of a department store executive, at a barfly who wears
a monocle and men's clothing, at the Little Mother whose
sixteen-year hulking son beats up older women, and at the
convict who smiles at the touch of lash of a whip....

Rowland Browns' films look better and better all the
time. Alas, his private life and many details of his career
are as obscure as ever. We are left with few clues as to
what interrupted and eventually terminated his promising career as a director. One legend has it that he punched a
producer and was subsequently blacklisted. Certainly his
films didn't do very well at the box-office--even Spencer
Tracy in an interview in Photoplay in 1932 admitted that
Quick Millions "went out and grossed about a dollar and
eighty cents."29 Brown's relative lack of concern for graphic
violence, his deliberate pacing, his eccentric characters, and
his lack of sentimentality--not to mention those odd, wobbly
storylines that are so fascinating now--all helped insure the
indifference of the public. Steve Zito theorizes that Brown's
"uncompromising, radical social vision was his undoing."30
After all, this was the same Brown that had Bill Bailey recognize that this world, contrary to Hollywood's traditional
view, was not a world open to the easy definition and subsequent eradication of crime: "The only difference between
a liberal and a conservative man is that the liberal recognizes
the existence of vice and controls it; while the conservative
turns his back and pretends that it doesn't exist." Whichever,
Bill knows, crime is here to stay--hardly a reassuring idea
coming at a moment of world depression.

I can't resist a personal note and the hope that whatever his disappointments, Rowland Brown was able to take a
cue from one of his characters, Drury Darling, in dealing
with them. Drury knows the game and the ways things are
done. When he's caught for bank robbery, he just shrugs his
shoulders affably. Fair is fair. Maybe that's the way it was
when Brown transgressed so many Hollywood formulas. Citing
one last time that filmmaker whom Brown so oddly resembles
in his work, those were the rules of the game.

Acknowledgments

The author wishes to thank the following people for
their generous assistance in the preparation of this article:

Paul Scaramazza, Union City, N.J.; Dr. James Loutzen-
heiser, Kansas City, MO; Clarissa Ann Snow, Lawrence,
KS; and, of course, to the redoubtable Frank Thompson. ...

Notes

1. Any research on Rowland Brown must be largely in the
    debt of Don Miller's pioneering article, "Rowland
    Brown: Notes on a Blighted Career," in Focus on
    Film, No. 7, 1971, pp. 43-52. It is especially valu-
    able for its biographical emphasis. See also Gerald
    Peary's "Doorway to Hell," in The Velvet Light Trap,
    No. 16, pp. 1-4; and Danny Peary's assessment of
    Blood Money in Cult Movies 2 (New York: Dell Pub.
    Co., Inc., 1983), pp. 28-31.
2. These three films are currently available for non-
    theatrical rental from Films Incorporated (Wilmette,
    Illinois branch).
3. André Bazin, Jean Renoir (New York: Simon and Schu-
    ster, 1973), p. 30.
4. Gerald Peary in "Doorway to Hell," The Velvet Light
    Trap, No. 16, claims that "A Handful of Clouds" was
    not a story but a play. The expression is explained
    when a policeman says to a hood: "You're going to
    treat yourself to a handful of clouds; I mean the kind
    that come out from the end of a .38 automatic."
5. For a recent discussion of this form of public hero wor-
    ship, see Eugene Rosow, Born to Lose (New York:
    Oxford University Press, 1978), pp. 3-21.
6. Quoted in Carlos Clarens, Crime Movies (New York: W.
    Norton and Co., 1980) p. 69.
7. The New Movie Magazine, Vol. 3, No. 2 (February 1931),
    p. 100.
8. Photoplay, Vol. 38, No. 6 (November 1930), p. 55.
9. Photoplay, Vol. 40, No. 1 (June 1931), p. 56.
10. Modern Screen, Vol. 2, No. 2 (July 1931), p. 98.
11. Mordaunt Hall, "Racketeering and Murder," The New
    York Times, April 18, 1931, p. 17.
12. Photoplay, Vol. 42, No. 2 (July 1932), p. 52.
13. Photoplay, Vol. 42, No. 3 (August 1932), p. 51.
14. Don Miller (p. 47) notes that the working title of the
    film was Liberty Road.
15. Photoplay, Vol. 42, No. 6 (November 1932), p. 58.
16. Mordaunt Hall, "Hell's Highway," The New York Times,
    September 26, 1932, p. 18.
17. Photoplay, Vol. 45, No. 2 (January 1934), p. 108.

18. Mordaunt Hall, "Blood Money," The New York Times,
     November 16, 1933, p. 30.
19. See Don Miller, p. 50.
20. Todd McCarthy and Charles Flynn, eds. Kings of the Bs
     (New York: E. P. Dutton & Co., Inc., 1975), p. 342.
21. See Carlos Clarens, p. 70.
22. See Eugene Rosow, p. 99.
23. Ibid., p. 23.
24. Ortega y Gasset, The Dehumanization of Art (Princeton,
     N.J.: Princeton University Press, 1972), p. 103.
25. Ibid., p. 66.
26. Ibid., p. 78.
27. Ibid., p. 78.
28. See Danny Peary, p. 31.
29. Ruth Biery, "Worry! Who--Me?", Photoplay, Vol. 43,
     No. 1 (December 1932), p. 60.
30. Taken from Steve Zito's program notes for "Cinema Club
     9," in conjunction with WTOP-TV's telecast of a series
     of Rowland Brown films, 1972.

CHARLES T. BARTON

by Frank Thompson

In his sixty-year career, Charles T. Barton worked within virtually every area of show business: he was a prop-boy, actor, writer, producer, and one of the most prolific and financially successful directors in Hollywood.   The phases of his career can be divided neatly: from 1910 to 1918 Barton acted in dozens of stage plays in San Francisco and was, for a time, the most popular juvenile performer in the city; the years 1920-34 saw him working his way through the motion picture industry as prop-boy and assistant to nearly every important director at Paramount--Cecil B. DeMille, William A. Wellman, William K. Howard, James Cruze, Herbert Brenon, Edward Sutherland, Mal St. Clair, Marshall Neilan and many others; in 1934 he directed his first feature, Wagon Wheels.   Before he was through, he would have over seventy features to his credit, including eleven Abbott and Costello vehicles, two Walt Disney films (The Shaggy Dog and Toby Tyler), numerous musicals and wartime comedies at Columbia featuring Ann Miller, Jinx Falkenburg, Larry Parks and others, and many programmers and "B" pictures for Paramount, Columbia and Universal.   His last feature, Swingin' Along, was released in 1962, but by that time Barton was firmly ensconced in the most prolific phase of his career, television. Between his first Amos 'n' Andy in 1951 to his last episode of Family Affair in 1972, he directed hundreds of segments of popular series such as The Real McCoys, Oh! Susannah, The Munsters, Hazel, Dennis the Menace, Spin and Marty and Zorro.

The range of his experience makes Barton an obvious case for further study, yet this very scope renders his career unwieldy and difficult to deal with.   This difficulty is compounded by the mediocrity of so much of his work.   Many of his programmers are rushed, vapid, visually uninteresting,

The later Charles Barton, 1971, as a successful television
director

and made more with schedule than art in mind, but his speed
and professionalism made Barton highly prized by studio executives, for he could always be counted upon to bring his
projects in ahead of schedule and under budget; his financial
track record was formidable and Barton put his name to few
money-losing films. Some of his features (Reveille with
Beverly, for instance) brought in receipts many times greater
than their original costs. Hollywood has always prized box-
office savvy over artistic achievement, and Barton knew what
the public wanted. He worked at breakneck pace, a method
which precluded much personal involvement in his projects,
and there is little evidence to prove that Barton looked at
motion pictures as a way of expressing himself. He was a
craftsman first and foremost. His major goal was to fulfill
his job efficiently and profitably. It was a goal he reached
repeatedly.

    This is not to say that Barton was incapable of turning
out good films. Among his Abbott and Costello movies are
two of their finest: Abbott and Costello Meet Frankenstein
(1948) and the gentle, whimsical The Time of Their Lives
(1946). (It must also be noted that Barton was responsible
for their worst feature: 1956's vapid Dance with Me Henry.)
At Disney, Barton directed The Shaggy Dog (1958), which
earned almost $8,000,000 and garnered a Best Director nom-
ination from the Directors' Guild. In 1960, his Toby Tyler,
also for Disney, proved to be a model of what Barton was
capable of: it is gentle, relaxed, amiable, charming, well
directed and well played.

    In fact, a great number of Barton's "B's" have spirit
and verve, if little style. Pictures like Island of Doomed
Men (1940), Jam Session (1944), Wagon Wheels (1934) and
Car 99 (1935) are modest, unpretentious and quite entertaining. Too, there is that quality that Barton's films share
with many "B" pictures: they seem a direct route to the
sensibilities of their age. Lacking the budgets that provided
elaborate sets, fanciful costumes, complex camera movement
and top scripts and scores, the "B's" had to use what was
at hand. As a result, the settings were often more ordinary
(and hence more realistic), while the characters talked, acted,
dressed, danced--not like Hollywood stars, but like the average people who flocked to these films. It may be minor
praise, but a simple, rather forgettable feature like Barton's
The Spirit of Stanford (1942) gives one a much more accurate
view of college life of the period than does a more main-
stream feature like M-G-M's Good News (1948). There is

no denying that Good News is the better film, but its college campus is an elaborate set, the people talk with cleverly scripted slickness and there is a general aura of fantasy. Barton never had the resources to create such a dreamlike environment, so he had to draw on what was available to him.

Barton was not a hack, but neither did he possess the drive, ambition or artistic craving to rise above his modest fare. His films lack--for want of a better term-- inspiration. The compulsion that led other directors in similar, or more meager, professional circumstances (Edgar G. Ulmer, Allan Dwan, Samuel Fuller) to turn the limitations of "B" production into artistic virtues was not to be found in Barton's character. His films are rarely more than they seem to be.

Typical of Barton's work is his 1943 Reveille with Beverly. It has a hurried, slapdash look (understandable, since it is one of thirty-five features he directed in his four years at Columbia), is broadly written and played, flatly photographed and unimaginatively staged. Its major virtues are its fine character actors (Tim and Irene Ryan, Franklin Pangborn, Eddie Kane, Doodles Weaver) and some of the top musical acts around: Duke Ellington, Count Basie, The Mills Brothers and, in only his third feature film appearance, Frank Sinatra. The character actors lend an urgency and fervor to even the most tired gags (and this film is densely populated with tired gags) and the inherent quality of the music does much to overcome the thoughtlessness of its presentation. Reveille with Beverly was obviously a rush job, designed for a quick play-off to wartime audiences eager for an hour or so of escape. As such, the film is surprisingly entertaining, if artless. However, if it is typical of Barton's weaknesses as a director, Reveille with Beverly is representative in another way, as well: it was Columbia's top-grossing "B" of the year.

Charles Barton was the sort of director that Hollywood has always preferred: competent, workmanlike, professional, non-tempermental. It would not be exaggeration to say that men like Barton "paid the bills" in the studio system for the artistic accomplishments of others. Filmmakers like John Ford advanced the art of the cinema; craftsmen like Barton kept the money rolling in. Not the stuff of legends, certainly, but an indispensable cog in the studio machinery. Barton's pictures brought uncomplicated pleasures to audiences

and many millions of dollars in profits to the studios for
which he worked. He was no artist and no auteur--in fact,
he was just the opposite--but his expertise in producing box-
office winners helped support an atmosphere in which the
true artists of the cinema could work and, on occasion, lose
money.

    Charles Thomas Barton, Jr. was born on May 25,
1902 in Oakland, California. His father owned a candy store
and manufactured his own chocolates. Barton's sweet shop
stood next door to the Liberty Theatre in San Francisco and
when Charlie was still an infant he was carried onstage by
actress Edith Chapman as part of a vaudeville turn. As soon
as he was old enough to learn lines, the child started appearing in plays at the Liberty. He quickly became a favorite in
the popular comedies and melodramas of the day: Bunty Pulls
the String, Alias Jimmy Valentine, The Little Gray Lady,
Broadway Jones, Puss in Boots, The Littlest Rebel. The
shows generally ran for about a week before closing to make
room for the next. It was marvelous training for a fledgling
actor and Charlie had appeared in more than thirty plays by
the time he was fourteen years old.

    In 1916, while appearing in The Miracle Man, Charlie
made the transition into the big time. He recalled, "[Pro-
ducer] Oliver Morosco sent a man up to talk to me because
they wanted me to come down to Los Angeles and do a show
for him: The Dummy. So I came down and did the show at
the Morosco Theatre. I think it ran about eighteen weeks. "[1]

    The Dummy was a detective comedy by Harvey J.
O'Higgins and Harriet Ford that had already had a successful
run on the Broadway stage. Charlie played the title role, a
street urchin who pretends to be deaf and dumb in order to
acquire the evidence which will solve the case of a kidnapped
girl. Critic Maitland Davies wrote: "His work is natural
and free from the brashness that usually spoils the efforts
of actors his age. He is ... direct in his methods, [with]
a wholesome, fresh personality that makes his work very attractive. "[2]

    Nearly all reviewers of Charlie's performances of the
period comment on his natural charm and believable personality. Similar reviews would greet the many performances
of children like Billy Lee, Dorothy Ann Seese and Kevin

Corcoran in Barton's films. It is, perhaps, Barton's strong point as a director; he never forgot what it was like to perform and he always went out of his way to make his actors feel comfortable and involved.

The Dummy was directed by Fred Butler, whose son, David, was the stage manager. David later became a director of note, too, known primarily for the gentle Americana of his Fox films of the early Thirties.

When The Dummy ended its run in Los Angeles, plans were made to take the show back to New York. It went, but without Charlie, who was suddenly taken ill. The show continued its success wherever it played and, in 1916, was made into a film with Jack Pickford in the title role. Charlie was disappointed at missing out on what would have been his first trip of any note, but he soon found a novel way of consoling himself: the movies.

"There was a motion picture company down in Niles Canyon," Barton recalled, "which was about thirty miles from Oakland. Broncho Billy [Anderson] had a company there. I heard that [he] was looking for young kids to work in one of his films [so] my sister took me down and I was interviewed in his office. "[3] Charlie was cast in the film and reported to the set the following week. He was fascinated by the peculiar working methods of the movie people.

He remembered, "It was a completely open stage. They had gauze on strings that cut off the shadows from the sharp sunlight. The sets were painted canvas with the windows open so that you could see right out into Niles Canyon. That gave [the filmmaker] an exterior, too. "[4]

Comic Ben Turpin was shooting a one-reeler on the same location. Barton said, "We were shooting in the bedroom and they had a camera facing [us] and right in back of [our] camera was another camera facing the other way. There was another set on the other side of the stage. At the same time that we were doing a scene with Broncho Billy, Ben Turpin was doing a comedy scene. At the same time!"[5]

His stint in the movie (unfortunately, the title is not known) lasted only three days. Soon Charlie was back on stage at the Morosco, this time in a play called Young America, which had been produced by George M. Cohan at New York's Astor Theatre. Charlie, whose co-stars in the play

included a young Richard Dix, was back in his element and
received his best notices yet.   He assumed that his brief
flirtation with the movies had been nothing but a pleasant
holiday.   He was wrong.   During Young America's run, he
was approached by a prestigious producer/director: Maurice
Tourneur.

     "My agents [Arthur Landau and Eddie Small] got a
call from Tourneur asking if I could ride a horse," Barton
said.   "What are you gonna say? 'Of course I can ride a
horse!' "6 He couldn't, of course, but after a frantic morning's training at a local stable, he was able to fake it well
enough to convince Tourneur.   He got the role of Tim Vail,
a jockey in County Fair.

     Charlie soon found out that movie making was fraught
with more hazards than stage-work.   He was thrown from
his horse twice; on the second occasion, his foot was caught
in the stirrup and Charlie was "dragged all the way over to
the stables.   [It's lucky] that I wasn't killed, because my
head was back next to the hooves. "7   He received a slight
concussion and spent five days in Riverside Hospital.   No
sooner did he report back to work than misfortune struck
again.

     "I was up in this hayloft for [a] fire scene," he re-
membered, "and they put too much gas on it and she really
went! I jumped ... but had quite a few burns. "8 Charlie's
bad luck caused the shooting schedule of the film to nearly
double.   As physically painful as the film turned out to be,
though, he was delighted with pictures.   It helped that there
were several old friends from the stage among his co-stars:
David Butler, Edith Chapman and Wesley Barry.   The filming of County Fair was further complicated by the sudden ill-
ness of Tourneur.   Mid-way through the shooting, assistant
director Clarence Brown took over the reins and completed
the film.   Brown would offically co-direct several of Tourneur's subsequent films before beginning his own stellar career as a director at M-G-M.

     County Fair was a success and Charlie was convinced
that he should forsake the stage and permanently settle in as
a movie actor.   His agents soon secured a contract for him
with Mary Pickford.   "It didn't mean a damn thing," he said.
"She signed me to a contract, but she had a brother, Jack,
and he was about my size.   I think I stayed with her about
six months and didn't work once.   At that point I decided

that I was going to get into the picture business any way
I could. "9

He was now seventeen, an awkward age for an actor--
neither juvenile nor adult. Too, he felt that his height was
a detriment to a serious career; 5'2" is as tall as he ever
got. Now living in the YMCA on Flower St. in Los Angeles,
he was faced with getting the first non-show business job of
his life. When he was younger, he had spent summers helping his brother George run a soda parlor in San Francisco
called The Magic Isle. The experience led Charlie to seek
employment as a soda jerk and before long he was gainfully
employed at a drugstore at the corner of Vermont and Prospect, near the Buster Keaton studio. Picture people frequented the lunch counter there and Charlie was soon known
to many of them. He became particularly friendly with Freddie Anderson, an office boy at the Lasky Studios. Anderson
knew that Charlie wanted to get into the picture business, so
when an opening came at the studio, he was able to use his
influence to get Charlie a job. Charlie worked in the mail
room and at the information desk, and when, two weeks later,
Anderson was promoted into the camera department, Charlie
was made Head Office Boy. This was a customary position
for those who wanted to work their way through the ranks and
Charlie kept his eye peeled for the first opportunity. It soon
came.

"After about six or seven months, they asked me, if
I wanted to go into the prop department or the camera department," he recalled. "I said I'd rather go into the prop
department and work up from there. "10 He had already decided that he wanted to be a director. It was not the power,
money, or hunger for artistic expression that fueled this de-
sire--it was the "clothes. Boy, seeing these guys coming in
there, oh they were great! Mickey Neilan, DeMille with his
riding breeches. I wanted to be a director so I could dress
like that! "11

Barton entered the prop department in December, 1923
and was immediately put to work with director Joseph Henabery on The Stranger (1924), starring Betty Compson and Barton's old friend from Young America, Richard Dix. Over the
next two years, he was to work with an impressive roster of
Paramount's top directing talent: James Cruze Irvan Willat, C.B. DeMille, Herbert Brenon, Alan Crosland, William
K. Howard, Edward Sutherland, Allan Dwan, William Beaudine, William A. Wellman and others.

"That was a great experience. I was in the labor department, then I was put on the 'swing gang' (that meant
striking the sets and dressing them),"[12] he remembered. It
was also a film school of the first order; his teachers were
the best directors in Hollywood, though some of their working
methods struck the young prop-boy as being a little odd. He
remembered Herbert Brenon as being a "mystery man. He
wouldn't let anybody on the set [when he was planning a scene].
I sneaked in [once] and hid under a piano. It was a beautiful
set that had a long stairway and a balcony with a rail around
it. [Brenon] played the parts of the three people in the scene.
He would run up the stairs and be this person over here, then
he would run down the stairs and be this person over there.
Finally, he ran up the stairs, took a position and said,
'Bang! Bang!' and grabbed himself and fell down the stairs.
Well, I started laughing and the chase started!"[13]

Barton's fourth assignment was Lily of the Dust (1924),
directed by Dimitri Buchowetski and starring Pola Negri.
"He [Buchowetski] had this custom that for the first shot he
had to have a friend and a pig on the set," Barton said, "a
good luck charm. I was chosen to go out and hold the pig and
this was his little ceremony for the picture. He was quite a
nice man."[14]

James Cruze, for whom Barton worked a total of eight
times, was eccentric in a more positive way. "He was one
of the nicest guys I ever worked for and ... one of the highest paid directors in the business. He got $1,000 a day,
seven days a week. He had a heart of gold. At his home,
he had homemade gin, a tremendous buffet of food, and it was
always open house on Sunday. He took in all the old friends
and when people would leave--say, an actor who hadn't worked
in a month or two--he'd shake your hand and [slip you] a
hundred, two hundred dollars."[15] Barton worked on some of
Cruze's best and most famous films, including Old Ironsides
(1926). The production of this sea epic was fraught with difficulties and Barton was glad to be called away early to accompany William A. Wellman to San Antonio, Texas to begin
work on Wings.

Wellman was the director with whom Barton would become most closely associated. They worked together on
eleven films and, in 1939, Barton acted in Wellman's Beau
Geste. "I was assistant prop-man on his first two pictures
at Paramount [You Never Know Women and The Cat's Pajamas, both 1926]," recalled Barton, "and we hit it off right

away and became very good friends. " Wings was shaping up
to be Paramount's major production of the year (indeed, it
was to win the first Academy Award as Best Picture at the
1928 ceremony) and it was to prove to be a pivotal point in
Barton's career, as well.   Once in San Antonio, Barton's
progression up the studio ladder was swift.   Barton started
production as assistant prop-boy, but "I was promoted three
times.   I became the assistant unit manager.   They found
out the unit manager was skimming a little off the top.   When
he found out they were gonna build a set, he'd go out and buy
the lumber and sell it to the studio at a higher price.   He
was doing pretty good! I think they asked him to quit.   The
assistant unit manager, Dick Johnson, became the Unit Manager and, I must say, also the first assistant, because I had
very little experience. "16

His lack of experience did not matter much, for he was
only passing through the job.   Soon he was promoted to second
assistant and, finally, First Assistant Director.

The importance of the assistant director has never been
adequately examined.   It was a particularly important post in
the early days of the motion picture industry before unioniza-
tion caused such strict segregation of the various duties to be
performed.   The assistant director often decided on camera
set-ups, rehearsed actors, coordinated special effects, worked
out shooting schedules and, on occasion, shot scenes.   Barton
proved adept at the job.   He was energetic, creative, organized and shrewd, and quickly came to be highly prized by the
studio and its directors.   From 1928 to 1934 he worked as
first or second assistant on nearly every important Paramount
release: Beau Sabreur, Legion of the Condemned, Beggars
of Life, The Dance of Life, Santa Fe Trail, City Streets,
Monkey Business, Horse Feathers, Sign of the Cross and If
I Had a Million.   On the last of these films he got his first
opportunity to direct when Norman McLeod became ill and
Barton completed the W. C. Fields sequence.

By now, Barton was familiar with most phases of filmmaking and was never averse to filling any job that came his
way.   He occasionally shot second-unit footage, filled in as a
gag writer or script doctor or even, as in Wings, did a little
acting.   In 1928, he was one of five assistant directors called
upon to shoot a complex carnival scene for Mauritz Stiller's
The Street of Sin; his fellow assistants were Bob Lee, Henry
Hathaway, George Yohalem and Sid Brod.

A director with whom Barton frequently worked was

Cecil B. DeMille. He served as assistant on Sign of the
Cross (1932), This Day and Age (1933), Four Frightened
People (1934) ("Hell, everybody was frightened on that picture!"[17]) and Cleopatra (1934). Barton was fond of the exuberant, often tyrannical DeMille and found him to be "a
very particular guy; he had eyes in the back of his head.
When you had people walking on the street, you, as the
assistant, had to stay up the night before and write out
pieces of business for them to do. "[18] Barton sooned learned
that DeMille's passion for detail was not just some conceit
of the director's; few things escaped his sharp eye. During
the filming of Sign of the Cross, Barton helped to supervise
a busy street scene which involved a large crowd of people
making way for a chariot being driven by Fredric March.
Barton stood beside DeMille on a parallel as the scene commenced. "We started the chariot down the road and everything was going fine. Suddenly, DeMille hollers through his
loud speaker, "Cut! Cut!' He gets off the parallel and walks
way up the street and picks out two extras. 'What did the
assistant tell you to do?' The guys got scared and said,
'Well, he just told us to walk up and down here. ' [DeMille]
came back up to the parallel, picks up the megaphone and
says, 'Mr. Assistant, get me my revolver and some live
ammunition. ' I said, 'Oh, Mr. DeMille, I can get you your
revolver, but I can't get you any live ammunition--we're in
a very tight position here. ' 'I told you to get me my gun
and live ammunition!' I said, 'I'll go to the front office if
you'll tell me what you want to use it for. ' He said, 'I want
to kill my assistant! '"[19]

     A great deal of Barton's experience as an assistant
director lay in the realm of comedy. He worked with the
Marx Brothers on Monkey Business (1931, Norman McLeod),
Horse Feathers (1932, McLeod), and Duck Soup (1934, Leo
McCarey). The Marx Brothers were particularly fond of
Barton; they nicknamed him "Echo Marx" and offered him
an exclusive contract as their permanent assistant. He also
worked often with W. C. Fields: If I Had a Million (1932,
McLeod), Million Dollar Legs (1932, Eddie Cline) and International House (1933, Eddie Sutherland). This training would
stand him in good stead in his own directing career, when
he was responsible for popular, if less talented comics such
as Abbott and Costello, Jackie Gleason, Joe Besser, Joan
Davis, Judy Canova, Bert Gordon and Joe E. Brown. Whatever his shortcomings in other areas, Barton always knew
his way around a gag and a great many of his comedies can
convince the viewer that they are far funnier than they actually are.

Ironically, when he finally became a director, his impressive apprenticeship in comedy was overlooked for several years. His output at Paramount consists of westerns, crime dramas, action stories and melodramas. It was not until he moved to Columbia in 1939 that he was able to work consistently in the genre with which he was most adept.

Just why it took Barton so long to receive a contract as a director is a little puzzling. Certainly he was highly prized as an assistant (in fact, he received an Academy Award as Paramount's best assistant director in 1933, the only year such an award was given.)[20] However, he stayed in the job a full seven years before being promoted. Then, once promoted, he was relegated to "B" films, a level from which he was never really to escape.

Former assistant director Henry Hathaway had recently started directing at Paramount, working on westerns for "B" producer Harold Hurley. Hathaway and Barton were good friends and when Hurley was casting about for new directing talent, Hathaway suggested Barton. Hurley was making a series of Zane Grey Westerns that could make use of stock footage from the more elaborate silent versions directed by Victor Fleming, John Waters, George B. Seitz, William K. Howard and others. He felt that Barton could "audition" by making one of these as co-director with another assistant, Arthur Jacobson. The film was Wagon Wheels, a re-make of the 1931 Fighting Caravans which had been directed by Otto Brower and on which Barton had served as assistant director. Thus, he found himself in the unique position of padding out his first directorial effort with stock footage that he himself had shot. Just before Wagon Wheels went into production, Hurley decided that Jacobson was not quite ready for the responsibility and he served on the film as Barton's First Assistant. It was understood that when Jacobson's debut as a director rolled around, Barton would return the favor. He never did; Jacobson never directed a film.

When it became known that Barton was about to direct his first feature, his director friends gathered around to offer advice. Bill Wellman congratulated Barton and told him, "You're going to get stuck so many goddamn times that you won't know which end is up. So, do what I do: when you get stuck, act as crazy as you can, raise Hell and storm off the set. People will stay away from you and you'll have time to think. " Barton replied, "Jesus Christ! You must be stuck

all the time!"21   Other, more ordinary, directors like Otto
Brower advised Barton to use a storyboard.

"It sounded very good," he remembered, "so I went
ahead and laid out all the scenes on a storyboard--it looked
easy.   The first day of shooting was on location [at night] in
the Sequoias of Sonora.   Randy Scott was to ride into the
scene, which took place at the end of a big wagon where Gail
Patrick, Billy Lee and I were standing.   I [lined up the shot
according to the] storyboard and it was fine ... except the
cameraman [William C. Mellor] said, 'We'll have to be back
so far, to hold Randy's height on the horse, that you won't
see the little boy on the ground.'

"'I'll put the kid up on the big wheel of the wagon.'

"That worked fine [until] Gail said, 'I can't play the
scene from where I'm standing because that's my wrong
side.'

"Now the electrician spoke up.   'You got them so
close to the wagon, I can't get any back light on any of
them.'

"Well, there goes the storyboard in the first scene.
The Hell with it!"22

Barton worked on Wagon Wheels with what was to be
recognized as his usual swift pace.   The company was on
location at Sonora for two weeks, then returned to the studio
on Marathon Street in Los Angeles for four days to wrap up
production.   It was released to generally good reviews and
brisk box-office.

While there are certainly no surprises in Wagon
Wheels, it is quite respectable as a debut film.   The cast
performs with an understated, likable ease, Mellor's photography is crisp and lovely, and, at 56 minutes, the whole
thing moves at quite a clip.   While at Paramount, Barton
was to make a total of six westerns based on Zane Grey
stories: Rocky Mountain Mystery (1935, with Randolph Scott),
Nevada (1936, with Buster Crabbe), Forlorn River (1937, with
Crabbe), Thunder Trail (1937, with Gilbert Roland), and Born
to the West (1938, with John Wayne).   Their qualities do not
vary much, though each has little quirks that make it of interest.   Rocky Mountain Mystery eschewed many traditional
western factors to emerge a rather neat murder mystery.

Of Nevada, Variety wrote, "Picture has received more than
casual production attention and is photographed particularly
well, many of the exteriors giving it a slight spectacle perspective.   In his direction, Charles Barton has moved his
story along carefully and piloted his cast for action that carries a convincing note, unlike most westerns in which anything goes."[23] Born to the West (re-released as Hell Town)
had the advantage of a particularly good cast: John Wayne,
John Mack Brown, Monte Blue and Marsha Hunt.   Beyond
the good performances, though, the film is simply too flat
and predictable to warrant a second look.   It was released
at a tidy 50 minutes, but when it was re-released several
years later, several minutes of aimless stock footage (cattle
drives and the like) were added.   This worthless and tire-
some footage is usually included when the film is revived on
television today.

          Aside from his series of westerns, Barton turned his
hand to several fine, hard-boiled crime/action pictures while
at Paramount.   The best are Car 99 (1935), a police-themed
comedy/thriller with Fred MacMurray, William Frawley and
Ann Sheridan, and two mysteries featuring Lew Ayres, Murder with Pictures (1936), a newspaper melodrama, and The
Crime Nobody Saw (1937).

          The most striking element of Barton's direction that
can be easily discerned in these formative films at Paramount is his obvious rapport with actors; it is what his co-
workers of the period remember best about him.   Billy Lee,
who first appeared in a Barton film--Wagon Wheels--at age
six, remembered, "He was like a second father to me,
literally.   He bought me my first tricycle.   He was always
very patient with me, always explained what I was supposed
to do.   He made doing scenes like playing a game.   He was
fun to work with."[24]   Billy Lee worked with Barton a total
of four times.   Another actor who worked frequently with
Barton was character actor Fritz Feld.   He wrote in 1936,
"Charlie's democratic nature is the key-note to his success.
His secret is laughter.   With that he captivates everyone.
With his amusing gags he puts his whole company in a gay
spirit and therefore gets successful results."[25]

          Though his Paramount films were successful and his
direction consistently well-reviewed, Barton soon felt con-
stricted by the seemingly never-ending string of "B" pictures that were perpetually his lot.   He began to badger the
front office for better assignments and his resentment grew

as the studio ignored his pleas.   Finally, perhaps taking a
cue from his more headstrong director friends like Wellman,
Barton put his foot down.   He was assigned another "B" and,
to the studio's amazement, he refused the project.   He did
not, however, have quite the clout that he believed, for the
studio called his bluff and put him on suspension.   When his
contract ran out in 1937, it was not renewed.

        Barton was stunned.   He had rightfully believed that
his pictures were very profitable for the studio and that he
was perfectly justified in asking for better projects.   He also
found that being, in essence, fired from Paramount made
finding work at other studios difficult.   As his bank account
dwindled through the year that he was out of work, he began
to wonder if he should have been so particular about his projects.   It is likely that, at this point, he vowed to himself
that he would never indulge in acts of temperament again.
It was better to work on any sort of picture than to go through
another such period of inactivity.   Whether or not he experienced such an epiphany at this time is not certain.   What is
certain is that Barton began 1939 with the first job that came
his way: as Cecil B. DeMille's Assistant Director on Union
Pacific.   Barton was probably too relieved at the prospect of
a steady paycheck again to notice that his pay as DeMille's
assistant would be about one-third of his last pay check as a
Paramount director.   He was glad to be working again, any-
way, and settled easily into his relationship with his old boss.
He found that DeMille had not changed much: he was still a
tyrant with a violent temper, an eagle's eye for detail and an
uncanny sense of what the American public wanted to see.

        The year 1939 must have seemed like an experience
in déjà vu all the way around for Barton, for no sooner did
his DeMille production wrap up than he found himself on location with another former boss: William Wellman.   Wellman had been assigned one of Paramount's plum projects of
the year, a re-make of the 1926 classic of the French Foreign Legion, Beau Geste.   Most of the cast had already been
lined up; it included Gary Cooper, Ray Milland, Robert Preston, Brian Donlevy, J. Carrol Naish, and Susan Hayward.
The search was still on for an actor to play a very short,
very tough cowboy who joins the Foreign Legion with his
partner (played by Broderick Crawford).   As soon as Wellman found out that Barton was out of work, he realized
that his friend was the perfect size and type to play the
role.   Wellman called Barton into his office, handed him
a contract and said, "Sign here, you little squirt.   You're

Barton and William Wellman struggle over the script of
<u>Beau Geste</u> as filming commences in 1939. Wellman won.

an actor now.   And you'd better be funny, you little son of
a bitch!"26   A month later, Barton found himself on the
Beau Geste location in Buttercap Valley, an area of desert
near Yuma, Arizona.   He thoroughly enjoyed the experience of performing the small role.   The location, though
tense and rugged at times, had the friendly, raucous atmosphere of a slightly deadly boys' camp.   The brawls,
blow-ups and endless practical jokes that characterized the
location rivaled anything that reached the screen.   At the
end of shooting, Barton was surprised to be offered a contract with Paramount as a director/actor, but after some
consideration, he turned it down.

        In the spring of 1939, Barton was offered a contract
with Columbia Pictures.   At first hesitant to commit to the
inevitable string of "B" pictures which were Columbia's almost exclusive province, he eventually decided that he would
rather keep working than hold out for better projects that
might never appear.   His first film under his new contract
was a prison melodrama, Numbered Men, which featured
his Beau Geste co-star, Brian Donlevy.   Eventually released
as Behind Prison Gates, the film was, according to Variety,
"tightly directed.   Careful mounting of sets and substantial
production values are evident, despite moderate negative
cost. "27   The same could be said of nearly all of Barton's
Columbia work.

        As a whole, Barton's Columbia canon is inferior to
his Paramount output, the low budgets are far more obvious,
the acting and scripting of lower caliber.   The Paramount
films could at least make use of stock footage from big-
budgeted "A" pictures, giving the programmers a glossy
veneer far beyond their meager budgets.   Columbia had no
backlog of expensive "A" films to cannibalize and Barton's
films there often look drab and cheap.   Though he was to
get the opportunity to try his hand at comedy much more
frequently at Columbia, it is striking how somber and humor-
less his non-comedies at the studio are; the films seem so
turgid and slow that even at their short running times (rarely
longer than an hour) some seem to go on forever.

        Barton helmed a successful series of films based on
Margaret Sidney's The Five Little Peppers and How They
Grew, but the films are annoyingly saccharine and spineless.
His adeptness at directing children is certainly in evidence in
all these films and the performance of the "Little Peppers"
are the main reason to watch the films; Edith Fellows,

Dorothy Ann Seese, Tommy Bond and others became popular
child stars partly as a result of the Five Little Peppers films.
The series was financially lucrative, though the critics lashed
it unmercifully. With good reason.

Others of Barton's films of the period are particularly
frustrating, for there is so much promise there: My Son Is
Guilty boasts an original story by the great photographer and
director, Karl Brown; Babies for Sale concerns a reporter
who exposes a home for un-wed mothers in which the girls
are persuaded to sign over the rights to their unborn infants,
as part of a baby-selling ring; Island of Doomed Men starred
Peter Lorre as the sadistic head of a prison camp who likes
to listen to Chopin before flogging his unfortunate prisoners
or mistreating his wife (Rochelle Hudson). Though each of
the films is fairly well directed and exerts a certain fascination due to its subjects or stars, none is particularly satisfying.

As the 1940s got underway, Barton took on many
films with a war theme or that had patriotism as the core
emotion: Reveille with Beverly (1943) was about a disc
jockey (Ann Miller) who dedicates her radio show to the
various armed services camps; Tramp Tramp Tramp (1942)
featured Jackie Gleason as a 4-F draft reject who takes it
upon himself to protect the home front; Sweetheart of the
Fleet and Parachute Nurse (both 1942) are concerned with
service men and women. Jam Session (1944), set in a
movie studio, makes no overt references to the war, though
the plot hinges on the housing shortage and other topical
references. Ann Miller plays a beauty contest winner who
comes to Hollywood to break into the movies and ends up
living under the stairs in a rooming house. She ends the
film with a large production number, "The Victory Polka,"
but the war is never otherwise mentioned.

Jam Session is, in fact, one of Barton's brighter
projects at Columbia. It boasts an above-average script
and a solid line-up of musical guests: Charlie Barnet,
Louis Armstrong, Alvino Rey, Jan Garber, Glen Gray (and
their accompanying orchestras) and The Pied Pipers. Whereas his handling of the musical scenes in the similarly struc-
tured Reveille with Beverly seemed almost purposefully uninspired and dull, Jam Session's musical acts come off with
style. Barton obviously spent more time in the planning of
these scenes, for they are imaginatively staged. To be fair,
Columbia never gave Barton the resources to turn out a

Barton with actress Jean Parker on the set of Hello Annapolis.

---

really first-class musical, even if he had had it within himself to produce one, but Jam Session is a sprightly and enjoyable film, despite its shortcomings. He was not so lucky with several others of his musical comedies of the period: Honolulu Lu (1941), Sing for Your Supper (1941), Two Latins from Manhattan (1941), Laugh Your

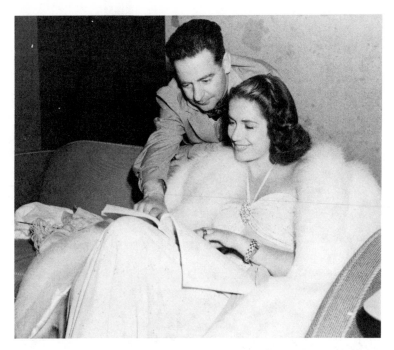

Barton gives much needed direction to model-turned-actress Jinx Falkenburg while filming Two Latins from Manhattan (1941).

Blues Away (1942) and Lucky Legs (1943) each have individual bright spots, but, in the end, little to distinguish or recommend them.

It must be stressed that Barton's films continued to perform well at the box office. Reveille with Beverly, What's Buzzin' Cousin? (1943), Louisiana Hayride, and the surprisingly funny Beautiful But Broke (1944) kept the cash receipts rolling into Columbia's coffers. Barton's excellent track record was noticed by other studios and, as his contract neared completion at Columbia, he began to receive offers. By this time, he had virtually given up any idea of graduating to the big budgets and top stars of "A" features and, all things considered, Universal made him the most promising offer: his salary would go up, his quota of films would go down, and he would helm a fair number of Universal's major releases.

To cinch the deal, Universal dangled a plum: Barton would
get to produce, on occasion, as well as direct.

   He signed on with Universal in the spring of 1945 and
immediately got to work on The Beautiful Cheat, the first of
his dual capacity films.   This picture and the one that followed, Men in Her Diary showed a marked improvement in
quality over the Columbia programmers.   Both are well
mounted and, though modest and unpretentious, a cut above
what they would have been had Barton made them a year
earlier in his former position.   The director was always
at his best with character and secondary actors and Universal gave him a fine list to choose from; Irene Ryan,
Milburn Stone, Ernest Truex, Eric Blore, Sig Rumann,
Maxie Rosenbloom and Minerva Urecal are just some of
the fine performers who appeared in these first two Universal projects.   Because of the greater resources available to him at Universal, none of his films there would
emerge as completely worthless and unwatchable, as some
of the Columbia pictures (Harmon of Michigan, for example)
had.

   One trait that did not leave Barton in his more important position at the new studio was his willingness to do
odd jobs for other directors.   Thus in 1946 he shot second-
unit footage for Alfred Hitchcock's Spellbound and Jacques
Tourneur's Canyon Passage.   In the latter, he was responsible for some truly stunning Technicolor vistas, a valuable
ingredient in this, one of the finest westerns of the decade. 28
He also found time that year to direct three features: Smooth
as Silk with Kent Taylor and Virginia Grey; White Tie and
Tails with Dan Duryea, Ella Raines and William Bendix; and,
arguably the finest film of his career, The Time of Their
Lives with Bud Abbott and Lou Costello.

   Since making their first film for Universal in 1940,
One Night in the Tropics, Abbott and Costello had become
the studio's most valuable assets.   From 1941 to 1944 they
were among the top ten box office draws, and 1942 saw them
as the most popular stars in Hollywood.   Their popularity
had slipped a little in the ensuing years because, in Barton's
opinion, "Universal was making so much money that they
flooded the market with [the team].   The same time a new
film came out, a re-release would also be on the market.
Instead of sitting down and waiting for [the public] to say,
'When are we going to have another Abbott and Costello
film?' [the studio kept] the films there all the time.   You
can only stand so much."29

Barton and Dan Duryea talk over a scene in <u>White Tie and</u> <u>Tails</u>.

Whether by accident or design, 1946 saw the release
of two of the team's most unusual films, The Time of Their
Lives and William A. Seiter's Little Giant. Neither film
teamed the comics in the traditional sense. In the latter,
they play separate characters who meet in the course of the
film; in the former, they do not meet at all in the film prop-
er, since Costello plays a ghost whom Abbott never sees.
(Abbott plays two roles, one a Revolutionary War character,
the other a modern day psychiatrist; in the period prologue,
the comics play a scene together, but once the story shifts
to modern times, they are no longer teamed.) The Time of
Their Lives is unique for Abbott and Costello, and sadly so,
for few of their films ever probed the more subtle, gentle
side of their talents. Costello, particularly, had a wistful
air that made him perfect for the sort of Chaplinesque pathos
that so many comics tried and failed at, and this appealing
quality is in evidence in this film as in practically no other.
The team considered themselves justified in resisting any attempts to change or color their usual characters, for their
two "experimental" films of 1946 did not do well at theaters;
for the rest of their careers, Abbott and Costello stayed with
tried-and-true characterizations and techniques. Barton was
to guide them back to major box-office success but, with few
exceptions (like the superior Abbott and Costello Meet Frankenstein [1948]) his films with the team are virtually indistinguishable from those of their other major directors: Seiter, Arthur Lubin, Erle C. Kenton and Jean Yarbrough.

This is all the more frustrating because The Time of
Their Lives shows both the duo and their director at peak
form, the team's usual bag of tricks--slapstick and moth-
eaten routines--augmented by a gentleness, a sense of purpose, whimsy, a belief in the above-average story and the
atmosphere of charm and fantasy that it creates. The film
concerns two innocent people (Costello and Marjorie Reynolds), shot as traitors during the Revolutionary War, who
are bound to earth as ghosts until their innocence is proven.
The period scenes that begin the film are eloquent of Universal's ability to make low budgets stretch beyond their limits.
Barton wisely has the scenes played completely straight.
There are several fresh aspects to Costello's character: he
is a tinker by trade and, unexpectedly, is shown to be a
superior craftsman; he is allowed a serious romance with a
girl who admires and respects him; finally, apart from an
innate clumsiness (the better for a few pratfalls), Horatio
Prim is neither stupid nor gullible--something that can be
said for few Costello parts. Costello's scenes with Ann

Gillis (as his fiancée Nora) are sweet and delightful. It is a
pity that the two were never teamed again, for Gillis's comic
timing is masterly and she never resorts to the adversarial
aspects that usually define Costello's romantic entanglements.

Once the story reaches modern times, some of the
charm is replaced by the more standard slapstick-and-slang
with which the team felt more comfortable.   There is some
humor in the wisecracks of Binnie Barnes and it is quite
satisfying to see Abbott getting the rough end of it for once.
The special effects are good examples of the "Invisible Man"
school of walking dresses and so forth, but the real humor
of the film is drawn from the characters.   Gale Sondergaard
has a standout role as a psychic housekeeper (one character
asks her, "Didn't I see you in Rebecca?") and Bud Abbott
gives an atypical, sympathetic performance.   Though both
Abbott and Costello resisted doing the film, The Time of
Their Lives represents the level that they were capable of
and it is a pity that they and their audiences so consistently
settled for less.

The Time of Their Lives marked the first of eleven
times that Barton worked with the team.   He would eventually
get used to their eccentricities, but on this first film he often
found himself caught by surprise.

"Lou acted as if he owned the studio.   During production of The Time of Their Lives, there was a beautiful grandfather's clock in the hallway.   I [shot] scenes around it.   One
day, we went to lunch and when we came back, the clock was
gone.   I went around asking, 'Who took the clock?   Where is
it?'   Finally, it leaked out.   Lou said, 'I took it.   Get another clock.'   I said, 'How can I get another clock?   I've
gotta match shots!   God, I'd have to go back and re-shoot
everything!'   Finally I asked Bob Arthur, the producer, to
tell Lou to bring the clock back.   The studio sent a truck
out and the clock was returned so the remaining scenes could
be shot."30

"Another time," Barton recalled, "there was a canoe
lined with buckskin near the water.   Next day we returned to
the set and the canoe [was] gone.   It is now a planter in front
of Lou's home.   Lou was able to keep both the clock and the
canoe after the production was over."31

Barton spent the next three years directing nothing but
Abbott and Costello vehicles.   All of the entries in the series

are funny and each has moments of real hilarity, often provided by the veteran character actors whom Barton loved to
work with: Fritz Feld has a wonderfully amusing scene in
Mexican Hayride (1948) as a diction coach teaching Costello
how to make a speech; Joe Besser and Shemp Howard provide a great many of the laughs in Africa Screams (1949);
Mike Mazurki, usually cast as a brutish thug, showed his
excellent comic timing in The Noose Hangs High (1948).

Without a doubt, the best of the bunch is Bud Abbott
and Lou Costello Meet Frankenstein (1948), a remarkably
sustained horror-comedy that (like The Time of Their Lives)
brings out the best in the team by squelching their penchant
for trotting out their vaudeville routines and inserting them
at random at any opportune moment.   The humor in Abbott
and Costello Meet Frankenstein arises from the situations;
nothing is extraneous.   The horror elements are played
straight, adding a welcome sense of respect and authenticity
to the proceedings.   Not only is the film one of their best,
it was one of their most popular, and at the end of 1948 Abbott and Costello once again found themselves listed among the
top ten box-office attractions of the year.

Ironically, they were reluctant to do the film.   When
Costello read the script (originally titled The Brain of Frankenstein) he fumed, "You don't think I'll do that crap, do you?
My five-year-old daughter can write something better than
that!"32   Producer Robert Arthur thought that the project had
so much promise that he wheedled and cajoled the team into
doing it (his wheedling was helped along a little when he offered Costello a $50,000 advance on his percentage if he
would agree to do the film).

Production began on February 14, 1948 with a cast
composed of the veterans of so many of Universal's famous
monster movies.   Bela Lugosi, lately reduced to working in
Poverty Row quickies and, since 1944, battling a drug ad-
diction, appeared once more as Count Dracula, now the master of Frankenstein's monster played by Glenn Strange.   Lon
Chaney, Jr. appeared once more as Larry Talbot, the Wolf-
man.   In the original script, these monsters were to have
been joined by more of Universal's inventory: Kharis, the
Mummy, Count Alucard (Dracula's son), and The Invisible
Man.   The first two were dropped from the script and The
Invisible Man makes only a cameo "appearance" at the end
of the film (with a voice provided by Vincent Price).

Throughout the filming, Abbott and Costello were tem-
peramental and difficult. "All the 'monsters' were the nicest;
the real monsters were Abbott and Costello," Barton told author Gregory Mank. "Bud and Lou had quite a chip on their
shoulders about doing it and they'd fight me like hell. Our
budget was very cheap--maybe $1,000,000--not very much
for that time. The only thing that cost us money was when
the boys got on their high horse and wouldn't show up. Another trick they loved to pull was to sit over on the side of
the set and play cards for three days. Yet, during all these
problems, we never had any trouble with Lon or Bela or
Glenn. "The 'monsters' were sweet as little babies. Isn't
that wonderful? God, they were great!"[33]

Except for the stars, there existed a spirit of generosity and camaraderie among the cast. When Strange fell
and broke his foot, Barton was told that production would be
halted for three days, at a cost of many thousands of dollars.
Lon Chaney came to the rescue. Having played the monster
in The Ghost of Frankenstein (1942), Chaney volunteered to
play the role until Strange could get back to work. Chaney
appears as the monster in only one shot in the film, when
Lenore Aubert as the evil Dr. Mornay is hurled to her death
through a laboratory window by the malevolent creature.

It is a testament to Barton's speed and skill that,
though the company did not work week-ends and the star
team's contrary behavior cost at least six working days, Abbott and Costello Meet Frankenstein completed filming on
March 20, only one month and six days after shooting commenced. The film opened in New York on July 28, 1948, and
despite an air conditioner engineers' strike, was soon doing
turnaway business. It was to be the team's last great success, though Universal never tired of trying to repeat the
magic by having Abbott and Costello meet Dr. Jekyll and Mr.
Hyde, The Invisible Man, The Mummy, and even The Key-
stone Kops and Captain Kidd. It was all to no avail.

In 1949, Barton was relieved to be assigned to something other than an Abbott and Costello vehicle, but Free for
All turned out to be a limp comedy with Robert Cummings,
Ann Blyth, and Percy Kilbride starring in the story of a
young inventor who comes up with a formula for turning water
into gasoline. To be fair, Barton had a sluggish and not particularly amusing script to work with, but his direction of the
film is perfunctory and lackluster. Things did not look up
much in his next two projects, either, though on paper they

would appear to be quite promising. The Milkman (1950)
and Double Crossbones (1951) both star Donald O'Connor,
who was being groomed for stardom by Universal. Though
the former co-stars Jimmy Durante and the latter is filmed
in beautiful Technicolor, neither film did well critically or
financially.

In 1952, Barton directed his final film for Universal,
Ma and Pa Kettle at the Fair. Mid-way through the filming,
his wife, Nancy Bowers Barton, 34, died and Frederick De
Cordova, later a television producer and director of note
(The Tonight Show) took over as director until Barton's return. (Barton was prolific in other areas of his life besides
show business--he was married eight times and widowed four
times in a row). By the time the film was released in April,
1952, Barton was already at work on his newest project: directing Amos 'n' Andy for television.

"My wife, at that time, was in the hospital with can-
cer," he remembered. "She was in very bad shape. One
day I went to see her and she said to me, 'I read today where
they are going to do a TV show [based on] Amos 'n' Andy. I
think that it would be your kind of comedy. You should look
into it and get away from Universal.' Well, with all the ex-
penses [due to her illness] I wasn't going to try and leave
Universal and look for a TV show, I can tell you that! So,
two days later, she said to me, 'What have you done about
the Amos 'n' Andy thing?' and I said, 'Oh, I've checked on it
and they're gonna let me know." Well, strangely enough,
within two days I got a call from Freeman Gosden, who was
the creator of Amos 'n' Andy. He asked, 'Would you be interested in doing a show of Amos 'n' Andy?' I said, 'Yes,
but I'm under contract to Universal.' So I went down to talk
with him a few days later and he said, 'You've got the job if
you want it.' I said, 'I'll take it.'"[34] Barton immediately
went to William Goetz and asked to be released from his
Universal-International contract, and within the month he was
at work bringing the popular radio show to television.

Freeman Gosden and Charles Correll had guided the
radio show through its long and popular run. They did the
voices of Amos and Andy on the air and even appeared (in
blackface) in movies as their famous characters. However,
they knew that for television they would have to assemble a
cast of black actors, and for nearly four years they conducted
a highly publicized search. Judging from the "oohs" and
"aahs" of the studio audience when, in the pilot for the series,

the cast is introduced, Gosden and Correll obviously made
the right choices: Alvin Childress, Tim Moore and Spencer
Williams conformed in every detail to the public's idea of
how the characters should look.   The show was an immediate
hit, though from its first broadcast it garnered criticism
from the NAACP and other organizations which protested its
"racist" aspects.   This pressure would eventually take the
show, still very popular, off the air only two years later.
It ran in syndication for a few years, though pressure-groups
finally had it removed there as well.   It remains fondly remembered and, happily, the shows are becoming available
once more via video cassette.   Barton directed every episode
save the pilot.

His success in television made Barton a sought-after
director in the still-new medium.   In the next five years he
directed dozens of episodes in series like Duffy's Tavern and
Joe Palooka (both 1954), Trouble with Father and The Great
Gildersleeve (both 1955), Tugboat Annie and Oh! Susannah
(both 1956).   In 1958, he was approached by Walt Disney to
direct episodes in the ABC series, Zorro, and segments of the
popular "Mickey Mouse Club" serial, Spin and Marty.   Between
the two series, Barton was responsible for nearly fifty episodes and was soon assigned to a Disney feature, The Shaggy
Dog, the studio's first live-action comedy.

Since leaving Universal in 1951, he had only directed
one feature, Abbott and Costello's dismal Dance with Me Henry (1956; Barton also produced).   He had concentrated entirely on television, and The Shaggy Dog shows it.   It looks
like nothing so much as a long situation comedy, filmed in
black and white and broadly directed and acted.   Still, it is
a landmark film for the Disney organization.   The enormous
public response (in its first release, the film earned back
about nine times its cost) to this first live-action comedy
set the stage for the seemingly endless list of puerile,
juvenile comedies to follow from the studio.   It was an important film for star Fred MacMurray, as well.   Though
he had occasionally performed in comedic roles, the bulk
of his career had been taken up with hard-boiled parts in
crime films or (more recently) westerns.   The Shaggy Dog
was such an enormous hit that it virtually gave MacMurray
a second career.   He was to be seen in many more Disney
films in similar roles the stage was set for his successful
television series, My Three Sons.

The critical response to The Shaggy Dog was generally

very positive as well. Barton received his only nomination
as Best Director from the Directors' Guild for his work on
the picture and expectations ran high around the Disney organization that The Shaggy Dog would be nominated for an
Academy Award. It was not. That year, the Academy selected Anatomy of a Murder, Ben-Hur, The Diary of Anne
Frank, The Nun's Story and Room at the Top as the five
nominees for Best Picture; there was obviously a serious
mood among the voters that allowed no room for a fanciful
comedy like The Shaggy Dog. Even in the Special Effects
nominations, the Academy could only think of two films
worthy of mention: Ben-Hur (the winner) and Journey to
the Center of the Earth. One wonders how Barton's career
might have changed if The Shaggy Dog had garnered any
"official" honors, as its director so hoped it would. Certainly it would have spurred him on to stay in feature production, for he still had twelve years of professional life
ahead of him. Too, it might have pushed Barton into a
higher echelon in the business, a place where he could consistently have projects to consider which were worthy of his
talents. The Shaggy Dog, however, turned out to be "only"
a huge commercial success and Hollywood had always expected no less of Barton.

        The Shaggy Dog is certainly not a bad film. Quite
often it is exuberant and fanciful. The scenes in which
young Wilby Daniels (Tommy Kirk) magically turns into a
sheepdog are eerily convincing. Barton's handling of the
mostly young cast is easy and natural and he invokes readings and bits of business that bring the most out of the material. Nevertheless, it is slightly galling that The Shaggy
Dog should have performed so spectacularly at the box-office
when other, far finer, Disney films did so poorly: Darby
O'Gill and the Little People, Sleeping Beauty, Pollyanna and
Barton's next film, the lovely Toby Tyler, or Ten Weeks
with a Circus.

        This story of a boy who, feeling unloved at home,
runs off to join the circus, is among Barton's most accomplished films. It is simple, earnest, and evokes diverse
emotions, from laughter to tears. It was rare in his prolific career that the director could concentrate almost solely
on characterizations, but Toby Tyler--comprised of a series
of vignettes rather than a rigid plot--was such an easygoing,
relaxed and ambling film that it gave Barton the opportunity
to work on that aspect of his art that was most accomplished.

Kevin Corcoran, who appeared in The Shaggy Dog as
well as the sixteen episodes of Spin and Marty that Barton
directed, starred as Toby Tyler. He recalled, "Toby Tyler
was a very rough film for me to make. The character runs
the whole range of emotions: his parents are dead, his
guardians sort of turn their backs on him, he goes off to
join the circus, his pet is shot. Well, ten-year-old boys
are taught that they're not supposed to cry and there were
several scenes in the film in which I had to shed tears.
It was very difficult for me because it's against what an
American boy is conditioned toward. Charlie knew how hard
it was for me to do the scenes and he was very, very patient."[35]

When Toby Tyler was in its first run, Barton told a
reporter that he enjoyed working with children. "Give them
time, understanding and have a levity or a running gag and
there are no problems," he said. "Like Kevin and I on Toby
Tyler. We had a thing whereby if Kevin blew a line we'd
pretend that 'Herman' had done it. We still refer to each
other as 'Herman.'"[36]

Corcoran added recently, "When you're a kid and
you're standing in front of a hundred adults and they're all
expecting you to perform well, you're put under a great deal
of pressure. You're aware of things; you're conscious of the
fact that if you don't perform well, a lot of people could suf-
fer. You know that if your picture shuts down, there are going to be a lot of people who aren't going to eat next week.
That's a lot of pressure for a kid to be under. That was
Charlie's great talent, that he could help you have fun with
it, but at the same time, get the job done. He was a 'people' director. He looked like a big rabbit to me and he was
so short that we could nearly work eye to eye. It was easy
to trust him."[37]

Toby Tyler did not find the enormous audience that
The Shaggy Dog had, but it is the finer film, filled with
delightful moments and even little in-jokes (one such joke
is the credit reading "and introducing Ollie Wallace"; Wallace was a long-time Disney composer who appears in the film
as the circus bandleader). The critics almost unanimously
approved of Toby Tyler. Howard Thompson of the New York
Times wrote, "The picture may seem tame to adults and
Charles Barton has directed the unstartling incidents with
frank, affectionate gentility. But Mr. Disney and his staff
have accomplished three very nice things. They have cast
Mr. Corcoran--and he is as manly and wide-eyed a tyke as

anyone could hope for. Better still, the circus is not the
greatest show in the world—just a colorful, one-ring affair.
Furthermore, here's one circus that is not mortgaged to the
hilt or terrorized by escaping animals ... this little picture
shines from within, mildly but sweetly."38

Barton was to direct only one other feature, the best-
forgotten Swingin' Along for 20th Century-Fox in 1962. The
script, cast, direction and musical acts (except Ray Charles,
whose talent can survive worse than this) are banal and triv-
ial. There are scenes in Swingin' Along (such as a recreation of Laurel and Hardy's famous Music Box sequence, wherein stars Peter Marshall and Tommy Noonan attempt to carry
a piano up an impossibly long flight of stairs) that go beyond
being unfunny; they are downright insulting.

Meanwhile, Barton's career in television was going at
full tilt. He directed 136 episodes of Dennis the Menace and
assorted segments of Grindl (1963), The Baileys of Balboa,
McHale's Navy, The Munsters and Broadside (all 1964), The
Smothers Brothers Show, Camp Runamuck and Hazel (all
1965), and Petticoat Junction (1966); and he produced and
directed over one hundred episodes of Family Affair. When
that series went off the air in 1972, Barton retired from the
business, a wealthy and successful veteran of sixty years in
motion pictures, television and theater. He spent his last
years happily married to singer-actress Julie Gibson and
found himself increasingly sought out by eager young film students who saw in him a personal link to the great days of
Hollywood's youth. He was unfailingly generous with his time
and knowledge and he kept until the day of his death the qualities that made him so beloved by the majority of his co-
workers through the years: he was eager, interested and
amused, a good talker and a good listener, a shrewd judge
of character and a deadly mimic. He was also an inherently
democratic soul; he remembered Cecil B. DeMille and Paramount bootblack Oscar Smith with equal respect and affection.

Charles T. Barton died of heart failure on December
5, 1981. If there are no aesthetic masterpieces among his
films, his career must still be regarded as an important one.
He worked steadily and produced many films that great numbers of viewers took pleasure in. His work was popular and
profitable, and a great deal of it can be returned to by those
seeking out the sensibilities of a by-gone age or simply an
uncomplicated good time. His is the sort of career that is
impossible to duplicate in today's industry, even if there

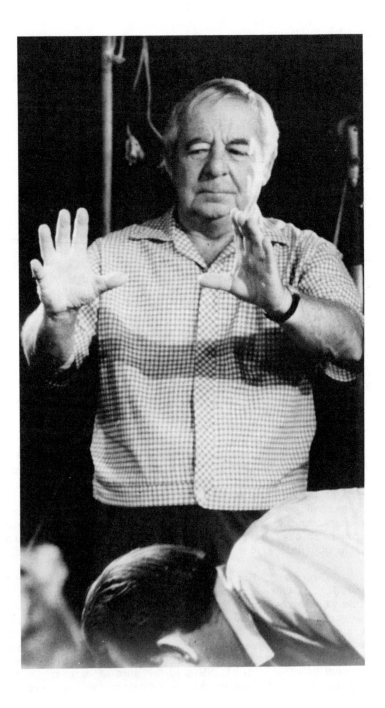

were a breed of filmmakers existing now with the versatility, talent, stamina and good humor to try it.

Acknowledgments

My deepest thanks are due many people who helped me in the research for this piece: Tom Holland, Alexa Foreman, Lee Tsiantis, Mike Durrett, John Gallagher, Tony Slide, Kevin Brownlow, Bill Schlensker, Benny Baker, Kit Parker Films, Kevin Corcoran, Jemi Nicoll. Special thanks to John Tibbetts and the nice folks at the National Film Society; it was in their magazine, American Classic Screen, that an early version of this piece first appeared.

My gratitude is extended to John Cocchi, for his heroic efforts in making the Barton filmography the most complete ever printed; to Greg Lenburg, a good friend and a tireless researcher, for sharing unselfishly the transcripts of his many hours of interviews with Barton; to Julie Gibson, Barton's widow, for her enormous help in providing me with Barton's papers and scrapbooks and for her unfailing generosity, hospitality, patience and good humor.

Finally, thanks to Charlie Barton, who answered questions about himself and his career with an enthusiasm that he could not always have felt. His merits as a director can be debated, but as a kind and gentle friend he had few peers.

Note: Copies of most of the research materials used in the preparation of this article have been deposited in Charles Barton's file at the Margaret Herrick Library of the Academy of Motion Picture Arts and Sciences.

Notes

1. Charles Barton interviewed by the author and Kevin Brownlow, October 23, 1980.
2. Maitland Davies, "Boy Hero, Morosco Drama, Unique," Los Angeles Tribune, October 30, 1916.
3. Barton interviewed by Greg Lenburg.
4. Ibid.
5. Ibid.
6. Brownlow, author, interview.

Opposite: Barton sets up a shot for TV's Family Affair, circa 1970.

7.   Lenburg, interview.
8.   Ibid.
9.   Ibid.
10. Ibid.
11. Brownlow, author, interview.
12. Lenburg, interview.
13. Ibid.
14. Ibid.
15. Ibid.
16. Barton interveiwed by author April 11, 1979.
17. Lenburg, interview.
18. Ibid.
19. Ibid.
20. This was a multiple award, given to one Assistant Direc-
     tor at each major studio. Barton was Paramount's
     winner and the others were: Scott Beal, Universal;
     Charles Dorian, M-G-M; Fred Fox, United Artists;
     Gordon Hollingshead, Warner Bros.; Dewey Starkey,
     RKO Radio; William Tummell, Fox.
21. Author, interview April 11, 1979.
22. Lenburg, interview.
23. "Nevada," Variety, April 15, 1936.
24. Bill "Billy Lee" Schlensker, interviewed by author,
     August 30, 1983.
25. Fritz Feld, "Key-Hole Portrait of Charles Barton," un-
     published, © 1936.
26. Author interview, April 11, 1979.
27. "Behind Prison Gates," Variety, August 23, 1939.
28. Canyon Passage also utilized footage from John Ford's
     Drums Along The Mohawk (Fox, 1939).
29. Lenburg, interview.
30. Author interview, October 24, 1980.
31. Lenburg, interview.
32. Bob Thomas, Bud and Lou (Philadelphia: J.B. Lippincott,
     Co., 1977).
33. Gregory William Mank, It's Alive (San Diego/New York:
     A.S. Barnes & Co., Inc., 1981).
34. Author interview, October 24, 1980.
35. Kevin Corcoran interviewed by author, November 15,
     1983.
36. Harold Hildebrand, "Barton Tames the Tots," Los
     Angeles Examiner, February 7, 1960.
37. Corcoran interview.
38. Howard Thompson, "Toby Tyler," New York Times,
     April 20, 1960.

FILMOGRAPHIES

Victor Fleming (Museum of Modern Art/Film Stills Archive)

Victor Fleming

<u>As Director of Photography</u>

BETTY OF GREYSTONE (Fine Arts-Triangle, 1916). Directed by
Allan Dwan. With Dorothy Gish, George Fawcett, Kate Bruce.
Produced by D. W. Griffith.

HIS PICTURE IN THE PAPERS (Fine Arts-Triangle, 1916). Directed
by John Emerson. With Douglas Fairbanks, Loretta Blake,
Clarence Handyside. Produced by D. W. Griffith.

THE HABIT OF HAPPINESS (Fine Arts-Triangle, 1916). Directed
by Allan Dwan. With Douglas Fairbanks, Dorothy West,
George Fawcett. Produced by D. W. Griffith.

THE GOOD BAD MAN (Fine Arts-Triangle, 1916). Directed by
Allan Dwan. With Douglas Fairbanks, Bessie Love, Sam
DeGrasse. Produced by D. W. Griffith.

THE MYSTERY OF THE LEAPING FISH (Triangle-Keystone, 1916).
Directed by John Emerson. With Douglas Fairbanks, Bessie
Love, A. D. Sears. Produced by D. W. Griffith.

THE HALF-BREED (Fine Arts-Triangle, 1916). Directed by Allan
Dwan. With Douglas Fairbanks, Alma Rubens, Jewel Carmen.
Produced by D. W. Griffith.

MANHATTAN MADNESS (Fine Arts-Triangle, 1916). Directed by
Allan Dwan. With Douglas Fairbanks, Jewel Carmen, George
Beranger. Produced by D. W. Griffith.

AMERICAN ARISTOCRACY (Fine Arts-Triangle, 1916). Directed by
Lloyd Ingraham. With Douglas Fairbanks, Jewel Carmen,
Albert MacQuarrie. Produced by D. W. Griffith.

THE MATRIMANIAC (Fine Arts-Triangle, 1916). Directed by Paul
Powell. With Douglas Fairbanks, Constance Talmadge, Winifred Westover. Produced by D. W. Griffith.

THE AMERICANO (Fine Arts-Triangle, 1916). Directed by John
Emerson. With Douglas Fairbanks, Alma Rubens, Spottis-
woode Aitken. Produced by D. W. Griffith.

IN AGAIN, OUT AGAIN (Artcraft-Paramount, 1917).   Directed by
    John Emerson.   With Douglas Fairbanks, Arline Pretty,
    Bull Montana, Albert Parker.   Produced by Douglas Fairbanks.

WILD AND WOOLLY (Artcraft-Paramount, 1917).   Directed by John
    Emerson.   With Douglas Fairbanks, Eileen Percy, Sam De-
    Grasse,   Produced by Douglas Fairbanks.

DOWN TO EARTH (Artcraft-Paramount, 1917).   Directed by John
    Emerson.   With Douglas Fairbanks, Eileen Percy, Gustav Von
    Seyffertitz.   Produced by Douglas Fairbanks.

THE MAN FROM PAINTED POST (Artcraft-Paramount, 1917). Directed
    by Joseph Henabery. With Douglas Fairbanks, Eileen Percy,
    Frank Campeau, Monte Blue. Produced by Douglas Fairbanks.

A MODERN MUSKETEER (Artcraft-Paramount, 1918).   Directed by
    Allan Dwan. With Douglas Fairbanks, Marjorie Daw, Kath-
    leen Kirkham, Tully Marshall, Frank Campeau, Zasu Pitts.
    Produced by Douglas Fairbanks.

HIS MAJESTY, THE AMERICAN (United Artists, 1919).   Directed
    by Joseph Henabery. With Douglas Fairbanks, Marjorie Daw,
    Lillian Langdon, Frank Campeau, Boris Karloff.   Produced
    by Douglas Fairbanks.

As Director

Dates given are: Copyright, release date, and New York premiere.

WHEN THE CLOUDS ROLL BY (1919).   Douglas Fairbanks Pictures
Corp. /United Artists.   Produced by Douglas Fairbanks.   Story by
Douglas Fairbanks.   Scenario by Tom J. Geraghty (and uncredited,
Lewis Weadon).   Photography: William C. McGann and Harry Thorpe.
Assistant Director: Theodore Reed.   Titles Designed by Henry Clive.
Art Direction: Edward M. Langley.   Publicity Director: Bennie F.
Zeidman.   6 reels.
    The Cast: Douglas Fairbanks (Daniel Boone Brown), Albert
MacQuarrie (Hobson), Ralph Lewis (Curtis Brown), Frank Campeau
(Mark Drake), Herbert Grimwood (Dr. Ulrich Metz), Daisy Robinson
(Bobbie DeVere), Kathleen Clifford (Lucette Bancroft), Bull Montana
(The Nightmare), Babe London (Switchboard Operator), Victor Flem-
ing, William C. McGann, Harry Thorpe (Themselves--Main Title
Sequence). December 21, 1919.   Released December 29, 1919.   New
York Premiere: December 28, 1919 at the Rivoli Theatre.

THE MOLLYCODDLE (1920).   Douglas Fairbanks Pictures Corp. /
United Artists.   Produced by Douglas Fairbanks.   Story by Harold
McGrath.   Scenario Editor (Screenplay): Tom J. Geraghty (and un-
credited, Douglas Fairbanks).   Photography: Harry Thorpe and
William C. McGann.   Assistant Director: Theodore Reed.   Art
Direction: Edward M. Langley.   Technical Effects: Robert Fair-
banks.   Publicity Director: Bennie F. Zeidman.   6 reels.

The Cast: Douglas Fairbanks (Richard Marshall III, Richard Marshall IV, Richard Marshall V), Wallace Beery (Henry Van Holkar), Morris Hughes (Patrick O'Flannigan), George Stewart (Ole Olsen), Paul Burns (Samuel Levinski), Ruth Renick (Virginia Hale), Adele Farrington (Mrs. Warren), Betty Bouton (Molly Warren), Albert MacQuarrie (Driver of the Desert Yacht), Charles Stevens (Yellow Horse, A Bad Indian), Lewis Hippe (First Mate), Victor Fleming (Sailor). June 15, 1920. Released June 14, 1920. New York Premiere: June 13, 1920 at the Strand Theatre.

MAMA'S AFFAIR (1921). Constance Talmadge Film Co. /Associated First National Pictures. Produced by Joseph M. Schenck. Screenplay by John Emerson and Anita Loos. Photography: Oliver T. Marsh. 6 reels. Based on the play, Mamma's Affair by Rachel Barton Butler.
The Cast: Constance Talmadge (Eve), Effie Shannon (Mrs. Orrin), Katherine Kaelred (Mrs. Marchant), George LeGuere (Henry Marchant), Kenneth Harlan (Dr. Harmon), Gertrude LeBrandt (Bundy). February 23, 1921. Released January 1921.

WOMAN'S PLACE (1921). Joseph M. Schenck Productions /Associated First National Pictures. Presented by Joseph M. Schenck. Screenplay: John Emerson and Anita Loos. Photography: Oliver T. Marsh and J. Roy Hunt. 6 reels.
The Cast: Constance Talmadge (Josephine Gerson), Kenneth Harlan (Jim Bradley), Hassard Short (Freddy Bleeker), Florence Short (Amy Bleeker), Ina Rorke (Mrs. Margaret Belknap), Marguerite Linden (Miss Jane Wilson), Jack Connolly (Dan Dowd). October 6, 1921. Released October 17, 1921.
Honorable Mention, New York Times Best Films of the Year.

THE LANE THAT HAD NO TURNING (1922). Paramount /Famous Players-Lasky. Presented by Adolph Zukor. Screenplay: Eugene Mullin. Adaptation by Gilbert Parker, from his short novel in The Lane That Had No Turning and Other Tales Concerning the People of Pontiac. Photography: Gilbert Warrenton. 5 reels.
The Cast: Agnes Ayres (Madelinette), Theodore Kosloff (Louis Racine), Mahlon Hamilton (George Fournel), Wilton Taylor (Joe Lajeunesse), Frank Campeau (Tardiff), Lillian Leighton (Marie), Charles West (Havel), Robert Bolder (Monsieur Poire), Fred Vroom (Governor General). January 17, 1921. Released January 15, 1922.

RED HOT ROMANCE (1922). John Emerson and Anita Loos Productions /Associated First National Pictures. Original Screenplay: John Emerson and Anita Loos. Photography: Ernest Palmer and Oliver T. Marsh. 6 reels.
The Cast: Basil Sydney (Rowland Stone), Henry Warwick (Lord Howe-Greene), Frank Lalor (King Caramba XIII), Carl Stockdale (General deCastanet), Olive Valerie (Madame Puloff de Plotz), Edward Connelly (Colonel Cassius Byrd), Mae Collins (Anna Mae Byrd), Roy Atwell (Jim Conwell), Tom Wilson (Thomas Snow), Lillian Leighton (Mammy), Snitz Edwards (Signor Frijole). February

8, 1922. Released February 13, 1922. New York Premiere: January 22, 1922 at the Criterion Theatre.

ANNA ASCENDS (1922). Paramount/Famous-Players Lasky. Presented by Adolph Zukor. Screenplay: Margaret Trumbull. Based on the play by Harry Chapman Ford. Photography: Gilbert Warrenton. 6 reels.

The Cast: Alice Brady (Anna Ayyob), Robert Ellis (Howard Fisk), David Powell (The Baron), Nita Naldi (Countess Rostoff), Charles Gerrard (Count Rostoff), Edward Durand (Siad Coury), Florence Dixon (Bessie Fisk), Grace Griswold (Miss Fisk), Frederick Burton (Mr. Fisk). November 20, 1922. Released November 19, 1922.

DARK SECRETS (1923). Paramount/Famous-Players Lasky. Presented by Adolph Zukor. Original Screenplay: Edmund Goulding. Photography: Harold Rosson. 6 reels.

The Cast: Dorothy Dalton (Ruth Rutherford), Robert Ellis (Lord Wallington), Jose Ruben (Dr. Mohammed Ali), Ellen Cassidy (Mildred Rice), Pat Hartigan (Biskra), Warren Cook (Dr. Case), Julia Swayne Gordon (Mrs. Rutherford). January 17, 1923. Released February 5, 1923. New York Premiere: January 21, 1923 at the Rialto.

THE LAW OF THE LAWLESS (1923). Paramount/Famous Players-Lasky. Presented by Jesse L. Lasky. Screenplay: E. Lloyd Sheldon and Edfrid Bingham. Based on the story in Ghitza, and Other Romances of Gypsy Blood by Konrad Bercovici. 67 minutes.

The Cast: Dorothy Dalton (Sahande), Theodore Kosloff (Sender), Charles DeRoche (Costa), Tully Marshall (Ali Mechmet), Fred Huntley (Osman), Margaret Loomis (Fanutza). May 30, 1923. Released July 22, 1923. New York Premiere: June 18, 1923 at the Rivoli Theatre.

TO THE LAST MAN (1923). Paramount/Famous Players-Lasky. Presented by Jesse L. Lasky. Screenplay: Doris Schroeder. Based on the novel by Zane Grey. Photography: James Wong Howe and Bert Baldridge. Assistant Director: Henry Hathaway. 75 minutes.

The Cast: Richard Dix (Jean Isbel), Lois Wilson (Ellen Jorth), Noah Beery (Colter), Robert Edeson (Gaston Isbel), Frank Campeau (Blue), Fred Huntley (Lee Jorth), Edwin Brady (Daggs), Eugene Pallette (Simm Bruce), Leonard Clapham, later Tom London (Guy), Guy Oliver (Bill), Winifred Greenwood (Mrs. Guy). August 29, 1923. Released September 23, 1923. New York Premiere: August 27, 1923 at the Rialto Theatre.

Remade in 1933 by Paramount, directed by Henry Hathaway, with Randolph Scott, Buster Crabbe, Esther Ralston, Jack LaRue, Noah Beery, Barton MacLane, Muriel Kirkland, Fuzzy Knight, Egon Brecher, Shirley Temple.

THE CALL OF THE CANYON (1923). Paramount/Famous Players-Lasky. Presented by Jesse L. Lasky. Screenplay: Doris Schroeder and Edfrid Bingham. Based on the novel by Zane Grey.

Photography: James Wong Howe.   Assistant Director: Henry Hatha-
way.   75 minutes.
        The Cast: Richard Dix (Glenn Kilbourne), Lois Wilson (Car-
ley Burch), Marjorie Daw (Flo Hutter), Noah Beery (Haze Ruff),
Ricardo Cortez (Larry Morrison), Fred Huntley (Tom Hutter), Lillian
Leighton (Mrs. Hutter), Helen Dunbar (Aunt Mary), Leonard Clapham,
later Tom London (Lee Stanton), Edward Clayton (Tenney Jones),
Dorothy Seastrom (Eleanor Harmon), Laura Anson (Beatrice Lovell),
Charles Richards (Roger Newton), Ralph Yearsley (Charlie Oatmeal),
Arthur Rankin (Virgil Rust), Mervyn LeRoy (Jack Rawlins).   Decem-
ber 25, 1923.   Released December 16, 1923.   New York Premiere:
December 16, 1923 at the Rivoli Theatre.

CODE OF THE SEA (1924).   Paramount/Famous Players-Lasky.
Presented by Adolph Zukor and Jesse L. Lasky.   Screenplay: Bert-
ram Millhauser.   Story: Byron Morgan.   Photography: Charles Ed-
gar Schoenbaum.   61 minutes.
        The Cast: Rod LaRocque (Bruce McDow), Jacqueline Logan
(Jenny Hayden), George Fawcett (Captain Hayden), Maurice B. Flynn
(Ewart Radcliff), Luke Cosgrave (Captain Jonas), Lillian Leighton
(Mrs. McDow), Sam Appel (John Swayne).   June 4, 1924.   Released
June 2, 1924.   New York Premiere: May 25, 1924 at the Rivoli
Theatre.

EMPTY HANDS (1924).   Paramount/Famous Players-Lasky.   Pre-
sented by Adolph Zukor and Jesse L. Lasky.   Screenplay: Carey
Wilson.   Based on the novel by Arthur Stringer.   Photography:
Charles Edgar Schoenbaum.   80 minutes.
        The Cast: Jack Holt (Grimshaw), Norma Shearer (Claire
Endicott), Charles Clary (Robert Endicott), Hazel Keener (Mrs.
Endicott), Gertrude Olmstead (Gypsy), Ramsey Wallace (Montie),
Ward Crame (Milt Bisnet), Charles Stevens (Indian Guide), Hank
Mann (Spring Water Man), Charles Green (Butler).   August 26, 1924.
Released October 13, 1924.   New York Premiere: August 17, 1924
at the Rivoli Theatre.

THE DEVIL'S CARGO (1925).   Paramount/Famous Players-Lasky.
Presented by Adolph Zukor and Jesse L. Lasky.   Screenplay: A.P.
Younger.   Story: Charles E. Whittaker.   Photography: Charles
Edgar Schoenbaum.   75 minutes.
        The Cast: Wallace Beery (Ben), Pauline Starke (Faro Samp-
son), Claire Adams (Martha Joyce), William Collier, Jr. (John
Joyce), Raymond Hatton (Mate), George Cooper (Jerry Dugan), Dale
Fuller (Millie), Spec O'Donnell (Jimmy), Emmett C. King (Square
Deal Sampson), John Webb Dillon (Farwell), Louis King (Briggs).
January 27, 1925.   Released February 2, 1925.   New York Pre-
miere: February 2, 1925 at the Rivoli Theatre.

ADVENTURE (1925).   Paramount/Famous Players-Lasky.   Presented by Adolph Zukor and Jesse L. Lasky.   Screenplay: A.P.
Younger and L.G. Rigby.   Based on the novel by Jack London.   Photography: Charles Edgar Schoenbaum.   78 minutes.
        The Cast: Tom Moore (David Sheldon), Pauline Starke (Joan

Lackland), Wallace Beery (Morgan), Raymond Hatton (Raff), Walter
McGrail (Tudor), Duke Kahanamoku (Noah Noa), James Spencer
(Adam), Noble Johnson (Googomy).   April 28, 1925.   Released
April 27, 1925.   New York Premiere: April 14, 1925 at the Ri-
alto Theatre.

A SON OF HIS FATHER (1925).   Paramount/Famous Players-Lasky.
Presented by Adolph Zukor and Jesse L. Lasky.   Screenplay: Anthony Coldeway.   Based on the novel by Harold Bell Wright.   Photography: Charles Edgar Schoenbaum.   75 minutes.
        The Cast: Bessie Love (Nora), Warner Baxter ("Big Boy"
Morgan), Raymond Hatton (Charlie Grey), Walter McGrail (Holdbrook),
Carl Stockdale (Zobester), Billy Eugene (Larry), James Farley (Indian Pete), Charles Stevens (Pablo), Valentina Zimina (Dolores),
George Kuwa (Wing), Nelson McDowell (Ranch Hand).   October 15,
1925.   Released September 21, 1925.   New York Premiere: September 28, 1925 at the Rialto Theatre.

LORD JIM (1925).   Paramount/Famous Players-Lasky.   Presented
by Adolph Zukor and Jesse L. Lasky.   Screenplay: George C. Hull.
Adaptation: John Russell, based on the novel by Joseph Conrad.
Photography: Faxon Dean.   Technical Adviser: Captain H. J. Jacob-
son.   67 minutes.
        The Cast: Percy Marmont (Lord Jim), Shirley Mason (Jewel),
Noah Beery (Captain Brown), Raymond Hatton (Cornelius), Joseph
Dowling (Stein), George Magril (Dain Waris), Nick DeRuiz (Sultan),
J. Gunnis Davis (Scoggins), Jules Cowles (Yankee Joe), Duke Ka-
hanamoku (Tamb Itam).   December 14, 1925.   Released December
14, 1925.   New York Premiere: November 15, 1925 at the Rialto
Theatre.
        Remade in 1965 by Columbia Pictures, directed by Richard
Brooks, with Peter O'Toole, Eli Wallach, James Mason, Daliah
Lavi, Curt Jurgens.

THE BLIND GODDESS (1926).   Paramount/Famous Players-Lasky.
Presented by Adolph Zukor and Jesse L. Lasky.   Screenplay: Ger-
trude Orr.   Adaptation: Hope Loring and Louis Duryea Lighton,
based on the novel by Arthur Chesney Train.   Photography: Alfred
Gilks.   77 minutes.
        The Cast: Jack Holt (Hugh Dillon), Ernest Torrence (Big
Bill Devens), Esther Ralston (Moira Devens), Louise Dresser (Mrs.
Eileen Clayton), Ward Crane (Tracy Redmond), Richard Tucker (Henry Kelling), Louis Payne (Taylor), Charles Clary (District Attorney),
Erwin Connelly (Chief of Detectives), Charles Lane (Judge).   April
12, 1926.   Released: April 12, 1926.   New York Premiere: April
4, 1926.

MANTRAP (1926).   Paramount/Famous Players-Lasky.   Presented
by Adolph Zukor and Jesse L. Lasky.   Associate Producers: B. P.
Schulberg and Hector Turnbull.   Screenplay: Adelaide Heilbron and
Ethel Doherty.   Based on the novel by Sinclair Lewis.   Titles:
George Marion, Jr.   Photography: James Wong Howe.   Assistant
Director: Henry Hathaway.   68 minutes.

The Cast: Clara Bow (Alverna Easter), Ernest Torrence (Joe Easter), Percy Marmont (Ralph Prescott), Eugene Pallette (E. Wesson Woodbury), Tom Kennedy (Curly Evans), Josephine Crowell (Mrs. McGavity), William Orlamond (Angus McGavity), Charles Stevens (Lawrence Jackfish, Indian Guide), Miss DuPont (Mrs. Barker), Charlot Bird (Stenographer), Rolfe Sedan (Barber), Chief John Big Tree (Joe's Guide), Edwin Brady and Kalla Pasha (Party Guests), Lon Poff (Tall Man). August 30, 1926. Released July 24, 1926. New York Premiere: July 10, 1926 at the Rivoli Theatre.

THE ROUGH RIDERS (1927). Paramount/Famous Players-Lasky. Presented by Adolph Zukor and Jesse L. Lasky. Associate Producer: B. P. Schulberg. Screenplay: Robert N. Lee and Keene Thompson. Adaptation by John Fish Goodrich. Original Story and Technical Adviser: Hermann Hagedorn. Titles: George Marion, Jr. Photography: James Wong Howe. Special Music Score: Hugo Reisenfeld. Assistant Director: Henry Hathaway. 100 minutes.
    The Cast: Noah Beery (Hells' Bells), Charles Farrell (Stewart Van Brunt), George Bancroft (Happy Joe), Charles Emmett Mack (Bert Henley), Mary Astor (Dolly), Frank Hooper (Colonel Theodore Roosevelt), Colonel Fred Lindsay (Leonard Wood), Fred Kohler (Sergeant Stanton). October 1, 1927. Released October 1, 1927. New York Premiere: March 15, 1927 at the George M. Cohan Theatre.

THE WAY OF ALL FLESH (1927). Paramount/Famous Players-Lasky. Presented by Adolph Zukor and Jesse L. Lasky. Screenplay: Jules Furthman. Adaptation by Lajos Biro. From a story by Perley Poore Sheehan. Titles: Julian Johnson. Photography: Victor Milner. Assistant Director: Henry Hathaway. 90 minutes.
    The Cast: Emil Jannings (August Schiller), Belle Bennett (Mrs. Schiller), Phyllis Haver (Mayme), Donald Keith (August Schiller, Jr.), Fred Kohler (The Tough), Philippe De Lacey (August as a child), Mickey McBan (Evald), Betsy Ann Lisle (Charlotte), Carmencita Johnson (Elizabeth), Gordon Thorpe (Karl), Jackie Coombs (Heinrich), Dean Harrell, Anne Sheridan, Dorothy Kitchen. October 1, 1927. Released October 1, 1927. New York Premiere: June 25, 1927 at the Rialto Theatre.
    Won Academy Award for Best Actor (Emil Jannings). Nominated for Best Picture.
    Remade by Paramount in 1940, directed by Louis King, with Akim Tamiroff and Gladys George.

HULA (1927). Paramount/Famous Players-Lasky. Presented by Adolph Zukor and Jesse L. Lasky. Associate Producer: B. P. Schulberg. Screenplay: Ethel Doherty, Adaptation by Doris Anderson, based on the novel Hula, a Romance of Hawaii by Armine Von Tempski. Titles: George Marion, Jr. Photography: William Marshall. Editor: Eda Warren. Assistant Director: Henry Hathaway. 60 minutes.
    The Cast: Clara Bow ("Hula" Calhoun), Clive Brook (Anthony Haldane), Arlette Marchal (Mrs. Bane), Arnold Kent (Harry Dehan) Maude Truax (Margaret Haldane), Albert Gran (Old Bill Calhoun),

Agostino Borgato (Uncle Edwin).   August 27, 1927.   Released August
27, 1927.   New York Premiere: August 25, 1927 at the Paramount Theatre.

ABIE'S IRISH ROSE (1928).   Paramount/Famous Players-Lasky.
Presented by Adolph Zukor and Jesse L. Lasky.   Associate Producer: B. P. Schulberg.   Screenplay: Jules Furthman.   Based on the
play by Anne Nichols.   Titles: Herman J. Mankiewicz, Julian John-
son, Anne Nichols.   Photography: Harold Rosson.   Editor: Eda
Warren.   Musical Score: J. S. Zamecnik.   Songs, "Rosemary,"
"Little Irish Rose" by J. S. Zamecnik.   120 minutes.
      The Cast: Charles "Buddy" Rogers (Abie Levy), Nancy Car-
roll (Rosemary Murphy), Jean Hersholt (Solomon Levy), J. Farrell
MacDonald (Patrick Murphy), Bernard Gorcey (Isaac Cohen), Ida
Dramer (Mrs. Isaac Cohen), Nick Cogley (Father Whalen), Camillus
Pretal (Rabbi Jacob Samuels), Rosa Rosanova (Sarah).   January 8,
1929.   Released January 5, 1929.   New York Premiere: April 19,
1928 at the Forty-fourth Street Theatre.
      Remade in 1946 by United Artists, directed by Edward Suth-
erland, with Joanne Dru, Richard Norris, Michael Chekhov, Eric
Blore, Art Baker, J. M. Kerrigan.

THE AWAKENING (1928).   Samuel Goldwyn/United Artists.   A Vic-
tor Fleming Production.   Produced by Samuel Goldwyn.   Screenplay:
Carey Wilson.   From an original story by Frances Marion.   Titles:
Katherine Hilliker and H. H. Caldwell.   Photography: George Barnes.
Assistant Camera: Gregg Toland.   Editor: Viola Lawrence.   Art
Director: William Cameron Menzies.   Musical Score: Hugo Risen-
fled.   Song, "Marie" by Irving Berlin.   Technical Adviser: Eric
von Brincken.   105 minutes.
      The Cast: Vilma Banky (Marie Ducrot), Walter Byron (Count
Karl von Hagen), Louis Wolheim (Le Bête), George Davis (The Orderly), William H. Orlamond (Grandfather Ducrot), Carl von Hart-
mann (Lieutenant Franz Geyer), Yola D'Avril (Cabaret Girl), General
Wiatsheslav Savitsky (Top Sergeant), Ferdinand Schuman-Heink (Officer of Uhlans), Owen Corin, Paul Vasel (Soldiers).   December 5,
1928.   Released November 17, 1928.   New York Premiere: December 30, 1928 at the Rivoli.

WOLF SONG (1929).   Paramount/Famous Players-Lasky.   Presented
by Adolph Zukor and Jesse L. Lasky.   Produced and Directed by
Victor Fleming.   Associate Producer: B. P. Fineman.   Screenplay:
John Farrow and Keene Thompson.   Based on the novel by Harvey
Fergusson.   Titles: Julian Johnson.   Photography: Allen Siegler.
Editor: Eda Warren.   Musical Director: Irvin Talbot.   Supervising
Musical Recorder: Max Terr.   Songs, "Mi Amado," "Yo Te Amo
Means I Love You" by Richard Whiting (music) and Alfred Bryan
(lyrics).   Assistant Director: Henry Hathaway.   75 minutes.
      The Cast: Gary Cooper (Sam Lash), Lupe Velez (Lola Sala-
zar), Louis Wolheim (Gullion), Constantine Romanoff (Rube Thatcher),
Michael Vavitch (Don Solomon Salazar), Ann Brody (Duenna), Russell "Russ" Columbo (Ambrosia Guiterrez), Augustina Lopez (Loui-
sa), George Regas (Black Wolf), Leone Lane (Dance Hall Girl).

March 29, 1929. Released March 30, 1929. New York Premiere: February 24, 1929 at the Embassy Theatre.

THE VIRGINIAN (1929). Paramount/Famous Players-Lasky. Presented by Adolph Zukor and Jesse L. Lasky. Produced by Louis D. Lighton. Screenplay: Howard Estabrook. Adaptation by Grover Jones and Keene Thompson. Dialogue: Edward E. Paramore. Based on the novel by Owen Wister, and the play by Wister and Kirk LaShelle. Photography: J. Roy Hunt and Edward Cronjager. Assistant Cameraman: Harold E. Wellman. Editor: William Shea. Titles: Joseph L. Mankiewicz. Assistant Director: Henry Hathaway. Recording Engineer: M. M. Paggi. Gary Cooper's Dialogue Coach: Randolph Scott. 90 minutes.
      The Cast: Gary Cooper (The Virginian), Walter Huston (Trampas), Mary Brian (Molly Stark Wood), Richard Arlen (Steve), Helen Ware ("Ma" Taylor), Chester Conklin (Uncle Hughey), Eugene Pallette ("Honey" Wiggin), Victor Potel (Nebraskey), E. H. Calvert (Judge Henry), Tex Young (Shorty), Charles Stevens (Pedro), Jack Pennick (Slim), George Chandler (Ranch Hand), Willie Fung (Hong, the Cook), George Morrell (Reverend Doctor McBride), Ernie S. Adams (Saloon Singer), Ethan Laidlaw (Posse Man), Ed Brady (Greasy), Bob Kortman (Henchman), James Mason (Jim), Fred Burns (Ranch Hand), Nena Quartero (Girl in Bar). November 8, 1929. Released November 9, 1929. New York Premiere: December 22, 1929 at the Rialto Theatre, Re-released in 1935.
      Previously filmed in 1914 by the Lasky Company, directed by Cecil B. DeMille, with Dustin Farnum, Winifred Kingston, Redwing, Dick LaStrange, Foster Knox, Monroe Salisbury, Fred Montague; also in 1923 by B. P. Schulberg Productions/Preferred Pictures, directed by Tom Forman, with Kenneth Harlan, Florence Vidor, Russell Simpson, Pat O'Malley, Raymond Hatton, Milton Ross, Sam Allen; remade in 1946 by Paramount, directed by Stuart Gilmore, with Joel McCrea, Brian Donlevy, Sonny Tufts, Barbara Britton, Fay Bainter, William Frawley, Henry O'Neill, Vince Barnett, NBC Television series from 1962 to 1966, with James Drury, Lee J. Cobb, Doug McClure.

COMMON CLAY (1930). Fox Film Corporation. Presented by William Fox. Directed by Victor Fleming. Screenplay: Jules Furthman. Based on the play by Cleves Kincaid. Photography: Glen MacWilliams. Editor: Irene Morra. Art Director: William Darling. Assistant Director: William Tummel. Sound: B. J. Kroger and Eugene Grossman. Costumes by Sophie Wachner. 68 minutes.
      The Cast: Constance Bennett (Ellen Neal), Lew Ayres (Hugh Fullerton), Tully Marshall (W. H. Yates), Matty Kemp (Bud Coakley), Beryl Mercer (Mrs. Neal), Hale Hamilton (Judge Samuel Filson), Purnell B. Pratt (Richard Fullerton), Ada Williams (Anne Fullerton), Charles McNaughton (Edwards), Genevieve Blinn (Mrs. Fullerton). June 14, 1930. Released August 13, 1930. New York Premiere: August 1, 1930 at the Roxy Theatre.
      Previously filmed in 1919 by Pathé, directed by George Fitzmaurice, with Fannie Ward, Mary Alden, E. W. Lawrence.

RENEGADES (1930). Fox Film Corporation. Presented by William
Fox. Screenplay: Jules Furthman. Based on the novel Le Rénégat
by Andre Armandy. Photography: L. William O'Connell. Editor:
Harold Schuster. Art Director: William Darling. Assistant Direc-
tor: William Tummel. Sound: Arthur L. von Kirbach. Costumes:
Sophie Wachner. Technical Adviser: Louis Van Den Ecker. Song,
"I Got What I Wanted" by Cliff Friend and Jimmy Monaco. 84 min-
utes.
    The Cast: Warner Baxter (Deucalion), Myrna Loy (Eleanore),
Noah Beery (Machwurth), Gregory Gaye (Vologuine), George Cooper
(Biloxi), C. Henry Gordon (Captain Mordiconi), Colin Chase (Ser-
geant-Major Olson), Bela Lugosi (The Marabout), Victor Jory (Young
Officer), Noah Beery, Jr., Fred Kohler, Jr. (Young Legionnaires).
October 3, 1930. Released October 26, 1930. New York Premiere:
November 7, 1930 at the Roxy Theatre.

AROUND THE WORLD WITH DOUGLAS FAIRBANKS (1931). The El-
ton Corporation/United Artists. Produced by Douglas Fairbanks.
Written by Douglas Fairbanks and Robert E. Sherwood. Photography:
Henry Sharp. Production Manager/Sound: Chuck Lewis. Animated
Sequence by Walt Disney. Alternate Title: AROUND THE WORLD IN
EIGHTY MINUTES. 80 minutes.
    The Cast: Douglas Fairbanks, Victor Fleming, Henry Sharp,
Chuck Lewis, Sessue Hayakawa, Sojin, Duke Kahanamoku, Dr. Mei
Lan Fang, King Prajadhipok of Siam, General Emilio Aguinaldo,
Maharanee of Cooch-Behar, Mickey Mouse (Themselves). November
18, 1931. Released December 12, 1931. New York Premiere: No-
vember 19, 1931 at the Rivoli Theatre.

THE WET PARADE (1932). Metro-Goldwyn-Mayer. A Victor Flem-
ing Production. Produced by Hunt Stromberg. Screenplay: John
Lee Mahin. Based on the novel by Upton Sinclair. Photography:
George Barnes. Editor: Anne V. Bauchens. Musical Score: Dr.
William Axt. Orchestra under the direction of Oscar Radin. Art
Director: Cedric Gibbons. Recording Engineer: Douglas Shearer.
122 minutes.
    The Cast: THE PARADE (In the South)--Dorothy Jordan
(Maggie May), Lewis Stone (Colonel Roger Chilcote), Neil Hamilton
(Roger Chilcote, Jr.), Emma Dunn (Mrs. Chilcote), Frederick Bur-
ton (Judge Brandon), Reginald Barlow (Major Randolph), John Larkin
(Moses), Gertrude Howard (Angeline). THE PARADE (In the North)
--Robert Young (Kip Tarleton), Walter Huston (Pow Tarleton), Jim-
my Durante (Abe Schilling), Wallace Ford (Jerry Tyler), Myrna Loy
(Eileen Pinchon), Joan Marsh (Evelyn Fessenden), John Miljan (Ma-
jor Doleshal), Clarence Muse (Taylor Tibbs), Clara Blandick (Mrs.
Tarleton), Forrester Harvey (Mr. Fortesque), John Beck (Mr. Gar-
rison), Ben Alexander (Dick), Cecil Cunningham (Mrs. Twombey).
September 22, 1932, Released April 16, 1932. New York Premiere:
April 21, 1932 at the Rialto Theatre.

RED DUST (1932). Metro-Goldwyn-Mayer. A Victor Fleming Production. Produced by Hunt Stromberg. Screenplay: John Lee
Mahin (and uncredited, Donald Ogden Stewart and Howard Hawks).

Based on the play by Wilson Collison. Photography: Harold Rosson.
Editor: Blanche Sewell. Art Director: Cedric Gibbons. Recording
Engineer: Douglas Shearer. Costumes by Adrian. 84 minutes.
     The Cast: Clark Gable (Dennis Carson), Jean Harlow (Van-
tine), Gene Raymond (Gary Willis), Mary Astor (Barbara Willis),
Donald Crisp (Guidon), Tully Marshall (McQuarg), Forrester Harvey
(Limey), Willie Fung (Hoy). November 7, 1932. Released October
22, 1932. New York Premiere: November 4, 1932 at the Capital
Theatre.
     Remade as MOGAMBO in 1953 by M-G-M, directed by John
Ford, with Clark Gable, Ava Gardner, Grace Kelly, Donald Sinden,
Phillip Stainton. Also the basis for CONGO MAISIE (1940, M-G-M),
directed by H. C. Potter, with Ann Sothern, John Carroll, and Rita
Johnson.

THE WHITE SISTER (1933). Metro-Goldwyn-Mayer. A Victor Flem-
ing Production. Produced by Hunt Stromberg. Screenplay: Donald
Ogden Stewart and Walter Hackett. Based on the novel by F. Marion
Crawford. Photography: William Daniels. Editor: Margaret Booth.
Art Director: Cedric Gibbons. Musical Score: Herbert Stothart.
Recording Engineer: Douglas Shearer.
     The Cast: Helen Hayes (Angela Chiaromonte), Clark Gable
(Lieutenant Giovanni Severi), Lewis Stone (Prince Guido Chiaromonte),
Louise Closser Hale (Mina), May Robson (Mother Superior), Edward
Arnold (Monsignor Saracinesca), Alan Edwards (Ernesto Severi), Don-
ald Ogden Stewart (Rear end of a Horse), Gino Corrado (Chauffeur),
Nat Pendleton (Corporal), Frank Puglia (Soldier), Agostino Borgato
(Citizen). March 23, 1933. Released April 14, 1933. New York
Premiere: March 17, 1933 at the Astor Theatre.
     Previously filmed in 1923 by Inspiration Pictures/United Art-
ists, directed by Henry King, with Lillian Gish, Ronald Colman, Gail
Kane, J. Barney Sherry, and Charles Lane; also in 1915 by Essanay,
with Viola Allen and Richard Travers.

BOMBSHELL (1933). Metro-Goldwyn-Mayer. A Victor Fleming
Production. Associate Producer: Hunt Stromberg. Screenplay:
Jules Furthman and John Lee Mahin. Based on the play by Caroline
Francke and Mack Crane. Photography: Harold Rosson and Chester
Lyons. Editor: Margaret Booth. Art Director: Merrill Pye. In-
terior Decorations: Edwin B. Willis. Recording Engineer: Douglas
Shearer. Gowns by Adrian. Assistant Director: Cullen Tate. Re-
titled BLONDE BOMBSHELL. 98 minutes.
     The Cast: Jean Harlow (Lola Burns), Lee Tracy (E. J.
"Space" Hanlon), Frank Morgan (Pop Burns), Franchot Tone (Gifford
Middleton), Pat O'Brien (Jim Brogan), Una Merkel (Miss Mac), Ted
Healy (Junior Burns), Ivan Lebedeff (Marquis Hugo di Binelli di
Pisa), Isabel Jewell (Junior's Girl), Louise Beavers (Loretta),
Leonard Carey (Winters), Mary Forbes (Mrs. Middleton), C. Aubrey
Smith (Mr. Middleton), June Brewster (Alice Cole), William Newell
(Delivery Man), Donald Kerr (Marty, makeup man), James Burke,
Edward Gargan (immigration officers), Ed Brady (Reporter), Mor-
gan Wallace (A. G. Gillette), Dennis O'Keefe (Dance Extra), Ethel
Griffies, Mary Carr (Orphanage Representatives), Gus Arnheim and

his Orchestra (Themselves). October 11, 1933. Released October
13, 1933. New York Premiere: October 20, 1933 at the Capitol
and Loew's Metropolitan.
    Includes a shot from HOLD THAT MAN (1933, M-G-M), di-
rected by Sam Wood, with Clark Gable and Jean Harlow.

TREASURE ISLAND (1934), Metro-Goldwyn-Mayer. Produced by
Hunt Stromberg. Screenplay: John Lee Mahin. Adaptation: Leonard Praskins and John Howard Lawson. Based on the novel by Robert Louis Stevenson. Photography: Ray June, Clyde DeVinna, and
Harold Rosson, Musical Score: Herbert Stothart. Editor: Blanche
Sewell. Art Director: Cedric Gibbons; associates: Merrill Pye
and Edwin B. Willis. Recording Director: Douglas Shearer. Cos-
tume Design and Technical Adviser: Dwight Franklin. Unit Manager:
Ulrick Bush. Properties: Harry Edwards. Firearms: Jack Leg-
gett. 102 minutes.
    The Cast: Wallace Beery (Long John Silver), Jackie Cooper
(Jim Hawkins), Lionel Barrymore (Billy Bones), Otto Kruger (Dr.
Livesey), Lewis Stone (Captain Alexander Smollett), Nigel Bruce
(Squire Trelawney), Charles "Chic" Sale (Ben Gunn), William V.
Mong (Pew), Charles McNaughton (Black Dog), Dorothy Peterson
(Mrs. Hawkins), Douglass Dumbrille ("Ugly Israel" Hands), Edmund
Breese (Anderson), Olin Howland (Dick), Charles Irwin (Abraham
Gray), Edward Pawley (O'Brien), Richard Powell (William Post),
James Burke (George Merry), John Anderson (Harry Sykes), Charles
Bennett (Dandy Dawson), J.M. Kerrigan (Tom Morgan), Westcott
Clark (Allan), Yorke Sherwood (Mr. Arrow), Harry Cording (Henry),
Tom Mahoney (Redruth), Sidney D'Albrook (Joyce), Frank Dunn (Hun-
ter), Robert Adair (Tom, seaman), Cora Sue Collins (Child at Inn),
Harold Entwistle (Ship's chandler), Harold Wilson (Oldster), Bernice
Beatty (Woman at Inn), Vernon Downing (Boy at Inn), Bobby Bolder
(Mild Man at Inn), Edith Kingdon (Wife at Inn), Wilson Benge (Friend
at Inn), Shirlee Simpson (Woman Friend at Inn), Matt Gillman, Bob
Anderson, A.B. Lane, John Kerr, Tom Wilson, James Mason, Ed-
win J. Brady, Frank Hagney, Bill Dooley, Bob Stevenson, Red Burg-
er, Jack Hill, King Mojave (Pirates), Kay Deslys, Jane Tallent,
Ethel Ransome, Jill Bennett (Streetwalkers). August 7, 1934. Released August 17, 1934. New York Premiere: August 17, 1934 at
the Capitol and Loew's Metropolitan.
    Previously filmed in 1917 by Fox, directed by Chester and
Sidney Franklin; in 1920 by Paramount, directed by Maurice Tourneur, with Shirley Mason and Lon Chaney. Remade in 1950 by Walt
Disney/RKO, directed by Byron Haskin, with Robert Newton and
Bobby Driscoll; in 1972, directed by John Hough, with Orson Welles
and Walter Slezak.

RECKLESS (1935). Metro-Goldwyn-Mayer. Produced by David O.
Selznick. Screenplay: P.J. Wolfson (and uncredited, Arthur Sheek-
man). From a story, "A Woman Called Cheap," by Oliver Jeffries
(pseudonym for David O. Selznick, and uncredited, Victor Fleming).
Photography: George Folsey, Editor: Margaret Booth. Art Director: Cedric Gibbons; associates: Merrill Pye and Edwin B. Willis.
Recording Director: Douglas Shearer. Gowns by Adrian. Makeup:

Jack Dawn. Dances staged by Carl Randall and Chester Hale. Orchestra conducted by Victor Baravalle. Songs, "Reckless," music
by Jerome Kern, lyrics by Oscar Hammerstein II; "Hi-Diddle-Dee-
Dum," music by Con Conrad, lyrics by Herb Magidson; "Ev'rything's
Been Done Before," music and lyrics by Harold Adamson, Edwin H.
Knopf, and Jack King; "Hear What My Heart Is Saying" and "Troca-
dero," music and lyrics by Harold Adamson and Burton Lane; "Cy-
clone," music and lyrics by Gus Kahn and Walter Donaldson. Jean
Harlow's singing voice dubbed by Virginia Verrell. 99 minutes.
     The Cast: Jean Harlow (Mona Leslie), William Powell (Ned
Riley), Franchot Tone (Bob Harrison), May Robson (Granny), Ted
Healy (Smiley), Nat Pendleton (Blossom), Robert Light (Paul Mer-
cer), Rosalind Russell (Josephine), Henry Stephenson (Harrison),
Louise Henry (Louise), James Ellison (Dale Every), Leon Waycoff,
later Leon Ames (Ralph Watson), Man Mountain Dean (Himself),
Farina, aka Allen Hoskins (Gold Dust), Allan Jones (Allan), Carl
Randall ("Trocadero" Dance Partner), Nina Mae McKinney (Herself),
Robert Andrews (Mona's Baby), Jeanie Gunn (Little Girl Singer),
Hans Steinke, Ernie Haynes (Wrestlers), and Mickey Rooney, Dick
Elliott, Kay Sutton, Mae Madison, Rafael Storm, Wade Boteler, Don
Brodie, Sam Ash, Joe Sawyer, Henry Kolker, Hooper Atchley, Libby
Taylor, Charles R. Moore, Paul Fix, Sam Flint, Akim Tamiroff,
Lee Phelps, Jack Mulhall, Larry Steers, Charles Middleton, Theo-
dore Lorch, Edward LeSaint, Charles C. Wilson, John Davidson,
Ed Peil, Claudia Coleman, Margaret Dumont, Harold Huber, Irene
Thompson, Lorna Lowe, Donna Roberts, Marian Ladd, Edna Waldron,
Lynn Carleton, Earlene Heath, Billie Lee.   April 16, 1935.   Re-
leased April 17, 1935. New York Premiere: April 17, 1935 at the
Capitol and Loew's Metropolitan.
     Clip used in THAT'S ENTERTAINMENT (1974, M-G-M/UA).

THE FARMER TAKES A WIFE (1935).   Fox Film Corporation.   Pro-
duced by Winfield Sheehan.   Screenplay: Edwin Burke.   From Max
Gordon's production of the stage play by Frank B. Elser and Marc
Connelly, based on the novel, Rome Haul, by Walter D. Edmonds.
Photography: Ernest Palmer.   Editor: Harold Schuster.   Art Di-
rector: William Darling.   Musical Director: Oscar Bradley.
Sound: Joseph Aiken.   Costumes: Rene Hubert.   Apprentice Editor:
William H. Reynolds.   81 minutes.
     The Cast: Janet Gaynor (Molly Larkins), Henry Fonda (Dan
Harrow), Charles Bickford (Jotham Klore), Slim Summerville (For-
tune Friendly), Andy Devine (Elmer Otway), Roger Imhof (Samson
Weaver), Jane Withers (Della), Margaret Hamilton (Lucy Gurget),
Siegfried "Sig" Rumann (Blacksmith), John Qualen (Sol Tinker), Kitty
Kelly (Ivy), Robert Gleckler (Freight Agent), Dick Foran (Lansing),
Louis Mason (Barfly), Max Davidson (Seller), Mitchell Lewis (Man
in Office), Wade Boteler (Patron), James Burtis (Sailor), Chief
Thundercloud (Chief), Iron Eyes Cody (Indian), Esther Howard (Cook),
James Burke (Farmer), J.M. Kerrigan (Angus), Irving Bacon (Man
on Bridge), Stanley Blystone (Worker), DeWitt Jennings (Agent),
Frederick Burton (Butterfield), Zeffie Tilbury (Old Lady), Billy
Benedict (Boy), and Robert Warwick, Frank Melton, Lee Kohlmar,
J. Farrell MacDonald, Philip Cooper, Robert Adair, Lilyan Irene,

Bert Hanlon.   August 2, 1935.   Released August 2, 1935.   New York
Premiere: August 8, 1935 at Radio City Music Hall.
    Remade in 1953 by 20th Century-Fox, directed by Henry
Levin, with Betty Grable, Dale Robertson, John Carroll, Eddie Foy,
Jr., Thelma Ritter.

CAPTAINS COURAGEOUS (1937).   Metro-Goldwyn-Mayer.   A Victor
Fleming Production.   Produced by Louis D. Lighton.   (Uncredited
additional direction by Jack Conway.)   Screenplay: John Lee
Mahin, Marc Connelly, Dale Van Every (and uncredited, Howard
Hawks).   Based on the novel by Rudyard Kipling.   Photography:
Harold Rosson.   Musical Score: Franz Waxman.   Editor: Elmo
Vernon.   Marine Director: James C. Havens.   Art Director: Ced-
ric Gibbons; associates: Arnold Gillespie and Edwin B. Willis.   Re-
cording Director: Douglas Shearer.   Makeup: Jack Dawn.   Tech-
nical Advisers: James B. Connelly and Olaf Olsson.   Associate
Marine Director: Harry Marble.   Second Unit Photography: Harold
Marzorati and Bob Roberts.   Production Managers: Frank Barnes
and Ewing Scott.   Wardrobe Man: Bill Beattie.   Chanty Vocal Coach:
Arthur Rosenstine.   Songs, "Don't Cry Little Fish" and "Ohhh, What
a Terrible Man!" by Franz Waxman and Gus Kahn.   116 minutes.
    The Cast: Freddie Bartholomew (Harvey Cheyne), Spencer
Tracy (Manuel), Lionel Barrymore (Captain Disko Troop), Melvyn
Douglas (Mr. Cheyne), Mickey Rooney (Dan Troop), Charley Grape-
win (Uncle Salters), Christian Rub (Old Clement), Walter Kingsford
(Dr. Finley), Donald Briggs (Tyler), Sam McDaniel (Doc), Dave
Thursby (Tom), John Carradine (Long Jack), William Stack (Elliott),
Leo G. Carroll (Burns), Charles Trowbridge (Dr. Walsh), Richard
Powell (First Steward), Billy Burrud (Charles), Jay Ward (Pogey),
Kenneth Wilson (Alvin), Roger Gray (Nate Rogers), Jack LaRue
(Priest), Oscar O'Shea (Cushman), Bobby Watson (Reporter), Billy
Gilbert (Soda Steward), Norman Ainsley (Robbins), Gladden James
(Secretary Cobb), Tommy Bupp, Wally Albright (Boys), Katherine
Kenworthy (Mrs. Troop), Dave Wengren (Lars), Murray Kinnell
(Minister), Dora Early (Appleton's Wife), Gertrude Sutton (Nate's
Wife), Dennis O'Keefe, Francis X. Bushman, Jr. (Gloucester Fish-
erman), Goldie Sloan (Colored Woman), Frank Sully (Taxi Driver),
Don Brodie, David Kerman, Billy Arnold (Reporters), Lester Dorr
(Corridor Steward), Jimmy Conlin (Thin Man), Lloyd Ingraham (Skip-
per of Ship), Jack Kennedy (Captain of the Flying Swan), Monte
Vandergrift (Sailor on the Flying Swan), Charles Coleman (Butler),
Wade Boteler (Skipper of Blue Gill), Myra Marsh (Chester's Wife),
Philo McCullough, James Kilgannon, Bill Fisher, Dick Howard,
Larry Fisher, Gil Perkins, Jack Sterling, Stubby Kreuger (Members
of Crew), Art Berry, Sr., Captain Anderson, Edward Peil, Sr.
(Fisherman), Myra McKinney, Lee Van Atta, Gene Reynolds, Sherry
Hall, Jr., Henry Hanna, Betty Alden, Reggie Streeter (Bits).
April 21, 1937.   Released June 25, 1937.   New York Premiere:
May 11, 1937 at the Astor.
    Won Academy Award for Best Actor (Spencer Tracy).   Nomin-
ated for Best Picture, Best Written Screenplay, Best Editing.
    Remade in 1977 for TV, directed by Harvey Hart, with Karl
Malden, Jonathan Kahn.

TEST PILOT (1938). Metro-Goldwyn-Mayer. A Victor Fleming
Production. Produced by Louis D. Lighton. Screenplay: Vincent
Lawrence and Waldemar Young (and uncredited, Howard Hawks).
Original Story: Frank "Spig" Wead. Photography: Ray June.
Musical Score: Franz Waxman. Editor: Tom Held. Art Director:
Cedric Gibbons; associate: John Detlie. Set Decorations: Edwin B.
Willis. Montage Effects: Slavko Vorkapich. Special Effects: Ar-
nold Gillespie; associate: Donald Jahraus. Recording Director:
Douglas Shearer. Costumes: Dolly Tree. Makeup: Jack Dawn.
Aerial Photography: Paul Mantz and Ray Moore. Camera Operator:
Joseph Novak. Second Camera: Charlie Marshall. South Tech-
nician: Charles "Wally" Wallace. Location Manager: Lou Strohm.
Produced with the cooperation of the United States Army. 118 min-
utes.

The Cast: Clark Gable (Jim Lane), Myrna Loy (Ann Barton
Lane), Spencer Tracy (Gunner Sloane), Lionel Barrymore (Howard B.
Drake), Samuel S. Hinds (General Ross), Marjorie Main (Landlady),
Ted Pearson (Joe), Gloria Holden (Mrs. Benson), Louis Jean Heydt
(Benson), Virginia Grey (Sarah), Priscilla Lawson (Mabel), Claudia
Coleman (Mrs. Barton), Arthur Aylesworth (Frank Barton), Gregory
Gaye (Grant), Dudley Clements (Mr. Brown), Henry Roquemore (Fat
Man), Jack Mack, Wally Maher (Mechanics), Richard Kipling, Arthur
Stuart Hull (Floorwalkers), Charlie Sullivan, Ernie Alexander, Buddy
Messenger (Field Mechanics), Donald Kerr, Nick Copeland (Drake
Mechanics), Byron Foulger (Designer), Frank Jaquet (Motor Expert),
Roger Converse (Advertising Man), Tom Rutherford (First Photog-
rapher), James Donlan (Second Photographer), Phillip Terry (Third
Photographer), Robert Fiske, Jack Cheatham (Attendants), Alonzo
Price (Weatherman), Mitchell Ingraham (First N. A. A. Official),
Frank DuFrane (Second N. A. A. Official), Cyril Ring (Third N. A. A.
Official), Lester Dorr, Charles Waldron, Jr. , Garry Owen (Pilots),
Bobby Caldwell, Marilyn Spinner, Tommy Tucker (Benson Children),
William O'Brien (Waiter), Hudson Shotwell, Dick Winslow, Richard
Tucker, James Flavin, Forbes Murray, Don Douglas, Hooper Atch-
ley, Ray Walker (Pilots in Cafe), Martin Spellman (First Kid),
Knowlton Levenick (Second Kid), Ralph Gilliam (Third Kid), Dix
Davis (Fourth Kid), Dorothy Vaughan (Fat Woman), Billy Engle
(Little Man), Brent Sargent (Movie Leading Man), Mary Howard
(Movie Leading Woman), Gladden James (Interne), Frank Sully
(Drunk Pilot in Cafe), Douglas McPhail (Singing Pilot in Cafe),
Fay Holden (Saleslady), Tom O'Grady (Bartender), Syd Saylor (Boss
Loader), Lulumae Bohrman, Estella Ettaire (Salesladies), Ken Bar-
ton (Announcer). April 15, 1938. Released April 22, 1938. New
York Premiere: April 15, 1938 at the Capitol Theatre.

Nominated for Academy Awards for Best Picture, Best Original Story, Best Editing.

THE WIZARD OF OZ (1939). Metro-Goldwyn-Mayer. A Victor
Fleming Production. Produced by Mervyn LeRoy. Directed by
Victor Fleming (and uncredited, Richard Thorpe, George Cukor,
King Vidor). Associate Producer: Arthur Freed. Screenplay:
Noel Langley, Florence Ryerson, Edgar Allan Woolf (and uncredited,
John Lee Mahin, Samuel Hoffenstein, Herman J. Mankiewicz, Ogden

Nash, Herbert Fields, Jack Mintz, Sid Silvers). Adaptation: Noel
Langley. Based on the book, The Wonderful Wizard of Oz, by L.
Frank Baum. Color by Technicolor. Opening and Closing Sequences
in Sepia. Photography: Harold Rosson; associate: Allen Davey.
Technicolor Color Consultant: Natalie Kalmus; associate: Henri
Jaffa. Editor: Blanche Sewell. Art Direction: Cedric Gibbons
and William A. Horning. Set Decorations: Edwin B. Willis. Re-
cording Director: Douglas Shearer. Character Makeup created by
Jack Dawn. Special Effects: Arnold Gillespie. Electrical Effects:
Kenneth Strickfaden. Assistant to Mervyn LeRoy: Bill Cannon.
Musical Score: Herbert Stothart. Musical Numbers staged by Bob-
by Connolly. Associate Conductor: George Stoll. Orchestral/Vocal
Arrangements: George Bassman, Murray Cutter, Paul Marquardt,
Ken Darby. Songs by E. Y. "Yip" Harburg and Harold Arlen: "Over
the Rainbow," "Follow the Yellow Brick Road," "If I Only Had a
Brain," "We're Off to See the Wizard," "Merry Old Land of Oz,"
"If I Only Had the Nerve," "Laugh a Day Away," "If I Were King,"
"Welcome to Munchkinland," "Ding, Dong, the Witch is Dead," "If
I Only Had a Heart," "The Jitterbug" (cut). Mussorgsky's "Night on
Bald Mountain" used in musical score. 101 minutes.

The Cast: Judy Garland (Dorothy Gale), Frank Morgan (Pro-
fessor Marvel/A Guard/The Wizard), Ray Bolger (Hunk/Scarecrow),
Bert Lahr (Zeke/Cowardly Lion), Jack Haley (Hickory/Tin Woods-
man), Billie Burke (Glinda), Margaret Hamilton (Miss Gulch/The
Wicked Witch of the West), Charley Grapewin (Uncle Henry), Pat
Walshe (Nikko), Clara Blandick (Auntie Em), Toto (Toto the Dog),
The Singer Midgets (Munchkins), Jerry Marenghi, later Jerry Maren
(A Munchkin), Mitchell Lewis (Monkey Officer). August 7, 1939.
Released August 25, 1939. New York Premiere: August 17, 1939
at the Capitol Theatre.

Won Academy Award for Best Song ("Over the Rainbow") and
Best Original Score, with Special Oscar awarded to Judy Garland.
Nominated for Best Picture, Best Special Effects, Best Art Direction,
Best Interior Decoration.

Previously filmed in 1910 as THE WONDERFUL WORLD OF
OZ, DOROTHY AND THE SCARECROW, and THE LAND OF OZ
(one-reelers by the Selig Company); in 1914 as THE PATCHWORK
GIRL AND HIS MAJESTY, THE SCARECROW OF OZ; in 1925 by
Chadwick Pictures with Larry Semon and Oliver Hardy. Remade
as THE WIZ in 1978 by Universal, directed by Sidney Lumet, with
Diana Ross, Michael Jackson, Nipsey Russell, Richard Pryor, Lena
Horne.

GONE WITH THE WIND (1939). A Selznick International Picture.
Released by Loew's Incorporated. Produced by David O. Selznick.
Directed by Victor Fleming (and uncredited, George Cukor, Sam
Wood, William Cameron Menzies, Sidney Franklin). Screenplay:
Sidney Howard (and uncredited, Ben Hecht, Oliver H. P. Garrett,
Jo Swerling, Winston Miller, F. Scott Fitzgerald, John Van Druten,
John Lee Mahin, Charles MacArthur, Michael Foster, John Balder-
ston, Edwin Justus Mayer, David O. Selznick). Based on the novel
by Margaret Mitchell. Color by Technicolor. Photography: Ern-
est Haller (and uncredited, Lee Garmes). Production Designer:

William Cameron Menzies. Assistant to Menzies: J. MacMillan
Johnson. Technicolor Associates: Ray Rennahan and Wilfred M.
Cline (and uncredited, Paul Hill). Technicolor Company Super-
vision: Natalie Kalmus. Musical Score: Max Steiner. Musical
Director: Louis Forbes. Art Director: Lyle Wheeler (and un-
credited, Hobe Erwin). Interiors: Joseph B. Platt. Interior Dec-
oration: Edward G. Boyle. Costumes Designed by Walter Plunkett.
Supervising Film Editor: Hal C. Kern. Associate Film Editor:
James E. Newcom. Assistant Editors: Richard Van Enger, Ernest
Leadley, Stuart Frye, Hal Kern, Jr. Special Photographic Effects:
Jack Cosgrove (and Fred Albin, Arthur Johns). Fire Effects: Lee
Zavitz. Special Effects Photography: Clarence Slifer. Production
Manager: Raymond Klune. Associate Production Manager: Edward
W. Butcher. Scenario Assistant: Barbara Keon. Production Con-
tinuity: Lydia Schiller and Connie Earle. Second Unit Drector: B.
Reeves "Breezy" Eason (and uncredited, Chester Franklin). Assistant
Director: Eric Stacey. Second Assistant Director: Ridgeway Cal-
low. Dance Directors: Frank Floyd and Eddie Prinz. Sound Re-
corder: Frank Maher. Sound Supervisor: Thomas T. Moulton.
Makeup and Hairstyling: Monty Westmore, Hazel Rogers, Ben Nye,
Paul Stanhope. Scarlett's Hats: John Frederics. Historian: Wil-
bur G. Kurtz. Technical Advisers: Susan Myrick and Will Price.
Research: Lillian K. Deighton. Southern Location Footage: James
A. Fitzpatrick. Executive Assistant to Selznick: Marcella Rabwin.
Story Editor for Selznick International: Katherine "Kay" Brown. Key
Grip: Fred Williams. Camera Operators: Arthur Arling and Vin-
cent Farrar. Clapper Boy: Harry Wolf. Mechanical Engineer:
R. Don Musgrave. Construction Superintendent: Harold Fenton. In
Charge of Wardrobe: Edward P. "Ned" Lambert; associates: Marian
Dabney and Elmer Ellsworth. Wardrobe Woman: Helene Henley.
Casting Managers: Charles Richards and Fred Schuessler. Location
Manager: Mason Litson. Scenic Department Superintendent: Henry
J. Stahl. Electrical Superintendent: Wally Oettel. Chief Electrician:
James Potevin. Property Manager: Harold Coles. Set Property
Man: Arden Cripe. Greensman: Roy A. McLaughlin. Drapes:
James Forney. Special Props Made by Ross B. Jackman. Tara
Landscaped by Florence Yoch. Still Photographer: Fred Parrish.
Production Accountant: Ernest Scanlon, Clark Gable's Makeup:
Stanley Campbell. Gable's Wardrobe: Eddie Schmidt. Gable's
Stand-In: Lew Smith. Stunt Doubles for Burning of Atlanta: Yakima
Canutt and Dorothy Fargo. Scarlett O'Hara Painting by Helen Carl-
ston. Publicity Directors: Russell Birdwell and Victor M. Shapiro.
222 minutes.

    The Cast (in order of appearance): AT TARA--Fred Crane
(Brent Tarleton), George Reeves (Stuart Tarleton), Vivien Leigh
(Scarlett O'Hara), Hattie McDaniel (Mammy), Everett Brown (Big
Sam), Zack Williams (Elijah), Thomas Mitchell (Gerald O'Hara),
Oscar Polk (Pork), Barbara O'Neil (Ellen O'Hara), Victor Jory
(Jonas Wilkerson), Evelyn Keyes (Suellen O'Hara), Ann Rutherford
(Careen O'Hara), Butterfly McQueen (Prissy).

    AT TWELVE OAKS--Howard Hickman (John Wilkes), Alicia
Rhett (India Wilkes), Leslie Howard (Ashley Wilkes), Olivia de
Havilland (Melanie Hamilton), Rand Brooks (Charles Hamilton),

Carroll Nye (Frank Kennedy), Marcella Martin (Cathleen Calvert),
Clark Gable (Rhett Butler), James Bush (Gentleman), Marjorie Rey-
nolds (Gossip), Ralph Brooks (Gentleman), Philip Trent (Gentleman,
later bearded Confederate on steps at Tara).
     AT THE BAZAAR IN ATLANTA--Laura Hope Crews (Aunt
Pittypat Hamilton), Harry Davenport (Doctor Meade), Leona Roberts
(Caroline Meade), Jane Darwell (Dolly Merriwether), Albert Morin
(Rene Picard), Mary Anderson (Maybelle Merriwether), Terry Shero
(Fanny Elsing), William McClain (Old Levi).
     OUTSIDE THE EXAMINER OFFICE--Eddie "Rochester" Ander-
son (Uncle Peter), Jackie Moran (Phil Meade), Tommy Kelly (Boy).
     AT THE HOSPITAL--Cliff Edwards (Reminiscent Soldier), Ona
Munson (Belle Watling), Ed Chandler (The Sergeant), George Hacka-
thorne (Wounded Soldier), Roscoe Ates (A Convalescent Soldier), John
Arledge (A Dying Soldier), Eric Linden (An Amputation Case), Guy
Wilkerson (Wounded Card Player).
     DURING THE EVACUATION--Tom Tyler (A Commanding Of-
ficer), Frank Faylen (Soldier Aiding Dr. Meade), Junior Coghlan
(Exhausted Boy).
     DURING THE SIEGE--William Bakewell (A Mounted Officer),
Lee Phelps (Bartender).
     GEORGIA AFTER SHERMAN--Paul Hurst (A Yankee Deserter),
Ernest Whitman (Carpetbagger's Friend), William Stelling (A Return-
ing Veteran), Louis Jean Heydt (A Hungry Soldier), Isabell Jewell
(Emmy Slattery), William Stack (Minister).
     DURING RECONSTRUCTION--Robert Elliott (A Yankee Major),
George Meeker, Wallis Clark (His Poker-Playing Captains), Irving
Bacon (The Corporal), Adrian Morris (A Carpetbagger Orator), J.M.
Kerrigan (Johnny Gallagher), Olin Howland (A Yankee Businessman),
Yakima Canutt (A Renegade), Blue Washington (His Companion), Ward
Bond (Tom, a Yankee Captain), Cammie King (Bonnie Blue Butler),
Mickey Kuhn (Beau Wilkes), Lillian Kemble Cooper (Bonnie's Nurse),
Si Jenks (Yankee on Street), Harry Strang (Tom's Aide), Emerson
Treacy, Trevor Bardett, Lester Dorr, John Wray (Bits). December
31, 1939. Released January 17, 1941. World Premiere: Decem-
ber 15, 1939 at the Grand Theatre, Atlanta, Georgia. New York
Premiere: December 19, 1939 at the Capitol and Astor Theatres.
Re-released by Metro-Goldwyn-Mayer in 1947, 1961, and 1968.
     Won Academy Awards for Best Picture, Best Director (Victor
Fleming), Best Actress (Vivien Leigh), Best Supporting Actress (Hat-
tie McDaniel), Best Written Screenplay, Best Color Cinematography,
Best Editing, Best Interior Decoration, with Special Oscars to Wil-
liam Cameron Menzies; Don Musgrave and Selznick International for
use of coordinated equipment; and the Irving G. Thalberg Memorial
Award to David O. Selznick. Nominated for Special Effects, Original
Score, Sound Recording, Best Actor (Clark Gable), Best Supporting
Actress (Olivia de Havilland).

DR. JEKYLL AND MR. HYDE (1941). Metro-Goldwyn-Mayer. A
Victor Fleming Production. Produced and directed by Victor Fleming, Co-Producer: Victor Saville. Screenplay: John Lee Mahin.
Based on the novel, The Strange Case of Dr. Jekyll and Mr. Hyde,
by Robert Louis Stevenson. Photography: Joseph Ruttenberg.

Musical Score: Franz Waxman. Editor: Harold F. Kress. Art
Director: Cedric Gibbons: associate: Daniel B. Cathcart. Set
Decorator: Edwin B. Willis. Special Effects: Warren Newcombe.
Montage: Peter Ballbusch. Recording Director: Douglas Shearer.
Dance Director: Ernst Matray. Gowns by Adrian. Men's Costumes:
Gile Steele. Makeup: Jack Dawn. Sound Technician: Charles "Wal-
ly" Wallace. 127 minutes.

The Cast: Spencer Tracy (Dr. Henry Jekyll/Mr. Hyde), Ing-
rid Bergman (Ivy Peterson), Lana Turner (Beatrix Emery), Donald
Crisp (Sir Charles Emery), Ian Hunter (Dr. John Lanyon), Barton
MacLane (Sam Higgins), C. Aubrey Smith (The Bishop), Peter God-
frey (Poole), Sara Allgood (Mrs. Higgins), Frederic Worlock (Dr.
Heath), Frances Robinson (Marcia), Denis Green (Freddie), Billy
Bevan (Mr. Weller), Olaf Hytten (Hobson), Forrester Harvey (Old
Prouty), Brandon Hurst (Briggs), Martha Wentworth (Landlady), Wil-
liam Tannen (Interne Fenwick), John Barclay (Constable), Lionel Pape
(Mr. Marley), Doris Lloyd (Mrs. Marley), Gwen Gaze (Mrs. French),
Lawrence Grant (Dr. Courtland), Winifred Harris (Mrs. Weymouth),
Lumsden Hare (Colonel Weymouth), Lydia Bilbrook (Lady Copewell),
Gwendolen Logan (Mrs. Courtland), Hillary Brooke (Mrs. Arnold),
Susanne Leach (Dowager in Church), Milton Parsons (Choir Master),
C. M. "Slats" Wyrick (Thug), Harold Howard (Blind Man), Jimmy
Aubrey (Hanger-on), Alec Craig (Waiter), Yorke Sherwood (Chair-
man), Cyril McLaglen, Pat Moriarty (Drunks), Bobby Hale (Cart
Driver), Mary Field (Wife), Eric Lonsdale (Husband), Clare Reid
(Old Woman), John Power, Al Ferguson, Colin Kenny (Constables),
Claude King (Uncle Geoffrey), Aubrey Mather (Inspector), Vangie
Beilby (Spinster), Rudolph Andrian (Art Student), Frank Hagney
(Drunk), Jacques Vanaire (French Attendant), Jimmy Spencer (Young
Man), Frances McInerney (Young Girl), Herbert Clifton (Bit Hustler),
Eldon Gorst (Messenger), Patrick J. Kelley (Man), Rita Carlyle
(Woman), David Dunbar (Footman), Jack Stewart (Constable), Mel
Forrester, Stuart Hall (Men), Pat Walker (Woman), Douglas Gordon
(Cockney Bit). July 17, 1941. Released September 1941. New
York Premiere: August 12, 1941.

Nominated for Academy Awards for Best Cinematography,
Best Music Score for a Dramatic Picture, Best Editing.

Previous versions in 1908 by the Selig Company; in 1909
in Denmark; in 1912 with James Cruze; in 1913 with King Baggot;
in 1920 by Pioneer Film Corp.; in 1920 by Paramount, directed
by John S. Robertson, with John Barrymore, Nita Naldi, Louis
Wolheim; in 1920 by UFA in Germany, directed by F.W. Murnau
as DER JANUSKOPF, with Conrad Veidt; in 1931 by Paramount,
directed by Rouben Mamoulian, with Fredric March, Miriam Hop-
kins, Rose Hobart, Holmes Herbert, Halliwell Hobbes. Later variations included TWO FACES OF DR. JEKYLL/HOUSE OF FRIGHT
(1961, Hammer), directed by Terence Fisher, with Paul Massie,
Dawn Addams, Christopher Lee, Oliver Reed; and even ABBOTT
AND COSTELLO MEET DR. JEKYLL AND MR. HYDE (1953, Universal), directed by Charles Lamont, with Bud Abbott, Lou Costello, Boris Karloff, Craig Stevens.

TORTILLA FLAT (1942). Metro-Goldwyn-Mayer. A Victor Fleming

Production. Produced by Sam Zimbalist. Screenplay: John Lee
Mahin and Benjamin Glazer. Based on the novel by John Steinbeck.
Photography: Karl Freund. Musical Score: Franz Waxman. Edi-
tor: James E. Newcom. Art Director: Cedric Gibbons; associate:
Paul Groesse. Set Decorations: Edwin B. Willis. Special Effects:
Warren Newcombe. Recording Director: Douglas Shearer. Gowns:
Kalloch. Men's Costumes: Gile Steele. Makeup Created by Jack
Dawn. Sound Technician: Charles "Wally" Wallace. Songs, "Oh
How I Love a Wedding" and "Ai, Paisano" (based on Mexican folk
song melody). Lyrics by Frank Loesser. Dialect Coach: Dr. Simon
R. Mitchneck. 105 minutes.

The Cast: Spencer Tracy (Pilon), Hedy Lamarr (Dolores
"Sweets" Ramirez), John Garfield (Danny), Frank Morgan (The Pi-
rate), Akim Tamiroff (Pablo), Sheldon Leonard (Tito Ralph), John
Qualen (Jose Maria Corcoran), Donald Meek (Paul D. Cummings),
Connie Gilchrist (Mrs. Torrelli), Allen Jenkins (Portagee Joe), Hen-
ry O'Neill (Father Ramon), Mercedes Ruffino (Mrs. Marellis), Nina
Campana (Senora Teresina Cortez), Arthur Space (Mr. Brown), Bet-
ty Wells (Cesca), Harry Burns (Torrelli), Louis Jean Jeydt (Young
Doctor), Willie Fung (Chin Kee), Roque Ybarra (Alfredo), Tim Ryan
(Rupert Hogan), Charles Judels (Joe Machado), Yvette Duguay (Little
Girl), Tito Renaldo (Boy), Harry Strang, Walter Sande (Firemen),
Jack Carr (Owner), Shirley Warde (Nurse), Emmett Vogan (Doctor),
Bob O'Conor and George Magrill (Cannery Workers), Fleeta, Hobo,
Pumpkin, Scooter, Fluff (The Pirate's Dogs). April 23, 1942. Re-
leased May, 1942. New York Premiere: May 21, 1942 at Radio
City Music Hall.

Nominated for Academy Award for Best Supporting Actor
(Frank Morgan).

A GUY NAMED JOE (1943). Metro-Goldwyn-Mayer. A Victor Flem-
ing Production. Produced by Everett Riskin. Screenplay: Dalton
Trumbo. Adaptation: Frederick Hazlitt Brennan. From an original
story by Chandler Sprague and David Boehm. Novelization: Randall
M. White. Photography: George Folsey and Karl Freund. Musical
Score: Herbert Stothart. Editor: Frank Sullivan. Art Director:
Cedric Gibbons; associate: Lyle Wheeler. Set Decorations: Edwin
B. Willis; associate: Ralph Hurst. Special Effects: Arnold Gilles-
pie, Donald Jahraus, and Warren Newcombe. Recording Director:
Douglas Shearer. Costume Supervision: Irene. Assistant Director:
Horace Hough. Makeup: Jack Dawn. South Technician: Charles
"Wally" Wallace. Technical Adviser: Major Edward G. Hillery,
U.S.A.A.C. Songs, "I'll Get By as Long as I Have You" by Roy
Turk and Fred Ahlert, and "I'll See You in My Dreams" by Isham
Jones and Gus Kahn. Waltz Instructor: Jeannette Bate. 118 min-
utes.

The Cast: Spencer Tracy (Pete Sandidge), Irene Dunne (Dor-
inda Durston), Van Johnson (Ted Randall), Ward Bond (Al Yackey),
James Gleason (Col. "Nails" Kilpatrick), Lionel Barrymore (The
General), Barry Nelson (Dick Rumney), Esther Williams (Ellen
Bright), Henry O'Neill (Colonel Sykes), Don Defore ("Powerhouse"
James J. Rourke), Charles Smith (Sanderson), Addison Richards
(Major Corbett), Mary Elliott (Dance Hall Girl), Earl Schenck

(Colonel Hendricks), Maurice Murphy (Captain Robertson), Gertrude Hoffman (Old Woman), Mark Daniels (Lieutenant), William Bishop (Ray), Eve Whitney ("Powerhouse" 's Girl), Kay Williams (Girl at Bar), Walter Sande (Mess Sergeant), Gibson Gowland (Bartender), John Whitney, Kirk Alyn (Officers in Heaven), James Millican (Orderly), Ernest Severn (Davy), Edward Hardwicke (George), Raymond Severn (Cyril), Yvonne Severn (Elizabeth), Christopher Severn (Peter), John Frederick (Lieutenant Ridley), Frank Faylen, Phillip Van Zandt (Majors), Blake Edwards, Marshall Reed, Robert Lowell, Michael Owen, Stephen Barclay, Neyle Morrow (Fliers), Irving Bacon (Corporal), Peter Cookson (Sergeant Hanson), Matt Willis (Lieutenant Hunter), Jacqueline White (Helen), Bill Arthur, John Bogen, Herbert Gunn, Harold S. Landon, Bob Sully, Johnny Dunn, James Martin, Richard Woodruff, Ken Scott, Louis Hart, Fred Beckner (Cadets), Craig Flannagan, Melvin Nix, Earl Kent, Michael Owen (U.S. Lieutenants), Joan Thorsen, Leatrice Gilbert, Mary Ganley (Girls in Chinese Restaurant), Charles King III (Lieutenant Collins, Radio Operator), Eddie Borden (Taxi Driver), Arthur Space (San Francisco Airport Captain), Alan Wilson (Sergeant in Jeep), Leslie Vincent (Sentry), Elizabeth Valentine (Washerwoman's Child), Arthur Stenning, George Kirby (Fishermen), Mary McLeod, Aileen Haley (Hostesses), Oliver Cross (American Major), Wyndham Standing (English Colonel), Violet Seton (Bartender's Wife), Becky Bohannon (English Girl), Harold S. Landon (Cadet), Jean Prescott (Mother), Simon Olivier (Boy), Richard Graham (Crew Member), James Warren (Irish Guard), George Atkinson (Waiter), Howard Davies (Bartender), Carlie Taylor (English Captain), Jack Saunders (American Captain), Stanley Orr (English Captain), William Bishop (Ray), Allen Wood (Tough Corporal), Eddie Coke (Corporal), Carey Harrison (American Major in Red Lion Inn), Dora Baker (Scrub Woman), Clarence Straight (Flight Sergeant), Vernon Downing (English Liason Officer), William Manning (Co-Pilot), Jesse Tai Sing (Headwaitress), Martin Ashe (Sergeant in Chinese Restaurant). January 18, 1944. Released March, 1944. New York Premiere: December 23, 1943.

Clip used in POLTERGEIST (1982, M-G-M/UA), directed by Tobe Hooper, produced by Steven Spielberg. Projected remake, ALWAYS, by Spielberg and M-G-M/UA.

ADVENTURE (1946). Metro-Goldwyn-Mayer. A Victor Fleming Production. Produced by Sam Zimbalist. Screenplay: Frederick Hazlitt Brennan and Vincent Lawrence. Adaptation: Anthony Veiller and William H. Wright. Based on the novel, The Anointed, by Clyde Brion Davis. Photography: Joseph Ruttenberg. Musical Score: Herbert Stothart. Song, "Nora Girl," by Frederick Hazlitt Brennan. Editor: Frank Sullivan. Art Direction: Cedric Gibbons and Urie McCleary. Set Decorations: Edwin B. Willis. Special Effects: Warren Newcombe. Recording Director: Douglas Shearer. Orchestrations: Murray Cutter. Costumes: Irene; associate: Marion Herwood-Keyes. Makeup: Jack Dawn. Hairstyles: Sidney Guilaroff. Sound Technician: Charles "Wally" Wallace. Working Title: THIS STRANGE ADVENTURE. 125 minutes.

The Cast: Clark Gable (Harry Patterson), Greer Garson (Emily Sears), Joan Blondell (Helen Melohn), Thomas Mitchell

(Mudgin), Tom Tully (Gus), John Qualen (Model T). Richard Haydn
(Limo), Lina Romay (Maria), Philip Merivale (Old Ramon Estado),
Harry Davenport (Dr. Ashlon), Tito Renaldo (Young Ramon Estado),
Pedro de Cordoba (Felipe), Garry Owen (Jabbo), Ralph Peters (Joe),
Joseph Crehan (Ed), Ray Teal (Tom Burke), Byron Foulger (Little-
ton), Audrey Totter (Ethel), Marta Linden (Adele), Harry Tyler
(Doctor), Bess Flowers (Modiste), Kay Medford (Red), Rex Ingram
(Preacher), Joan Thorsen (Model), Max Davidson, Claire McDowell,
Jack Kenny, Carli Elinor, Blanche Rose, Bill Beaumann, Alex Pal-
asthy, Pete Sosso, John Piffle, Charles Millsfield, Alex Novinsky,
Charles Meakin, William Wagner, D'Arcy Corrigan, Count Stefanelli,
Fred Fox, Eric Mayne, Harry Denny, Gene Leslie, William Musset-
ter, Margaret Millsfield, Genevieve Bell, Vangie Beilby (People in
Library), Chef Joseph Milani (Rodolf), Martin Garralaga (Nick the
bartender), Jack Young (Capitan), Dorothy Granger (Cashier), Eliza-
beth Russell (First Dame), Esther Howard (Blister), Florence Auer
(Landlady), Harry Wilson (Big Mug), Betty Blythe (Mrs. Buckley),
Pierre Watkin (Mr. Buckley), Charles La Torre (Tony), Dorothy
Vaughan (Mrs. Ludlow), Morris Ankrum (Mr. Ludlow), Dick Elliott
(George), Gladden James, Billy Newell (Barbers), Barbara Billings-
ley, Rebel Randall, Sue Moore (Dames), Myron Geiger (Bartender),
George Suzanne (Barfly), Eddie Hart (Milkman), Lee Phelps (Bar-
tender), Richard Abbott (Clerk), Fred Hoose, Major Farrell, Frank
Pharr, Joe Kamaryt (Readers), Aileen Carlyle (Matron), Jack Sterl-
ing (First Bouncer), Paul Stader (Second Bouncer), Frank Hagney
(Boss), Johnny Berkes (Bum), Martha Wentworth (Woman), John
Harmon (Taxi Driver), James Darrell (Officer), June Terry Picker-
ell, Marjorie Wood (Nurses), Tim Murdock (Interne), Ray H. Mc-
Kay, Al Maxiello (Barbers), Walter Knox (Bootblack), Ila Lee,
Barbara Coombs (Girls), Charles Haefli (Faro Dealer), Jeffrey Say-
re (Wheel of Fortune), Ed Randolph (Crap Man), Charles Regan,
Tom Kingston (Chip Men), Sayer Dearing (Roulette Man), Nina Bara,
Zedra Conde, Toni LaRue, Kanza Omar (Tomoatoes), Augie Gomez
(Hack Driver), Roque Ybarra (Foreign Cab Driver), Paul Smith
(First Mate), Charles Sherlock (Cab Driver), Miguel Contreras,
George Derrick, Hercules Mendez (Bits in Cantina), George Peters,
Cliff Powell (Navy Gun Crew Members), Clay Anderson (Young Doc-
tor), John Gilbreath (Seaman), Robert Emmett O'Connor, Charles
Stevens (Bits in Cantina), Franco Corsaro (Waiter in Cantina), Stan-
ley Andrews (Third Officer), Martha Bamattre (Bit Woman), Lita
Cortez, Helen McLeod, Connie Montoya (South American Girls in
Cantina). January 8, 1946. Released February, 1946. New York
Premiere: Feb. 7, 1946 at Radio City Music Hall.

JOAN OF ARC (1948). Released by RKO-Radio. Presented by
Sierra Pictures. A Victor Fleming Production. Produced by Walter Wanger. Screenplay by Maxwell Anderson and Andrew Solt.
Based on the play, Joan of Lorraine, by Maxwell Anderson. Color
by Technicolor. Photography: Joseph Valentine. Technicolor Photographers: William V. Skall and Winton C. Hoch. Technicolor
Direction: Natalie Kalmus and Richard Mueller. Associate Director: Slavko Vorkapich. Second Unit Director: Richard Rosson.
Editor: Frank Sullivan. Music by Hugo Friedhofer. Musical

Director: Emil Newman. Orchestral Arrangements: Jerome Mor-
oss. Vocal Direction: Charles Henderson, with the Roger Wagner
Choir. Art Director: Richard Day. Set Decorations: Edwin Rob-
erts and Joseph Kish. Main Title Sequence: William Cameron Men-
zies. Assistant Director: Edward Salven. Second Unit Assistant
Director: Horace Hough. Sound: William Randall and Gene Garvin.
Special Photographic Effects: Jack Cosgrove and John P. Fulton.
Research: Ruth Roberts, Michel Bernheim, Noel Howard. Techni-
cal Adviser: Father Paul Doncoeur. Costume Supervision: Herschel
McCoy. Costume Design: Karinska and Dorothy Jeakins. Makeup:
Jack Pierce. Produced on stage by the Playwrights' Company. 146
minutes.

The Cast: Ingrid Bergman (Jeanne D'Arc), Jose Ferrer (The
Dauphin, Charles VII), Francis L. Sullivan (Pierre Cauchon), J.
Carroll Naish (Count John of Luxembourg), Ward Bond (La Hire),
Shepperd Strudwick (Father Jean Massieu), Gene Lockhart (Georges
La Tremouille), Leif Erickson (Jean Dunois), Cecil Kellaway (Jean
Le Maistre), Selena Royle (Isabelle D'Arc), Robert Barrat (Jacques
D'Arc), James Lydon (Pierre D'Arc), Rand Brooks (Jean D'Arc),
Roman Bohnen (Durand Laxart), Irene Rich (Catherine LeRover),
Nestor Paiva (Henri Le Royer), Richard Derr (Jean De Metz), Ray
Teal (Bertrand de Poulengy), David Bond (Jean Fournier), George
Zucco (Constable of Clervaux), George Coulouris (Sir Robert De
Baudricort), John Emery (Duke of Alencon), Nicholas Joy (Arch-
bishop of Thiems), Richard Ney (Duke of Claremont), Vincent Dona-
hue (Alain Chartier), John Ireland (St. Severe), Henry Brandon
(Giles De Raiz), Morris Ankrum (Poton De Xantrailles), Tom Brown
Henry (Raoul De Gaucourt), Gregg Barton (Admiral De Culan), Ethan
Laidlaw (Jean D'Aulon), Hurd Hatfield (Father Pasquerel), Frederic
Worlock (Duke of Bedford), Dennis Hoey (William Glasdale), Colin
Keith-Johnston (Duke of Burgundy), Mary Currier (Jeanne, Countess
of Luxembourg), Roy Roberts (Wandamme, a Captain), Taylor Holmes
(Bishop of Avranches), Alan Napier (Earl of Warwick), Philip Bour-
neuf (Jean D'Estivet), Aubrey Mather (La Fontaine), Stephen Roberts
(Thomas de Courcelle), Herbert Rudley (Isombard De La Pierre),
Frank Puglia (Nicholas de Houppeville), William Conrad (Guillaume
Erard), John Parrish (Jean Beaupere, a judge), Victor Wood (Nicho-
las Midi), Houseley Stevenson (Winchester), Jeff Corey (Prison
Guard), Bill Kennedy (Thirache the Executioner), James Kirkwood
(Judge Mortemer), Herbert Rawlinson (Judge Marguerie), Matt
Moore (Judge Courneille), Frank Elliott (Dr. Tiphane), Barbara
Woodell (Woman with Baby), Arthur Space (Luxembourg Guard),
Eve March (Peasant Woman), Greta Granstedt, Marjorie Wood,
Julia Faye (Townswomen), James Fallet (Louis De Conte), Lee
Miller (Colet De Vienne/Townsman/French Soldier), Leo McMahon
(Richard, archer/French Solider), Henry Wills (Julian), Chuck
Hamilton (Jean De Honeycourt/French Soldier), Kate Lawson (Mar-
guerite), James Logan (Beaudricourt's Clerk), Charles Wagenheim
(Calot, Taxpayer), Robert Bice (Dying English Archer), Jean Ahlin
(Hauviette), Victor Travers (Bishop of Therouanne), Robert E. Burns
(Bishop of Norwich), Mike Donovan (Bishop of Noyon), Joseph Gran-
by (Giles de Fecamp), Patrick O'Conner (Guillaume Manchon), Lon
Poff (Guillaume Colles), Ed Biby (Nicholas Taquel), Alex Harford

(Lyonnel), Alvin Hammer (Court Jester), Jack Lindquist (Beaudri-
court's Page), James Garner, Walter Cook, Raymond Saunders, Rus-
sell Saunders, George Suzanne (Tumblers), June Lavere, William
Wagner, Symona Boniface, June Le Pre, Lester Dorr, Beatrice
Gray, Hazel Keener (Peasants), Phyllis Hill, Sally Cooper, Jean
La Vell, Dorothy Tuttle, June Harris (Court Ladies), Eve Whitney,
Beverly Loyd (Court Ladies/Camp Followers), Carl Knowles (Guard),
Babe London, Lorna Jordan, June Harris, Gloria Grafton, June Ben-
how (Camp Followers), Clancy Cooper (First Soldier), Lee Phelps
(Second Soldier), Frank Hagney (Third Soldier), Herschel Graham
(Constable), John Epper (Demetz), Art Dupuis (First Peasant),
George Dee (Second Peasant), Jack Gargan (Third Peasant), Bob
Whitney, John Pedrini (Deacons), Gregory Marshall (Boy), Mary
Field (Boy's Mother), Vernon Steele (Boy's Father), Wally Cassell
(French Soldier), Harry Hays Morgan (Guard), Art Foster (Marksman),
Burt Stevens, Jim Drum, George Magrill, John Moss, Allen Pinson
(English Knights), George Backus (English Knight/English Man at
Arms), Minerva Urecal (Old Woman), Raymond Bond (Hauviette's
Father), Russell Simpson (Old Man with Pipe), Robert Anderson (Sol-
dier at the Inn), Leo Borden (Pot Boy), Benjamin Litrenta (Second
Pot Boy), George Davis (Farmer), Jack George (Merchant), Frances
Morris, Eula Guy (Women at the Inn), Jean Ransome, Maurice
Brierre, Al Winters, Stella Le Saint, Stan Jolley (Domremy Peas-
ants), Pete Sosso (Domremy Peasant/Townsman), Manuel Paris
(Judge Chatillon), Peter Seal (Judge Albane), Vincent Neptune (Judge
Alespee), Tom Leffingwell (Judge Grouchet), Charles Meakin (Judge
Barbier), Stuart Holmes (Judge Benoit), Allen Schute (Judge Etienne),
Scott Seaton (Judge Edmond), Curt Furberg (Judge Jerome), Albert
Godderis (Judge Tobie), Louis Payne (Judge Thibault), John Bohn
(Judge Gustinel), Phillip Keiffer (Judge Haiton), Frank Marlowe,
Michael Cirillo (Guards), Everett Glass (Judge Anselene), Percival
Vivien (Judge Laurent), Pat Lane (Luxembourg Guard), Bob Thom,
Bob McLean (Burgundian Guard), Bob Bentley (English Man at Arms),
George Robotham (English Knight), Leland Hodgson (English Guard
at First Trial/English Soldier), Jerry Elliott, Gretchen Gailing,
Maria Tavares, Frances Sanford, Kiki Kellett (Townspeople), Dave
Dunbar, Clive Morgan, Sanders Clark (English Soldiers), Dick Alex-
ander (Man on Boulevard), Herbert Evans (Bailiff), Julius Aicardi,
Sam Calprice, Jim Cooley, Erno Kiraly, William Wagner, Ford
Raymond (Priests in Cauchon's Box), Henry Hebert (Winchester's
Secretary), Charles Quirk (Townsman/French Soldier), Fred Zendar
(Townsman/French Soldier), Bill Cody, J. W. Cody (English Guards),
John Roy, George Barrows, Philip Ahlm, Shephard Houghton, Roger
Creed, Bob Crosby, Byron Poindexter, Harry Raven, Eric Alden,
Victor Romito, Bob St. Angelo, Zane Megowan, George Bruggeman,
Lyle Moraine (French Soldiers), Ann Roberts (Riding Double), Jerry
Elliott (Running Double), Peggy O'Neil, Gail Goodson (Armor Doubles),
Patricia Marlowe (Stand-in).   November 11, 1948. Released Septem-
ber 2, 1950. New York Premiere: November 11, 1948 at the Vic-
toria Theatre.

    Won Academy Awards for Best Color Cinematography, Best
Color Costume Design, with Special Award to Walter Wanger, Nominated for Best Actress (Ingrid Bergman), Best Supporting Actor

(Jose Ferrer), Best Musical Scoring, Best Editing, Best Color Art Direction.

Victor Fleming also contributed uncredited direction to the following films:

THE GOOD EARTH (1936). Metro-Goldwyn-Mayer. Directed by Sidney Franklin. With Paul Muni, Luise Rainer, Walter Connelly, Tilly Losch.

THE GREAT WALTZ (1937). Metro-Goldwyn-Mayer. Directed by Julian Duvivier (and, uncredited, Josef von Sternberg). With Luise Rainer, Fernand Gravet, Miliza Korjus, Hugh Herbert, Lionel Atwill.

BOOM TOWN (1940). Metro-Goldwyn-Mayer. Directed by Jack Conway. With Clark Gable, Spencer Tracy, Claudette Colbert, Hedy Lamarr, Frank Morgan.

Bibliography

Ingrid Bergman and Alan Burgess, My Story (New York: Delacorte, 1978).

Peter Bogdanovich, Allan Dwan: The Last Pioneer (New York: Praeger, 1971).

Michael Conway and Mark Ricci, The Films of Jean Harlow (New York: Citadel, 1965).

Jackie Cooper with Dick Kleiner, Please Don't Shoot My Dog: The Autobiography of Jackie Cooper (New York: William Morrow, 1981).

Donald Deschner, The Films of Spencer Tracy (New York: Citadel, 1968).

Homer Dickens, The Films of Gary Cooper (Secaucus: Citadel, 1970).

John Douglas Eames, The M-G-M Story: The Complete History of Fifty Roaring Years (New York: Crown, 1976).

Gabe Essoe, The Films of Clark Gable (New York: Citadel, 1970).

Henry Fonda as told to Howard Teichmann, Fonda: My Life (New York: New American Library, 1981).

John Gallagher, "Victor Fleming," Films in Review, March 1983.

Joseph McBride, Hawks on Hawks (Berkeley: University of Califor-
    nis Press, 1982).

James Robert Parish and Gregory W. Mank, The Best of M-G-M:
    The Golden Years (1928-59), (Westport: Arlington House,
    1981).

John Howard Reid, "The Man Who Made G. W. T. W. ," Films and
    Filming, December 1967 (Part One) and January 1968 (Part
    Two).

Irving Shulman, Harlow: An Intimate Biography (New York: Dell,
    1964).

Bob Thomas, Thalberg (New York: Doubleday, 1969).

_____, Selznick (New York: Doubleday, 1970).

Lyn Tornabene, Long Live the King: A Biography of Clark Gable
    (New York: G. P. Putnam's Sons, 1976).

Lana Turner, Lana: The Lady, the Legend, the Truth (New York:
    E. P. Dutton, 1982).

John C. Tibbetts and James M. Welsh, His Majesty the American:
    The Films of Douglas Fairbanks, Sr. (South Brunswick:
    A. S. Barnes, 1977).

                        On The Wizard of Oz

Aljean Harmetz, The Making of the Wizard of Oz (New York: Al-
    fred Knopf, 1977).

Doug McClelland, Down the Yellow Brick Road (New York: Pyramid,
    1976).

                        On Gone with the Wind

Roland Flamini, Scarlett, Rhett, and a Cast of Thousands: The
    Filming of Gone with the Wind (New York: Macmillan, 1975).

Gerald and Harriet Gardner, The Tara Treasury (Westport: Arling-
    ton House, 1980).

Ron Haver, David O. Selznick's Hollywood (New York: Alfred Knopf,
    1980).

Gavin Lambert, GWTW, The Making of Gone with the Wind (Boston:
    Atlantic-Little, Brown, 1973).

William Pratt, Scarlett Fever (New York: Macmillan, 1977).

Malcolm Vance, <u>Tara Revisited</u> (New York: Award,   1976).

By Victor Fleming

<u>Action Is the Word: The Life Story of Victor Fleming</u>, Metro-
Goldwyn-Mayer Publicity Department, 1939.   Howard Strickling, Director of Publicity at M-G-M, prepared this 51-page
manuscript with Fleming, which was excerpted in newspapers
and magazines.   Through an error by Strickling, Fleming is
credited with the direction of three Fairbanks films of the
Twenties--<u>Robin Hood</u>, <u>Don Q, Son of Zorro</u>, and <u>The Black
Pirate</u>.   They were actually directed by Allan Dwan, Donald
Crisp, and Albert Parker respectively.

WILLIAM K. HOWARD

Notes on Filmography Credits

Since virtually all of the films are directed by William K. Howard, a director credit is given only when it is a shared credit, or on the infrequent (early) films where Howard's contribution was limited to the scenario.

The abbreviation Sc: indicates Scenario (for the silent films) and Screenplay (the term more usually used for sound films). Orig: indicates the writer of the original story; if it is a published play or novel, that fact is so indicated.

Additional credits such as Art Director or Special Effects are included only when those credits are of particular importance to an individual film, and where their qualities and or importance have been discussed in the body of the text relative to those films.

In the interests of consistency, the length of the silent films is given in number of reels. A full reel runs for one thousand 35mm feet. However, in the silent period, depending both on the speed at which the film had been shot, and on the whim of the projectionist, actual projection speed could vary considerably. Thus a four-reel film could logically be listed at either 40 minutes or 60 minutes-- and a projectionist needing to save time or prolong a program could present the film at faster or slower speeds than either of those two extremes. A five-reel film was any film that exceeded 4000 feet and thus needed to be mounted on five reels. Actually many of the early Howard melodramas had lengths in the area of 4,100 feet, and thus were actually closer to four-reelers than five. The invaluable American Film Institute Catalogue of Feature Films 1921-30 does provide the exact 35mm footage of each film, along with useful synopses of all films released in that period. In the sound period, of course, there could be no deviation in projection speeds, and thus with the transition to sound, the length of each film is given in minutes rather than in the number of reels. It should be emphasized that not only do many reference sources disagree, but in some cases films have been reissued with lost or deliberately deleted footage. Running times, in every case, are of the full original release.

FILMOGRAPHY

GET YOUR MAN (1921). Fox. Co-directed by William K. Howard and George Hill. Sc: John Montague. Orig: Alan Sullivan. Cam: Frank B. Good. 5 reels.
    With: Buck Jones, Beatrice Burnham, William Lawrence, Helen Rosson, Paul Kamp.

THE ONE MAN TRAIL (1921). Fox. Directed by Bernard Durning. Sc: Howard. Orig: Jack Strumwasser, Clyde C. Westover. Cam: Frank B. Good. 5 reels.
    With: Buck Jones, Beatrice Burnham, Helen Rosson, James Farley.

PLAY SQUARE (1921). Fox. Sc. and Orig: Jack Strumwasser. Cam: Victor Milner. 5 reels.
    With: Johnnie Walker, Edna Murphy, Laura La Plante, Hawyward Mack, Jack Brammall, Wilbur Higby, Nanine Wright, Al Fremont, Harry Todd.

WHAT LOVE WILL DO (1921). Fox. Sc: Jack Strumwasser. Orig: L. G. Rigy. Cam: Victor Milner. 5 reels.
    With: Johnnie Walker, Edna Murphy, Glen Cavender, Barbara Tennant, Richard Tucker, Edwin B. Tilton.

CAPTAIN FLY BY NIGHT (1922). Robertson-Cole Pictures, distributed by F.B.O. Sc.: Eve Unsell. Orig: Johnston McCulley. Cam: Lucien Andriot. 5 reels.
    With: Johnnie Walker, Shannon Day, Francis McDonald, Eddie Gribbon, Victory Bateman, Bert Wheller, Charles Stevens, James McElhern, Fred Kelsey.

THE CRUSADER (1922). Fox. Directed by Howard M. Mitchell. Sc: William K. Howard, Jack Strumwasser. Cam: David Abel. 5 reels.
    With: William Russell, Gertrude Claire, Helen Ferguson, Fritzi Brunette, George Webb, Carl Grantvoort.

DESERTED AT THE ALTER (1922). Phil Goldstone Productions. Directed by William K. Howard and Al Kelley. Sc: Grace Miller White. Orig: (Play) Pierce Kingsley. 7 reels.
    With: Bessie Love, Tully Marshall, William Scott, Barbara Tennant, Eulalie Jensen, Fred Kelsey, Frankie Lee, Wade Boteler, Les Bates, Edward McWade, Helen Howard.

EXTRA! EXTRA! (1922). Fox. Sc: Arthur J. Zellner. Orig: Julien Josephson. Cam: George Webber. 5 reels.
    With: Johnnie Walker, Edna Murphy, Herschel Mayall, John Steppling, Wilson Hummell, Gloria Woodthorpe, Theodore von Eltz, Edward Jobson.

LUCKY DAN (1922). Phil Goldstone Productions. 5 reels.

   With: Richard Talmadge, Dorothy Woods, George A. Williams, S. E. Jennings.

TROPPER O'NEILL (1922). Fox. Directed by Scott R. Dunlap.
Scenario: William K. Howard. Camera: Lucien Andriot. 5 reels.
   With: Buck Jones, Beatrice Burnham, Francis McDonald,
Claude Payton, Jack Rollins, Karl Formes.

THE FOURTH MUSKETEER (1933). Robertson-Cole Pictures–F. B. O.
release. Produced by J. G. Caldwell. Scenario by Paul Schofield,
from the Cosmopolitan story of the same title by H. C. Witwer.
Camera: William O'Connell. 6 reels.
   With: Johnnie Walker, Eileen Percy, Eddie Gribbon, William
Scott, Edith Korkie, Georgie Stone, James McElhern, Philo McCullough, Kate Lester.

DANGER AHEAD (1923). Phil Goldstone Productions. Scenario:
Keene Thompson. Camera: Reginald Lyons. 5 reels.
   With: Richard Talmadge, Helen Rosson, J. P. Lockney, David
Kirby, Fred Stanton.

LET'S GO (1923). Truart. Richard Talmadge Productions. Produced by A. Carlos. Scenario: Keene Thompson. Camera: W. E.
Shepherd. Titles: Ralph Spence. 5 reels.
   With: Richard Talmadge, Eileen Percy, George Nicholls,
Matthew Betz, Tully Marshall, Bruce Gordon, Al Fremont, Louis
King, Aggie Herring, John Steppling.

BORDER LEGION (1924). Paramount. Scenario by George Hull,
from the novel by Zane Grey. Camera: Alvin Wyckoff. 7 reels.
   With: Antonio Moreno, Helene Chadwick, Rockliffe Fellowes,
Gibson Gowland, Charles Ogle, Eddie Gribbon, James Corey, Luke
Cosgrave.

EAST OF BROADWAY (1924). Encore Pictures for Associated Exhibitors, dist. Scenario/adaptation by Paul Scofield, from the short
story "Tropic of Capricorn" by Richard Connell. Camera: Lucien
Andriot. 6 reels.
   With: Owen Moore, Marguerite De La Motte, Mary Carr,
Eddie Gribbon, Francis McDonald, George Nicholls, Betty Francisco,
Ralph Lewis.

CODE OF THE WEST (1925). Paramount. Scenario by Lucien Hubbard, from the novel by Zane Grey. Camera: Lucien Andriot. 7
reels.
   With: Owen Moore, Constance Bennett, Mabel Ballin, Charles
Ogle, George Bancroft, David Butler, Gertrude Short, Lillian Leighton, Eddie Gribbon, Pat Hartigan, Frankie Lee.

THE THUNDERING HERD (1925). Paramount. Scenario by Lucien
Hubbard, from the novel by Zane Grey. Camera: Lucien Andriot.
7 reels.
   With: Jack Holt, Lois Wilson, Noah Beery, Raymond Hatton,

Tim McCoy, Lilliam Leighton, Eulalie Jensen, Stephen Carr, Elliott
Hicks, Ed Brady, Pat Hartigan, Fred Kohler, Robert Perry.

THE LIGHT OF WESTERN STARS (1925). Paramount. Scenario:
George C. Hull, Lucien Hubbard, from the novel by Zane Grey.
Camera: Lucien Andriot. 7 reels.
    With: Jack Holt, Billie Dove, Noah Beery, Alma Bennett,
William Scott, George Nicholls, Mark Hamilton, Eugene Pallette,
Robert Perry.

RED DICE (1926). DeMille Pictures-Producers Dist. Corp. Scenario by Jeanie Macpherson and Douglas Doty, from "The Iron Chal-
ice" by Octavius Roy Cohen. Camera: Lucien Androit. 7 reels.
    With: Rod LaRocque, Marguerite De La Motte, Ray Hallor,
Gustav von Seyffertitz, Walter Long, George Cooper, Edith Yoke,
Clarence Burton, Charles Clary, Alan Brooks.

BACHELOR BRIDES (1926). De Mille Pictures-Producers Dist. Corp.
Scenario by Garrett Fort and C. Gardner Sullivan, from the play of
the same title by Charles Horace Malcolm. Camera: Lucien An-
driot. Assistant Director: Henry Hathaway. 6 reels.
    With: Rod LaRocque, Eulalie Jensen, Elinor Fair, George
Nichols, Julia Faye, Lucien Littlefield, Sally Rand, Eddie Gribbon,
Paul Nicholson.

VOLCANO (1926). Paramount. Scenario: Bernard McConville,
from the play "Martinique" by Laurence Eyre. Camera: Lucien
Andriot. 6 reels.
    With: Bebe Daniels, Ricardo Cortez, Wallace Beery, Arthur
Edmund Carewe, Dale Fuller, Eulalie Jensen, Brandon Hurst, Rob-
ert Perry, Marjorie Gay, Snitz Edwards, Emile Barrye, Bowditch
Turner, Edith Yorke, Mathilde Comont.

GIGOLO (1926). DeMille Pictures-Producers Dist. Corp. Scenario:
Garrett Fort and Marion Orth, from the novel by Edna Ferber.
Camera: Lucien Andriot. Costumes: Adrian. 7 reels.
    With: Rod LaRocque, Jobyna Ralston, Louise Dresser, Cyril
Chadwick, George Nichols, Ina Anson, Sally Rand.

WHITE GOLD (1926). DeMille Pictures-Producers Dist. Corp.
Scenario: Garrett Fort, Marion Orth and Tay Garnett, with titles
by John Farrow and John Krafft, from the play of the same name
by J. Palmer Parsons. Camera: Lucien Andriot. Art Direction:
Anton Grot. 6 reels.
    With: Jetta Goudal, Kenneth Thompson, George Bancroft,
George Nichols, Clyde Cook, Robert Perry.

THE MAIN EVENT (1926). DeMille Pictures-Pathe Dist. Scenario
and Art Direction: Rochus Glieses, from the story "That Makes Us
Even" by Paul Allison. Camera: Lucien Andriot. Costumes:
Adrian. 7 reels.
    With: Vera Reynolds, Rudolph Schildkraut, Julia Faye,
Charles Delaney, Robert Armstrong, Ernie Adams.

A SHIP COMES IN (1928). DeMille Pictures-Pathé Dist. Scenario
by Sonya Levien, from a story by Julien Josephson. Camera:
Lucien Andriot. Art Direction: Anton Grot. Costumes: Adrian.
7 reels.
    With: Rudolph Schildkraut, Louise Dresser, Robert Edeson,
Milton Holmes, Linda Landi, Lucien Littlefield, Fritz Feld, Louis
Natheaux.

THE RIVER PIRATE (1928). Fox. (Part talkie, music and effects.)
Scenario by John Reinhardt and Benjamin Karkson, from the story by
Charles Francis Coe. Camera: Lucien Andriot. 77 mins.
    With: Victor McLaglen, Lois Moran, Nick Stuart, Earle Fox,
Donald Crisp, Robert Perry.

SIN TOWN (1928). DeMille Pictures-Pathé Dist. Directed by J.
Gordon Cooper. Original story and scenario: J. Gordon Cooper and
William K. Howard. Camera: Harold Stein. 5 reels.
    With: Elinor Fair, Ivan Lebedeff, Hugh Allan, Jack Oakie,
Robert Perry.
    (Note: director Cooper had been an assistant director on
some prior Howard films, and returned to that capacity on "The
Valiant.")

THE VALIANT (1929). Fox. (All-talkie.) Screenplay: John Hunter
Booth, Tom Barry, from the play of the same title by Robert Mid-
dlemass and Holworthy Hall. Camera: Lucien Andriot, Glen Mac-
Williams. 59 mins.
    With: Paul Muni, Marguerite Churchill, John Mack Brown,
Edith Yorke, DeWitt Jennings, Richard Carlyle, Clifford Dempsey,
Henry Kolker, Don Terry, George Pearce.

LOVE, LIVE AND LAUGH (1929). Fox. Screenplay: Dana Burnet,
with dialogue by Edwin Burke and George Jessel from the play "The
Hurdy Gurdy Man" by LeRoy Clemens and John B. Hymer. Camera:
Lucien Andriot. Art Direction: William S. Darling. Asst. Direc-
tors: Phil Ford and Henry Kolker. 89 mins.
    With: George Jessel, Lila Lee, David Rollins, Henry Kolker,
John Loder, John Reinhardt, Dick Winslow, Henry Armetta, Marcia
Manon, Jerry Mandy.

CHRISTINA (1929). Fox. Screenplay by Marion Orth, with dialogue
by S.K. Lauren from a story by Tristram Tupper. Camera: Lucien
Andriot. Asst. Director: Phil Ford. 83 mins. (also released in
7-reel silent version).
    With: Janet Gaynor, Charles Morton, Rudolph Schildkraut,
Harry Cording, Lucy Dorraine.

GOOD INTENTIONS (1930). Fox. Screenplay by George Manker
Watters, with dialogue by William K. Howard from an original story
by Howard. Camera: George Schneiderman. 70 mins.
    With: Edmund Lowe, Marguerite Churchill, Regis Toomey,
Earle Fox, Eddie Gribbon, Robert McWade, Georgia Caine, Owen Davis
Jr., Pat Somerset, J. Carrol Naish, Henry Kolker, Hale Hamilton.

SCOTLAND YARD (1930). Fox. Produced by Ralph Block. Screenplay by Garrett Fort, from the play of the same title by Denison Clift. Camera: George Schneiderman. 73 mins.

With: Edmund Lowe, Joan Bennett, Donald Crisp, Georges Renevant, Lumsden Hare, David Torrence, Barbara Leonard, Halliwell Hobbes, J. Carrol Naish, Arnold Lucy.

DON'T BET ON WOMEN (1931). Fox. Screenplay by Leon Gordon and Lynn Starling, from "All Women Are Bad" by William Anthony McGuire. Camera: Lucien Andriot. Editor: Harold Schuster. 70 mins.

With: Edmund Lowe, Jeanette MacDonald, Roland Young, J. M. Kerrigan, Henry Kolker, Una Merkel, Helene Millard.

TRANSATLANTIC (1931). Fox. Screenplay and original story: Guy Bolton. Additional dialogue, Lynn Starling. Camera: James Wong Howe. Art Director: Gordon Wiles. 78 mins.

With: Edmund Lowe, Lois Moran, Myrna Loy, Jean Hersholt, John Halliday, Greta Nissen, Earle Fox, Billy Bevan, Ruth Donnelly, Goodee Montgomery, Jesse DeVorska, Rosalie Roy, Claude King, Crauford Kent, Henry Sedley, Louis Natheaux, Bob Montgomery.

SURRENDER (1932). Fox. Screenplay by S. N. Behrman and Sonia Levien, from the play "Axelle" by Pierre Benoit. Camera: James Wong Howe. Art Director: Anton Grot. 72 mins.

With: Warner Baxter, Leila Hyams, Ralph Bellamy, Alexander Kirkland, C. Aubrey Smith, William Frawley, Howard Phillips, Bert Hanlon, Tom Ricketts, Bodil Rosing, Andre Beranger, William von Brincken, Frank Swales, Joseph Sawyer, Albert Burke, J. Carrol Naish, Jack Conrad.

THE TRIAL OF VIVIENNE WARE (1932). Fox. Screenplay by Philip Klein and Barry Conners, from a story by Kenneth Ellis. Camera: Ernest Palmer. 58 mins.

With: Joan Bennett, Donald Cook, Sketts Gallagher, ZaSu Pitts, Herbert Mundin, Noel Madison, Christian Rub, Alan Dinehart, Lillian Bond, Howard Phillips, J. Maurice Sullivan, Ruth Selwyn, William Frawley, Maude Eburne, Eddie Dillon, Jameson Thomas, Dale Fuller, Nora Lane, Bert Hanson, Ward Bond, Stanley Blystone.

THE FIRST YEAR (1932). Fox. Screenplay by Lynn Starling, from the play by Frank Craven. Camera: Hal Mohr. 80 mins.

With: Janet Gaynor, Charles Farrell, Minna Gombell, Leila Bennett, Dudley Digges, Robert McWade, George Meeker, Maude Eburne, Henry Kolker, Elda Fokel.

SHERLOCK HOLMES (1932). Fox. Screenplay by Bertram Milhauser, suggested by William Gillette play based on a story by Sir Arthur Conan Doyle. Camera: George Barnes. 68 mins.

With: Clive Brook, Ernest Torrence, Miriam Jordan, Reginald Owen, Alan Mowbray, Howard Leeds, Herbert Mundin, C. Montague

Shaw, Arnold Lucy, Lucien Prival, Roy D'Arcy, Stanley Fields, Eddie Dillon, Robert Graves, Jr. , Brandon Hurst, Claude King.

THE POWER AND THE GLORY (1933). Fox. A Jesse Lasky Producation. Screenplay and original story: Preston Sturges. Camera: James Wong Howe. 76 mins.
     With: Spencer Tracy, Colleen Moore, Ralph Morgan, Helen Vinson, Clifford Jones, Henry Kolker, Sarah Padden, Billy O'Brien, Cullen Johnston, J. Farrell MacDonald.

THIS SIDE OF HEAVEN (1934). M-G-M. Screenplay by Zelda Sears, Eve Green, Edgar Allan Woolf and Florence Ryerson, from "It Happened One Day" by Marjorie Bartholomew Paradis. Camera: Hal Rosson. 76 mins.
     With: Lionel Barrymore, Fay Bainter, Mae Clarke, Tom Brown, Una Merkel, Mary Carlisle, Onslow Stevens, Henry Wadsworth, Eddie Nugent, C. Henry Gordon, Dickie Moore.

THE CAT AND THE FIDDLE (1934). M-G-M. Screenplay by Bella and Samuel Spewack, from an original by Jerome Kern and Otto Harbach. Camera: Hal Rosson and Charles Clarke. 90 mins. (Technicolor sequence.)
     With: Jeanette MacDonald, Ramon Novarro, Frank Morgan, Charles Butterworth, Jean Hersholt, Vivienne Segal, Frank Conroy, Henry Armetta, Joseph Cawthorn, Adrienne D'Ambricourt.

EVELYN PRENTICE (1934). M-G-M. Screenplay by Lenore Coffee, from an original story by W. E. Woodward. Camera: Charles Clarke. 80 mins.
     With: William Powell, Myrna Loy, Rosalind Russell, Una Merkel, Isabel Jewell, Harvey Stephens, Edward Brophy, Henry Wadsworth, Cora Sue Collins, Jessie Ralph, Frank Conroy.

VANESSA, HER LOVE STORY (1935). M-G-M. Produced by David O. Selznick. Screenplay by Lenore Coffee and Hugh Walpole, from the novel by Hugh Walpole. Camera: Ray June. 84 mins.
     With: Helen Hayes, Robert Montgomery, Otto Kruger, May Robson, Lewis Stone, Henry Stephenson, Violet Kemble-Cooper, Donald Crisp, Jessie Ralph, Agnes Anderson, Lionel Belmore, Lawrence Grant, Crauford Kent, Howard Leeds, Ethel Griffies, Elspeth Dudgeon, Mary Gordon, George K. Arthur.

RENDEZVOUS (1935). M-G-M. Produced by Lawrence Weingarten. Screenplay by Bella Spewack, Samuel Spewack, P. J. Wolfson and George Oppenheimer, from "American Black Chamber" by Herbert O. Yardley. Camera: William Daniels. 91 mins.
     With: William Powell, Rosalind Russell, Binnie Barnes, Lionel Atwill, Cesar Romero, Samuel S. Hinds, Henry Stephenson, Frank Reicher, Charles Grapewin, Sterling Holloway, Leonard Mudie, Howard Hickman, Charles Trowbridge.

MARY BURNS, FUGITIVE (1935). Paramount. 84 mins.
     With: Sylvia Sidney, Melvyn Douglas, Alan Baxter, Brian

Donlevy, Wallace Ford, Pert Kelton, Frank Sully, Frances Gregg,
Charles Waldron, William Ingersoll, Boothe Howard, Norman Willis,
Joe Twerp, William Pawley, Ivan Miller, Charles Wilson, Kerman
Cripps.

THE PRINCESS COMES ACROSS (1936).   Paramount.   Produced by
Arthur Hornblow, Jr.   Screenplay by Walter DeLeon, Frances Mar-
tin, Frank Butler and Don Hartman, from a story by Philip Mac-
Donald and Louis Lucien Rogger.   Camera: Ted Tetzlaff.   Art Di-
rection: Hans Dreier and Ernst Fegte.   76 mins.
    With: Fred MacMurray, Carole Lombard, Douglas Dumbrille,
Alison Skipworth, William Frawley, Porter Hall, George Barbier,
Lumsden Hare, Sig Rumann, Tetsu Komai, Mischa Auer, Bradley
Page, David Clyde, Edward Keane, Tom Herbert, George Sorel,
Jacques Vanaire, Gladden James, Gaston Glass, William Newell,
Milburn Stone, Phil Tead, Jean de Briac, Nanette Lafayette, Charles
Fallon, Andre Cheron.

FIRE OVER ENGLAND (1937).   Alexander Korda/London Films for
United Artists.   Produced by Erich Pommer.   Screenplay: Clemence
Dane and Sergei Nolbandoz, from the novel by A. E. W. Mason.   Cam-
era: James Wong Howe.   Art Director: Lazar Meerson.   92 mins.
    With: Flora Robson, Laurence Olivier, Vivien Leigh, Ray-
mond Massey, Leslie Banks, Morton Selton, Robert Newton, Tamara
Desni, Lyn Harding, George Thirlwell, James Mason, Henry Oscar,
Robert Rendel, Donald Calthrop, Charles Carson.

THE SQUEAKER (1937).   Alexander Korda/London Films for United
Artists.   Produced by Alexander Korda.   Screenplay by Edward
Berkman and Bryan Wallace, from the novel by Edgar Wallace.
Camera: Georges Perinal.   77 mins.
    With: Edmund Lowe, Ann Todd, Sebastian Shaw, Robert
Newton, Tamara Desni, Alastair Sim, Allan Jeayes, Stewart Rome,
Mabel Terry-Lewis, Gordon McLeod.
    Released in the U. S. under the title "Murder on Diamond
Row. "

OVER THE MOON (1937).   Alexander Korda/London Films for United
Artists.   Technicolor.   Produced by Alexander Korda.   Directed by
Thornton Freeland.   Additional direction (uncredited): William K.
Howard.   Screenplay by Anthony Pelissier and Alec Coppell, from
an original story by Robert Sherwood and Lajos Biro.   78 mins.
    With: Rex Harrison, Merle Oberon, Ursula Jeans, Robert
Douglas, Louis Borell, Zena Dare, Peter Haddon, David Tree, Mac-
kenzie Ward, Carl Jaffe, Elizabeth Welch.
    Not released in the U. S. until 1941.

THE GREEN COCKATOO (1937) 20th Century Fox-British.   Pro-
ducer: Robert T. Kane.   Director: William Cameron Menzies.
Screenplay by Arthur Wimperis and O. E. Berkman, from a story by
Graham Greene.   66 mins.
    With: John Milla, Rene Ray, Robert Newton, Bruce Seton,
Charles Oliver, Julian Veddey, Allan Jeayes, Frank Atkinson.

Note: Additional direction (uncredited) by William K. Howard, who, however, received a producer credit on later releases of the film, replacing Robert Kane.

Produced and originally reviewed under the title Four Dark Hours.

Not released in the U.S. until 1947, when it was distributed with six minutes cut by Devonshire Films.

BACK DOOR TO HEAVEN (1938).   Paramount (distribution only). Screenplay: John Bright, Robert Tasker from an original story by William K. Howard.   Camera: Hal Mohr, Bill Kelly, Don Malkames.   Art Direction: Gordon Wiles, William Saulter.   Asst. Producer: Johnnie Walker.   85 mins.

With: Wallace Ford, Patricia Ellis, Aline MacMahon, Van Heflin, Stuart Erwin, Bert Frohman, Bruce Evans, George Lewis, Doug McMullen, Helen Christian, Robert Vivian, Iris Adrian, Georgette Harvey, Jimmy Lydon, Anita Magee, William Harrigan, Jane Seymour, Robert Wildhack, Billy Redfield, Kenneth LeRoy, Raymond Roe, Al Webster, Joe Garry, William K. Howard, Johnnie Walker.

Note: Kent Smith, listed in most reference sources for this film, was replaced by Van Heflin.

Filmed at the Astoria Studios in Long Island, with location work in Cleveland.

MONEY AND THE WOMAN (1940).   Warner Brothers.   Screenplay by Robert Presnell, from "The Embezzler" by James M. Cain.   Camera: L. W. O'Connell.   Associate Producer: William Jacobs.   67 minutes.

With: Jeffrey Lynn, Brenda Marshall, Roger Pryor, Henry O'Neill, Lee Patrick, Henry Kolker, Guinn "Big Boy" Williams, John Litel, William Gould, Edward Keane, William Marshall, Peter Ashley, Mildred Coles, Willie Best, Susan Peters, Stuart Holmes, Creighton Hale, Tom Wilson, Leo White, Dane Clark.

BULLETS FOR O'HARA (1941).   Warner Brothers.   Screenplay by Raymond Shrock, from "Pat and Mike" by Richard Connell.   Camera: Ted McCord.   50 mins.

With: Joan Perry, Roger Pryor, Anthony Quinn, Maris Wrixon, Dick Purcell, Hobart Bosworth, Richard Ainley, DeWolf Hopper, Joan Winfield, Roland Drew, Joseph King, Victor Zimmerman, Hank Mann, Frank Mayo, Jack Mower, Sidney Bracey, Leah Baird.

Remake of the 1936 Public Enemy's Wife, with interpolated footage from that film.

KLONDIKE FURY (1942).   Monogram Pictures.   Produced by the King Brothers.   Screenplay by Henry Blankfort, from 'Klondike" by Tristram Tupper.   Camera: L. W. O'Connell.   68 mins.

With: Edmund Lowe, Lucille Fairbanks, Ralph Morgan, William Henry, Robert Middlemass, Jean Brooks, Mary Forbes, Vince Barnett, Clyde Cook, Marjorie Wood, Kenneth Harlan, Monte Blue.

Remake of Klondike, Monogram, 1932.

JOHNNY COME LATELY (1943).   United Artists.   Produced by Wil-
liam Cagney.   Screenplay by John Van Druten, from "McLeod's
Folly" by Louis Bromfield.   Camera: Theodor Sparkuhl.   97 mins.
      With: James Cagney, Grace George, Marjorie Main, Mar-
jorie Lord, Hattie McDaniel, Ed McNamara, Bill Henry, Robert
Barrat, George Cleveland, Margaret Hamilton, Norman Willis,
Lucien Littlefield, Edwin Stanley, Irving Bacon, Tom Dugan, Charles
Irwin, John Sheehan, Clarence Muse, John Miller, Arthur Hunnicutt,
Victor Kilian, Wee Willie Davis.
      Released in England under the title Johnny Vagabond.

WHEN THE LIGHTS GO ON AGAIN (1944).   Producers Releasing
Corp.   Produced by Leon Fromkess.   Screenplay by Milton Lazarus,
from a story by Frank Craven.   Camera: Ira Morgan.   74 mins.
      With: James Lydon, Regis Toomey, George Cleveland, Grant
Mitchell, Dorothy Peterson, Harry Shannon, Lucien Littlefield, Luis
Alberni, Emmett Lynn, Joseph Crehan, Warren Mills, Jill Browning,
Roberta Carling, Larry Thompson, James Hope, Barbara Belden.

A GUY COULD CHANGE (1946).   Republic.   Screenplay by Al Martin,
from a story by F. Hugh Herbert.   Camera: John Alton.
      With: Allan Lane, Jane Frazee, Twinkle Watts, Bobby Blake,
Wallace Ford, Adele Mara, Mary Treen, Joseph Crehan, Eddie
Quillan, Gerald Mohr, George Chandler, William Haade, Betty Shaw.
      Howard received Associate Producer as well as Director
credit on this film.

ROLAND WEST

As Director

A WOMAN'S HONOR. Roland West Film Corporation/William Fox
Films, 1916. 45 minutes in 5 reels. Presented by William Fox.
Produced and Directed by Roland West. Copyright April 7 under the
title LOST SOULS; copyright June 11 as A WOMAN'S HONOR. Based
on the Snappy Stories magazine story, "La Terribula" by George L.
Knapp. Scenario: Donald I. Buchanan. Cameraman: Ed Wynard.
    Cast: Jose Collins (Helena), Arthur Donaldson (Tochetti),
Devore Palmer (Minotti), Ruby Hoffman (Mrs. Minotti), Mrs. Cecil
Raleigh (La Terribula), Bradley Barker (Guido Ferrari), Anna Reedor
(Maria), Armand Cortez (Roberto).

DE LUXE ANNIE. Norma Talmadge Productions, 1918. Presented
by Joseph M. Schenck. Adapted by Paul West. From a play based
on the Saturday Evening Post story by Edward Clarke.
    Cast: Norma Talmadge (Julie Kendall), Frank Mills (Walter
Kendall), Edward Davis (Dr. Fernand Niblo), Edna Hunter ("De Luxe
Annie"), Eugene O'Brien.

THE SILVER LINING. Iroquois Film Corporation/Metro Pictures,
January 1921. 6 reels. Presented by Roland West. Producer,
Director, Story: Roland West. Adaptation & Scenario: D. J. Bu-
chanan & Charles H. Smith. Photography: Edward Wynard & Frank
Zucker. Sets: Charles O. Seessel.
    Cast: Jewel Carmen ("The Angel"), Leslie Austen (Robert El-
lington), Coit Albertson (George Johnson), Virginia Valli (Evelyn
Schofield), Julia Swayne Gordon ("Gentle Annie"), J. Herbert Frank
("Big Joe"), Edward Davis (George Schofield), Marie Coverdale (Mrs.
Schofield), Gladden James (Billy Dean), Theodore Babcock (Eugene
Narcom), Charles Wellesley (Burton Hardy), Henry Sedley (Mr. Bax-
ter), Jule Powers (Mrs. Baxter), Arthur Donaldson (Friend of the
Baxters), Paul Everton (A Detective), Carl Hyson (Dancer), Dorothy
Dickson (Dancer).

NOBODY. Roland West Productions/Associated First National Pictures, July 1921. 7 reels, 6396 feet. Producer, Director, Story:
Roland West. Scenario: Charles H. Smith & Roland West. Photography: Harry Fischbeck. Assistant Director: Joseph Rothman.
    Cast: Jewel Carmen (Little Mrs. Smith), William Davidson

(John Rossmore), Kenneth Harlan (Tom Smith), Florence Billings
(Mrs. Fallon), J. Herbert Frank (Hedges), Grace Studiford (Mrs.
Rossmore), George Fawcett (Hiram Swanzey), Lionel Pape (Noron
Ailsworth), Henry Sedley (Rossmore's Secretary), Ida Darling (Mrs.
Van Cleek), Charles Wellesley (Clyde Durand), William de Grasse
(Rossmore's skipper), Riley Hatch (The "Grouch" Juror).

THE UNKNOWN PURPLE.   Carlos Productions/Distributed by Truart
Film Corporation, 1923.   7 reels; 6950-7800 feet.   Copyright De-
cember 8th.   From the play by Roland West & Carlyle Moore.   Ad-
aptation by Roland West & Paul Schofield.   Titles by Alfred A. Cohn.
Photography: Oliver T. Marsh.   Set Design by Horace Jackson.
Film Editor: Alfred A. Cohn.
        Cast: Henry B. Walthall (Peter Marchmont, alias Victor
Cromport), Alice Lake (Jewel Marchmont), Stuart Holmes (James
Dawson), Helen Ferguson (Ruth Marsh), Frankie Lee (Bobbie),
Ethel Grey Terry (Mrs. Freddie Goodlittle), James Morrison (Les-
lie Bradbury), Johnny Arthur (Freddie Goodlittle), Richard Wayne
(George Allison), Brinsley Shaw (Hawkins), Mike Donlin (Burton).

THE MONSTER;   Metro-Goldwyn-Mayer, 1925.   72 minutes; 6425
feet in 7 reels.   Copyright March 9th.   Released March 16th.   Scen-
ario by Willard Mack & Albert Kenyon.   From the 1922 play by
Crane Wilbur.   Titles by C. Gardner Sullivan.   Photography: Hal
Mohr.   Editor: A. Carle Palm.   Production Manager: W. L.
Heywood.
        Cast: Lon Chaney (Dr. Ziska), Gertrude Olmstead (Betty
Watson), Hallam Cooley (Hal), Johnny Arthur (Johnny), Charles A.
Sellon (The Constable), Walter James (Caliban), Knute Erickson
(Daffy Dan), George Austin (Rigo), Edward McWade (Luke Watson),
Ethel Wales (Mrs. Watson).

THE BAT.   Feature Productions/Distributed by United Artists, 1926.
91 minutes; 8219 feet in 9 reels.   Released on March 14th.   Direction & Screenplay by Roland West.   Story by Julien Josephson.   From
the play The Bat by Mary Roberts Rinehart & Avery Hopwood, inspired by Miss Rinehearts' 1908 novel, The Circular Staircase.   Titles: George Marion, Jr.   Photography: Arthur Edeson.   Second
Cameraman: Gregg Toland.   Art Director: William Cameron Menzies.   Production Assistants: Frank Hall Crane, Thornton Freeland, Ned Herbert Mann.   A Roland West Production.   Film Editor:
Hal C. Kern.
        Cast: André de Beranger (Gideon Bell), Charles W. Hert-
zinger (Man in Black Mask, alias Courtleigh Fleming), Emily Fitz-
roy (Cornelia Van Gorder), Louise Fazenda (Lizzie Allen), Arthur
Houseman (Richard Fleming), Robert McKim (Dr. Wells), Jack
Pickford (Brooks Bailey), Jewel Carmen (Dale Ogden), Kamiyama
Sojin (Billy, the Houseboy), Tullio Carminati (Detective Moletti,
alias The Bat), Eddie Gribbon (Detective Anderson), Lee Shumway
(The Unknown).

THE DOVE.   Norma Talmadge Productions/Distributed by United

Artists, 1928. Released January 7. 9100 feet in 9 reels. Presented
by Joseph M. Schenck. Continuity by Wallace Smith & Paul Bern.
Titles: Wallace Smith. Adaptation: Roland West, Wallace Smith &
Willard Mack. Photography: Oliver Marsh. Art Director: William
Cameron Menzies. Film Editor: Hal Kern. From a play by Wil-
lard Mack & story by Gerald Beaumont.

Cast: Norma Talmadge (Dolores), Noah Beery (Don José
María y Sandoval), Gilbert Roland (Johnny Powell), Eddie Borden
(Billy), Harry Myers (Mike), Michael Vavitch (Gómez), Brinsley
Shaw (The Patriot), Kalla Pasha (The Comandante), Charles Darvas
(The Comandante's Captain), Michael Dark (Sandoval's Captain), Wal-
ter Daniels (The Drunk).

Academy Award: Art Direction: William Cameron Menzies,
for his work on both THE DOVE and TEMPEST.

ALIBI. Feature Productions/Distributed by United Artists. April
20, 1929. Sound and silent versions. Silent: 7263 feet. Sound:
90 minutes. 8167 feet in 10 reels. Released in England as THE
PERFECT ALIBI. A Roland West Production. Presented by Joseph
M. Schenck. Produced & Directed by Roland West. Screenplay,
Titles & Dialogue: Roland West & C. Gardner Sullivan. From the
play Nightstick by John Griffith Wray, J.C. Nugent & Elaine S.
Carrington. Photography: Ray June. Art Director: William Cam-
eron Menzies. Film Editor: Hal C. Kern. Sound by Movietone.
In Charge of Sound: Howard Campbell. Music Synchronization:
Hugo Risenfeld. Dance Arrangements: Fanchon. Make-up: Robert
Stephanoff. Police Advisor: Captain John McCaleb.

Cast: Chester Morris (Chick Williams), Harry Stubbs (Buck
Bachman), Mae Busch (Daisy Thomas), Eleanor Griffith (Joan Man-
ning), Irma Harrison (Toots), Regis Toomey (Danny McGann), Al
Hill (Brown), James Bradbury, Jr. (Trask), Purnell E. Pratt (Pete
Manning), Pat O'Malley (Tommy Glennon), DeWitt Jennings (O'Brien),
Edward Brady (George Stanislaus David), Edward Jardon & Virginia
Flohri (Singers in theater).

THE BAT WHISPERS. Art Cinema Corporation/Distributed by United
Artists, 1930. 35mm & 65mm "Magnifilm" versions. 89 minutes;
7991 feet in 10 reels. Previewed November 6th at 8100 feet. Extant UA release print: 82 mins. Extant Altantic Pictures re-issue
print: 71 minutes. Released November 29th. MPPA Certificate
3339R. A Roland West Production. Presented by Joseph M. Schenck.
Director, Screenplay: Roland West. From the play The Bat by
Mary Roberts Rinehart & Avery Hopwood, originally produced on the
stage by Wagenhals and Kempner. Inspired by Miss Rinehart's 1908
novel The Circular Staircase. 35 mm photography: Ray June. 65mm
photography: Robert H. Planck, supervised by Ray June. Assistant
Cameramen: Stuart Thompson & Bert Shipman. Film Editors:
James Smith, Hal C. Kern. Settings Designed & Executed by Paul
Roe Crawley. Scenic Artist: Harvey Meyers. Original Oil Paint-
ings: Thomas Lawless. Sound by Movietone. In Charge of Sound:
J.T. Reed. Sound Technician: Oscar E. Lagerstrom. Rehearsal
Director: Charles H. Smith. Assistant Director: Roger H. Heman.
Electrician: William McClellan. Technical Staff: Charles Cline.

Miniatures: Ned Herbert Mann. Production Ass't: Helen Hallet.
     Cast: Chester Morris (Detective Anderson, alias The Bat),
Una Merkel (Dale Van Gorder), Grace Hampton (Mrs. Cornelius
Van Gorder), Maude Eburne (Lizzie Allen), Gustav Von Seyffertitz
(Dr. Venrees), Spencer Charters (The Caretaker), Charles Dow
Clarke (Detective Jones), William Bakewell (Brooks Bailey), Ben
Bard (The Unknown), Hugh Huntley (Richard Fleming), S. E. Jen-
nings (Man in Black Mask, Courtleigh Fleming), Sidney D'Albrook
(Police Sergeant), DeWitt Jennings (Police Captain), Richard Tucker
(Mr. Bell), Wilson Benge (The Butler), Chance Ward (Police Lt.).

CORSAIR. Art Cinema Corporation/Distributed by United Artists,
1931. 73 minutes, 8 reels. Released in September. A Roland West
Production. Produced and Directed by Roland West. Screenplay
by Roland West & Josephine Lovett. From the Liberty magazine
serial by Walton Green. Photography: Ray June & Robert H.
Planck. Art Director: Richard Day. Editor: Hal C. Kern.
Sound: Frank Maher. Co-Directors: Robert Ross, Rollo Lloyd
& Robert Webb. Musical Score & Direction: Alfred Newman.
Gowns: Sophie Wachner.
     Cast: Chester Morris (John Hawks), Alison Loyd (Thelma
Todd) (Alison Corning), Fred Kohler ("Big John"), Ned Sparks
("Slim"), Frank McHugh ("Chub" Hopping), Mayo Methot (Sophie),
Frank Rice ("Fish Face"), Emmett Corrigan (Stephen Corning),
William Austin (Richard Bentinck), Gay Seabrook (Susie Grenoble),
Addie McPhail (Jean Phillips), Al Hill (Gangster).

Screenplay/Adaptations

     By the account of West and his PR folks, West wrote "many"
produced motion picture scenarios prior to 1918. These projects
remain unknown and undocumented.

DARING LOVE. Hoffman Productions/Truart, 1924. Directed by
Roland G. Edwards. From the Redbook story, "Driftwood" by Albert Payson Terhune. Adaptation: Roland West & Willard Mack.

THE PURPLE MASK (Unproduced). Adaptation: Wallace Smith.
Adaptation: Roland West. Continuity: Charles H. Smith.

Other Versions of the Motion Pictures

THE CIRCULAR STAIRCASE. Selig, 1915. 60 minutes. Directed
by Edward J. Le Saint. From the novel by Mary Roberts Rinehart.
     Miss Rinehart's 1908 novel, The Circular Staircase was her
root source for her 1920 play, The Bat, and the 1926 novelization
of the play. The story and characters are nearly identical--except
that "The Bat" is not a dramatis personae! No print of the 1915
motion picture is known to exist.

THE BAT. Liberty Pictures/Allied Artists, 1959. 80 minutes. Direction & Screenplay: Crane Wilbur.

ROWLAND BROWN

POINTS WEST (1929). Universal-Jewel. Screenplay by Rowland Brown from the novel by B. M. Bower. Directed by Arthur Rosson. Photography: Barry Neumann.

The Cast: Hoot Gibson (Cole Lawson, Jr.), Alberta Vaughn (Dorothy), Frank Campeau (McQuade), Jack Raymond (His Nibs), Martha Franklin (The Mother), Milt Brown (Parsons), Jim Corey (Steve).

THE DOORWAY TO HELL (1930). Warner Brothers Pictures. Original story by Rowland Brown ("A Handful of Clouds") with adaptation and additional dialogue by George Rosener. Directed by Archie Mayo. Photography: Barney McGill. Editor: Robert Crandall.

The Cast: Lew Ayres (Louis Ricarno), Charles Judels (Sam Margoni), Dorothy Matthews (Doris), Leon Janney (Jackie Lamarr), Robert Elliott (Captain O'Grady), James Cagney (Steve Mileaway), Kenneth Thomson (captain of military academy), Jerry Mandy (Joe), Noel Madison (Rocco), Eddie Kane (Dr. Morton), Edwin Argus (Midget).

QUICK MILLIONS (1931). Fox. From a screenplay written in collaboration with Courtenay Terrett. Additional dialogue: John Wray. Photography: Joseph August. Art Direction: Duncan Cramer. Editor: Harold Schuster.

The Cast: Spencer Tracy ("Bugs" Raymond), Marguerite Churchill (Dorothy Stone), Sally Eilers (Daisy De Lisle), Robert Burns ("Arkansas" Smith), John Wray (Kenneth Stone), Warner Richmond ("Nails" Markey), George Raft (Jimmy Kirk), John Swor (Contractor).

WHAT PRICE HOLLYWOOD? (1932). RKO-Pathé. Screenplay by Rowland Brown in collaboration with Gene Fowler, from the original story by Adela Rogers St. John. Additional dialogue by Jane Murfin and Ben Markson. Directed by George Cukor.

The Cast: Constance Bennett, Lowell Sherman, Neil Hamilton, Gregory Ratoff, Brooks Benedict, Louise Beavers, Eddie Anderson.

STATE'S ATTORNEY (1932). RKO Radio. Screenplay by Rowland Brown in collaboration with Gene Fowler, from the original story by Louis Stevens. Directed by George Archainbaud (begun by Brown, who was first replaced by Irvin Pichel).

The Cast: John Barrymore (Tim Cardigan), Helen Twelvetrees, Jill Esmond, William Boyd, Mary Duncan, Oscar Apfel, Raoul

Roulien, Ralph Ince, Frederick Burton, Ethel Sutherland, Leon Waycoff, C. Henry Gordon.

HELL'S HIGHWAY (1932).   RKO Radio.   Produced: David O. Selz-
nick.   Screenplay written with Samuel Ornitz and Robert Tasker.
Photography: Edward Cronjager.   Art Direction: Van Nest Polglase.
Music: Max Steiner.   Editor: William Hamilton.
    The Cast: Richard Dix (Frank "Duke" Ellis), Tom Brown
(Johnny Ellis), Rochelle Hudson (Mary Ellen), C. Henry Gordon
(Blacksnake Skinner), Warner Richmond (Pop Eye Jackson), Sandy
Roth (Blind Maxie), Charles Middleton (Matthew the Hermit), Clar-
ence Muse (Rascal), Stanley Fields (Whiteside), Jed Kiley (Romeo
Schultz), Fuzzy Knight (Society Red), Oscar Apfel (Billings).

BLOOD MONEY (1933).   20th Century-United Artists.   Produced by
Darryl Zanuck.   Assoc. Producers: William Goetz & Raymond
Griffith.   Screenplay: Rowland Brown & Hal Long.   Photography:
James Van Trees.   Art Director: Al D'Agostino.   Music: Alfred
Newman.   Editor: Lloyd Nosler.
    The Cast: George Bancroft (Bill Bailey), Frances Dee
(Blaine Talbert), Chick Chandler (Drury Darling), Judith Anderson
(Ruby Darling), Blossom Seely (nightclub singer), J. Carrol Naish
(Charley), Etienne Girardot (Bailey's co-worker), Joe Sawyer (Red),
Sandra Shaw, Paul Fix.

LEAVE IT TO BLANCHE (1934).   Warner Bros.-First National
British.   Original story by Rowland Brown.   Director: Harold
Young.
    The Cast: Henry Kendall, Olive Blakeney, Miki Hood,
Griffiths Jones, Hamilton Keene, Rex Harrison, Julian Joyce,
Elizabeth Jenns, Molly Clifford, Phyllis Stanley, Harold Warrender,
Denise Sylvester, Margaret Gunn.

WIDOW'S MIGHT (1935).   Warner Bros.-First National British.
Screenplay by Rowland Brown with Brock Williams, from the play
by Frederick Jackson.   Director: Cyril Gardner.
    The Cast: Laura La Plante, Yvonne Arnaud, Barry Clifton,
Gary Marsh, George Curzon, Margaret Yarde, Davina Craig, Joan
Hickson, Hugh E. Wright, Hal Walters, Ray Plumb, Walter Amner.

THE DEVIL IS A SISSY (1936).   M-G-M.   Original story by Rowland
Brown.   Screenplay by John Lee Mahin and Richard Schayer.   Di-
rector: W.S. Van Dyke.
    The Cast: Freddie Bartholomew, Jackie Cooper, Mickey
Rooney, Ian Hunter, Peggy Conklin, Katharine Alexander, Gene
Lockhart, Kathleen Lockhart, Jonathan Hale.

BOY OF THE STREETS (1937).   Monogram.   Original story by
Rowland Brown.   Screenplay by Gilson Brown and Scott Darling.
Director: William Nigh.
    The Cast: Jackie Cooper, Maureen O'Connor, Kathleen
Burke, Robert Emmet O'Connor, Marjorie Main, Matty Pain, George
Cleveland, Gordon Elliott, Guy Usher.

ANGELS WITH DIRTY FACES (1938). Warner Bros. Original story
by Rowland Brown. Screenplay by John Wexley, Warren Duff. Pro-
duced by Sam Bischoff. Director: Michael Curtiz. Art Director:
Robert Hass. Music: Max Steiner. Photography: Sol Polito. Edi-
tor: Owen Marks.
        The Cast: James Cagney (Rocky Sullivan), Pat O'Brien (Jer-
ry Connelly), Humphrey Bogart (James Frazier), Ann Sheridan
(Laury Martin), George Bancroft (Mac Keefer), Billy Halop (Soapy),
Bobby Jordan (Swing), Leo Gorcey (Bim), Bernard Punsley (Hunky),
Gabriel Dell (Pasty), Huntz Hall (Crab), Frankie Burke (Rocky as a
Boy).

THE LADY'S FROM KENTUCKY (1939). Paramount. Original story
by Rowland Brown. Screenplay by Malcolm Stuart Boylan. Director: Alexander Hall.
        The Cast: George Raft, Ellen Drew, Hugh Herbert, ZaSu
Pitts, Louise Beavers, Lew Payton, Forrester Harvey, Harry Tyler,
Edward Pawley, Gilbert Emery, Eugene Jackson, Jimmy Bristow.

JOHNNY APOLLO (1940). 20th Century-Fox. Screenplay by Row-
land Brown with Philip Dunne from a story by Hal Long and Samuel
G. Engel. Director: Henry Hathaway.
        The Cast: Tyrone Power, Dorothy Lamour, Edward Arnold,
Lloyd Nolan, Charles Grapewin, Marc Lawrence, Lionel Atwill, Jon-
athan Hale, Harry Rosenthal, Russell Hicks, Fuzzy Knight, Charles
Lane, Selmar Jackson.

NOCTURNE (1946). RKO. Original story by Rowland Brown with
Frank Fenton. Screenplay by Jonathan Latimer. Producer: Joan
Harrison. Director: Edwin L. Marin. Photography: Harry J.
Wild. Music: Leigh Harline. Editor: Harold Palmer.
        The Cast: George Raft (Joe Warne), Lynn Bari (Frances
Ranson), Virginia Huston (Carol Page), Joseph Pevney (Fingers),
Myrna Dell (Susan), Edward Ashley (Vincent), Walter Sande (Hal-
berson), Mabel Paige (Mrs. Warne), Bernard Hoffman (Torp),
Queenie Smith (Queenie).

THE NEVADAN (1950). Ranown, for Columbia. Additional dialogue
by Rowland Brown. Screenplay by George W. George and George
F. Slavin. Director: Gordon Douglas.
        The Cast: Randolph Scott, Dorothy Malone, Forrest Tucker,
Frank Faylen, George Macready, Charles Kemper, Jeff Corey, Tom
Powers, Jack O'Mahoney, Stanley Andrews, James Kirkwood, Kate
Drain Lawson, Olin Howlin, Louis Mason.

KANSAS CITY CONFIDENTIAL (1952). United Artists. Original
story by Rowland Brown and Harold R. Greene. Screenplay by George
Bruce and Harry Essex. Producer: Edward Small. Director: Phil
Karlson. Photography: George E. Diskant. Music: Paul Sawtell.
Art Direction: Edward L. Ilou. Editor: Buddy Small.
        The Cast: John Payne (Joe Rolfe), Coleen Gray (Helen),
Preston Foster (Timothy Foster), Dona Drake (Teresa), Jack
Elam (Harris), Neville Brand (Kane), Lee Van Cleff (Tony),

Mario Seletti (Timaso), Howard Negley (Andrews), Ted Ryan (Morelli), George Wallace (Olson), Vivi Janiss (Mrs. Rogers), Helen Keeb (Mrs. Crane).

CHARLES BARTON

As Actor

c. 1915

Two-Reel Short with Bronco Billy Anderson (title unknown).

1920

COUNTY FAIR. Produced by Maurice Tourneur, Directed by Clarence Brown. Barton played the part of Tim Vail.

1927

WINGS. Directed by William A. Wellman. Barton appears in a cameo role as a soldier who is hit by Clara Bow's ambulance.

1939

BEAU GESTE. Directed by William A. Wellman. Barton appears as Buddy McGonigal.

As Assistant Prop. Boy

(All features are Paramount unless noted otherwise)

1924

THE STRANGER. Dir: Joseph Henabery.
THE FIGHTING COWARD. Dir: James Cruze.
WANDERER OF THE WASTELAND. Dir: Irvin Willat.
LILY OF THE DUST. Dimitri Buchowetski.
FEET OF CLAY. Cecil B. DeMille.
MERTON OF THE MOVIES. James Cruze.
THE CITY THAT NEVER SLEEPS. James Cruze.
PETER PAN. Herbert Brenon.

1925

CONTRABAND. Alan Crosland.
THE THUNDERING HERD. William K. Howard.

264

THE GOOSE HANGS HIGH. James Cruze.
CODE OF THE WEST. William K. Howard.
BEGGAR ON HORSEBACK. James Cruze.
THE PONY EXPRESS. James Cruze.

1926

MANNEQUIN. James Cruze.
BEHIND THE FRONT. Edward Sutherland.
SEA HORSES. Allan Dwan.
HOLD THAT LION. William Beaudine.

As Second Assistant Prop. Boy

1926

YOU NEVER KNOW WOMEN. William A. Wellman.
THE CAT'S PAJAMAS. William A. Wellman.
OLD IRONSIDES. James Cruze.

1927

MAN POWER. Clarence Badger.
FIREMAN SAVE MY CHILD. Edward Sutherland.
WINGS. William A. Wellman. Also served in the capacities of
        First Propboy, Second Assistant Director, First Assistant
        Director and Assistant Unit Manager.

As Assistant Director

1927

WINGS. (see above)

1928

BEAU SABREUR. John Waters.
DOOMSDAY. Rowland V. Lee.
LEGION OF THE CONDEMNED. William A. Wellman.
THE VANISHING PIONEER. John Waters.
LADIES OF THE MOB. William A. Wellman.
WARMING UP. Fred Newmeyer.
THE FLEET'S IN. Mal St. Clair.
BEGGARS OF LIFE. William A. Wellman.
AVALANCHE. Otto Brower.

1929

THE SHOPWORN ANGEL. Richard Wallace.
SUNSET PASS. Otto Brower.
CHINATOWN NIGHTS. William A. Wellman.

CLOSE HARMONY. John Cromwell/Edward Sutherland.
THE MAN I LOVE. William A. Wellman.
DANGEROUS CURVES. Lothar Mendes.
WOMAN TRAP. William A. Wellman.
DANCE OF LIFE. John Cromwell/Edward Sutherland.
FAST COMPANY. Edward Sutherland.

1930

DANGEROUS PARADISE. William A. Wellman.
ONLY THE BRAVE. Frank Tuttle.
YOUNG EAGLES. William A. Wellman.
THE SOCIAL LION. Edward Sutherland.
BORDER LEGION. Otto Brower.
THE SEA GOD. George Abbott.
THE SANTA FE TRAIL. Otto Brower.
DERELICT. Rowland V. Lee.

1931

FIGHTING CARAVANS. Otto Brower.
JUNE MOON. Eddie Sutherland.
CITY STREETS. Rouben Mamoulian.
MONKEY BUSINESS. Norman Z. McLeod.
TOUCHDOWN. Norman Z. McLeod.
LADIES OF THE BIG HOUSE. Marion Gering.
CONFESSIONS OF A CO-ED. Dudley Murphy.

1932

MILLION DOLLAR LEGS. Edward Cline.
HORSE FEATHERS. Norman Z. McLeod.
NIGHT AFTER NIGHT. Archie Mayo.
HE LEARNED ABOUT WOMEN. Lloyd Corrigan.
IF I HAD A MILLION. James Cruze, H. Bruce Humberstone, Steph-
        en Roberts, William A. Seiter, Ernst Lubitsch, Norman
        Taurog, Norman Z. McLeod.
SIGN OF THE CROSS. Cecil B. DeMille.

1933

INTERNATIONAL HOUSE. Edward Sutherland.
THIS DAY AND AGE. Cecil B. DeMille. Barton served as Second
        Assistant.
DUCK SOUP. Leo McCarey.
ISLAND OF LOST SOULS. Erie C. Kenton.

1934

FOUR FRIGHTENED PEOPLE. Cecil B. DeMille.
LITTLE MISS MARKER. Alexander Hall.
CLEOPATRA. Cecil B. DeMille.

As Writer

<u>1934</u>

MANY HAPPY RETURNS. Stephen Roberts. Barton worked as gag
   writer.

<u>1935</u>

LIVES OF A BENGAL LANCER. Henry Hathaway. Barton worked
   on early drafts of the script.

As First Assistant Director

<u>1939</u>

UNION PACIFIC. Cecil B. DeMille.

As Second Unit Director

<u>1945</u>

SPELLBOUND. Alfred Hitchcock.

<u>1946</u>

CANYON PASSAGE. Jacques Tourneur.

As Director

WAGON WHEELS. Paramount, 9-21-34. Presented by Adolph Zuk-
or. Prod: Harold Hurley. Scr: Jack Cunningham, Charles Logue,
Carl A. Buss, from the book <u>Fighting Caravans</u> by Zane Grey.
Photog: William C. Mellor. Ed: Jack Daniels. Art Dir: Earl
Hedrick, Asst Dir: Art Jacobson. Song: "Wagon Wheels" by Billy
Hill. 56 min.
   Television Title: CARAVANS WEST. Re-make of FIGHTING
CARAVANS (1931, Otto Brower) and uses stock footage from the '31
film.
   Cast: Randolph Scott (Clint Belmet), Gail Patrick (Nancy
Wellington), Billy Lee (Sonny Wellington), Monte Blue (Murdock),
Raymond Hatton (Jim Burch), Jan Duggan (Abby Masters), Leila
Bennett (Hetty Masters), Olin Howland (Bill O'Meary), J. P. McGow-
an (Couch), James Marcus (Jed), Helen Hunt (Mrs. Jed), James B.
"Pop" Kenton (Masters), Alfred Del Cambre (Ebe), John Marston
(Orator), Sam McDaniels (Negro Coachman), Howard Wilson (Per-
mit Officer), Michael S. Visaroff (Russian), Julian Madison (Les-
ter), Eldred Tidbury (Chauncey), E. Alyn Warren (The Factor),
Fern Emmett (Settler), Ann Sheridan (extra), Lew Meehan (listener),

Harold Goodwin (Nancy's brother).   (Gary Cooper appears in stock
footage from 1931 FIGHTING CARAVANS).

ROCKY MOUNTAIN MYSTERY.   Paramount, 2-8-35.   Presented by
Adolph Zukor.   Prod: Harold Hurley.   Scr: Edward E. Paramore,
Jr.   Adapt: Ethel Doherty, from an unpublished story "Golden Dreams"
by Zane Grey.   Art Dir: Hans Dreier, Dave Garber.   Photog: Ar-
chie Stout.   Ed: Jack Daniels.   66 min.
       Working title: VANISHING PIONEER.   Re-issued as: THE
FIGHTING WESTERNER.
       Cast: Randolph Scott (Larry Sutton), Charles 'Chic' Sale
(Tex Murdock), Mrs. Leslie Carter (Mrs. Borg), Kathleen Burke
(Flora), George Marion, Sr. (Ballard), Ann Sheridan (Rita Ballard),
James C. Eagles (John Borg), Howard Wilson (Fritz), Willie Fung
(Ling Yat), Florence Roberts (Mrs. Ballard).

CAR 99.   Paramount, 3-1-35.   Presented by Adolph Zukor.   Prod:
Bayard Veiller.   Scr: Karl Detzer and C. Gardner Sullivan, from
a story by Karl Detzer.   Photog: William C. Mellor.   Art Dir:
Hans Dreier, John Goodman.
       Cast: Fred MacMurray (Ross Martin), Ann Sheridan (Mary
Adams), Sir Guy Standing (Prof. Anthony/John Viken), Frank Craven
(Sheriff Pete Arnot), William Frawley (Sgt. Barrel), Marina Schu-
bert (Nan Anthony), Dean Jagger (Officer Jim Burton), John Cox
(Howard) (Recruit Carney), Douglas Blackley (Robert Kent) (Recruit
Blatsky), Alfred Del Cambre (Recruit Jamison), Nora Cecil (Granny),
Joseph Sauers (Sawyer) (Whitey), Mack Gray (Smoke), Eddie Dunn
(Mac/servant), Peter Hancock (Eddie), Howard Wilson (Dutch), Al
Hill (Hawkeye), Eddy Chandler (Recruit Haynes), John Sinclair (Crook
in Sedan), Charles G. Wilson (Captain Ryan), Russell Hopton (Operator Harper), Hector Sarno (French Charlie), Sam Flint (President
1st Nat. Bank--cut from final release print), Jack Cheathom (Radio
Sgt. Meyers), Gordon Jones (Mechanic--cut from release print), Harry Strang (Dispatch Sgt.), Ted Oliver (Sgt.), Duke York (Cop), Charles Sullivan (Green Gang hood), Malcolm McGregor (pilot).

THE LAST OUTPOST.   Paramount, 10-11-35.   Prod: E. Lloyd Shel-
don.   Co-Dir: Louis Gasnier.   Scr: Philip MacDonald.   Adapt:
Frank Partos, Charles Brackett based on the book Drums by Fred-
erick Britten Austin.   Photog: Theodore Sparkuhl.   Ed: Jack Dan-
iels.   77 mins.
       Cast: Cary Grant (Michael Andrews) Claude Rains (John
Stevenson) Gertrude Michael (Rosemary Haydon), Kathleen Burke
(Ilya), Colin Tapley (Lt. Prescott), Jameson Thomas (Cullen),
Margaret Swope (Nurse Rowland), Billy Bevan (Corp. Foster), Nick
Shaid (Haider), Harry Semels (Amrak), Georges Renevent (Turkish
Major) Meyer Cuhayoun (Armenian Patriarch), Frazier Acosta (of-
ficer) Malay Clu (guard), Elspeth Dudgeon (Head Nurse), Beulah
McDonald (Nurse), Claude King (General), William Brown (Sgt.
Bates), Olaf Hytten (Doctor), Robert "Bob" A'Dair (Sgt. in General's
office), Akim Tamiroff (Mirov), Frank Elliott (Col.), Frank Daw-
son (Surgeon), Ramsay Hill (Capt.) Ward Lane (Col.), Carey Harrison (Bit officer), Mark Strong (bit officer).

NEVADA. Paramount, 11-29-35. Prod: Harold Hurley. Scr: Garnett Weston, Stuart Anthony based on the book by Zane Grey. Photog: Archie Stout. Ed: Jack Daniels. 59 min.

Cast: Larry "Buster" Crabbe (Nevada), Kathleen Burke (Hattie Ida), William Duncan (Ben Ida), Monte Blue (Clem Dillon), Raymond Hatton (Sheriff), Sid Saylor (Cash Burridge), Leif Glenn Erikson (Bill Ida), Richard Carle (Judge Franklidge), Stanley Andrews (Cawtherne), Frank Sheridan (Tom Blaine), Jack Kennedy (McTurk), Albert Taylor (Hedge), Murdock MacQuarrie (Watson), Robert E. Homans (Carver), William L. Thorne, Harry Dunkinson (card players), Barney M. Furey (Bystander-card game), Henry Roquemore (Bartender), William Desmond (Wilson), Frank Rice (Shorty), Dutch O. G. Hendrian (Cawtherne's benchman).

TIMOTHY'S QUEST. Paramount, 1-31-36. Presented by Adolph Zukor. Prod: Harold Hurley. Scr: Virginia Van Upp, Dore Schary, Gilbert Pratt from the book by Kate Douglas Wiggin. Art Dir: Hans Dreier, Robert Odell. Photog: Harry Fischbeck. Ed: Jack Dennis. Asst Camera: Skippy Sanford. 65 min.

Cast: Eleanore Whitney (Martha), Tom Keene (David Young), Dickie Moore (Timothy), Virginia Weidler (Samantha Tarbox), Esther Dale (Hitty Tarbox), Elizabeth Patterson (Vilda Cummins), Irene Franklin (Flossie), Samuel S. Hinds (Fellows), Raymond Hatton (Jabe Doolittle), J. M. Kerrigan (Dr. Cudd), Bonnie Bartlett (Jimmy), Sally Martin (Gay), Ralph Ramley (Joe), Robert Perry (Bartender), Otto Fries (Timid Tenor), Irving Bacon (Henry, drunken wagon driver), Clarence H. Wilson (Mr. Simpson), Tempe Pigott (Mrs. Simpson), George Cuhl (Policeman), Jack Clifford (Ed, tramp), John Kelley (Herb), Lew Kelly (sheriff).

AND SUDDEN DEATH. Paramount 6-19-36. Prod: A. M. Botsford. Scr: Joseph Moncure March from a story by Theodore Reeves and Madeleine Ruthven. Photog: Alfred Gilks. Ed: Hugh Bennett. Presented by Adolph Zukor. Art Dir: Hans Dreier, Earl Hedrick. Makeup: Max Asher. 68 min. Filmed in LaCanada, California.

Cast: Randolph Scott (Lt. James Knox), Frances Drake (Betty Winslow), Tom Brown (Jackie Winslow), Billy Lee (Bobby Sanborn), Fuzzy Knight (Steve Bartlett), Terry Walker (Bangs), Porter Hall (District Attorney), Charles Quigley (Mike Andrews), John Hyams (J. R. Winslow), Joseph Sawyer (Sgt. Sanborn), Oscar Apfel (Anderson, defense council), Don Rowan (Sgt. Maloney), Jimmy Conlin (Mr. Tweets), Maidel Turner (Dodie Sloan), Charles E. Arnt (Archie Sloan), Wilma Francis (Nurse), Herbert Evans (Meggs), Bryant Washburn (Bill Arden), Fred Blanchard (Blakely), Harry Depp (Collins), John Dilson (Judge), Janet Elsie Clark (Class member), Hal Davis (sour-faced driver), Russ Clark (Dan), Jerry Fletcher (Attendant), Sam Ash (Cook), Florence Wix (Miss Allenby), Eddie Dunn (Gas station attendant), Hal Price (Bus driver), Tom Hanlon, Lee Shumway (cops), Harry Geise (radio announcer), Robert Littlefield (intern), Eddy Chandler (Adams), Earl Pingree (McCarthy), Lee Phelps (Court Clerk), William Ingersoll (Judge), Howard Mitchell (Court Attendant), Don Brodie (Newspaperman), Hilda Vaughn (Prison girl), Jane Keckley (Matron), Edwin Stanley (Dr. Drayson), Dora

Clement (Nurse), Eddie Fetherston (Newspaperman), Jack Mack (gas station attendant).

MURDER WITH PICTURES. Paramount, 9-25-36. Presented by Adolph Zukor. Prod: A. M. Botsford. Scr: John C. Moffit and Sidney Salkow based on the book by George Harmon Coxe. Art Dir: Hans Dreier, John Goodman. Photog: Ted Tetzlaff. 71 min.

    Cast: Lew Ayres (Kent Murdock), Gail Patrick (Meg Archer), Paul Kelly (I. B. McGoogin), Benny Baker, (Phil Doans), Ernest Cossart (Stanley Redfield), Onslow Stevens (Nate Girard), Joyce Compton (Hester Boone), Anthony Nace (Sam Cusick), Joseph Sawyer (Inspector Bacon), Don Rowan (Siki), Frank Sheridan (Police Chief), Irving Bacon (Keogh), Purnell Pratt (Eastern Editor), Christian Rub (Olaf), Mike Pat Donovan (Foreman), Eddie Dunn (bailiff), Howard C. Hickman (Judge), Pat West, Phil Tead (reporters), Robert Perry, Lee Phelps, Jack Mulhall, Harry Jordan (Girard Henchman), Robert Burkhardt, Edmund Burns, Paddy O'Flynn, Jerry Fletcher, Jack Chapin, Nick Lukats, Martin Lamont, Paul Barrett, Frank Losee, Jr., Allen Saunders (reporters), Wolfe "William" Hopper (photographer), Margaret Harrison, Beatrice Coleman, Dorothy Stevens, Dorothy Thompson, Kay Gordon, Larry Steers, William Norton Bailey, Kai Schmidt, Patsy Bellamy, Jack Clark (guests), Earl M. Pingree (taxi driver), Lee Shumway (cop), Rex Moore (newsboy), Davison Clark (Overholt), Frank Marlowe (pipe smoker), Art Rowland (asst. editor), George Ovey (trunk man), Harry Wallace (Girard Henchman), Pat O'Malley, Hal Price, Howard Joslin (policeman), Harry C. Bradley (Gas station attendant), Milburn Stone (operator).

ROSE BOWL. Paramount, 10-30-36. Prod: A. M. Botsford. Scr: Marguerite Roberts from the book O'Reilly of Notre Dame by Francis Wallace. Presented by Adolph Zukor. Songs: Charlie Rosco, Leo Robin. Mus. Dir: Boris Morros. Photog: Henry Sharp. Ed: William Shea. Contributor to Treatment: Francis Wallace. Contributor to Scr. Construction: Ray Harris. 75 min.

    Cast: Eleanore Whitney (Cheers Reynolds), Tom Brown (Paddy O'Riley), Larry "Buster" Crabbe (Ossie Merrill), William Frawley (Coach Soapy Moreland), Benny Baker (Dutch Schultz), Nydia Westman (Susie Reynolds), Priscilla Lawson (Florence "Flossie" Taylor), Adrian Morris (Doc), James Conlin (Browning Hills), Nick Lukats (Donavan), Terry Ray (Ellen Drew) (Mary Arnold), Bud Flanagan (Dennis O'Keefe) (Jones), William Moore (Peter Potter) (Holt), Lon Chaney, Jr., Ray Wehba, Donald McNeil, Gil Kuhn, Phil J. Duboski, Gene Hibbs, Joe Preininger, Charles Williams, Owen Hansen, Jim Henderson, Boyd "Red" Morgan, Nick Pappas, Angelo Peccianti, James Jones, Leavitt Thurlow, Jr., Miles Norton, Lyman H. Russell, Edward Shuey, Glen Galvin, Tod Goodwin, David Newell, David Horsley (football players), Louis Mason (Thornton), John Sheehan (Orville Jensen), Joe Ploski (Swenski), Hugh McArthur (Russell), Charles Judels (Mrs. Schultz), Sid Saylor, George Ovey, Milburn Stone, Henry Roquemore, Jerry Fletcher (Rubber Band), Billy Lee (Little Boy), Bodil Ann Rosing (Mrs. Schultz), Bert Moorhouse, Hal Price, Earl Jamison, Arthur Rowlands, Buck Mack, (reporters) Pat O'Malley, Hooper Atchley,

Charles Sherlock (Photographers), Herbert Ashley (Pitt Fan), Ber-
nard Suss (spectator), Thomas Pogue (Rooter), Anthony Pawley,
Donald Kerr (reporters), Edward Peil, Jr. (Undergraduate), Dick
Winslow (boy), Gertrude Messinger, June Johnson (girls), Joseph
Sawyer, Garry Owen (announcers), Ray Hanford (football fan), Jack
Murphy (player), Spec O'Donnell (underclassman), Paul Perry (Mana-
ger), Paul Kruger (Team Manager), Harry Depp (King), William
Jeffrey (Hay), Wheaton Chambers (Wallace), Antrim Short (asst.
director) Frances Morris (assistant publicist), Richard Kipling (bar-
ber), Charles C. Wilson (Burke).

THE CRIME NOBODY SAW. Paramount. 3-12-37. Presented by
Adolph Zukor. Prod: William Le Baron. Scr: Bertram Millhauser
from the play Crime Incorporated by Ellery Queen and Lowell
Brentano. Art Dir: Hans Dreier, Robert Odell. Photog: Harry
Fischbeck. Ed: James Smith. 60 min.
     Cast: Lew Ayres (Nick Milburn), Ruth Coleman (Kay Mallory),
Eugene Pallette (Babe), Benny Baker (Horace Dryden), Vivienne Os-
borne (Mrs. Duval), Colin Tapley (Dr. Brookes), Howard C. Hick-
man (Robert Mallory), Robert Emmet O'Connor (Tim Harrigan), Jed
Prouty (William Underhill), Hattie McDaniel (Ambrosia), Ferdinand
Gottschalk (John Atherton), Terry Ray (Ellen Drew) (Secretary)
Ivan Miller (Inspector Duffy), Geraldine Hall (Maid), Stanhope Wheat-
croft (designer), Frank O'Connor (policeman).

FORLORN RIVER. Paramount, 7-2-37. Presented by Adolph Zuk-
or. Prod: Harold Hurley. Scr: Stuart Anthony, Stuart Yost from
the book by Zane Grey. Ed: John Link. Mus: Boris Morros.
Photog: Harry Hallenberger. 56 min.
     Re-issued as RIVER OF DESTINY.
     Re-make of 1926 version directed by John Waters, utilizing
some stock footage from the earlier production. Songs: "Sweet
Betsy from Pike," "Red River Valley."
     Cast: Larry "Buster" Crabbe (Nevada), June Martel (Ina
Blaine), John Patterson (Ben Ida), Harvey Stephens (Les Setter),
Chester Conklin (Sheriff Alec Grundy), Lew Kelly (Sheriff Jim Hen-
ry Warner), Syd Saylor (Weary Pierce), William Duncan (Blaine),
Raphael "Ray" Bennett (Bill Hall), Ruth Warren (Millie Moran),
Lee Powell (Duke), Oscar G. "Dutch" Hendrian (Sam), Robert E.
Homans (Jeff Winters), Purnell Pratt (David Ward), Larry Lawrence
(Ed), Barlowe Borland (Cashier), Tom Ung (Barber), Merrill McCor-
mick (Deputy Chet Parker), Vester Pegg (Deputy Hank Gordon),
Spike Spackman, Jack Moore, Cecil Kellogg, Frank Cordell, Bob
Clark (cowboys), Gordon Jones (Lem Watkins), Jay Wilsey (Buffalo
Bill, Jr.), (Pete Hunter).

THUNDER TRAIL. Paramount, 10-22-37. Presented by Adolph
Zukor. Scr: Robert Yost, Stuart Anthony. Photog: Karl Struss.
Ed: John Link. Mus: Boris Morros, adapted from George Antheil's
score for DeMille's THE PLAINSMAN (1936). Based on the book
Arizona Ames by Zane Grey. 56 min.
     Working Titles: ARIZONA AMES, BUCKAROO, RIDERS OF
THE PANAMINT, GUN SMOKE. Television Title: THUNDER PASS.

Cast: Gilbert Roland (Arizona Dick Ames), Marsha Hunt (Amy Morgan), Charles Bickford (Lee Tate), J. Carroll Naish (Rafael Lopez), James Craig (Bob Ames), Monte Blue (Jeff Graves), Barlowe Borland (Jim Morgan), Billy Lee (Bob Ames as a child), William Duncan (John Ames), Gene Reynolds (Richard Ames at 14), Edward Coxen (Martin), Vester Pegg (Lee), Earl Askam (Flinty), Bob Clark, Frank Cordell, Slim Hightower, Pardner Jones, Cecil Kellogg, Jack Moore, Guy Schultz, Ed Warren, Tommy Coats, Alan Burk, Danny Morgan (Cowboys), Carol Halloway, Gertrude Simpson, Mary Foy (women), Jack Daley (bartender), Lee Shumway, Ray Hanford (miners), Hank Bell (barfly).

BORN TO THE WEST. Paramount, 12-10-37. Prod: William Lackey. Scr: Stuart Anthony, Robert Yost from the novel by Zane Grey. Photog: J. D. "Dev" Jennings. Ed: John Link. Mus: Boris Morros.   59 min.

Re-make of BORN TO THE WEST, 1926 directed by John Waters.

Re-issued in 1950 as HELL TOWN.

Cast: John Wayne (Dare Rund), Johnny Mack Brown (Tom Fillmore), Marsha Hunt (Judith Worstall), John Patterson (Lynn Hardy), Monte Blue (Bart Hammond), Sid Saylor (Dink Hooley), Lucien Littlefield (John, cattle buyer), Nick Lukats (Jim Fallon), James Craig (Buck Brady), Johnny Boyle (Sam), Jack Kennedy (sheriff Pete Starr), Lee Prather (Lightning rod salesman), Jack Daley (Gambler), Vester Pegg (Bartender), Jim Thorpe (bit), Earl Dwire (cowhand), Al Ferguson (bartender), Neal Hart (Man at slot machine), Art Dillard (Hench).

BEHIND PRISON GATES. Columbia, 7-28-39. Prod: Wallace MacDonald. Story and Scr: Arthur T. Horman, Leslie T. White. Mus Dir: M. W. Stoloff. Photog: Allen G. Siegler. Ed: Richard Fantl. 61 min.

Working titles: NUMBERED MEN and ESCAPE FROM ALCATRAZ.

Cast: Brian Donlevy (Red Murray), Jacqueline Wells (Julie Bishop) (Sheila Murray), Joseph Crehan (Warden O'Neill), Paul Fix (Petey Ryan), George Lloyd (Marty Conroy), Dick Curtis (Capt. Simmons), Richard Fiske (Lyman), George Pearce (Dad Prentiss), Ralph Dunn (guard, Evans), James Craig (Jenkins), John Tyrell (Martin), Ed Lesaint (Dr. Mason), George Anderson (Matthews), Al Hill (Betts), George McCay (Walsh), Ky Robinson (Guard Slade), Ernie Adams (Voight), Dick Botiller (Graves), Charles McMurphy (guard), Al Herman (guard), Douglas Williams (guard), Kit Guard (convict), C. L. Sherwood (convict), Jack Evans (convict), Lester Dorr (Floyd), Earl Bunn (Machine Gun guard), Al Ferguson (Thornton), Ed Brady (guard), Shemp Howard (waiter), Del Lawrence (Turnkey), Chuck Hamilton (Parker), Harry Strang (Hastings), Abe Reynolds (prisoner), Eddie Foster (convict), Cy Schindell (convict).

FIVE LITTLE PEPPERS AND HOW THEY GREW. Columbia, 8-22-39. Scr: Nathalie Bucknall, Jefferson Parker based on the book by Margaret Sidney. Photog: Henry Freulich. Ed: James Sweeney.

Art Dir: Lionel Banks. Mus Dir: M.W. Stoloff. Story: J. Robert Bren, Gladys Atwater. Asst Dir: William Mull. 60 min.
    Cast: Edith Fellows (Polly Pepper), Clarence Kolb (Mr. King), Dorothy Peterson (Mrs. Pepper), Ronald Sinclair (Jasper), Charles Peck (Ben Pepper), Tommy Bond (Joey Pepper), Jimmie Leake (Davie Pepper), Dorothy Ann Seese (Phronsie Pepper), Leonard Carey (Martin), Bruce Bennett (chauffeur), Paul Everton (Townsend), George Lloyd (truck driver), Ed La Saint (Dr. Emery), Linda Winters (Dorothy Comingore), (bit nurse), Harry Hayden (Dr. Spence), Betty Roadman (cook), Bessie Wade (asst. cook), Harry Bernard (caretaker), Maurice Costello (Hart), Flo Campbell (bit woman).

MY SON IS GUILTY. Columbia, 12-28-39. Scr: Harry Shumate, Joseph Carole from a story by Karl Brown. Photog: Benjamin Kline. Ed: William Lyon. Asst. Dir: Arthur Black. Sound Engineer: Edward Bernds. 63 min.
    Cast: Bruce Cabot (Ritzy Kerry), Jacqueline Wells (Julie Bishop) (Julia Allen), Harry Carey (Tim Kerry), Glenn Ford (Barney), Wynne Gibson (Claire Morelli), Don Beddoe (Duke Mason), John Tyrell (Whitey Morris), Bruce Bennett (Lefty), Dick Curtis (Monk), Edgar Buchanan (Dan), Al Bridge (Police Lt.), Robert Sterling (Clerk), Edmund Cobb (Detective), Howard Hickman (Commissioner), Ivan "Dusty" Miller (Capt. Hespelt), Hermine Sterler (Barney's mother), Mary Gordon (Mrs. Monticelli), Stanley Brown (Police announcer), Richard Fiske (Cop), Beatrice Blinn (telephone girl), Eddie Fetherston (Harry), Hal Price (Gateman), Josef Forte (First Aid man), Forrest Taylor, Ed Peil, Sr. (cops), Julian Madison (taxi driver), Joe Scully (peddler), Roger Gray (workman), Roger Haliday (young man), Hugh Chapman (boy), Bessie Wade (woman), Jack Gardner, James Coughlin, Victor Travers (men). The Nicholas Brothers and extra Dennis O'Keefe in a dance sequence from DON'T GAMBLE WITH LOVE (1936).

FIVE LITTLE PEPPERS AT HOME. Columbia, 2-8-40. Scr: Harry Sauber from the book by Margaret Sidney. Photog: Allen G. Siegler. Ed: Viola Lawrence. Asst Dir: William Mull. Art Dir: Lionel Banks. Mus Dir: M.W. Stoloff. Sound: Edward Bernds. 65 min.
    Cast: Edith Fellows (Polly Pepper), Dorothy Ann Seese (Phronsie Pepper), Clarence Kolb (Mr. King), Dorothy Peterson (Mrs. Pepper), Ronald Sinclair (Jasper), Charles Peck (Ben Pepper), Tommy Bond (Joey Pepper), Bobby Larson (Davie Pepper), Rex Evans (Martin), Herbert Rawlinson (Mr. Decker), Laura Treadwell (Aunt Martha), Spencer Charters (Mr. Shomer), Bruce Bennett (King's chauffeur), Jack Rice (Bainbridge), Ed LeSaint (Dr. Emery), Ann Doran (nurse), Paul Everton (Townsend), John Dilson (Daniels), Joe DeStafani (Hart), Richard Fiske (Wilcox chauffeur), Tom London (miner), Sam Ash (Hartley), Marin Sais (neighbor woman).

BABIES FOR SALE. Columbia, 5-16-40. Prod: Ralph Cohn. Scr: Robert D. Andrews from a story by Robert Chapin, Joseph Carole. Photog: Benjamin Kline. Ed: Charles Nelson. Asst Dir: Thomas Flood. Sound: Lodge Cunningham. 64 min.

Cast: Rochelle Hudson (Ruth Williams), Glenn Ford (Steve Burton),
Miles Mander (Dr. Rankin), Joseph de Stefani (Dr. Gaines), Georgia
Caine (Miss Talbor), Isabel Jewell (Edith Drake), Eva Hyde (Gerda
Bonaker), Selmor Jackson (Mr. Kingsley), Mary Currier (Mrs. King-
sley), Edwin Stanley (Mr. Edwards), Douglas Wood (Dr. Aloshire),
John Qualen (Mr. Anderson), Helen Brown (Mrs. Anderson), Bruce
Bennett (cop), Dorothy Adams (mother), Ben Taggart (Mike Burke),
Edward Cassidy (Police capt.), Ed Thomas (Butler), Lew Kelly
(gardener), Joan Fowler (Mrs. Parker), Louis Payne (Mr. Foster),
Bill Lally (cop), John Bock (Relief collector).

ISLAND OF DOOMED MEN. Columbia, 5-20-40. Prod: Wallace
MacDonald. Story and Scr: Robert D. Andrews. Photog: Ben-
jamin Kline. Ed: James Sweeney. Asst Dir: Tomas Flood. Art
Dir: Lionel Banks. Gowns: Kalloch. Mus Dir: M.W. Stoloff.
Sound: Lodge Cunningham. 67 min.
    Cast: Peter Lorre (Stephen Danel), Rochelle Hudson (Lor-
raine Danel), Robert Wilcox (Mark Sheldon), Don Beddoe (Brand),
George E. Stone (Siggy), Kenneth MacDonald (Doctor), Charles Mid-
dleton (Capt. Cort), Stanley Brown (Eddie), Earl Gunn (Mitchell),
Don Douglas (official), Bruce Bennett (Hazen, guard), Sam Ash
(Ames), Eddie Laughton (Borgo), John Tyrell (Durkin), Richard
Fiske (Hale), Al Hill (Clinton), Trevor Bardette (Dist. Attorney),
Howard Hickman (Judge), Addison Richards (Jackson), Ray Bailey
(Mystery man), Lee Prather (Warden), Forbes Murray (Parole Board
chairman), George McKay (bookkeeper), Bernie Breakston (Townsend),
Harry Strang, Charles "Chuck" Hamilton (cops), Walter Miller (detec-
tive).

OUT WEST WITH THE PEPPERS. Columbia, 6-30-40. Scr: Harry
Rebuas from the book by Margaret Sidney. Photog: Benjamin Kline.
Ed: James Sweeney. Asst Dir: George Rhein. Art Dir: Lionel
Banks. Mus Dir: M.W. Stoloff. Sound: Lodge Cunningham. 62
min.
    Cast: Edith Fellows (Polly Pepper), Dorothy Ann Seese
(Phronsie Pepper), Dorothy Peterson (Mrs. Pepper), Charles Peck
(Ben Pepper), Tommy Bond (Joey Pepper), Bobby Larson (Davie
Pepper), Victor Killian (Jim Anderson), Helen Brown (Alice Ander-
son), Emory Parnell (Ole), Pierre Watkin (Mr. King), Ronald Sin-
clair (Jasper King), Walter Soderling (Caleb) Roger Gray (Tom), Hal
Price (Bill), Rex Evans (Martin), Millard Vincent, Wyndham Standing
(specialists), Andre Cheron (Frendhman), John Rogers (Ship steward),
Ernie Adams (telegraph operator), Kathryn Sheldon (Abbie), Eddie
Laughton (Lumberjack), Harry Bernard (Checker player).

FIVE LITTLE PEPPERS IN TROUBLE. Columbia, 9-1-40. Scr:
Harry Rebuas from the book by Margaret Sidney. Photog: Ben-
jamin Kline. Ed: Richard Fantl. Asst Dir: George Rhein. Art
Dir: Lionel Banks. Sound: Lodge Cunningham. 64 min.
    Cast: Edith Fellows (Polly Pepper), Dorothy Ann Seese
(Phronsie Pepper), Dorothy Peterson (Mrs. Pepper), Pierre Watkin
(Mr. King), Ronald Sinclair (Jasper King), Charles Peck (Ben Pep-
per), Tommy Bond (Joey Pepper), Bobby Larson (Davie Pepper),

Rex Evans (Martin), Kathleen Howard (Mrs. Wilcox), Mary Currier
(Mrs. Lansdowne), Helen Brown (Miss Roland), Betty Jane Graham
(May), Shirley Mills (June), Shirley Jean Rickert (Kiki), Antonia
Oland (Pam), Rita Quigley (Peggy), Beverly Michelson (Dorothy),
Judy Lynn (Betty), Bess Flowers (Miss Roberts), Reginald Simpson
(Mr. Corman), Carlton Griffin (Mr. Barnes), Sue Ann Burnett (Mad-
eline), Fred Mercer (Tim), Billy Lechner (Tom), Ruth Robinson
(Miss Simpson), Robert Carson (King's chauffeur), Eddie Laughton
(Wilcox's chauffer), Ann Barlow (Cynthia).

NOBODY'S CHILDREN. Columbia, 10-17-40. Adapted from the
radio program "Nobody's Children" by Walter White, Jr. Story:
Doris Malloy. Photog: Benjamin Kline. Ed: Richard Fantl.
Asst Dir: George Rhein. Art Dir: Lionel Banks. Sound: Lodge
Cunningham. 65 min.
     Cast: Edith Fellows (Pat), Billy Lee (Tommy), Georgia Caine
(Mrs. Marshall), Lois Wilson (Miss Jamieson), Walter White, Jr.
(himself), Ben Taggart (Mr. Miller), Mary Currier (Mrs. Miller),
Mary Gordon (Mary), Lillian West (Miss Spellman), William Gould
(Dr. Tovar), Russell Hicks (Sen. Hargreave), Janet Chapman (Peg-
gy), Mary Ruth (Carol), Cynthia Crane (Selma), Ivan Miller (Mr.
Stone), Dorothy Adams (Mrs. Stone), John Marston (Mr. Ferber),
Mira McKinney (Mrs. Ferber), William Forrest (Mr. Gregg), Ed-
ward Earle (Mr. Rogers), Edythe Elliott (Mrs. King), Lloyd Whit-
lock (Mr. Gibney), Georgia Backus (Mrs. Wynn), Jean Hunt (Flo),
James Crane (Jimmie), Jerry Mackey (Mickey), Fred Chapman (Hal),
Charles Flickinger (Walt), Sally Martin (June), Evelyn Young (Nurse),
Joel Friedkin (Grocery man), Nell Craig (receptionist), Lee Millar
(Dr. Gireaux), Stanley Brown (interne), Ed Thomas (Martin), Joel
Davis (Vincent), Ruddy Hartz (Junior Gregg).

THE PHANTOM SUBMARINE. Columbia, 12-20-40. Prod: Ralph
Cohn. Scr: Joseph Krumgold from a story by Augustus Muir.
Photog: Barney McGill. Ed: William Lyon. Art Dir: Lionel
Banks. Mus Dir: M. W. Stoloff. Asst. Dir: George Rhein.
Sound: George Cooper. 71 min.
     Cast: Anita Louise (Madeleine Neilson), Burce Bennett (Paul
Sinclair), Oscar O'Shea (Capt. Velsar), John Tyrell (Dreux), Pedro
de Cordoba (Henri Jerome), Victor Wong (Willie Ming), Charles
McMurphy (2nd mate), Harry Strang (chief engineer), Don Beddoe,
(Bartlett), Richard Fiske, Eddie Laughton (cab drivers), Budd Fine
(Chalon), Henry Zynda (Sub commander), Mildred Shay (cigarette
girl), Jacques Vanaire (head waiter), William Ruhl (Lt. Morrissey),
William Forrest (Jonas), Paul Scott (asst editor), Max Barwyn (But-
ler), Charles Sullivan (helmsman), Brick Sullivan, Al Rhein, George
Barton, Myron Geiger, John Kascier, Ward Arnold, Bernard Break-
ston, Dutch Hendrian (sailors).

THE BIG BOSS. Columbia, 4-28-41. Prod: Wallace MacDonald.
Scr: Howard J. Green. Photog: Benjamin Kline. Ed: Viola
Lawrence. 70 min.
     Cast: Otto Kruger (Jim Maloney), Gloria Dickson (Sue Pe-
ters), John Litel (Bob Dugan), Don Beddoe (Cliff Randall), Robert

Fiske (George Fellows), George Lessey (Sen. Williams), Joe Conti (Tony), Ralph Dunn (Detective), George Hickman (Jimmie), George McKay (Blake), Stanley Brown (radio announcer), Edmund Elton (Chief justice), Eddie Laughton (Robins), Ben Taggart (Dugan), Martin Spellman (Frankie), Schuyler Standish (Bob), Roger Gray (1st companion), Ted Oliver (2nd companion), John Tyrell (man), Al Bridge (man), Ernie Adams (prisoner).

RICHEST MAN IN TOWN. Columbia, 6-12-41. Prod: Jack Fier. Scr: Fanya Foss, Jerry Sackheim from a story by Jerry Sackheim. Art Dir: Lionel Banks. Photog: Philip Tannura. Ed: Al Clark, Mus: M. W. Stoloff. 69 min.
    Cast: Frank Craven (Abbott Crothers), Edgar Buchanan (Pete Martin), Eileen O'Hearn (Mary Martin), Roger Pryor (Tom Manning), Tom Dugan (Jack Leslie), George McKay (Jerry Ross), Jimmy Dodd (Bill Williams), Jan Duggan (Penelope Kidwell), John Tyrell (Oliver), Harry Tyler (Cliff Smithers), Will Wright (Frederick Johnson), Joel Friedkin (Ed Gunther), Edward Earle (Berton), Erville Alderson (Frank Jaquet, barber), Thomas W. Ross (Dr. Dickinson), Ferris Taylor (W. Hawkins, grocer), George Guhl (sheriff), Netta Packer, (Miss Andrews), William Gould (Thorpe), Kathryn Sheldon (Martha), Lee Prather (Game Warden), Edythe Elliott (elderly woman), Harry Depp, Ralph Peters (townsmen), James Farley (elderly man), Glenn Turnbull (dancer), Billy Benedict (young man), Harry Johnson (juggler), Ned Glass, Milburn Morante (men), Dorothy Vernon, Jessie Arnold (women), Ernie Adams (porter), Abe Reynolds (lounger) Murdock MacQuarrie (postman), Harry Bailey (teller), Edward McWade (old timer), Richard Fiske (son).

HARMON OF MICHIGAN. Columbia, 9-11-41. Prod: Wallace MacDonald. Scr: Howard J. Green from a story by Richard Goldstone, Stanley Rauh, Fredric Frank. Art Dir: Lionel Banks. Mus Dir: M. W. Stoloff. Photog: John Stumar. Ed: Arthur Seid. 66 min.
    Cast: Tom Harmon (himself), Anita Louise (Peggy Adams), Forest Evashevski (himself), Oscar O'Shea (Pop Branch), Warren Ashe (Bill Dorgan), Stanley Brown (Freddy Davis), Ken Christy (Joe Scudder), Tim Ryan (Flesh Regan), William Hall (Jimmy Wayburn), Larry Parks (Harvey), Lloyd Bridges (Ozzie), Chester Conklin (Gasoline Chuck), Bill Henry, Sam Balter, Wendell Niles, Tom Hanlon, Ken Niles (announcers), Harold "Hal" Landon (Calahan), David Durand (Perkins), Tommy Seidel (Smedovitch), Kenneth MacDonald (doctor), Nick Lukats (Pepper), Edythe Elliott (Mrs. Davis), Ben Taggart (Mr. Davis), Arthur Howard (Doctor), Cy Ring (Carter), Hal Cooke (Doctor), Dick Hogan (Bonetti), Franklin Parker (Bates), Edward Keane (city editor), Jack Carr (Jake), Jack O'Malley (Chuck).

TWO LATINS FROM MANHATTAN. Columbia, 10-2-41. Prod: Wallace MacDonald. Scr: Albert Duffy. Mus/Lyrics: Sammy Cahn, Saul Chaplin. Art Dir: Lionel Banks. Photog: John Stumar. Ed: Arthur Seid. 65 min.
    Cast: Joan Davis (Joan Daley), Jinx Falkenburg (Jinx Terry), Joan Woodbury (Lois Morgan), Fortunio Bonanova (Armando Rivero), Don Beddoe (Don Barlow), Marquita Madero (Marianela), Carmen

Morales (Rosita), Lloyd Bridges (Tommy Curtis), Sig Arno (Felipe
Rudolfo MacIntyre), Boyd Davis (Charles Miller), Antonio Moreno
(1st Latin), Rafael Storm (2nd Latin), John Dilson (Jerome Kittle-
man), Dick Elliott (Sylvester Kittleman), Tim Ryan (sgt.), Chuck
Morrison, Jack Cheatham (cops), Tyler Brooke (Hotel clerk), Don
Brodie (advertising man), Ed Bruce (Jed), Ed Fetherston (steward),
Lester Dorr (information attendant), Tony Merrill (steward), Ernie
Andams (stage Doorman), Bruce Bennett, Ralph Dunn (two Ameri-
cans), Stanley Brown (M. C.), Eddie Kane (manager), Mel Ruick
(radio announcer).

SING FOR YOUR SUPPER. Columbia, 12-4-41. Prod: Leon Bar-
sha. Scr: Harry Rebuas. Photog: Franz F. Planer. Art Dir:
Lionel Banks. Songs: "Why Is It So?" and "Boogie Woogie Piggy"
by Sammy Cahn and Saul Chaplin.   65 min.
        Cast: Jinx Falkenburg (Evelyn), Charles "Buddy" Rogers
(Larry), Bert Gordon (Russian), Eve Arden (Barbara), Don Beddoe
(Wing), Bernadene Hayes (Kay), Henry Kolker (Hayworth), Benny
Baker (William), Dewey Robinson ("Bonzo") Luise Squire (Mildred),
Larry Parks (Mickey), Lloyd Bridges (Doc), Harry Barris (Jimmy),
Walter Sande (Irv), Berni Gould (Art), Red Stanley, Pere Launders,
Harry Lang (musicians), Don Porter (Tim), Virginia Pherrin (Helen),
Jessie May Jackson (Mary), Dona Dax (Dorothy), Patricia Knox (Sue),
Sig Arno (Raskalnifoff), Eve Carlton, Franchon Estes, Valeri Grat-
ton, Betty Brooks, Dorothy Trail (hostesses), Earle Hodgins (Yokel),
Judith Linden (ticket girl), Ed Bruce (Jerk), Glenn Turnbull (Seaman),
Dink Freeman (seaman), Earl Bunn (counter man), Mildred Gover
(Nancy).

HONOLULU LU. Columbia, 12-11-41. Exec Prod: Irving Briskin.
Prod: Wallace MacDonald   Scr: Eliot Gibbons, Paul Yawitz from
a story by Eliot Gibbons. Addtnl Dialog: Ned Dandy. Ed: James
Sweeney. Mus Dir: M. W. Stoloff. Photog: Franz F. Planer.
Songs: "Honolulu Lu" and "That's The Kind of Work I Do" by Sam-
my Cahn and Saul Chaplin. 72 min.
        Cast: Lupe Velez (Consuelo Cordoba), Bruce Bennett (Skelly),
Leo Carillo (Don Estaban Cordoba), Marjorie Gateson (Mrs. Van
Derholt), Don Beddoe (Bennie Blanchard), Larry Parks (boy), For-
rest Tucker (Barney), George McKay (Horseface), Nina Campana
(Aloha), Roger Clark (Bill Van Derholt), Helen Dickson (Mrs.
Smythe), Curtis Railing (Mrs. Frobisher), Romaine Callender (Hotel
Manager), Ray Mala (Native cop), Lloyd Bridges (Desk clerk), John
Tyrell (Duffy), Eddie Laughton (Joe, Stagehand), Eileen O'Hearn,
Janet Shaw (debutantes), Joe Bautista (bellboy), Rudy Robles (eleva-
tor boy), Ed Mortimer, Elinor Counts, Mary Bovard (tourists),
Charlie Lung (cab driver), Dick Jensen, George Barton, Earl Bunn,
Charles D. Freeman, Kit Guard, Harry Anderson (Sailors), Ed
Mundy (magician), Hank Mann, Chester Conklin (comedians), Grace
Lenard (Soubrette), Blanche Payson (mezzo soprano), Ernie Adams
(Pierre), Sam Appel (Sgt.), Harry Depp (Dentist), Mickey Simp-
son (Strong man), Jack Raymond (Mr. Astouras), Kay Hughes
(Nurse), Al Hill (Detective), Jamiel Hasson (Police Sgt.), John Har-
mon (clerk), Al Bridge (shooting gallery proprietor).

SHUT MY BIG MOUTH. Columbia, 2-19-42. Prod: Robert Sparks.
Scr: Oliver Drake, Karen De Wolf, Francis Martin from a story by
Oliver Drake. Mus Dir: M. W. Stoloff. Dance Dir: Eddie Prinz.
Photog: Henry Freulich. Ed: Gene Havlick. 71 min.
    Cast: Joe E. Brown (Wellington Holmer), Adele Mara (Con-
chita Montoya), Victor Jory (Buckskin Bill), Fritz Feld (Robert
Oglethorpe), Don Beddoe (Hill), Will Wright (Long), Russell Simp-
son (Mayor Potter), Pedro De Cordoba (Don Carlos Montoya), Joan
Woodbury (Maria), Ralph Peters (Butch), Joe McGuinn (Hank), Lloyd
Bridges (Skinny), Forrest Tucker (Red), Noble Johnson (Chief Standing Bull), Chief Thundercloud (interpreter), Art Mix, Blackjack Ward
(bandits), Hank Bell (stage coach driver), Earle Hodgins (stage coach
guard), Eddy Waller (Happy), Fern Emmett (Maggie), Lew Kelly
(westerner), Dick Curtis (Joe), Edmund Cobb (stage agent), Bob
Folkerson (boy), Clay De Roy (Spanish driver), Ed Peil, Sr. (hotel
proprietor), Al Ferguson (Pursuer), John Tyrell (man), Georgia
Backus (woman).

TRAMP TRAMP TRAMP. Columbia, 3-12-42. Prod: Wallace Mac-
Donald. Scr: Harry Rebuas, Ned Dandy from a story by Shannon
Day, Hal Braham, Marian Grant. Photog: John Stumar. Ed: Wil-
liam Lyon. 68 min.
    Working title: CAMP NUTS.
    Cast: Jackie Gleason (Hank), Jack Durant(Jed), Florence
Rice (Pam Martin), Bruce Bennett (Tommy Lydell), Hallene Hill
(granny), Billy Curtis (midget), Mabel Todd (Vivian), Forrest Tuck-
er (Blond Bomber), James Seay (Biggie Waldron), John Tyrell
(Lefty), John Harmon (Mousey), Eddie Foster (Blackie), Al Hill
(Tim), Heinie Conklin (soldier), Kenneth MacDonald, Eddie Kane
(doctors), Walter Sande, Bud Geary (guards), William Gould (Col.),
Chuck Morrison (Col.'s guard), Herbert Rawlinson (ex-soldier com-
mander), Bud Jamison (Fat Man), Glenn Turnbull (Tall man), James
Millican (draftee), John Dilson (Judge Smith), Harry Strang, George
Turner, Lloyd Bridges, Eddie Laughton (guards).

HELLO ANNAPOLIS. Columbia, 4-23-42. Prod: Wallace Mac-
Donald. Scr: Ronald Davis, Tom Reed from a story by Tom Reed.
Art Dir: Lionel Banks. Mus Dir: M. W. Stoloff. Photog: Philip
Tannura. Ed: Arthur Seid. 62 min.
    Cast: Tom Brown (Bill Arden), Jean Parker (Doris Henley),
Larry Parks (Paul Herbert), Phil Brown Kansas City), Joseph Cre-
han (Evans Arden), Thurston Hall (Capt. Wendell), Ferris Taylor
(Capt. Forbes), Herbert Rawlinson (Capt. Dugan), Mae Busch (Miss
Jenkins), Robert Stevens (Robert Kellard), (George Crandall), Stan-
ley Brown (Norman Brennan), William Blees (Hazlett Houston),
Georgia Caine (Aunt Arabella), John Tyrell (male nurse), Charles
Jordan (Joe Jenkins), Jack Gardner, Cyril Ring (reporters), James
Millican (Lt. Blake), Wallis Clark (Nolan), Sam Flint (Admiral
Jones), Eddie Laughton (Hank), Barbara Brown (Mrs. Nolan), Glad-
den James (doctor), Forbes Murray (man), Arthur O'Connell (Phar-
macist's mate), Clayton Moore (Charles), Larry Williams (Under-
wood), William Forrest (Lt. Burns), Kip Good (Plebe), Eddie

Dew (watch officer), Boyd Davis (Exeuctive officer), Donald Curtis (Chief petty officer).

SWEETHEART OF THE FLEET. Columbia, 5-21-42. Prod: Jack Fier. Scr: Albert Duffy, Maurice Tumbragel from a story by Albert Duffy. Mus Dir: M. W. Stoloff. Photog: Philip Tannura. Ed: Richard Fantl. Addtnl Dialog: Ned Dandy. 65 min.

Cast: Joan Davis (Phoebe Weyms), Jinx Falkenburg (Jerry Gilbert), Joan Woodbury (Kitty Leslie), Blanche Stewart (Brenda), Elvia Allman (Cobina), William Wright (Lt. Philip Blaine), Robert Stevens (Kellard), (Ensign George "Tip" Landers), Tim Ryan (Gordon Crouse), George McKay (Hambone Skelly), Walter Sande (Daffy Bill), Dick Elliott (Chamley), Charles Trowbridge (Commander Howes), Tom Seidel (Bugsy), Irving Bacon (Standish), Stanley Brown (Call boy), Lloyd Bridges (Sailor), Boyd Davis (Mayor), John Tyrell (bell boy), Gary Breckner (radio announcer).

PARACHUTE NURSE. Columbia, 6-18-42. Prod: Wallace MacDonald. Scr: Rian James. Story: Elizabeth Meehan. Art Dir: Lionel Banks. Asst Dir: George Rhein. Ed: Mel Thorsen. Mus Dir: M. W. Stoloff. Art Assoc: Arthur Royce. Sound: Edward Bernds. Photog: Philip Tannura. 65 min.

Cast: Marguerite Chapman (Glenda White), William Wright (Lt. Woods), Kay Harris (Dottie Morrison), Lauretta M. Schimmeler (Jane Morgan), Louise Allbritten (Helen Ames), Frank Sully (Sgt. Peters), Diedra Vale (Ruby Stark), Evelyn Wahl (Gretchen Ernst), Shirley Patterson (Katherine Webb), Eileen O'Hearn (Mary Mack), Roma Aldrich (Nita Dominick), Marjorie Reardon (Riordan) (Wendie Holmes), Catherine Craig (Lt. Mullins), Douglas Wood (Major Devon), Forrest Tucker (Lt. Tucker), John Tyrell (Sgt. Tyrell), Ed Laughton (Sgt. Laughton), Mary Zavian, Sally Cairns, Ann Markall, Gwen Holubar, Ninette Crawford, Dona Dax, Helen Foster, Mary Milburn, Dorothy Trail, Diane Royal, Audrene Brier, Mary Windsor (Company "C" Girls), Barbara Brown (Mrs. Jordan), Elizabeth Dow (Doris), Alma Carroll (Mae), Kit Guard (truck driver), Theo Coleman (nurse), June Melville (Meehan), Jan Wiley (Tenderfeet).

THE SPIRIT OF STANFORD. Columbia, 9-10-42. Prod: Sam White. Scr: Howard J. Green, William Brent, Nick Lucats. Art Dir: Lionel Banks. Mus Dir: M. W. Stoloff. Photog: Franz F. Planer, Charles Stumar. Ed: James Sweeney. 75 min.

Cast: Frankie Albert (himself), Marguerite Chapman (Fay Edwards), Matt Willis (Link Wyman), Shirley Patterson (June Rogers) Kay Harris (Edna), Robert Stevens (Kellard) (Cliff Bonnard), Lloyd Bridges (Don Farrell), Forrest Tucker (Buzz Costello), Billy Lechner (Skeats), Harold Landon (Butch), Volta Boyer (Mrs. Bixby), Ernie Nevers (himself), Dale Van Sickel (Frosh backfield coach), John Gallaudet (Frosh coach), Arthur Loft (Varsity coach), Jim Westerfield (man), Stanley Brown (Kenny), Ed Laughton (asst. coach), John Tyrell (reporter), Ray Walker (Duke Conners), Winstead Sheffield, "Doodles" Weaver, Richard Hogan (men), Frank Ferguson (psychology professor), Ralph Brooks (sports reporter), Ken Carpenter (sports announcer), Lester Dorr (reporter), Jack Gardner (photographer), Knox Manning (sports announcer--himself), Thomas Quinn (sports reporter).

A MAN'S WORLD. Columbia, 9-17-42. Exec Prod: Irving Briskin. Prod: Wallace MacDonald. Scr: Edward T. Lowe, Jack Roberts. Story: Jack Roberts, George Buckner. Ed: Richard Fantl. Mus Dir: M. W. Stoloff. Photog: George Meehan. 60 min.

   Cast: William Wright (Dan O'Driscoll), Marguerite Chapman (Mona Jackson), Larry Parks (Chick O'Driscoll), Wynne Gibson (Blossom Donovan), Roger Pryor (Bugsy Nelson), Frank Sully (Sammy Collins), Ferris Taylor ("Chief" DeShon), Edward Van Sloan (Doc Stone), Clancy Cooper (John Black), James Millican (Parks), Lloyd Bridges (Brown), Al Hill (Eddie Dartlett), Ralph Peters (Vince Carrol), Alan Bridge (Capt. Peterson), Eddie Kane (Doc Drake), Beaulah Parkington, Grace Lenard, Diana Snyder, Thelma White (girls), Frank Richards (Thomas), Shirley Patterson (Nurse Bentley).

LUCKY LEGS. Columbia, 10-1-42. Exec Prod: Irving Briskin. Prod: Wallace MacDonald. Story, Scr: Stanley Rubin, Jack Hartfield, Mus Dir: M. W. Stoloff. Photog: Philip Tannura. Ed: Arthur Seid. 64 min. Title Song: Sammy Cahn, Saul Chaplin.
   Cast: Jinx Falkenburg (Gloria Carroll), Leslie Brooks (Jewel Perkins), Kay Harris (Calamity Jane), Elizabeth Patterson (Annabelle Dinwiddie), Russell Hayden (James Abercrombie), William Wright (Pinkie Connors), Don Beddoe (Ned McLane), Adele Rowland (Hettie Dinwiddie), Edward Marr (Mike Manley), George McKay (Red Fenton), James C. Morton (Pat), Eddie Kane (J. N. Peters), Shirley Patterson (chambermaid), Dick Talmadge (Sam), Charles Sullivan (Lou), Harry Tenbrook (Dan), Ralph Sanford (bartender), Rita and Rubins (dance team), Brick Sullivan (policeman), Adele Mara (secretary), Billy Curtis (newsboy), Romaine Callender (Crump), John Tyrell (dance director), Jack Gardner, Al Hill (reporters), Ethan Laidlaw (Duke), Tyler Brooke (Jenkins), Gohr Van Vleck (Doorman), Jack Rice (jewelry salesman), John Holland (fur salesman), Franklin Parker (real estate salesman), Frank Swales (inventor), Jack Carr (food vendor), Cyril Ring (yacht salesman), Ernest Hilliard (salesman), Blake McEdwards (Red Arrow messenger), Frank Skully (bit).

LAUGH YOUR BLUES AWAY. Columbia, 11-12-42. Exec Prod: Irving Briskin. Prod: Jack Fier. Story, Scr: Harry Sauber. Addtnl Dial: Ned Dandy. Songs: "Dark Eyes," "Prairie Parade," "Down in the Heat of Smetna," "Gin Rhumba," "He's My Guy" by Larry Markes, Dick Charles. Ed: Richard Fantl. Art Dir: Lionel Banks. Art Assoc: Paul Murphy. Int Dec: Robert Priestley. Mus Dir: M. W. Stoloff. Photog: Philip Tannura. 70 min.
   Cast: Jinx Falkenburg (Pam Crawford), Bert Gordon (Boris Rascalnikoff, the "Mad Russian"), Douglass Drake (Johnny Mitchell), (Jimmy Westerly), Isobel Elsom (Mrs. Westerly), George Lessey (Mr. Westerly), Vivian Oakland (Mrs. Conklin), Dick Elliott (Mr. Conklin), Phyllis Kennedy (Priscilla Conklin), Robert Grieg (Wilfred), Nora

Lou (Martin), and Her Pals of the Golden West (musical act), Roger
Clark (Blake Henley), Frank Sully (Buck), Clyde Fillmore (Sen. Hargrave), Barbara Brown (Mrs. Hargrave), Edna Holland (Mrs. Watson), Edward Earle (Mr. Larkin), Wyndham Standing (Mr. Jamison),
Florence Wix (Mrs. Jamison), Joel Friedkin, James Morton, Earle
Hodgins (actors), Walter Baldwin (clerk), Eddie Kane (headwaiter),
John T. Murray (Judge Watson), Bess Flowers (Mrs. Larkin), Shirley Patterson (Mrs. Knox), Ken Christy (Mr. Burke), Louise Squires
(blonde), Hallene Hill (woman), Eddie Laughton (man), John Tyrell
(decorator), Nora Lou Martin, Arthur A. Wenzel, Richard Robert
Rinehart, Eugene Walsh, Jack Lewis (musicians).

REVEILLE WITH BEVERLY. Columbia, 2-4-43. Prod: Sam White.
Scr: Howard J. Green, Jack Henley, Albert Duffy. Art Dir: Lion-
el Banks. Mus Dir: M. W. Stoloff. Photog: Philip Tannura. Ed:
James Sweeney. 78 min.
    Cast: Ann Miller (Beverly Ross), William Wright (Barry
Lang), Dick Purcell (Andy Adams), Franklin Pangborn (Vernon
Lewis), Tim Ryan (Mr. Kennedy), Larry Parks (Eddie Ross), Bar-
bara Brown (Mrs. Ross), Douglas Leavitt (Mr. Ross), Adele Mara
(Evelyn Ross), Walter Sande (Canvassback), Wally Vernon (Stomp
McCoy), Andrew Tombes (Mr. Smith), Eddie Kane (medical officer),
Boyd Davis (Col. Humphrey), Eddy Chandler (top sgt.), Doodles
Weaver (Elmer), Eugene Jackson (Jackson), Harry Anderson (Sgt.
Anderson), Si Jenks (Jenks), David Newell (sentry), Jack Rice (Dav-
is), Irene Ryan (Elsie), John T. Murray (director), Virginia Sale
(Mrs. Browning), Herbert Rawlinson (announcer), Ernest Hilliard,
Jean Inness (Mr. and Mrs. Oliver), Shirley Mills (Laura Jean),
Maude Eburne (Maggie), Bobby Barber (Collins), and the following
musical acts: Bob Crosby and His Orchestra, Freddie Slack
and His Orchestra with Ella Mae Morse, Duke Ellington and
His Orchestra, Count Basie and His Orchestra, Frank Sinatra,
The Mills Brothers, The Radio Rogues.

LET'S HAVE FUN. Columbia, 3-4-43. Prod: Jack Fier. Scr:
Harry Sauber. Art Dir: Lionel Banks. Mus Dir: M. W. Stoloff.
Photog: Philip Tannura. Ed: William Claxton. 63 min.
    Working Title: LAUGH YOUR BLUES AWAY.
    Cast: Bert Gordon (Boris Rascalnikoff), Margaret Lindsay
(Florence Blake), John Beal (Richard Gilbert), Dorothy Ann Seese
(Toni Gilbert), Constance Worth (Diana Crawford), Leonid Kinskey
(Gregory Loosnikoff), Sig Arno (Ivan Bloosnikoff), Edward Keane
(James Bradley), Ernest Hilliard ("Pepe" J. Morgan), John Tyrell
(Jimmy Wood), Nedda Packer (Miss Berkley), Louise Squire (Bur-
lesque Queen), Hallene Hill (Woman), John T. Murray (actor),
James Morton (Character man), Walter Baldwin (hotel clerk), Shir-
ley Patterson (bit girl), Jayne Hazard (Norma), Al Herman (bit
man), Edward Kane (Norton), Beryl Wallace (Sonia), Reginald Simpson, Ray Johnson, Wedgwood Nowell (reporters), Gwen Seager (bit
woman), Joe Novak (bit man), Dick Rush (doorman), Pat McVey
(Bates).

SHE HAS WHAT IT TAKES. Columbia, 4-15-43. Prod: Colbert
Clark. Story: Robert Lee Johnson, Paul Yawitz. Scr: Paul
Yawitz. Art Dir: Lionel Banks. Mus Dir: M. W. Stoloff. Photog:
Philip Tannura. Ed: Al Clark. 66 min.
     Cast: Jinx Falkenburg (Fay Morris), Tom Neal (Roger Rut-
ledge), Constance Worth (June Leslie), Douglas Leavitt (Paul Miloff),
Joe King (Lee Schuleman), Matt Willis ("One-Round" Beasley), Dan-
iel Ocko (Nick Partos), George McKay (Mike McManus), George
Lloyd ("Shocker" Dodie), Robert Homans (Capt. Pat O'Neal), Joseph
Crehan (George Clarks), John H. Dilson (Chamberlein Jones), Bar-
bara Brown (Mrs. Walters), Harry Hayden (Mr. Jason), Armand
(Curley) Wright (Tony), Jack Rice (Kimball) Cy Ring (Photographer),
Michael Owen (call boy), Frank O'Connor (police sgt.), Tyler Brooke
(stage mgr.), Ernie Adams (actor), Jayne Hazard, Alma Carroll,
Elizabeth Russell (Chorus girls), Frank Ragney (trainer), Eddie
Dunn, Dave Willock (cab drivers), Eddie Chandler, Ray Teal, Wil-
liam Heade (cops), David McKim (Call boy), Jack Gardner (clerk),
Harry Tyler (hotel mgr.), Richard Chandler (Western Union Boy),
Netta Packer (receptionist), Milt Kibbee, Wilbur Mack (men), John
Estes (elevator boy), Ann Evers (Janesy), Eddie Kane (Dillway).

WHAT'S BUZZIN' COUSIN? Columbia, 7-8-43. Prod: Jack Fier,
Story: Aben Kandel. Scr: Harry Sauber. Art Dir: Lionel Banks.
Mus Dir: M. W. Stoloff. Dance Dir: Nick Castle. Photog: Joseph
Walker. Ed: James Sweeney. Set Dec: Jospeh Kish. Songs:
"1875" by Wally Anderson; "Ain't That Just Like a Man, " "Short,
Fat, and 4-F" by Don Raye, Gene DePaul; "Nevada" by Mort Greene,
Walter Donaldson; "Knocked-Out Nocturne" by Jacques Press. Other
songs by Walter Samuels, Saul Chaplin, Charles Newman, Lew Pol-
lack and Eddie Cherkose. 75 min.
     Cast: Ann Miller (Ann Crawford), Eddie Anderson (Rochester),
John Hubbard (Jimmie Ross), Leslie Brooks (Josie), Jeff Donnell
(Billie), Carol Hughes (May), Theresa Harris (Blossom), Roy Gordon
(Jim Langford), Bradley Page (Pete Hartley), Warren Ashe (Dick
Bennett), Dub Taylor (Jed), Betsy Gay (Saree), Louis Mason (Hill
Billy), Eugene Jackson (bellboy), Jessie Arnold (Mrs. Hill Billy),
Erville Alderson (gas station attendant), Harry Tyler (hotel clerk),
Walter Soderling (Mr. Hayes), Eddie Fetherstone (Radio repairman),
John Tyrrell, Craig Woods (henchman), Freddy Martin and His
Orchestra.

IS EVERYBODY HAPPY? Columbia, 10-28-43. Prod: Irving Bris-
kin. Scr: Monte Brice. Art Dir: Lionel Banks. Mus Dir: M. W.
Stoloff. Photog: L. W. O'Connell. Ed: James Sweeney. 73 min.
     Cast: Ted Lewis (himself), Michael Deane (Tom), Nan Wynn
(Kitty), Larry Parks (Jerry), Lynn Merrick (Ann), Bob Haymes
(Artie), Dick Winslow (Joe), Harry Barris (Bob), Robert Stanford
(Frank), Fern Emmett (Mrs. Broadbelt), Eddie Kane (Salbin), Ray
Walker (Lou Merwin), Anthony Marlowe (Carl Muller), George Reed
(Mississippi), Perc Launders (Rod), Sally Cairns, Odessa Lauren,
Sheila Stuart (pretty girls), Paul Bryant (Snowball), Herbert Heyes
(Colonel), Madeline Grey (Colonel's wife), Broderick O'Farrell

(Justice of the Peace), Billy Bletcher (Waiter), Charles D. Wilson (Mr. Smaltz), Donald Kerr (Bouncer), George McKay (cop), Tom Kennedy (Desk Sgt), Phyllis Kennedy (Daley), Dick Rush (jailer), Clinton Rosemond (doorman), Jesse Graves (doctor), Vi Athens (girl), John Tyrrell (caller bit), Eddie Laughton (clerk bit), Eddie Bruce (proprietor), Kit Guard, Jack Gardner, Sidney Melton (players), Kirk Alyn (Thew), Muni Seroff (Maitre d'Hotel), Jack Salling (newsboy), William Sloan (Boy).

BEAUTIFUL BUT BROKE. Columbia, Prod: Irving Briskin. Story: Arthur Houseman. Scr: Monte Brice. Art Dir: Lionel Banks. Mus Dir: M. W. Stoloff. Photog: L. W. O'Connell. Ed: Richard Fantl. Songs by L. Wolfe Gilbert and Ben Oakland; James Cavanaugh and Walter G. Samuels; Jimmy Paul, Dick Charles and Walter Markes; Mort Greene and Walter Donahue; Phil Moore. Songs: "Take the Door to the Left," "Mama, I Want to Make Rhythm" "Shoo-Shoo Baby," "We're Keeping It Private (Me and Private Jones)," etc; 72 min.
    Cast: Joan Davis (Dottie), John Hubbard (Bill Drake), Jane Frazee (Salty Richards), Judy Clark (Sue Ford), Bob Haymes (Jack Foster), Danny Mummert (Rollo), Byron Foulger (Maxwell McKay), George McKay (station master), Ferris Taylor (Mayor), Isabel Withers (Mrs. Grayson), John Eldridge (Waldo Main), Grace Hayle (Birdie Benson), John Dilson (Putnam), Janice Simmons, Gloria Chappell, Helen Ireland (sax players), Lorraine Paige (drums or trumpet player), Joe King (Mr. Martin), Emmett Vogan (Hotel manager), Joanne Frank (secretary), Evelyn Porter (Minnie), George Bronson (shy soldier), John Tyrrell (Sgt), Lew Kelly (vendor), Thomas Kingston (waiter), Joseph Palma, Brian O'Hara, Kernan Cripps, Chuck Hamilton (defense workers), Robert Williams (train conductor), Ben Taggart (Pullman conductor), Lewis Wilson, Ronnie Rondell (pilots), Christine McIntyre (telephone operator), Gerald Pierce (elevator boy), Wesley Bilson, Arthur Carrington, Bunky Fleischman, Gary Gray, Jack O'Brian, Kathleen Earhart, Patsy Patterson, Geraldine Tinker, Jean Vanderwilt (Bunny Sunshine), June Arleen Wilson (children), Laura Gruver, Marguerite Campbell (trumpet players), Genevieve Duran (guitar player), Ruth Gordon (Bass player), Dorothy Frons (trombone player).

HEY ROOKIE. Columbia, 3-9-44. Prod: Irving Briskin. Assoc. Prod: Henry Myers, Edward Eliscu, Jay Gorney. Scr: Henry Myers, Edward Eliscu, Jay Gorney. Art Dir: Lionel Banks. Mus Dir: M. W. Stoloff. Dance Dir: Val Raset. Photog: L. W. O'Connell. Ed: James Sweeney. Based upon the musical play by E. B. (Zeke) Colvan and Doris Colvan. Title "Hey Rookie" originated by John Percy Hallowell Walker. Originally produced by The Yardbirds of Fort MacArthur, Cal. Songs: "Hey Rookie" by Henry Myers, Edward Eliscu, Jay Gorney; "He's Got a Wave in His Hair" by Sonny Burke, Hughie Prince; "So What! Serenade" by James Cavanaugh, John Redman, Nat Simon; "Take a Chance," "There Goes Taps," "It's Great to Be in Uniform," "It's a Swelluva Life in the Army," "When the Yardbirds Come to Town" by Sgt. J. C.

Lewis, Jr.; "Rockin' and Ridin'" by S. La Pertche, Danny Hurd;
"American Boy" by Al Dubin, Jimmy V. Monaco; "Streamlined Sheik,"
"You're Good for My Morale" by Myers, Eliscu, Gorney. Asst Dir:
Wilbur McGaugh, 71 min. Filmed at Fort MacArthur, California.
    Cast: Joe Besser (Pudge Pfeiffer), Ann Miller (Winnie Clark),
Larry Parks (Jim Lighter), Joe Sawyer (sgt), Jimmy Little (Bert
Pfeiffer), Selmer Jackson (Col Robbins), Larry Thompson (Capt.
Jessop), Barbara Brown (Mrs. Clark), Charles Trowbridge (General
Willis), Charles Wilson (Sam Jonas), Syd Saylor (Corp. Trupp),
Doodles Weaver (Maxon), Mel Shubert (Capt.), Bill Shawn (dancer),
Jack Lee (officer), Eddie Dunn (doctor), Philip Van Zandt (psychia-
trist), Ralph Dunn (Sgt, examiner), Sidney Melton (bored soldier),
Robert Lowell (Jitterbug), Tom Dugan (sourpuss soldier), Buddy
Yarus (George Tyne), (Cheerful) Bob Haymes (Farm boy), Eddie
Acuff (Jokester), Harry Barris (pianist), Jimmy Dodd (Bopkins),
Jack Rice (Highbrow), Joey Ray (M.C.), Dick Curtis (sgt), Ed
Laughton (Stage mgr), Teddy Mangean (call boy), George Eldredge
(Capt. Mulligan), John Tyrrell, Tim Morris (soldiers), Jeanne Bates
(Chief VAAC), Bonnie Shelley (dancer), Spot (dalmation), and fea-
turing Hi-Lo-Jack and the Dame, the Condos Bros., The Johnson
Bros., Jack Gilford, Judy Clark and the Six Solid Senders, Ventrilo-
quist Bob Evans and his dummy "Jerry O'Leary," Hal McIntyre and
His Orchestra, and The Vagabonds (Pete Peterson, Till Risso, Al
Torrieri, Don Germano),

JAM SESSION. Columbia. Prod: Irving Briskin. Story: Harlan
Ware, Patterson McNutt. Scr: Mann Seff. Art Dir: Lionel Banks,
Paul Murphy. Mus Dir: M.W. Stoloff. Photog: L.W. O'Connell.
Ed: Richard Fantl. 77 min.
    Cast: Ann Miller (Terry Baxter), Jess Barker (George Car-
ter Haven), Charles D. Brown (Raymond Stuart), Eddie Kane (Lloyd
Marley), George Eldredge (Berkley Tell), Renie Riano (Miss Tobin),
Clarence Muse (Henry), Pauline Drake (Evelyn), Charles La Torre
(Coletta), Anne Loos (Cavenish), Ray Walker (Fred Wylie), Mar-
guerite Campbell (girl jitterbug), George McKay (policeman), Robert
Williams (taxi driver), Vernon Dent (Butler), John Dilson (man),
Ethan Laidlaw (Jackson), Victor Travers (actor), Charles Haefell
(Rostler), Allen Fox (Cutter), Eddie Hall (smart young man), Eddie
Bruce (guide), Bill Shawn (dancer), Ted Mapes (guard), Hank Bell
(driver), John Tyrrell (director), Terry Frost (asst. dir.), Paul
Zeremba (Rip), Marilyn Johnson (stenographer), Constance Worth
(Miss Dooley), Nelson Leigh (Blake), Joanne Frank (girl), Jay Eaton
(designer), George Carleton (cop), Margaret Fealy (Old Lady), Ben
Taggart (Willie), Eddie Laughton (asst. dir.), Thomas Kingston
(sound engineer), J. Reilly Thompson (boy jitterbug), and featuring
the orchestras of Charlie Barnet, Louis Armstrong, Alvino Rey,
Jan Garber, Teddy Powell, Glen Gray and His Casa Loma Orchestra,
The Pied Pipers and Nan Wynn.

LOUISIANA HAYRIDE. Columbia, 7-13-44. Story: Paul Yawitz,
Manny Seff, Scr: Paul Yawitz. Asst Dir: Rex Bailey. Art Dir:
Lionel Banks, Walter Holschier. Mus Dir: M.R. Bakaleinikoff.

Photog: L. W. O'Connell. Ed: Otto Meyer. Set Dir: John W. Pascoe. Sound: Philip Falkner. Songs: "You Gotta Go Where the Train Goes," "Rainbow Road" by Kim Gannon and Walter Kent; "I'm a Woman of the World" by Jerry Seelen and Saul Chaplin; "Put Your Arms Around Me, Honey" by Junie McCree and Albert Von Tilzer. 67 min.

Cast: Judy Canova (Judy Crocker), Ross Hunter (Gordon Pearson), Richard Lane (J. Huntington McMasters), Matt Willis (Jed Crocker), George McKay (Canada Brown), Minerva Urecal (Maw Crocker), Hobart Cavanaugh (Malcolm Cartwright), Eddie Kane (War- burton), Nelson Leigh (Wiffle), Arthur Loft (director), Robert Hom- ans (Officer Conlon), Russell Hicks (Forbes), Jessie Arnold (Aunt Hepzibah), Walter Baldwin (Uncle Lem), Jack Rice (hotel clerk), Lew Meehan, Charles Sullivan, Jack Gardner, Brian O'Hara (cabbies), Syd Saylor, Pat West (boarders), Ernie Adams (pawnbroker), Si Jenks (man), Ben Taggart (conductor), Eddie Bartell (salesman), Earl Dewey (governer), Bud Jamison (Doorman), George Ford, Geroge Magrill (troopers), Reba King, Betty Jane Graham, (girls), Teddy Mangean (messenger), Joe Palma (cameraman), Constance Purdy (Mrs. Vandergriff), Danny Desmond (bellboy), Charles Sher- lock, Charles Marsh (photographers), Buddy Yarus (George Tyne), (Joe, asst. dir.), Gene Stutenroth (studio guard), Christine McIntyre (movie star), Frank Hagney (bartender), Eddy Chandler, Lane Chand- ler (plainclothesmen), Art Miles (brakeman), Louis Mason (farmer), Edwin Stanley (producer), Fred Graff (casting dir.), Harry Wilson, Dirk Thane (listeners on train).

THE BEAUTIFUL CHEAT. Universal, 7-20-45. Prod: Charles Barton. Scr: Ben Markson. Story: Manny Seff, Fritz Rotter. Addtnl Dial: Elwood Ullman. Art Dir: John B. Goodman, Abraham Grossman. Photog: Woody Bredell. Ed: Ray Snyder. Set Dec: Russell A. Gausman, Ted Von Hemert. Sound: Bernard Brown. Sound Tech: Jack A. Bolger, Jr. Asst Dir: Ronnie Rondell. Gowns: Vera West. Dial Dir: Escha Bledsoe. Songs: "Is You Is Or Is You Ain't?" by Billy Austin and Louis Jordan; "Stop and Make Love" by Jack Brooks; "Ooh, What You Do to Me" by Jack Brooks and Edgar Fairchild. 59 min.

Working title: IT'S NEVER TOO LATE.

Cast: Bonita Granville (Alice) Noah Beery, Jr. (Prof. Haven), Margaret Irving (Olympia Haven), Sarah Selby (Athena Haven), Irene Ryan (Miss Kent), Carol Hughes (Dolly), Milburn Stone (Lucius Hav- en), Tom Dillon (Officer Cassidy), Edward Gargan (Blue Moon man- ager), Lester Matthews (Harley), Edward Fielding (Dr. Pennypacker), Tommy Bond (Jimmy), Sandra Morgan (neighbor), John Kelley (Dr. McGinty), Mary Currier (Mrs. Woodside), Johnny Berkes (waiter), Perc Launders (Patron in flight), Charles Saggau (teammate), Fred Walton (cab driver), Eddy Chandler, Lee Phelps (cops).

MEN IN HER DIARY. Universal, 9-14-45. Exec Prod: Howard Welsch. Assoc Prod: Charles Barton. Story: Kerry Shaw. Scr: F. Hugh Hubert, Elwood Ullman. Adapt: Lester Cole. Mus: Mil- ton Rosen. Art Dir: John B. Goodman, Richard H. Riedel. Dance

Dir: Carlos Romero. Photog: Paul Ivano. Ed: Paul Landres.
Sets: Russell A. Gausman, E. R. Robinson. Sound: Bernard
Brown. Assoc Set Dec: E. R. Robinson. 73 min.
    Cast: Peggy Ryan (Dorie Mann), Jon Hall (Randolph Glen-
ning), Louise Allbritton (Isabel Glenning), William Terry (Tommy
Burton), Virginia Grey (Diana Lee), Ernest Truex (Williams), Jac-
queline De Wit (Marjorie), Alan Mowbray (Douglas Crane), Eric
Blore (Florist), Lorraine Miller (Pat Mann), Samuel S. Hinds (Judge
Moran), Maxie Rosenbloom (Moxie), Sig Rumann (Madame Irene),
Addison Richards (Cavanaugh), Arthur Loft (Attorney Reynolds), Min-
erva Urecal (Mrs. Braun), Robin Raymond (Stella), Vivian Austin
(Linda), Lorin Baker (man).

SMOOTH AS SILK. Universal, 3-1-46. Exec Prod: Howard Welsch.
Assoc Prod: Jack Bernhard. Story: Florence Ryerson, Colin
Clements. Scr: Dane Lussier, Kerry Shaw, Mus: Ernest Gold.
Art Dir: Jack Otterson, Robert Clatworthy. Photog: Woody Bren-
dell. Ed: Ray Snyder. Set Dec: Russell A. Gausman, Ted Von
Hemert. Sound: Bernard Brown. 65 min.
    Working Title: NOTORIOUS GENTLEMAN.
    Cast: Kent Taylor (Mark Fenton), Virginia Grey (Paula),
Jane Adams (Susan), Milburn Stone (John Kimble), John Litel (Stephen
Elliott), Danny Morton (Dick Elliott), Charles Trowbridge (Fletcher
Holliday), Theresa Harris (Louise), Harry Cheshire (Wolcott), Bert
Moorhouse, Ralph Brooks (detectives), Joe Kirk (Joe), Regina Wallace
(woman), Boyd Davis (Eddie), Helen Chapman (daughter), Stuart
Holmes (old friend), Chester Conklin (doorman), Jack Davidson (Sam),
Jack Frank, Frank Marlowe (reporters), William O'Brien (headwait-
er), Claire Whitney (woman).

THE TIME OF THEIR LIVES. Universal, 8-16-46. Exec Prod:
Joe Gershenson. Prod: Val Burton. Scr: Val Burton, Walter De
Leon, Bradford Ropes. Addtnl Dial: John Grant. Mus: Milt
Rosen. Art Dir: Jack Otterson, Richard H. Reidel. Photog:
Charles Van Enger. Spec. Photog: D. S. Horsley, Jerome Ash.
Ed: Phillip Cahn. Sound: Bernard Brown. Asst Dir: Seward
Webb. Sound: Jack A. Bolger. Dial Dir: Morgan Farley. 82
min.
    Working Title: THE GHOST STEPS OUT.
    Cast: Bud Abbott (Cuthbert and Dr. Greenway), Lou Costello
(Horatio Prim), Marjorie Reynolds (Melody Allen), Binnie Barnes
(Mildred Prescott), John Shelton (Sheldon Gage), Jess Barker (Tom
Danbury), Gale Sondergaard (Emily), Robert Barrat (Maj. Putnam),
Donald MacBride (Lt. Mason), Anne Gillis (Nora), Lynne Baggett
(June Prescott), William Hall (Connors), Rex Lease (Sgt. Make-
peace), Harry Woolman (motorcycle rider), Harry Brown (2nd sgt.)
Walter Baldwin (Bates), Selmer Jackson (curator), George Carlton,
Wheaton Chambers (guards), Vernon Downing (Leigh), Boyd Irwin
(Cranwell), Marjorie Eaton (Bessie), Kirk Alyn, Myron Healey,
Scott Thomson, John Crawford (dandies).

WHITE TIE AND TAILS. Universal-International, 8-30-46. Prod:

Howard Benedict. Story: "Victoria Docks At Eight" by Rufus King and Charles Beaham. Scr: Bertram Millhauser. Mus Dir: Milton Rosen. Art Dir: Jack Otterson, John De Cuir. Photog: Charles Van Enger. Ed: Ray Snyder. 74 min.
Re-issued as THE SWINDLERS.
Cast: Dan Duryea (Charles Dumont), Ella Raines (Louise Bradford), William Bendix (Larry Lundie), Richard Gaines (Archer Ripley), Barbara Brown (Mrs. Latimer), Clarence Kolb (Mr. Arkwright), Donald Curtis (Nate Romano), Frank Jenks (George), Samuel S. Hinds (Mr. Bradford), John Miljan (Mr. Latimer), William Trenk (Emil), Scotty Beckett (Bill Latimer), Nita Hunter (Betty Latimer), Patricia Alphin (Audrey Young) (Cynthia Bradford), Joan Fulton (Shawlee) (Virgie), Beatrice Roberts (Marie), Lois Austin (Agnes), Rex Lease (Briggs), Bert Moorhouse (Croupier), Earl Keen (dog impersonator), Ralph Brooks (Roger), Bob Wilke (starter), Roger Cole (cashier), Leo Z. Gray, Albin Robeling (waiters).

BUCK PRIVATES COME HOME. Universal-International, 4-21-47. Prod: Robert Arthur. Story: Richard Macauley, Bradford Ropes. Scr: John Grant, Frederic I. Rinaldo, Robert Lees. Art Dir: Bernard Herzbrun, Frank A. Richards. Mus Dir: Walter Schuman. Photog: Charles Van Enger. Ed: Edward Curtis. Set Dec: Russell A. Gausman, Charles Wyrick. Asst Dir: Joseph Kenney. Spec Photog: Davis S. Horsley. Sound: Charles Felstead. 77 min.
Cast: Bud Abbott (Slicker Smith), Lou Costello (Herbie Brown), Tom Brown (Bill Gregory), Joan Fulton (Shawlee) (Sylvia Hunter), Nat Pendleton (Sgt. Collins), Beverly Simmons (Yvonne Le-Bru "Evey") Don Beddoe (Mr. Roberts), Don Porter (Capt.), Donald MacBride (police captain), Lane Watson, William Ching (Lieutenants), Peter Thompson (Steve), George Beban, Jr. (Cal), Jimmie Dodd Whitey), Lennie Breman (Hank), Al Murphy (Murphy), Bob Wilke (Stan), William Haade (husband), Janna deLoos (wife), Buddy Roosevelt, Chuck Hamilton (cops), Patricia Alphin (Audrey Young) (girl), Joe Kirk (real estate salesman), Charles Trowbridge (Mr. Quince), Russell Hicks (Appleby), Ralph Dunn (Ed), John Sheehan (Drew), Cliff Clark (Quentin), Jean Del Val (Duprez), Harlan Warde, Lyle Lattel (Medics), Eddie Acuff, Milton Kibbee (passengers), Frank Marlowe (tie buyer), Ottola Nesmith (French matron), Eddie Dunn (Mulroney), Charles Sullivan (Harry), Billy Curtis (man with baby), Betty Alexander (Juliet), Jerry Farber (boy), Doris Kemper (Matron), Myron Healy (Medic), James Farley (bank guard), Ralph Brooks, Eddie Coke, Clarence Straight, Russell Conway (medics), Rex Lease (chauffeur), Thomas M. Skinner (medic), Frank Mayo (colonel), John Michaels, Dick Dickerson (soldiers), Lee Shumway (bank guard), Tony Merrill, Ernie Adams, Donald Kerr (tie buyers), Bob Bacon (Medic), George Barton (painter), Milburn Stone (announcer), Knox Manning (commentator).

THE WISTFUL WIDOW OF WAGON GAP. Universal-International, 10-8-47. Prod: Robert Arthur. Assoc Prod: Sebastian Cristillo. Story: D. D. Beauchamp, William Bowers. Scr: Robert Lees,

Frederic I. Rinaldo, John Grant.   Dial Dir: Norman Abbott.   Art
Dir: Bernard Herzbrun, Gabriel Scognamillo.   Mus Dir: Walter
Schuman.   Orch: David Tamkin.   Photog: Charles Van Enger.
Ed: Frank Gross.   Set Dec: Russell A. Gausman, Charles Wyrick.
Sound: Charles Felstead.   78 min.
      Cast: Bud Abbott (Duke Eagan), Lou Costello (Chester Wool-
ey), Marjorie Main (Widow Hawkins), Audrey Young (Juanita Hawk-
ins), George Cleveland (Judge Benbow), Gordon Jones (Jake Frame),
William Ching (Jim Simpson), Peter Thompson (Phil), Olin Howlin
(undertaker), Bill Clauson (Matt Hawkins), Billy O'Leary (Billy Hawk-
ins), Pamela Wells (Sarah Hawkins), Jimmie Bates (Jefferson Hawkins), Paul Dunn (Lincoln Hawkins), Diane Florentine (Sally Hawkins),
Rex Lease (Hank), Glenn Strange (Lefty), Edmund Cobb (Lem), Wade
Crosby (Lem), Dewey Robinson (miner/gambler), Murray Leonard
(bartender), Emmett Lynn (old codger), Billy Engle (undertaker's
asst.), Gilda Feldrais (hostess), Iris Adrian (dance hall hostess)
Lee Lasses White (shot-gun rider), George Lewis (cowpuncher),
Charles King (gunman), Jack Shutta (tough miner), Jerry Jerome
(cowboy), Zon Murray (cowpuncher), Frank Hagney (barfly), Harry
Evans (card dealer), Mickey Simpson (big miner), Monte Montague
(man), Frank Marlo, Ethan Laidlaw (cowboys), Ed Peil (Townsman),
Dave Sharpe (man thrown by the Widow).

THE NOOSE HANGS HIGH.   Eagle-Lion Studios, Inc., 4-17-48.
Prod: Charles Barton.   Story: Daniel Taradish, Julian Blaustein,
Bernard Fins, adapted from a screenplay by Charles Grayson and
Arthur T. Horman "For Love or Money."   Scr: John Grant, Howard Harris.   Art Dir: Edward L. Ilou.   Mus Dir: Irving Fried-
man.   Photog: Charles Van Enger.   Ed: Harry Reynolds.   77 min.
      Cast: Bud Abbott (Ted Higgins), Lou Costello (Tommy Hinch-
cliffe), Cathy Downs (Carol Scott), Joseph Calleia (Mike Craig), Leon
Errol (Julius Caesar McBride), Mike Mazurki (Chuck), Jack Over-
man (Joe), Fritz Feld (psychiatrist), Vera Martin (elevator girl),
Irmgard Dawson (girl), Joe Kirk, Matt Wills (gangsters), Joan Myles
(secretary), Ben Weldon (Stewart), Harry Brown (Upson), Jimmy
Dodd, Ben Hall (messengers), Ellen Corby (maid), Isabel Randolph
(Miss Van Buren), Frank O'Connor (postman), Benny Rubin (China-
man), Bess Flowers (patient), Murray Leonard (crazy dentist),
Sandra Spence (dentist's asst.), Pat Falherty (tough driver), Elvia
Allman (woman), Alvin Hammer (tipster), Jerry Marlowe (cashier),
Ralph Montgomery, Fred M. Browne (waiters), Lois Austin (woman
on the street), Herb Vigran (man with coat), James Flavin (traffic
cop), Lyle Latell (workman), Paul Maxey (jewelry proprietor), Fred
Kelsey (cop), Minerva Urecal (husky woman), James Logan (valet),
Tim Wallace, Chalky Williams (cab Drivers), Arno Frey (headwaiter),
Russell Hicks (manager), Oscar Otis (race track announcer).

BUD ABBOTT AND LOU COSTELLO MEET FRANKENSTEIN.   Universal-International, 7-22-48.   Prod: Robert Arthur.   Story/Scr:
Robert Lees, Frederic I. Rinaldo, John Grant.   Art Dir: Bernard

Herzbrun, Hilyard Brown. Mus: Frank Skinner. Photog: Charles
Van Enger. Ed: Frank Gross. Make-Up: Bud Westmore. Sound:
Leslie I. Carey, Robert Pritchard. Sets: Russell Gausman, Oliver
Emert. Spec Eff: David S. Horsley, Jerome H. Ash. Asst Dir:
Joseph E. Kenny. 92 min.
   Though the film is generally known as ABBOTT AND COSTEL-
LO MEET FRANKENSTEIN, all publicity and the title card in the
film itself give the title as BUD ABBOTT AND LOU COSTELLO,
etc.
   Cast: Bud Abbott (Chick Young), Lou Costello (Wilbur Grey),
Lon Chaney, Jr. (Lawrence Talbot), Bela Lugosi (Dracula), Glenn
Strange (monster), Lenore Aubert (Sandra Mornay), Jane Randolph
(Joan Raymond), Frank Ferguson (Mr. McDougal), Charles Broad-
Street (Dr. Stevens), Howard Negley (Mr. Harris), Joe Kirk (man),
Clarence Straight (man in armor), Harry Brown (photographer),
Helen Spring (woman at baggage counter), George Barton (man),
Carl Sklover (man), Paul Stader (sgt.), Joe Walls (man), Vincent
Price (voice of The Invisible Man), Bob Haymes (extra), Bobby Bar-
ber (waiter).

MEXICAN HAYRIDE. Universal-International, 12-13-48. Prod:
Robert Arthur. Scr: Oscar Brodney, John Grant based on the
musical play by Herbert and Dorothy Fields and Cole Porter. Art
Dir: Bernard Herzbrun, John F. DeCuir. Mus Dir: Walter Scharf.
Sets: Russell Gausman, John Austin. Sound: Leslie I. Carey,
Robert Pritchard. Song: "Is It Yes or Is It No?" by Walter Scharf
and Jack Brooks. Photog: Charles Van Enger. Ed: John Gross.
Choreography: Eugene Loring. 77 min.
   Cast: Bud Abbott (Harry Lambert), Lou Costello (Joe Bas-
com, alias Humphrey Fish), Virginia Grey (Montana), Luba Malina
(Dagmar), John Hubbard (David Winthrop), Pedro de Cordoba (Senor
Martines), Fritz Feld (Prof. Ganzmeyer), Tom Powers (Ed Mason),
Pat Costello (Tim Williams), Frank Fenton (Gus Adamson), Chris
Pin Martin (Mariachi leader), Sidney Fields (reporter), Flores broth-
ers Trio (trio), Argentina Brunetti (Indian woman), Mary Brewer,
Marjorie L. Carver, Lucille Casey, Toni (Mary) Castle, Lorraine
Crawford (girls), Eddie Kane (Mr. Clarke), Ben Chavez (magician),
Pedro Regas (proprietor), Charles Miller (Mr. Lewis), Harry Brown
(business man), Joe Kirk (2nd business man), Julian Rivero (ticket
seller), Donna deMario (Martell) (girl), Tony Roux (blanket weaver),
Roque Ybarra (basket weaver), Joe Dominguez (artist), Felipe Turich
(silversmith dealer), Alex Montoya (man), Julia Montoya (woman),
George Mendoza (photographer), Caroline Lopez (Mexican girl), Reed
Howes (man), Kippee Valez (girl), Fred Hoose (businessman), Robert
Lugo (man), Charles Rivero (ticket taker), Robert Elias (Mexican
boy), Rose Marie Lopez (child), Karen Randle, Yolanda Gonzalez
(girls), Alfonso Pedroza (Mexican man), Earl Spainard (bellboy),
Suzanne Ridgway (artist's model), Lalo Encinas (man), John L.
Sylvester, Sol Murgi, Rudy German, Hans Moebus (men), Cosmo
Sardo (headwaiter), Mary Castle (salesgirl).

AFRICA SCREAMS. Nassour Studios/United Artists, 5-27-49. A

Huntington Hartford Production.   Prod: Edward Nassour.   Story /
Scr: Earl Baldwin.   Art Dir: Lewis Creber.   Photog: Charles
Van Enger.   Ed: Frank Gross.   Assoc Prod: David S. Garber.
Asst Dir: Joe Kenny.   Set Dresser: Ray Robinson.   Spec Eff:
Carl Lee.   Prod Mgr: Joe C. Gilpin.   Dial Dir: Norman Abbott.
Mus Dir: Walter Schumann.   Sound: Robert Pritchard.   79 min.
          Cast: Bud Abbott (Buzz Johnson), Lou Costello (Stanley Liv-
ingston), Hillary Brooke (Diana Emerson), Max Baer (Boots), Buddy
Baer (Grappler), Shemp Howard (Gunner), Joe Besser (Harry), Clyde
Beatty (himself), Frank Buck (himself), Burton Wenland (Bobo),   Bob-
by Barber (Fat man).

ABBOTT AND COSTELLO MEET THE KILLER, BORIS KARLOFF.
Universal-International, 8-49.   Prod: Robert Arthur.   Story: Hugh
Wedlock, Jr. , Howard Snyder.   Scr: Hugh Wedlock, Jr. , Howard
Snyder, John Grant.   Art Dir: Bernard Herzbrun, Richard H. Rie-
del.   Mus: Milton Schwarzwald.   Photog: Charles Van Enger.   Ed:
Edward Curtiss.   Spec Eff: David S. Horsley.   Make-Up: Bud
Westmore.   94 min.
          Cast: Bud Abbott (Casey Edwards), Lou Costello (Freddie
Phillips), Boris Karloff (Swami Talpur), Lenore Aubert (Angela
Gordon), Gar Moore (Jeff Wilson), Donna Martell (Betty Crandall),
Alan Mowbray (Melton), James Flavin (Inspector Wellman), Roland
Winters (T. Hanley Brooks), Nicholas Joy (Amos Strickland), Mikel
Conrad (Sgt. Stone), Morgan Farley (Gregory Milford), Victoria
Horne (Mrs. Hargreave), Percy Helton (Abernathy), Claire Dubrey
(Mrs. Grimsby), Harry Hayden (Lawrence Crandell), Vincent Renno
(Mike Relia), Patricia Hall (Manicurist), Murray Alper (Joe), Mar-
jorie Bennett (Maid), Harry Brown (medical examiner), Gail Bonney
(Maid), Beatrice Gray (woman), Henrietta Taylor (maid), Billy Sny-
der, Eddie Coke (reporters), Ethan Laidlaw (man), Frankie Van
(Bozzo), Jack Chefe (barber), Billy Gray (boy with arrow), Arthur
Hecht (photographer), William H. O'Brien (waiter), Ed Randolph
(boot black), Jean Bane (manicurist), Phil Shepard (bellboy).

FREE FOR ALL.   Universal-International, 11-2-49.   Prod: Robert
Buckner.   Story: Robert Clyde Lewis.   Scr: Robert Buckner.   Art
Dir: Bernard Herzbrun, Nathan Juran.   Mus: Frank Skinner.
Photog: George Robinson.   Ed: Ralph Dawson.   Sound: Leslie I.
Carey, Joe Lapis.   Sets: Russell Gausman, Roland Fields.   83 min.
          Cast: Robert Cummings (Christopher Parker), Ann Blyth
(Alva Abbott), Percy Kilbride (Mr. Abbott), Ray Collins (Mr. Balir),
Donald Woods (Roger Abernathy), Mikhail Rasumny (Dr. Thorgel-
son), Percy Helton (Mr. Hershey), Harry Antrim (Mr. Whiting),
Wallis Clark (Mr. Van Alstyne), Frank Ferguson (Hap Ross), Dool-
ey Wilson (Aristotle), Russell Simpson (farmer), Lester Matthews
(Mr. Aberson), Murray Alper ("Gas Gat" McGuinness), Bill Walker
(Herbert), Kenneth Tobey (pilot), Harris Brown (col.), Willard
Waterman (commander), Robert D. Jellison (Penobscot), Joseph
Granby (stranger), Ruth Clifford (Miss Berry), Gaylord Pendleton
(Navy officer), Lois Austin (Miss Firby), Cajan Lee (receptionist),
Doris Karnes, Dee Carroll (stenographers), Edward Clark (doctor),

Charles Woolf (office boy), Forbes Murray, George Hyland (board of directors members).

THE MILKMAN. Universal-International, 11-50. Prod: Ted Richmond. Scr: Albert Beich, James Hanlon, Martin Ragaway, Leonard Stern. Art Dir: Bernard Herzbrun, Robert Boyld. Mus: Milton Rosen. Photog: Clifford Stone. Ed: Russell Schoengarth. Sets: Russell Gausman, Roland Fields. Sound: Leslie I. Carey, Rich DeWeese. 87 min.

Cast: Donald O'Connor (Roger Bradley), Jimmy Durante (Breezy Albright), Piper Laurie (Chris Abbott), Joyce Holden (Ginger Burton), Jess Barker (John Carter), Elizabeth Risdon (Mrs. Carter), William Conrad (Mike Morrel), Henry O'Neill (Bradley, Sr.), Paul Harvey (D. A. Abbott), Charles Flynn (Sgt. Larkin), Eddie Acuff (Herman Schultz), Garry Owen (Irving), John Cliff (Joe), Bill Nelson (Duke), Lucille Barkley (nurse), Frank Nelson (Mr. Green), Minerva Urecal (Mrs. Dillon), Howard Negley (Herman), John Skins Miller (Harry), Richard Powers (Tom Keene), (Dusik), Norman Field (Bradley Butler), Ruth Brady (Miss Williams), Therese Lyons (Bradley maid), Joe Kerr (man in window), Edward Clark (old man), Bob Stephenson (cop), Charmienne Harker (Lana), Hal Smith (milkman), Ralph Montgomery (Brown), David Newell (fireman), Perc Launders (police sgt.), Vesey O'Davoren (Carter's butler), Kippee Valez (Carmen), Hazel Keener (Bit Woman), Jerry Lewis (milkman), Marilyn Mercer (telephone operator), Dave Dunbar (Bill), Larry McGrath (Danny), Charles Hall (Ed), Audrey Betz (plump girl), Marian Dennish (pretty girl), John McKee, Donald Kerr, Frank Malet, Doug Carter, Wally Walker, Pat Combs, Bob Garvin (milkmen), Jewel Rose (secretary), Paul Power (butler), Parke MacGregor (photographer), John O'Connor, Chester Conklin (men), Paul Palmer (policeman), Carey Loftin, Dick Crockett, Eddie Parker, Frank McGrath, Frank McMahon, Tom Steele, Gordon Carveth, Jimmy Dundee, Wes Hopper, Wally Rose, Chick Collins, Cliff Lyons (ad lib lines).

DOUBLE CROSSBONES. Universal-International, 4-51. ("Film Daily" review 11-21-50). Prod: Leonard Goldstein. Story/Scr: Oscar Brodney. Art Dir: Bernard Herzbrun, Alexander Golitzen. Mus: Frank Skinner. Photog: Maury Gertsman. Ed: Russell Schoengarth. Addtnl Dial: John Grant. Technicolor consultant; William Fritzsche. Operating Cameraman: Harry Davis. Set Dec: Russell Gausman, John Austin. Sound: Leslie I. Carey, Richard DeWeese. Prod Mgr: Howard Christie. Asst Dir: Fred Frank. Script Sup: Betty Abbott. Hair Stylists: Joan St. Oegger, Doris Harris. Makeup: Bud Westmore, Emile LaVigne. Costumes: Yvonne Wood. Grip: Russ Frank. Gaffer: John Brooks. Songs: "Percy Had a Heart," "I'd Love to Take You Home," "Song of Adventure" by Dan Shapiro and Lester Lee. Color by Technicolor. 75½ min. Tech Adv: Lt. Cmmdr. K. D. Iain Murray. Fencing Master: Fred Cavens.

Cast: Donald O'Connor (Dave Crandall), Helena Carter (Lady Sylvia Copeland), Will Geer (Tom Botts), John Enery (Gov. Elden),

Stanley Hogan (Lord Montrose), Kathryn Givney (Lady Montrose),
Hayden Rorke (Malcolm Giles), Morgan Farley (Caleb Nicholas),
Hope Emerson (Mistress Ann Bonney), Charles McGraw (Capt.
Ben Wickett), Alan Napier (Capt. Kidd), Robert Barrat (Henry
Morgan), Louis Bacigalupi (Blackbeard), Glenn Strange (Capt. Ben
Avery), Gregg Martell (Isaac Wells), Frank Richards, James Ar-
ness, Chuck Hamilton (prisoners), Gavin Muir (Capt. Cavendish),
Ralph Byrd (Will), Lester Luther (tavern keeper), Howard J. Neg-
ley (Defiance capt.), Manuel Paris (Brethren of the Coast Pirate),
Fred Carson, Mickey Simpson, Duke York, Frank Hagney, Harry
Wilson (pirates). Narrated by Jeff Chandler.

MA AND PA KETTLE AT THE FAIR. Universal-International, 4-52.
Prod: Leonard Goldstein. Story: Martin Ragaway, Leonard Stern,
Jack Henley. Co-Dir (uncredited): Frederic De Cordova. Scr:
Richard Morris, John Grant. Art Dir: Bernard Herzbrun, Eric
Orbom. Mus Dir: Joseph Gershenson. Photog: Maury Gertsman.
Ed: Ted J. Kent. Sets: Russell Gausman, Ruby Levitt. Sound:
Leslie I. Carey, Corson Jowett. 78 min.
        Cast: Marjorie Main (Ma Kettle), Percy Kilbride (Pa Kettle),
Lori Nelson (Rosie Kettle), James Best (Marvin Johnson), Esther
Dale (Birdie Hicks), Russell Simpson (Clem Johnson), Emory Par-
nell (Billy Reed), Oliver Blake (Geoduck), Hallene Hill (Mrs. Hicks'
mother), James Griffith (medicine man), Rex Lease (sheriff), Teddy
Infuhr (Benjamin Kettle), George Arglen (Willie Kettle), Ronald R.
Rondell (Danny Kettle), Margaret Brown (Ruth Kettle), Billy Clark
(George Kettle), Jackie Jackson (Henry Kettle), Donna Leary (Sally
Kettle), Elana Schreiner (Nancy Kettle), Eugene Persson (Teddy Ket-
tle), Jenny Linder (Sara Kettle), Sherry Jackson (Susie Kettle), Gary
Lee Jackson (Billy Kettle), Beverly Mook (Eve Kettle), Zachary
Charles (Crowbar), Frank Ferguson (Sam the jailer), Syd Saylor
(postman), Harry Harvey (chairman), Frank Wilcox (driver), Harry
Cheshire (preacher), Sidney Mason (man), Lois Austin (woman), No-
lan Leary (elderly usher), Wheaton Chambers (injured man), Harry
Cording (Ed), George Eldredge (man), William Gould, Frank McFar-
land (judges), Forrest Taylor (man), Lester Dorr (man), Dick Ryan
(Spieler), Roy Regnier, Edmund Cobb (men), Sara Taft (Lucy),
Clair Meade (Sarah), Hal Smith (man), David Newell (man), James
Guilfoyle (Birdie's trainer), Margaret Bert (woman), Bob Donnelly
(clown), Harold De Garro (stilt walker), Elsie Baker (Woman), Jack
Harden (man), Helen Gibson (woman), Mel Pogue (Delivery Boy),
Roy Butler (man), Doug Carter (ticket seller), Juanita Close (ad lib
bit), Emily Marks (woman), Donald Kerr, John Barton, Philo McCul-
lough (bits).

DANCE WITH ME HENRY. United Artists, 12-56. Prod: Bob
Goldstein. Story: William Kozlenko, Leslie Kardos. Scr: Dev-
ery Freeman. Art Dir: Leslie Thomas. Mus: Paul Dunlap.
Photog: George Robinson. Ed: Robert Golden. Sound Ed: Verna
Fields. Sets: Morris Hoffman. Sound: Earl Snyder. Script Sup:
Eleanor Donahue. 79 min.
        Cast: Bud Abbott (Bud Flick), Lou Costello (Lou Henry),

Gigi Perreau (Shelley), Rusty Hamer (Duffer), Mary Wickes (Miss Mayberry), Ted de Corsia (Big Frank), Ron Hargrave (Ernie), Sherry Alberoni (Bottsie), Frank Wilcox (Father Mullahy), Richard Reeves (Mushie), Paul Sorenson((Dutch), Robert Shayne (Proctor), John Cliff (Knucks), Phil Garris (Mickey), Walter Reed (Drake), Eddie Marr (Garvey), David McMahon (Savoldi), Gil Rankin (McKay), Rod Williams (porter).

THE SHAGGY DOG. Walt Disney/Buena Vista, 4-59. Prod: Walt Disney. Assoc Prod: Bill Walsh. Story: Felix Salten ("The Hound of Florence") Scr: Bill Walsh, Lillie Hayward. Art Dir: Carroll Clark. Mus: Paul Smith. Photog: Edward Coleman. Ed: James D. Ballas. Set Dec: Emile Kuri, Fred MacLean. Costumes: Chuck Keehne, Gertrude Casey. Orch: Joseph Mullendore. Special Titles: T. Hee, Bill Justice, Xavier Atencio. Mus Ed: Evelyn Kennedy. Sound: Robert O. Cook, Harry M. Lindgren. Makeup: Pat McNalley. Hairstyles: Ruth Sandifer. Asst Dir: Arthur Vitarelli. Animal Sup: William R. Koehler. Song: Gil George, Paul Smith. 104 min.

    Cast: Fred MacMurray (Wilson Daniels), Jean Hagen (Frieda Daniels), Tommy Kirk (Wilby Daniels), Annette Funicello (Allison D'Allessio), Tim Considine (Buzz Miller), Kevin Corcoran (Moochie Daniels), Cecil Kellaway (Prof. Plumcutt), Alexander Scourby (Dr. Mikhail Andrassy), Roberta Shore (Franceska Andrassy), James Westerfield (Officer Hanson), Jacque Aubuchon (Stefano), Strother Martin (Thurm), Forrest Lewis (Officer Keely), Shaggy (himself), Ned Wever (E. P. Hackett), Gordon Jones (Capt. Scanlon), John Hart (police broadcaster), Jack Albertson (reporter), Mack Williams (Betz), Paul Frees (psychiatrist). Opening narration by Paul Frees.

TOBY TYLER, OR TEN WEEKS WITH A CIRCUS. Walt Disney/ Buena Vista. A Walt Disney Production. Assoc Prod: Bill Walsh. Story: James Otis Kaler (novel). Scr: Bill Walsh, Lillie Hayward. Art Dir: Carroll Clark, Stan Jolley. Mus; Buddy Baker. Orch: Walter Sheets. Song: "Biddle-Dee-Dee" by Diane Lampert and Richard Loring. Photog: William Snyder. Ed: Stanley Johnson. Set Dec: Emile Kuri, Fred MacLean. Costumes: Chuck Keehne, Gertrude Casey. Asst Dir: Arthur J. Vitarelli. Matte Artist: Peter Ellenshaw. Spec Effects: Ub Iwerks. Makeup: Pat McNalley. Hairstyles: Ruth Sandifer. Sound: Robert O. Cook, Dean Thomas. Mus Ed: Evelyn Kennedy. 96 min. Color by Technicolor.

    Cast: Kevin Corcoran (Toby Tyler), Henry Calvin (Ben Cotter), Gene Sheldon (Sam Treat), Bob Sweeney (Harry Tupper), Richard Eastman (Col. Sam Castle), James Drury (Jim Weaver), Barbara Beaird (Mademoiselle Jeanette), Dennis Joel (Monsieur Ajax), Edith Evanson (Aunt Olive), Tom Fadden (Uncle Daniel), Ollie Wallace (bandleader), Mr. Stubbs (himself), with The Flying Viennas, The Jungleland Elephants, The Marquis Family, The Ringling Brothers Clowns ("Eddie Spaghetti" Emerson, Abe "Korky" Goldstein, Duke Johnson, Harry Johnson).

294   Between Action and Cut

SWINGIN' ALONG. 20th Century-Fox, 2-62. Prod: Jack Leewood.
Scr: Jameson Brewer. Art Dir: Duncan Cramer, Gregory Van
Marter. Mus: Arthur Morton. Mus Con: Lionel Newman. Pho-
tog: Arthur E. Arling. Ed: Betty Steinberg. Set Dec: Walter
M. Scott, Lou Hafley. Sound: Don McKay, Frank W. Moran.
Makeup: Ben Nye. Hairstyles: Helen Turpin. Asst Dir: Ad
Schaumer. Color by DeLuxe. Filmed in CinemaScope. 74 min.
        Working Title: THE SCHNOOK. Released in January, 1961
as DOUBLE TROUBLE, pulled from release, re-edited and re-
released in February, 1962 in its current form.
        Cast: Tommy Noonan (Freddy Merkle), Peter Marshall (Duke),
Barbara Eden (Carol Walker), Connie Gilchrist (Aunt Sophie), Carol
Christensen (Ginny), Alan Carney (Officer Sullivan), Mike Mazurki
(Bookie), Lennie Breman (Willie), Tommy Farrell (Georgie), Don
Diamond (Tony), Terry Miele (Mrs. Crenshaw), Frank Wilcox (Psy-
chiatrist), Ted Knight (Priest), Sandra Warner (secretary), Bill
Bradley (TV announcer), Gregg Martell (man in manhole), Norman
Leavitt (cab driver), Edith Evanson (woman), Jimmy Ames, Robert
Foulk (piano movers), Earl Holmes (Western Union Boy), Blossom
Rock (Marie Blake) (Woman in apartment # 1), Sophania Whitney
(woman in apartment # 4).

                       Charles Barton TV Credits

                       Compiled by Greg Lenburg

1951:   The Amos 'n Andy Show (CBS/25 episodes)

1952:   The Amos 'n Andy Show (CBS/26 episodes)

1953:   The Amos 'n Andy Show (CBS/26 episodes/also
                               producer of last 13)
         Meet Mr. McNutley (CBS/37 episodes)

1954:   Duffy's Tavern (NBC/Pilot episode)
         Joe Palooka (Syndicated/Pilot episode)

1955:   Trouble with Father (ABC/18 episodes)
         The Great Gildersleeve (NBC/39 episodes)

1956:   Tugboat Annie (Syndicated/Pilot episode)
         Oh, Susanna! (CBS/11 episodes)

1957:   Oh, Susanna! (CBS/11 episodes)
         Spin and Marty (ABC/30 episodes)

1958:   Oh, Susanna! (CBS/11 episodes)
         Zorro (ABC/16 episodes)

1959:   Dennis the Menace (CBS /20 episodes)

1960:   Dennis the Menace (CBS /40 episodes)
          The Real McCoys (ABC /Various episodes)

1961:   Dennis the Menace (CBS /39 episodes)

1962:   Dennis the Menace (CBS /37 episodes)
          The Medicine Man (Never aired /Screen Gems pilot
                              with Ernie Kovacs, his last film,
                              and Buster Keaton)

1963:   Grindl (NBC /32 episodes)

1964:   The Baileys of Balboa (CBS /13 episodes)
          McHale's Navy (ABC /12 episodes)
          The Munsters (CBS /3 episodes)
          Broadside (ABC /14 episodes)

1965:   The Smothers Brothers Show (CBS /5 episodes)
          Camp Runamuck (NBC /5 episodes)
          Hazel (CBS /28 episodes)

1966:   Petticoat Junction (CBS /28 episodes)

1967:   Family Affair (CBS /28 episodes)

1968:   Family Affair (CBS /28 episodes)

1969:   Family Affair (CBS /26 episodes)
          To Rome with Love (CBS /11 episodes)

1970:   Family Affair (CBS /24 episodes)
          The Tim Conway Show (CBS /Pilot Episode)

Charles Barton also directed a series of commercials for "Beechnut
Peppermint Gum," featuring the likes of William Schallert, Kirk
Alyn, Mike Mazurki and a host of familiar Hollywood faces; one
episode of "The Patty Duke Show"; and two unsold pilots, one starring
Jayne Mansfield, Virginia Fields and Joanne Woodbury, and another
showcasing Paul Winchell and his dummies in a firehouse.

ABOUT THE CONTRIBUTORS

SCOTT MacQUEEN lives in New York where he works in motion picture and TV production. His credits include Alone in the Dark,
Come Back to the Five and Dime, Jimmy Dean, Jimmy Dean; Trad-
ing Places; and Rattlesnake in a Cooler. He has written about films
for Photon and American Classic Screen magazines. He and his
wife Elisabeth have a daughter.

JOHN GALLAGHER is a writer and filmmaker who lives in New
York. He wrote and directed Beach House, Long Walk to Forever,
Other Men's Wives and All That You Dream. His writings on film
have appeared in Rolling Stone, Films in Review, The Boston Globe,
The Real Paper and American Classic Screen, for which he serves
as New York Editor. He edited his own film journal, Grand Illu-
sions, while a student at Emerson College in Boston. His book on
director Tay Garnett is forthcoming from Scarecrow Press.

WILLIAM K. EVERSON is a noted film historian and prolific writer
and teacher. He has written for numerous magazines, lectured extensively throughout the United States, Great Britain and Europe and
has taught courses or seminars on film at Harvard, Berkeley, UCLA,
Dartmouth, Bard College, The Carnegie Institute and many other
schools. He currently teaches at The New School in New York City.
His books include The Art of W. C. Fields, Classics of the Horror
Film, The Western, The Films of Laurel and Hardy and American
Silent Film.

JOHN C. TIBBETTS is a writer, film historian, artist and musician.
He is the editor of American Classic Screen magazine and his duties
there include writing editorials, articles and reviews as well as
painting the star portraits that generally adorn the magazine's cover.
He is co-author with James Welsh of His Majesty the American, a
study of the life and career of Douglas Fairbanks. His book The
American Theatrical Film: Stages in Development will be published
in 1984. He works in radio and television broadcasting and teaches
at the University of Missouri at Kansas City.

FRANK THOMPSON studied musical composition and arranging at
Boston's Berklee College of Music before turning to film study as
both hobby and livelihood. He has written articles on a variety of
subjects for American Classic Screen, Atlanta Magazine and Motif,
an arts magazine of which he was co-founder and former editor.

296

He contributed several entries to the four-volume St. James film encyclopedia.   His book <u>William A. Wellman</u> was published by Scarecrow Press in 1983 as part of Anthony Slide's Filmmakers Series.   He is currently employed at Films Incorporated in Atlanta, Georgia.